CONSTRUCTING WOMEN AND MEN
Gender Socialization

Marlene Mackie
The University of Calgary
Calgary, Alberta

HOLT, RINEHART AND WINSTON OF CANADA, LIMITED
TORONTO

Canadian Cataloguing in Publication Data

Mackie, Marlene
  Constructing women and men

Bibliography: p.
ISBN 0-03-921845-7

1. Sex differences (Psychology). 2. Socialization.
3. Sex role.   I. Title.

HQ1075.M3 1987   305.3   C86-094296-1

Publisher: Anthony Luengo
Developmental Editor: Tessa McWatt
Copy Editor: Francine Geraci
Cover and Interior Design: John Zehethofer
Typesetting and Assembly: Cundari Group Limited

Printed in Canada
1 2 3 4 5 91 90 89 88 87

For Karen, my daughter and my friend.

Preface

Free to Be You and Me, a book for enlightened children, offers this new version of an old nursery rhyme:

> *What are little boys made of, made of?*
> *What are little boys made of?*
> *Love and care*
> *And skin and hair*
> *That's what little boys are made of.*
>
> *What are little girls made of, made of?*
> *What are little girls made of?*
> *Care and love*
> *And (SEE ABOVE)*
> *That's what little girls are made of.*
>
> (Laron, 1974:38)

Not snips and snails and puppy dog tails. Not sugar and spice and everything nice. Ms. Laron presents her youthful audience with an approximate summary of scientific research on sex differences: males and females share the same basic blueprint. Although inborn distinctions are few, most of us do not feel free to be simply people. Instead, we feel constrained to follow "female" or "male" rules, to play "female" or "male" roles. It is important to realize that these constraints are social constraints. Along with providing the "love and care" required to transform human infants into functioning adult members of Canadian society, the socialization process teaches children how boys and girls, men and women should think, feel, and behave.

Perhaps, the primary gender socialization lesson is the inequality of females and males. A true story illustrates this point. Sixty years ago, a small boy was fascinated by the trains that whistled through his Saskatchewan town. On several occasions, he disappeared from his backyard and was discovered eventually at the train station. Finally, his exasperated mother dressed her son in his sister's clothing and tied him to the front porch in sight of passersby. The demotion to girl was effective punishment. The little boy never again risked humiliation to run away from home. In recent years, the latest wave of the women's movement has criticized the notion of male superiority, as well as other traditional ideas about females and males. Nevertheless, gender continues to be an axis of both individual identity and social organization.

The theme of this book is the social construction of femininity and masculinity in Canadian society. Gender is regarded as a socially salient but, for the most part, arbitrary accretion upon relatively minor biological and psychological sex differences. In the words of Ortner and Whitehead (1981:1), the processes of sex and reproduction

> furnish only a suggestive and ambiguous backdrop to the cultural organization of gender and sexuality. What gender is, what men and women are, what sorts of relations do or should obtain between them — all of these notions do not simply reflect or elaborate upon biological "givens," but are largely products of social and cultural processes.

Therefore, this book emphasizes socialization: the genesis of gender identity in childhood; changing meanings of femininity and masculinity throughout the life cycle; primary, secondary, and symbolic agencies of socialization. These general questions are asked: What is the meaning of gender in Canadian society? How is it socially constructed? How are traditional gender definitions of the situation sustained in interaction? Is a "gender-blind" society possible?

Gender is understood to be a principle of social organization, not a property of individuals (Stacey and Thorne, 1985). The goal of *Constructing Women and Men* is to develop an innovative theoretical perspective that explains gender socialization as a social psychological process taking place within, and reflecting a social structural framework. Bernard's visionary article, "My Four Revolutions" (1973), observes, with apparent approval, that socialization has been "an all-but-overwhelming preoccupation" of post-women's liberation movement sociological theorizing:

> They have alerted us to aspects of it not previously recognized by male researchers, highlighting especially the processes by which women are socialized for weakness, dependency . . ., and even mild mental illness . . ., and thus shaped for marriage . . . (p. 779).

However, in a footnote, Bernard goes on:

> Hanisch (1971, p. 2) rejects this preoccupation with . . . socialization. She views it as a diversionary tactic, distracting attention from the real—power—basis for the position of women. She finds that male social scientists can cheerfully accept the socialization interpretation of the status of women because they gain greatly in substituting the socialization paradigm for a power paradigm (p. 779).

According to the view developed here, the "socialization paradigm" and "power paradigm" are not mutually exclusive.

This book is written in the tradition of symbolic interactionism, the framework that has provided sociology's theoretical treatment *par excellence* of problems of socialization. Moreover, interactionism is congruent with the conceptualization of gender as a processual, social construct, *not* an immutable attribute of the individual. According to this perspective, "the meanings of objects, their symbols, and our actions toward them evolve largely out of the contexts of our interactions with others" (Haas and Shaffir, 1978:4). Hierarchy and power are clearly the essence of gender. "The domination of women by men precedes the emergence of class domination and is structured deeply into the relations of production and reproduction of almost all known societies" (Miles, 1982:9). Therefore, theoretical analysis of socialization must attend to the power structure that underlies the socialization process and the institutional arrangements that buttress it (Rubin, 1976a). The ideas of George Herbert Mead, major progenitor of interactionism, are of some help here. According to Gerth and Mills (1953:xvi), Mead's concept of the generalized other enables "us to link the private and the public, the innermost acts of the individual with the widest kinds of social-historical phenomena." However, in order to facilitate further this combination of micro- and macro-analysis, central tenets from the sociology of knowledge are integrated with symbolic interactionism. As the "systematic study of the social conditions of knowledge" (Berger and Luckmann, 1966:12), the sociology of knowledge provides insight into the question, "How is gender accomplished in everyday life?"

The author writes as a feminist sociologist. The term "feminism" applies to people of both sexes who believe "in the full social-political equality of human beings" (Steinem, 1983b:15). Feminism, which also implies the equality of female and male in sociological analysis, provides the author's personal motivation for study, as the "revival of organized feminism" (Oakley, 1974:1) provided the stimulus for the social scientific study of gender. The women's movement provoked this fundamental realization: the sociology that had previously been accepted as the science of society was really the male science of male society (Bernard, 1973). "Women have been excluded as the producers of knowledge and as the subjects of knowledge . . ." (Spender, 1981b:1). Under the creative guidance of Smith (1974; 1975a) and Daniels (1975), feminists derived from the sociology of knowledge an appreciation of the politics of social science inquiry.

However, the most effective theoretical path to development of a sociology *for*, rather than *of* women (Smith, 1975a:367) is not necessarily the reinvention of "the world of knowledge, of thought, of symbols, and images" (p. 367). So far, the iconoclastic thrust of feminist thought has "worked better to criticize than to reconstruct most bodies of theoretical thought" (Stacey and Thorne, 1985:312). Refurbishing intellectual tools from the past, cleansing them of sexist assumptions and concepts may be one route to go. Several characteristics of symbolic interactionism make it congenial to feminists. As its label suggests, it focuses on language (the root of female invisibility in social life and social science) and on connectedness with others. Although inter-actionists use many methods, their traditional emphasis on "taking the role of the other," participant observation, small-sample depth-interviewing, and the like accord with the communal research style preferred by feminists (Bernard, 1973). Nevertheless, in this book, ideas from symbolic interactionism and the sociology of knowledge are augmented by "sparks for the sociological imagination" (Gould, 1980:460) found in the work of feminists inside and outside social science.

Finally, a few words about the content of *Constructing Women and Men*. The book attempts a balanced treatment of theory and up-to-date empirical studies. Although Canadian research, including the writer's own, is emphasized, extensive use is also made of ideas developed elsewhere. As the title indicates, the book deals with females and males.

> Feminism begins with the situation of women and
> analyzes the way that women's situation has been
> shaped by and in turn shapes the whole social world.
> *The focus is on women, but the basic enterprise is an attempt*
> *to understand and evaluate human affairs* (Benston, 1982:49,
> emphasis added).

Because the author is an Anglophone Canadian sociologist, the book is, of necessity, addressed to an Anglophone audience. It is intended for university or college students interested in the topics of gender rela-tions, socialization, or symbolic interaction theory. Although prior expo-sure to an introductory-level sociology course would be helpful, it is not necessary. Specialized concepts are italicized and defined in the text. In addition, it is hoped that professional social scientists will find useful the theoretical analysis of gender socialization and the presen-tation of the author's own research.

I incurred many debts in the writing of this book. I want to thank the Killam Foundation for the released time and research funds provided by a Killam Resident Fellowship. I am especially grateful to Cathy Schissel for her cheerful, capable research assistance. The advice and encouragement of Holt, Rinehart and Winston editors Tessa McWatt and Tony Luengo, and copy editor Francine Geraci has been very impor-tant to me. The thought-provoking suggestions of reviewers Barrie W. Robinson, Anne Duffy and Anne-Marie Ambert led to a greatly improved manuscript. The students in my gender relations classes, par-ticularly those in Sociology 303 and 503 in 1985-1986, contributed stimulation, criticism, and personal experiences. I benefitted greatly from my discussions of gender with Kathleen Cairns. Henry Zentner, Nan McBlane, Lynn Meadows, Arthur Frank, Tullio Caputo, and Bob Stebbins provided good ideas and advice. A conversation with Margaret Price inspired the Epilogue. Work done jointly with my colleague and collaborator, Merlin Brinkerhoff, forms a central part of Chapter 7. I wish to thank Diane Parsons, Valerie Matwick, and Bonnie Quan for typing and Thomas Huang for computer assistance. Finally, my love to Walter for understanding why I felt it necessary to be at the university seven days a week.

Publisher's Note to Instructors and Students

This text book is a key component of your course. If you are the instructor of this course, you undoubtedly considered a number of texts carefully before choosing this as the one that will work best for your students and you. The authors and publishers of this book spent considerable time and money to ensure its high quality, and we appreciate your recognition of this effort and accomplishment.

If you are a student, we are confident that this text will help you to meet the objectives of your course. You will also find it helpful after the course is finished, as a valuable addition to your personal library. So hold on to it.

As well, please don't forget that photocopying copyright work means the authors lose royalties that are rightfully theirs. This loss will discourage them from writing another edition of this text or other books, because doing so will simply not be worth their time and effort. If this happens, we all lose — students, instructors, authors, and publishers.

And since we want to hear what you think about this book, please be sure to send us the stamped reply card at the end of the text. This will help us to continue publishing high-quality books for your courses.

Contents

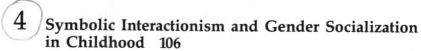

CHAPTER 1

Gender as Social Construct

Introduction

> *In modern industrial society, as apparently in all others, sex is at the base of a fundamental code in accordance with which social interactions and social structures are built up, a code which also establishes the conceptions individuals have concerning their fundamental human nature* (Goffman, 1977:301).

Male, female. The difference that makes a difference. He ejaculates and impregnates. She menstruates, gestates, lactates. She can identify 25 colors, including taupe and magenta. He can identify 25 cars (Aston Martin, Lamborghini). She smiles more. Except for anger, she finds it easier to express her feelings (Jourard, 1964), while he tends to be "emotionally constipated" (Farrell, 1974).

When an emergency occurs in a public place, he is more likely to help and she is more likely to be helped (Baron and Byrne, 1984:301). Moreover, he is usually both agent and object of aggression (Maccoby and Jacklin, 1974). He is more likely to cross the street against the light. When the traffic light is disobeyed, men "walk without hesitating and with a steady gait. Women, on the other hand, are more likely to pause, laugh, and then run" (Andersen, 1983:3). Indeed, across the world men commit more crime than women (Nettler, 1978:120).

In general, males enjoy more status and influence than females. When they are together, he does more of the talking and is more likely to interrupt her remarks. He initiates more touching and commands more personal space (Thorne and Henley, 1975). In informal task groups, he is more likely to be chosen leader and to influence the group's problem-solving processes (Unger, 1978:469). A petition sponsored by a male is more likely to be signed (Keasey and Tomlinson-Keasey, 1971). Political power is in male hands. After the 1984 Canadian federal election, women held a record high of 9.6 percent of the seats in the House of Commons.

Family life continues to be specialized by gender (Miller and Garrison, 1982). In our society, marriage is still the sign of the successful woman, while occupational achievement is the sign of the successful man (the "sex object" versus the "success object"). Therefore, it is women who show primary (though not exclusive) interest in makeup, cosmetic surgery for wrinkles and jowls, Weight Watchers meetings, and fashion shows. Men, on the other hand, still accept most of the responsibility for initiating contact with women (and the risk of rejection). Though "women are more likely than men to report emotional symptoms of love, such as feeling euphoric, having trouble concentrating, or feeling as though they are 'floating on a cloud', "men tend to have "more severe emotional reactions to the ending of a relationship" (Peplau, 1983: 242, 246). The burdens of decision making and economic support within marriage are carried disproportionately by men. Society expects them to achieve, to compete, to be aggressive. These "men of iron" do not have the option to be voluntarily unemployed or to fail occupationally (Safilios-Rothschild, 1974). On the other hand, the children belong to the women. Revolutionary changes in divorce custody awards have *not* occurred in recent years. Wives receive custody in 86 percent of Canadian divorce cases (McKie, Prentice and Reed, 1983).

Education and economic experiences also differ by sex. In the 20-to-24-year age category, more Canadian males than females have been enrolled full-time in school in every census year since 1911 (Hunter, 1981). The number of girls studying physics and mathematics in high school is less than half the number of boys, with a corresponding absence of women in the ranks of physical scientists (Shore, 1982). Despite news stories of pioneering women lumberjacks, judges, and a Governor General, most Canadian women are segregated into relatively few, mostly low-skilled, poorly paid occupations (Armstrong and Armstrong, 1984). The "micro-chip revolution" is making jobs for men and taking them away from women (Menzies, 1984). As Gloria Steinem (1983a:8) puts it, most women are "only one man away from welfare."

Old age is not easy for either sex. Compared to older men, older women are more likely to be poor and widowed, to be living alone, or to be institutionalized (Abu-Laban, 1980; Dulude, 1978; Matthews, 1980). Elderly men, on the other hand, generally lack the occupational prestige, income, physical strength, and sexual prowess that are considered prerequisites for masculinity in our society (Abu-Laban, 1980). In recent years, destitute women have joined homeless men on the Skid Rows of our cities (Ross, 1982).

Men and women differentially experience physical and mental health. Although women are ill more often than men (Thompson and Brown, 1980), the average woman outlives the average man by seven years (Statistics Canada, 1985). More females than males have been diagnosed with depression, phobia, anxiety, hysteria, and chronic schizophrenia. More males than females have been diagnosed with personality disorders, such as alcoholism and drug addiction, and psychophysiological disorders, such as ulcers, heart, and respiratory illness (Al-Issa, 1980). At every age, Canadian males are more likely than Canadian females to kill themselves (Cumming and Lazer, 1981).

Though changes are occurring, women and men are socialized differently, play different roles, and have somewhat different thoughts and experiences. They live out their lives in social worlds that are separate at some points and overlapping at others. The masculine world is more powerful and prestigious than the feminine world. "Men and women march to different drummers"; in some respects, "they are not even in the same parade" (Bernard, 1975).

The Sex/Gender Distinction

In the late 1960s, the feminist movement alerted social scientists to the fact that the world contains women as well as men. A preliminary problem faced by those motivated to study female and male experiences in society was to specify basic vocabulary. Eventually, a consensus emerged to define *sex* as the "biological dichotomy between females and males," and *gender* as that "which is recognized as feminine or masculine by a social world" (Gould and Kern-Daniels, 1977). In other words, "sex" refers to physiology and "gender" to the sociocultural elaborations upon physiology.[1]

To go a step further, *sex roles* (behaviors stemming from biological sexual differences) may be distinguished from *gender roles* (socially created behaviors differentially assigned to men and women) (Lipman-Blumen, 1984:1). Child bearer and sperm donor are examples of sex roles, and mother and father of social roles. Similarly, we may speak of *sex norms* and *gender norms* (standards guiding biologically relevant and socially relevant behavior, respectively).

At first, the sex/gender distinction seemed straightforward enough. However, it was soon noticed that even sophisticated researchers tend to use the terms interchangeably, not because they are careless, but because it is often difficult, even impossible, to disentangle biology from culture (Eichler, 1980:12). For example, though pregnancy is a biological fact, being pregnant in medieval England was a different experience from being pregnant in twentieth-century Canada. Similarly, sexual intercourse is interpreted and guided by social scripts (Laws and Schwartz, 1977). Witness the emergence in the 1980s of a *herpes simplex* etiquette. In short, culture conditions biology, and biology sets limits on culture.

A second problem with the sex/gender terminology is a tendency to view *both* sex and gender as inevitable, dichotomous qualities, deeply rooted in human nature. This thinking is more characteristic of laypersons than social scientists. The difficulty stems, in part, from the high degree of congruency between sex and gender. Most biological females and males also learn to display feminine and masculine behavior, respectively. Moreover, since sex is determined at conception and is, for the most part, immutable, there is a temptation to see gender as similarly constant. Perhaps because sexuality and gender arouse considerable emotion and touch the very core of human identity and social relationships, both tend to be regarded as "moral facts." That is, in everyday thinking, every person should be " 'naturally,' 'originally,' 'in the first place,' 'in the beginning,' 'all along,' and 'forever' " one hundred percent male or female (Garfinkel, 1967:116). Hence, many people feel that men should not weep and that women should not swear. Some people were quite disturbed by mid-1980s "gender-blender" rock stars, like Boy George, who sported pancake makeup, eyeliner, and lip gloss. A father, asked whether he would be upset by signs of femininity in his son, replied: "Yes, I would be. Very, very much. Terrifically disturbed — couldn't tell you the extent of my disturbance. I can't *bear* female characteristics in a man. I abhor them" (Goodenough, 1957:310).

A third and related difficulty is the propensity to understand gender as a property of individuals, not a principle of social organization (Stacey and Thorne, 1985). Put another way, social scientists emphasize that gender is a continuum of norms and behaviors "socially constructed, socially perpetuated and socially alterable" (Gould and Kern-Daniels, 1977:184). Gender is not an attribute of the individual, always there, like a nose!

> To be sure, individuals continuously display gender (e.g., through dress and speech) and are categorized by others as female or male, and gender forms a basic core of identity . . . But gender is more prominent in some situations than others, may wax and wane in visibility in an encounter, and may be verbally invoked on some occasions and not others (Thorne, 1983:62).

A study of children's play illustrates Thorne's point. Richer (1984) observed the sex-integrated play of three- and four-year-old children in two Ontario day-care centers. The children "displayed no reluctance whatsoever to play with one another." The boys were found playing "doctor" or "cook" with the girls, just as girls were found building with blocks and driving toy trucks and cars. Not once did sex-based name-calling occur. Not once was one child rejected by another on the basis of sex. By contrast, gender was very salient in the play of the somewhat older nursery school children observed by the same researcher (Richer, 1979). The game "Farmer in the Dell" demonstrated their preference for sex-segregated play. First of all, the teacher would choose one child to be farmer. Then the child would stand in the middle of a circle of children, while the nursery rhyme was sung. During the singing, the farmer would choose a wife, who would choose a child, who would choose a nurse, who would choose a dog, who would choose a cat, who would choose a rat, who would finally choose a cheese. Richer's research team observed four games of "Farmer in the Dell." Of the 28 choices made, 25 were same-sex choices. The male "farmers" even chose male "wives." Richer concludes that the significance of gender is learned and this learning coincides with the beginning of formal schooling.

A final point. Conceptualizing gender as an aspect of social organization, as a network of norms, implies the evaluation and control of behavior (Schur, 1984:11). For example, societal expectations that women should be nurturant and men tough mean that sanctions will likely be imposed on people who violate these norms.

Although the sex/gender distinction is imperfect, it is the best conceptual device currently available to label biological versus sociological maleness and femaleness. The distinction allows us to ask these questions: What relationships exist between gender and sex, i.e., what is biological and what is sociocultural? How, in modern society, do the minor biological differences between the sexes come to assume such vast social importance? How is gender related to sexuality? How is gender learned? When does gender become relevant in social situations? Relatedly, who makes gender relevant and why? And a final, very important query: How do disparities in female-male power and status enter into the answers to all these questions?

The Content of Gender

Gender has been distinguished from sex and then described as socially constructed and processual. Now we want to look more closely at gender and its content. Three interrelated dimensions may be specified: differentiation; traits; and hierarchy.

Gender as Differentiation

First of all, gender implies noticing the female-male sex difference. In our society, a great fuss is made over this biological distinction, and elaborate sets of meanings are built upon it. Indeed, this sex-typing begins even before birth. Lewis (1972) reports that pregnant women respond to the activity of fetuses in a sex-differentiated fashion. If the fetus kicks and moves a great deal, this behavior is often interpreted as a sign that the baby is male. There is a great deal of folk wisdom on this subject. For example, a child's pre-natal position supposedly indicates its sex, boys being carried high and girls low. Later, parents of a newborn infant ask, "Is it a boy or a girl?" (if amniocentesis has not already told them). Though at this stage, the baby is little more than a bundle of tissue with potentiality, members of society immediately begin to react to it in terms of its sex/gender.

Limitations in the English language partially explain early sex-typing. We cannot talk to or about a child without using a sex-specific personal pronoun. To refer to a child as "it" seems unfriendly (Maccoby, 1980:203). However, the behavior goes deeper. A mother, whose yellow snowsuited infant accompanies her as she does errands in a small Alberta city, reports that store clerks and strangers on the street seem annoyed that the child doesn't visibly signal its sex/gender. Infants are sorted into two (and only two) social categories, the male-female dichotomy being a moral fact. This initial placement or *gender assignment* is the beginning of a sustained sorting process, a streaming into different socialization experiences (Goffman, 1977:303).

As mentioned above, gender may or may not be evoked in everyday situations. For example, Canadian girls playing skipping rope have traditionally had many gender-relevant rhymes in their repertoire:

> *Ice cream soda, lemonade tart,*
> *Tell me the name of your sweetheart.*
> *A, B, C, D, E . . . .*
>
> *Bread and butter, sugar and spice,*
> *How many boys think I'm nice?*
> *1, 2, 3, 4, 5 . . . .*

However, there are other themes available, such as violence:

> *My mother and your mother*
> *Were hanging out the clothes.*
> *My mother gave your mother*
> *A punch on the nose.*
> *What color was the blood?*

Sometimes, gender and violence themes are mixed:

> *Girl Guide, Girl Guide, dressed in yellow,*
> *This is the way I treat my fellow.*
> *Hug him, kiss him, kick him in the pants.*
> *That is the way to find romance.*
>
> (Fowke, 1969: 54, 57, 48)

In some situations, gender may be relevant only in that actors are displaying gender. Gender would be irrelevant for university students concentrating on a chemistry lecture. However, a sociology lecture that focuses upon men's and women's contrasting labor-force experiences would make gender highly salient for the students. Similarly, gender would be more salient for students on a date than at home studying.

The social significance of sex differentiation extends beyond such interactional episodes. The female-male distinction has served as a basic organizing principle for every known society extant today and in those of the reconstructed historical past. Traditionally, family, work, politics, religion, and leisure have all employed a division of labor that makes gender roles and gender norms central. In addition to sexual anatomy, such other criteria as age, social class, ethnicity, and occupation provide ways of socially classifying people. Whether urban, industrial societies will continue to employ the principle of sex for organizing activities that have nothing to do with reproduction is a moot point. When aptitude and talent are ignored, both individuals and societies pay a price (Martin and Voorhies, 1975:406–407).

Gender as Traits

The second dimension of gender content consists of the societal norms specifying what individuals should be, feel, and do in order to be appropriately feminine or masculine. "Exaggerating both real and imagined aspects of biological sex, each society sorts certain polarized behaviors and attitudes into two sets it then labels 'male' and 'female'" (Lipman-Blumen, 1984:2). These two sets of traits are considered to be opposites. Males are expected to be assertive and females retiring. "Inappropriate" behavior is subject to sanctions (Wilson, 1982:143). Assertive females may find themselves labeled "bitches," and unassertive males "wimps."

One of the adventures of Huckleberry Finn, Mark Twain's (1884/1966) fictional character, illustrates gender as traits. For reasons that need not concern us, Huckleberry Finn has been masquerading as Mary Williams. Mrs. Loftus, suspicious of Huck's gender claims, puts him to the test. He fails, and she explains why:

> . . . You do a girl tolerable poor, but you might fool men, maybe. Bless you, child, when you set out to thread a needle, don't hold the thread still and fetch the needle up to it; hold the needle still and poke the thread at it — that's the way a woman most always does; but a man always does 'tother way. And when you throw at a rat or anything hitch yourself up on tip-toe, and fetch your hand up over your head as awkward as you can, and miss your rat about six or seven foot. Throw stiff-armed from the shoulder, like there was a pivot there for it to turn on — like a girl; not from the wrist and elbow, with your arm out to one side, like a boy. And mind you, when a girl tries to catch anything in her lap, she throws her knees apart: she don't clap them together, the way you did when you catched the lump of lead. Why, I spotted you for a boy when you was threading the needle; and I contrived the other things just to make certain (Twain, 1884/1966:116).

Twain's book, which was written a century ago, dealt with the southern United States of an even earlier period. Therefore, it is not surprising that the gender norms he describes sound quaint to modern ears. The qualities of masculinity and femininity vary considerably by culture and historical period.

Margaret Mead's classic anthropological study, *Sex and Tempera-ment in Three Primitive Societies* (1935), makes the point that what is regarded as masculine behavior in one society or era may be viewed as feminine in another place or time. More than fifty years ago, Mead (1935) set off to New Guinea to observe the relationship between sex and temperament in three tribes: the gentle, mountain-dwelling Arapesh; the fierce, cannibalistic Mundugumor; and the head-hunters of Tchambuli. Arapesh men and women alike displayed a gentle, mater-nal personality, which would seem feminine in our society.[2] On the other hand, the Mundugumor were pathologically "masculine": violent, aggressive, jealous, active, and competitive. Finally, among the Tcham-buli, gender roles and the accompanying temperament reversed Western notions of normalcy. The woman was the "dominant, impersonal, managing partner, the man the less responsible and the emotionally dependent person" (Mead, 1935:205). In short, Mead's results argue for the variability of female-male patterns. From her observations of the three tribes, she concluded:

> The material suggests that we may say that many, if not all, of the personality traits which we called masculine or feminine are as lightly linked to sex as are the clothing, the manners, and the forms of head dress that a society at a given period assigns to either sex . . . [The] evidence is overwhelmingly in favour of the strength of social con-ditioning (Mead, 1935:206).

Social scientists classify gender as traits according to two dimensions: communal-agentic (Bakan, 1966) or *expressive-instrumental* (Parsons, 1955). (The terms are synonymous but since both are frequently used, both are given here.) Traditionally, the essence of femininity has been a communal orientation, a concern for the relationship between self and other, and preoccupation with familial goals (the domestic sphere). The contrasting masculine agentic orientation has been concerned with active manipulation of the public sphere, especially with occupational goals. These gender-distinctive concerns and activities have been accompanied by corresponding attitudes and skills, for example, the feminine expressive qualities of nurturance, dependence, and the masculine instrumental qualities of aggressiveness, competitiveness. Traditional social organization has articulated with this instrumental/ expressive depiction of masculinity and femininity. Some social scien-tists have regarded social organization as inevitably grounded upon sex differences:

> In our opinion the fundamental explanation of the alloca-
> tion of the roles between the biological sexes lies in the
> fact that the bearing and early nursing of children estab-
> lish a strong presumptive primacy of the relation of
> mother to the small child and this in turn establishes a
> presumption that the man, who is exempted from these
> biological functions, should specialize in the alternative
> instrumental direction (Parsons, 1955).

Later on, we shall return to this interpretation.

Gender as Hierarchy

The third aspect of gender content is ranking of males and females.
Every society is gender-asymmetrical and values men's characteristics
and activities more than women's (Lipman-Blumen, 1984:6). According
to Confucius, "one hundred women are not worth a single testicle" (Cox,
1976: 238). As a result, males enjoy more status and resources than
females, and exercise more power and influence over others.[3]

Illustrations abound of the cultural devaluation of females.
Richer's (1983) study of Ottawa kindergarten children found evidence
of early understanding of gender inequality. The children maintained
that their school was rife with "girl germs" which threatened boys who
came into physical contact with girls. The only way for a boy to ward
off girl germs was to enact the purification ritual of crossing his fingers
as soon as possible after touching the girl. According to Richer
(1983:118),

> the fact that the expression "boy germs" was never used
> and that in general, the girls made no effort to challenge
> the girl germs label is indicative of the very early accep-
> tance by both sexes of a hierarchical division between
> males and females.

Parents' widespread preference for male children is another indicator of gender inequality. Although many folk remedies exist to
guarantee the production of male children (Long, 1983), folk wisdom
shows correspondingly little interest in female children. In order to
encourage conception of a son, Germanic tradition suggests taking an
axe into the marriage bed. Hebrew custom advises aligning the marriage
bed on a north-south axis, while Texan males are advised to wear boots
during sex if they want sons. Polynesian women are supposed to wear
men's clothing before intercourse to achieve the same goal. Many
methods reflect the ancient Chinese notion that the right side of the
body is masculine, the left feminine. (Parenthetically, the right side is
often described as the side of God in Western religions.) Sperm from
the right testicle was believed to produce male offspring and therefore,

the belief grew that sons could be conceived by tying off the left testicle. Indeed, eighteenth-century French noblemen, desperate for male heirs, are said to have had their left testicle amputated (Wolinsky, 1983).

All of the above methods work about half the time — that is, not at all. However, more sure-fire, if severe methods of guaranteeing a high sex ratio exist, such as infanticide:

> The birth of a female infant always caused some degree of dismay in China. She was not a member of her father's lineage and could not . . . provide even her father's descent line with descendants. By the time she was old enough to be of even minimal labor value she had to be sent to another family as a bride. Given the narrow margin between survival and starvation within which many Chinese peasants existed, the high rate of female infanticide in traditional China should not be surprising (Wolf, 1974:158).

Today, amniocentesis (a method that provides early identification of a fetus's sex) is reportedly used to abort female fetuses in such areas of the world as China and India, where the preference for boys is pronounced (Campbell, 1976). Though the preference for boys in the industrialized West is mild, it is still there. Parents prefer male first children, but sex-balanced completed families (Dixon and Levy, 1985). Asking what sort of social arrangements would result if Canadian parents could guarantee the sex of their children by taking a hypothetical blue pill or pink pill is an interesting science-fiction question (Campbell, 1976).

The cultural belief in the superiority of maleness translates into greater male power (Unger, 1978:464). (The sources of male prestige and the means of their translation into power will be considered in subsequent sections.) *Power* can be defined as the capacity of individuals or groups to control, influence, or manipulate others' behavior, whether these others wish to cooperate or not (Kopinak, 1983:405). Many feminist writers have characterized women in terms of their powerlessness: "the weak are the second sex" (Janeway, 1974); "where power is, women are not" (Nowotny, 1980:147). Simone de Beauvoir (1949) regards man as Subject and woman as Other:

> . . . woman has always been man's dependent, if not his slave; the two sexes have never shared the world in equality (de Beauvoir, 1949:xx).

Many of the behavioral differences between males and females are really power differences (Matthews, 1982; Unger, 1978). For example, folk knowledge depicts men as direct and forthright in their dealings with others and women as devious and manipulative. Assuming this description to be accurate, these interaction modes really describe the powerful and powerless in general, and not men and women in particular.

To say that males are more powerful than females means that males are situated in the highest stratum of every social institution — the family, the occupational system, the political and legal system, the religious system, the economic system. Though some women are more powerful than some men, women are consistently located in strata below men of their own social group (Lipman-Blumen, 1984:48):

> . . . in all known societies, despite differences in stage of development and political and economic structures, women's relative status and bargaining power are consistently less than that of men in their own cultures (Lipman-Blumen, 1984:48).

One facet of power, to which we shall return in the next chapter, is the fact that males are the creators and perpetrators of the dominant, authoritative world view. Where alternative perspectives exist, "he who has the bigger stick has the better chance of imposing his definitions of reality" (Berger and Luckmann, 1966:109). Social scientists disagree with the general public's stereotype of women as the talkative sex (Mackie, 1971). Instead, they find females to be "muted" and males "articulate" (Ardener, 1975). P. Fishman (1978), who taped conversations of three mixed-sex couples in their homes, documents the expression of power in the domestic sphere. She adopts a more specific definition of power as "the ability to impose one's definition of what is possible, what is right, what is rational, what is real" (p. 397). Fishman's research illustrates female muteness in the micro-world.

According to Fishman, women asked three times as many questions as men. Women used some version of the conversational opening, "D'ya know what?" twice as often as men. (Children use this strategy to ensure their right to speak.) Men often displayed minimal responses, indicating lack of interest. Men produced over twice as many statements as women, and they almost always got a response. For example, many times one or another of a couple were reading, then read a passage aloud or commented on what he was reading for the benefit of the other person. "The man's comments often engendered a lengthy exchange, the woman's comments seldom did" (P. Fishman, 1978:402). Fishman concludes that women do more of the interaction work than men; they keep the conversation going. However, the "definition of what is appropriate or inappropriate conversation becomes the man's choice" (P. Fishman, 1978:404).

Gender Deviance: The Case of Transsexuals

If gender is conceptualized as "a normative system . . . through which female (and male) behavior is evaluated and controlled" (Schur, 1984:11), the study of gender deviance becomes a matter of central concern. Since the powerful make and enforce the rules, the normative system of gender is a male product that serves to control females (Schur, 1984). "In our society, male is normal (not merely different) and female is deviant, or Other" (Laws, 1979:4). Femaleness carries a stigma in and of itself. However, there exist more specific cases of gender deviance: the "tomboy" who walks fences and jumps off garage roofs, clad in her Sunday best; the "sissy" with feminine mannerisms who prefers Barbie dolls to hockey; the homosexual who dates same-sex persons; the transvestite sexually aroused by cross-dressing. This section considers the most controversial of all gender deviants, the transsexual.

Renée Richards was born Richard Henry Raskind. Unusually intelligent and a superb athlete, Richard seemed to outsiders to be a "super-boy." Later, he became captain of the Yale University tennis team, and eventually an eye surgeon and army officer. He married and fathered a son. Richard, however, had a secret. From the age of three, he had felt that he was really a girl named Renée, trapped in someone else's body. Indeed, the highlight of his secret childhood was dressing up in his sister's clothing. Eventually, Richard underwent sex reassignment surgery and emerged as Renée Richards, professional tennis player and coach of Wimbleton champion Martina Navratilova (Richards, 1983).

Nearly everyone is familiar with the celebrity transsexuals who have written autobiographies — Renée Richards (1983), Jan Morris (1974), and Christine Jorgensen (1968). (Richard's story was made into the 1986 TV movie, *Second Serve*.) Until Christine Jorgensen's highly publicized 1952 sex-change operation in Denmark, few such operations were done and few people had heard of transsexuals. Since then, 3,000 to 4,000 transsexuals have undergone sex reassignment surgery in the United States (Geer et al., 1984:398). Between 1968 when it opened its doors and 1984, the Gender Identity Clinic at Toronto's Clarke Institute had seen more than 700 transsexuals and approved sex reassignment for 113 of them (MacFarlane, 1984). The world contains an estimated 30,000 self-labeled transsexuals (Lothstein, 1982:422). However, the surgery is becoming less popular (Geer et al., 1984:398).

The experiences of Renée Richards and other transsexuals shed considerable light on gender as a socially constructed phenomenon. *Transsexuals* are persons whose *gender identity* (their own conviction of being female or male) contradicts their biological sex. Such persons resent their own sex organs and "share an intense and insistent desire to transform their bodies into those of the opposite sex, in the conviction that they are victims of nature's mistake" (Restak, 1979:20). Transsexualism differs in degree rather than kind from transvestism and homosexuality (Benjamin, 1966). Male *transvestites* generally accept themselves as men, but are sexually motivated to dress occasionally in women's clothing. Because it is socially acceptable for women to dress as men, female transvestites are non-existent in our culture. For example, no one looks twice at females in pants, but the same cannot be said of males in dresses (Geer et al., 1984:395). There are practically no reports of females who experience sexual arousal by wearing men's clothes (Green, 1979:160). Technically speaking, transsexuals are *homosexual*, insofar as they prefer sexual contact with persons of the same physical sex. However, since they believe themselves to be trapped in the wrong body, they experience their desires as heterosexual. There-fore, most transsexuals prefer that their partners not be self-defined homosexuals. "Raj," a Toronto female-to-male transsexual, put it this way: "People say, 'if you like women, stay a lesbian.' But it's nothing to do with that . . . to be a lesbian you have to feel like a woman" (Mac-Farlane, 1984:S19). However, transsexuals, transvestites, and homo-sexuals may co-exist in the same subculture (Kando, 1973).

Sex reassignment can dramatically alter physical appearance and external genitals. However, reproductive capacity and chromosomal make-up remain unchanged. A man who wants to become a woman undergoes electrolysis and estrogen therapy. Then, penis and testes are removed and an artifical vagina constructed. Some male transsexuals seek cosmetic surgery for nose and Adam's apple and silicon breast implants. The female-to-male process involves hormones, hysterectomy, surgical removal of breasts, and perhaps, construction of an artificial penis (Geer et al., 1984:401).

Before genital surgery is performed, the patient is expected to live successfully as a member of the other sex for at least a year. In effect, the patient is told:

> If you believe you can function better socially as a female (or male), prove it. Dress all day, every day, in the role you desire. Get a job in that role. Move to a new neigh-borhood and live that new life. See how it really is (Green, 1979:160).

It is not surprising that transsexuals who have undergone, first, this social experiment and then surgery, talk about having been "re-born" (Kando, 1973:100).

The psychosocial adjustment of post-operative transsexuals is a matter of great controversy (Raymond, 1979). The patients themselves usually claim to be happy (Restak, 1979). After reviewing the evidence, Lothstein (1982:418) concluded that because of scarcity of sound follow-up studies, "very little is actually known about the medical-surgical and social-psychological effects of sex reassignment surgery." The one rigorous comparative study of operated and non-operated transsexuals (Meyer and Reter, 1979) reported that the latter do equally well. Such assessments have had "a chilling effect on the prevailing positive attitudes towards such surgery" (Geer et al., 1984:402).

Medical authorities also disagree over whether transsexualism is rooted in biology or faulty family dynamics (Benjamin, 1966; Green and Money, 1969; Stoller, 1968). Transsexuals themselves prefer a biological explanation, argue that they have no choice about the matter, and consider surgery repairing a "birth defect," not sex change. A medical problem is preferable to a moral problem (Kessler and Mc-Kenna, 1978:117). Gender relations specialists are especially interested in the social context that makes transsexualism possible (Raymond, 1979:xiv). These five issues are of particular concern:

First of all, the very existence of transsexualism is a dramatic (some say sad) commentary on the importance of gender in our society. In Eichler's (1980:88) words, "transsexuals are people who suffer so deeply from the sex structure that they are willing to endure terrible pain . . . in order to reduce their suffering." In a similar vein, Steinem (1983a:209) says transsexualism is a "testimony to the importance of sex roles as dictated by a society obsessed with body image, genitals, and 'masculine' or 'feminine' behavior."

Secondly, transsexualism emphasizes our society's construction of gender as a taken-for-granted dichotomy that parallels sexual dimorphism. The social definition of the situation holds that two, and only two, genders exist and that everyone, without exception, must be classified as a member of one or the other category. Transsexuals say, "I feel like I have a feminine brain trapped in a male body" (or the reverse). "A female mind in a male body only makes sense as a concept in a society that accepts the reality of both" (Raymond, 1979). A 26-year-old female-to-male transsexual expresses this point:

> There're only two alternatives in society. You're either a man or a woman. If I don't feel like a woman then it's got to be the other way . . . Because I didn't feel comfortable in the first position, I'm going into the second. I'll give it a try (Kessler and McKenna, 1978:112).

The fact that modern societies are willing to finance the very expensive sex reassignment process suggests both extreme intolerance of gender ambiguity (Eichler, 1980:72) and compassion for the suffering it produces.

Anthropologists' identification of mixed-gender statuses in quite a number of pre-industrial cultures shows gender to be a continuum of sociocultural attitudes, not an inevitable dichotomy. For example, the *berdache*, anatomical males dressed as women and performing women's tasks, occurred in most cultural areas of native North America about a century ago (Whitehead, 1981:84).

> Imagine a family in which there is a son. The child
> shows an interest in female tasks and shuns male tasks,
> so the parents decide to test him. They put their son in a
> small enclosure with a bow and arrow and some
> basketweaving material. Then they set fire to the
> enclosure and watch to see what he grabs as he runs out
> (Kessler and McKenna, 1978:21).

The child who grabs the basketry material is defined as neither male nor female, but something in between.

Thomas Berger's novel, *Little Big Man* (1964), portrays a berdache named Little Horse, who chose not to live up to the warrior ideal. Though Little Horse adopted women's dress and many feminine mannerisms, he was considered a "part man, part woman," not a woman. He interacted comfortably with both male and female members of the tribe (Doyle, 1983:82). "The transformation of a berdache was not a complete shift from his . . . *biological* gender to the opposite one, but rather an approximation of the latter in some of its social aspects" (Callender and Kochems, 1983). For these aboriginal tribes, the basis of masculine gender was occupation, clothing, and mannerisms, as much as physiology (Whitehead, 1981:88). The greater significance of women's anatomy explained the absence of female berdaches. Her menstruation and reproductive capabilities overwhelmed her occupational activities in defining her gender. In Whitehead's (1981:92) words, "female blood and its attendant associations seems to have anchored women more firmly in their womanly identity than male anatomy anchored the man in his masculinity." By the late nineteenth century, the phenomenon of the berdache disappeared as native construction of gender gave way to the dominant ideology of Western culture (Blackwood, 1984).

There is a third reason why transsexualism provides insight into the meaning of gender for the rest of the population. Transsexualism is a dramatic indicator of the primacy of biology in everyday thinking about gender. That is, the genitals are thought to be the natural basis, the source of gender. Researcher Kando (1973:53) asked a feminized transsexual, "What do you consider the ultimate difference between a man and a woman?" She answered, "Having sex organs . . . a vagina." For whatever reason, the transsexual experiences a discrepancy between gender identity and body. Instead of feeling free to give personality priority and relaxing traditional gender norms, the transsexual finds it necessary to change the body through "mutilating, irreversible, and drastic" surgery (Restak, 1979:20). Similarly, Steinem (1983a:210) asks,

"If the shoe doesn't fit, must we change the foot?" Transsexual authority Dr. Virginia Prince (1978:268) gives this advice:

> What the patient (and often the doctor) does not realize is that it is perfectly possible to change names, legal identification, passport, bank accounts, credit cards, diplomas, and other documents and *be* a woman without having sex surgery. I speak from personal, first-hand experience here because that is just what I did six and one half years ago. It is possible to shift one's identity into the head and away from the genitals and if this is accomplished, surgery is superfluous . . .

By contrast, ceremonial assumption of the occupation and dress of the other sex, but not genital alteration, marked the social birth of the berdache (Kessler and McKenna, 1978:39).

A fourth consideration. The reasons for the preponderance of male-to-female transsexuals is an intriguing gender relations puzzle. Estimates of the ratio of men to women requesting and obtaining sex reassignment surgery vary between two to one and seven to one (Raymond, 1979:24). While the possible motivation of the female-to-male transsexual as "status climber" is intuitively easier to understand, the male-to-female transsexual seems to be sacrificing status and power. The newly female Jan Morris (1974:159) was sensitive to her loss of rank:

> I know that by the very fact of my womanhood . . . I am treated in many petty situations as a second-class citizen — not because I lack brains, or experience, or character, but purely because I wear the body of a woman.

Male-to-female transsexual Sylvia says she does "the same work as before, secretary . . . but I get less now than I made before . . ." (Kando, 1973:60).

There are a number of explanations for the unequal proportions of female and male transsexuals. For one thing, there is the possibility that the condition is biologically caused by hormone accidents. If so, the prenatal error of female hormones in the brains of biological males is apparently more likely to occur than the reverse situation (Green, 1979:158). In addition, male-to-female surgery is less technically difficult, less expensive, better developed, and better publicized than that required by biological female transsexuals (Raymond, 1979:24–26). Devising a functional vagina is far easier than constructing an artificial penis that works (Geer et al., 1984:399). Also, success stories of people like Renée Richards have encouraged males to come forward. Once they do, there is comfort available in a subculture of males with gender-identity difficulties.

However, many authorities (Raymond, 1979) argue that the sexist nature of society is the most important explanation of the sex ratio. Contemporary society affords females more latitude for cross-sex expression. Women can dress in a masculine manner and, at least in young adulthood, live together without being stigmatized. Morgan (1978, cited in Geer et al., 1984:400) estimates that 30 percent of males requesting sex reassignment surgery are homophobics, seeking to avoid being stigmatized as homosexuals. Similarly, Kando's (1973:67) ethnographic study found a major reason for male-to-female transsexualism was "to gain greater social acceptance and respectability than they enjoyed prior to their operations, as homosexuals, transvestites, or some other category of social outcasts." Moreover, the higher incidence of male transsexualism may well be a graphic expression of the rigidity and unrealistic expectations of the male gender role (Raymond, 1979:24–26). A fictional character comments on the male role:

> For years, I bathed each morning, frosted my cheeks with
> Aqua Velva, donned a three-piece suit and snap-brim
> hat, and feeling like Superman emerging from a tele-
> phone booth, set forth to save the world from a lack of
> life insurance. I loathed the job so much that I did it
> quickly, urgently, almost violently (Kinsella, 1982:9).

In keeping with this final point, male-to-female transsexuals tend to glorify traditional masculinity. Jan Morris (1974:160) wrote about losing "the male stride, the male assurance, the problems and prerequisites of malehood, the constancy and the strength, the independence, the supremacy." As James Morris, he had lived what seemed a macho life — trained in military school, climbed Mt. Everest, been a war correspondent, fathered four children.

> Yet, according to his autobiography, no matter what feats
> he sets himself as a male or what his accomplishments,
> the high ideals of masculinity were never attained. By
> placing masculinity on a pedestal, the male-to-female
> transsexual finds himself unworthy and unable to live up
> to the honor of being a male; not meeting the ideal, he
> becomes a woman (Richardson, 1981:14).

These professional definitions of the transsexuals' situation should not be confused with the latter's own motives. Motivation has more to do with *current* interpretations or accounts (Lyman and Scott, 1970) of conduct to self and others, than prior causes (Mills, 1940).

Lastly, gender relations specialists are fascinated with transsexuality because these people's experiences in learning to "pass" provide a rich source of data on gender as social accomplishment. In the trial period before surgery, transsexuals manage themselves as persons of the gender they were not born to in order to be sure of their decision before it is irrevocable. Their performance must convince others. Though some post-operative transsexuals are quite open about their status, others pass successfully with friends, spouses, and sex partners (Kando, 1973).

> Genital surgery is often so successful that even experienced gynecologists do not question the authenticity of the transsexuals' genitals. Janet, a male-to-female transsexual, described a visit to a gynecologist who, not knowing that Janet was a transsexual, told her that there was a cyst on one of her ovaries. Janet protested that this was impossible. The doctor explained that he ought to know since he was a gynecologist, whereupon she countered with, "Well, I ought to know; I'm a transsexual" (Kessler and McKenna, 1978:130).

To pass, a new name must be adopted and a biography reconstructed. Motor patterns characteristic of males or females must be learned. Take leg crossing: a man tends to rest one ankle on the opposite knee; a woman is more likely to place one knee on top of the other. Voice pitch and resonance must be adjusted. "Proper" talk must be learned (Kessler and McKenna, 1978:126), as well as use of the other sex's washroom without being detected (Restak, 1979:24). The point to be emphasized is that although non-transsexuals must also accomplish gender, they do "naturally" what transsexuals do self-consciously (Kessler and McKenna, 1978:114) and with keen sensitivity to subtle cultural expectations most of us take for granted (Kando 1973:5).

In summary, in the critical eye of society, the deviance of transsexuals is twofold: "they are condemned in part for trying to 'steal' the other (biological) sex's appearance and 'body language,' and more generally for unacceptably blurring boundaries of sexual identity that people wish to believe are clear-cut" (Schur, 1984:58). Although to a lesser extent, gay men and women also challenge the moral facts of heterosexual masculinity and femininity.

Female-Male Differences

Our society emphasizes both sex and gender. Moreover, people tend to view anatomical distinctions and cultural elaborations upon them as equally natural. Therefore, it makes sense to determine just how important these differences really are before getting down to the real business of this book, namely, socialization. Possible origins of such differences are explored in succeeding sections.

FIGURE 1-1
Overlapping Normal Curves of Aggressiveness

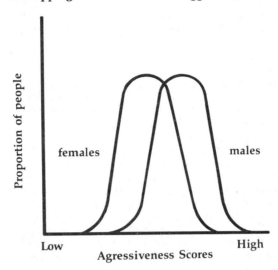

Misleading Female-Male Comparisons

Because so much emotion and mystery surround male-female relations, it is not surprising that many notions about male-female differences have been biased (Tresemer, 1975). We dwell on the differences between the sexes and ignore their similarities. Men and women are seen as *either* this *or* that, not both. We are fascinated with the anatomical differences required by intercourse and reproduction. However, we tend to overlook the fact that males and females really share much the same body blueprint.

Misleading comparisons are also made about psychological traits. We assume (correctly, as it happens [Deaux, 1985; Maccoby and Jacklin, 1974]) that males are more aggressive than females. However, this does not mean that *all* males are aggressive or that *all* females are unassertive. This logical pitfall is known as the *fallacy of the average* (Doyle, 1983:113). Research shows that this gender difference, as well as others, can be represented as an overlapping normal curve as in Figure 1-1. Both males and females vary between being highly aggressive and very unaggressive. However, the group average for males is somewhat higher. Nevertheless, a substantial number of females will be as or more aggressive than many males.

Primary Sex Differences

There is a chromosomal difference between the sexes. Women and men share 22 pairs of chromosomes. The one pair that differs determines the genetic sex of the individual. The female carries two X chromosomes and the male an X and a Y chromosome. The sexes also differ hormonally. The dominant sex hormones in males are androgens (the most powerful of them is called testosterone). In females, the dominant hormones are estrogen and progesterone. As Nicholson (1984:11) points out, "calling these 'male' and 'female' hormones is actually misleading, because both sexes produce both hormones, and the only difference lies in the balance between them." Females are equipped with ovaries, clitoris and vagina, and males with testes, penis and scrotum. Only females have the potential to give birth.

> Far from falling into two discrete groups, male and
> female have the same body ground-plan, and even the
> anatomical difference is more apparent than real. Neither
> the phallus nor the womb are organs of one sex only:
> the female phallus (the clitoris) is the biological equiva-
> lent of the male organ, and men possess a vestigial
> womb, whose existence they may well ignore until it
> causes enlargement of the prostrate gland in old age
> (Oakley, 1972:18).

Secondary Sex Differences

Females and males are also distinguished by a number of secondary sex characteristics which become more pronounced with puberty (Barfield, 1976). On the average, males are taller, heavier, and have a greater percentage of total body weight in muscle, and a smaller proportion of fat. Females have lighter skeletons, different shoulder/pelvis proportions, different pelvic bone shapes and different socket shapes at hip and shoulder. These differences contribute to women having less strength (especially in the upper body), less endurance for heavy labor, more difficulty in overarm throwing (as Huckleberry Finn discovered), and (thanks to that extra fat), a better ability to float. The overlapping nature of sex differences should be reiterated. Although the average man is taller and stronger than the average woman, the variation within the male or female categories may be greater than the male-female difference. For example,

> in the 1979 marathon race in New York City, the first
> woman to complete the race, Grete Waitz, ran faster than
> over 99 percent of the men who reached the finish line.
> There was roughly a sixteen-minute difference in running
> time between her and the first man to finish. There was
> over a five-hour difference in running time between the
> first man and the last man to finish (Hunter Collective,
> 1983:97).

Psychological Differences

With regard to psychological characteristics, the foremost expert in the area concludes that "the sexes are more alike than different" (Maccoby, 1980). Nevertheless, debate about such psychological traits as intelligence is centuries old. In 1879, Le Bon wrote:

> All psychologists who have studied the intelligence of women, as well as poets and novelists, recognize today that they represent the most inferior forms of human evolution and that they are closer to children and savages than to an adult, civilized man (quoted in Deaux, 1985:55).

Modern research shows no sex differences in general intelligence or creativity (Maccoby and Jacklin, 1974). To date, research has established that females have superior verbal ability, while males have superior mathematical ability and visual-spatial skills (Henley, 1985:108). However, these cognitive differences are slight (Hyde, 1981), and the sources for them unclear. Moreover, the performance of both sexes can be significantly altered by training (Deaux, 1985:55–56).

Because of the ease of administering personality questionnaires, psychologists have investigated sex differences in almost every imaginable personality disposition. Two lines of inquiry show current promise. First, men score somewhat higher on competitiveness. Researchers are scrutinizing subjective meaning of tasks to men and women (Deaux, 1985:57). Second, the sexes may differ in moral development, with caring and responsibility in relationships mattering more to women and individual rights and abstract rules being more characteristic of men (Gilligan, 1982). (See Chapter 4.)

Psychologists have established female-male differences in three major social behaviors. As mentioned earlier, males tend to be more aggressive than females. Males engage in more physical aggression, more verbal aggression, and more aggressive fantasies (Maccoby and Jacklin, 1974). Second, females are somewhat more likely than males to conform to group pressure (Eagley and Carli, 1981). Although females are not inherently more persuasible, they are sometimes more willing to go along with the group rather than risk disharmony. This is especially so when the issue falls outside their perceived expertise. Finally, the sexes differ in non-verbal behaviors. For example, women gaze more at men (Lamb, 1981) and are touched more by men (Henley, 1975) than vice versa. Women are more revealing senders of non-verbal cues and somewhat superior decoders of other people's non-verbal behavior (Deaux and Wrightsman, 1984:343). (See Chapter 6.)

The point to be emphasized is that research shows psychological sex differences to be statistically significant in large populations but a weak determinant of behavior. When "any particular behavior is considered, differences between males and females may be of relatively little consequence" (Deaux, 1984).[4] Considerations of gender in Canadian society involve such matters as fashion (trousers and hair length are no longer reliable guides); etiquette and demeanor (who drives the car on dates, who lights cigarettes for whom?); language (which sex is more often likened to food — a dish, tomato, peach, cookie, honey, cheese cake? [Eakins and Eakins, 1978]); social roles (nurses versus soldiers, mothers versus fathers); spheres of existence (the domestic world of women versus the public world of men). The psychological differences enumerated above have very little to do with these phenomena. For example, the fact of male superiority in spatial and mathematical skills cannot really explain why males outnumber females in architecture and engineering. Instead, socialization must be taken into account.

Siamese Twins and Gender Identity

In the summer of 1984, a well-publicized story of gender reassignment occurred at the Toronto Hospital for Sick Children. For two and a half years, Siamese twins from Burma, Lin and Win Htut, had shared the lower half of a body, including liver, intestines, and genitals. Joined at the pelvis in a Y-shape, they would never have walked. Indeed, they lived a "see saw" existence. When one twin wanted to sit up, the other had to lie down. The twins were separated in a 17-hour operation performed by a 43-member medical team.

The twins were genetically male but had only one penis between them. The doctors had to decide which one would retain a complete set of genitals. How to divide up the twin's body-in-common was a decision to challenge Solomon. "You wonder what happens when they grow up and say, 'How come you got that and I didn't?' " muses surgeon-in-chief Dr. Robert Filler. After consultation by telephone with the parents at home in Burma, the doctors agreed that Lin, the livelier and more aggressive (albeit smaller) of the two, should keep the male genitals. His sexuality is expected to be fully functional. During the surgery, the team constructed a vagina for Win from a tubelike section of colon. Though she will take female hormones when she reaches puberty, she will not be able to have children or a full sexual response. Win's favorite toy is reported to be a new tea set.

Sociologist Sylvia Hale made these observations in the Toronto *Globe and Mail* (August 11, 1984):

> There is something a lot more problematic about the so-called sex-change operation on the Siamese twins than that the more aggressive twin got the male genitalia . . . It has to do with the underlying concept of male and female, with female being defined solely in the negative — as "not having a penis."

The instant Win was surgically separated from the penis, everyone started referring to him as "her." A child, it seems, is only male when there is a penis present, while a child who does not have a penis is female, even when there are no ovaries, no uterus and genetically male chromosomes. But when female is defined from the female perspective as "capacity to bear offspring," then the child Win clearly did not "become a girl." Win is a male child without a penis.

Note also what is assumed in the doctor's statement that "they created a vagina for her." A vagina, defined from the female perspective, is the entrance to the uterus and the site of sexual pleasure. Defined thus, Win does not have a vagina. Win has an indentation between the legs from which some male might in the future get pleasure, but which is unlikely to give much sexual pleasure to Win.

Why, one wonders, was it unthinkable to give Win an artificial penis which might have looked like the real thing without having erectile or erotic capabilities, but quite acceptable to give Win an artificial vagina which may look like the real thing, but which is useless for reproductive or sexual pleasure? At least Win would not have had to "change sex."

Finally, note which child got most of the skin and muscle from the undeveloped third leg to close the abdominal wounds. He who gets the penis seems to get all the other perks as well. No doubt he will continue to do so for the rest of his life in this patriarchally defined world.

Sources: Anne Hollister, "From One Life to Two," *Life Magazine,* © October 1984 Time Inc. Reprinted with permission.
Sylvia M. Hale, "Siamese Twins and Gender Identity." Reprinted with permission of the Toronto *Globe and Mail,* August 11, 1984.

Biological Explanations of Gender

To what extent are women feminine and men masculine because they were born that way? In particular, is women's social subordination a reflection of their biological inferiority? Alternatively, are social structure and upbringing the real issues? These are enormously complex questions. They are questions that have been considered by many scientific disciplines. Nicholson (1984:3) describes it as "an over-researched area which is littered with contradictory findings . . ." For example, sociobiologists (e.g. Barash, 1979; Dawkins, 1976; Symons, 1979; Wilson, 1975) adopt an evolutionary perspective and try to explain twentieth-century gender relations by examining the way animals behave and "by making guesses about how our prehistoric ancestors might have organized their lives" (Nicholson, 1984:5). They espouse a "we're here because we're here" mentality and assume that any social practice, such as male supremacy, that has survived must be "good" (Tavris and Offir,

1977:266-277). Other biologists (Bleier, 1979) warn against extrapolating from one species to another.

The brain-lateralization approach to sex differences has become a trendy topic in popular books (Durden-Smith and deSimone, 1983) and magazines (Maynard, 1984). *Lateralization* refers to hypothesized specialization of each brain hemisphere. Efforts to explain slight sex differences in language fluency and visual-spatial abilities have focussed on apparent differences in the way male and female brains function (Bryden, 1979; Inglis and Lawson, 1981). People with psychosexual abnormalities, such as Siamese twins Win and Lin Htut (see insert), have functioned, to some extent, as natural experiments that provide some insight into the question of the relative weight of biological and social causation in the development of gender. Although central assumptions are open to scrutiny by outsiders, only practitioners of these disciplines are fully competent to sort out the intricacies of their own studies.

As it turns out, the questions outlined at the beginning of this section are *political* questions as well as scientific questions. They are "political" in that answers are preferred that enhance the image and position of one sex at the expense of the other. Even today some scientists suggest, in all sincerity, that "however well intentioned, the women's liberation movement . . . [wants] biologically unnatural changes that would bring grief to the human race" (Fausto-Sterling, 1985:4). Where knowledge is political, people with a stake in the outcome "have usually decided what the facts and their causes are prior to examining the data. Indeed, in many cases *despite* the data" (Weyant, 1979:373, emphasis in original). Grasping the political nature of the debate and cultivating a skeptical attitude is more critical than mastering all the details of the biological "stories." (For detailed discussions of this matter, see Ambert, 1976; Frieze et al., 1978; Mackie, 1983b; Nicholson, 1984; Oakley, 1972.)

The remainder of this section will first of all examine the feminist perspective on the nature-nurture debate. Then, after sketching some of the alternative treatments of this question, we will consider in detail the anthropological approach to gender's origins. Anthropology, sociology's sister discipline, offers findings that are here both cogent and transparent. At the end of this chapter, we will offer some conclusions concerning the whole matter.

The Politics of the Nature-Nurture Question

Feminists have charged that research on sex differences has often been a value-laden activity, used as "battle weapons against women" (Bernard, 1976:13). Specifically, the motive to seek knowledge was diverted by illegitimate attempts to document male superiority and to rationalize unequal social arrangements. Among the prerogatives of the more powerful sex is the ability to establish the ground-rules of the debate. (See Chapter 2.) For example, Eichler (1980:92) observed that those who have social power can decree which traits are hallmarks of inferiority and which of superiority. Steinem (1983a:337) elaborates:

> Whatever a "superior" group has will be used to justify
> its superiority, and whatever an "inferior" group has will
> be used to justify its plight. Black men were given poorly
> paid jobs because they were said to be "stronger" than
> white men, while all women were relegated to poorly
> paid jobs because they were said to be "weaker." As the
> little boy said when asked if he wanted to be a lawyer
> like his mother, "Oh no, that's women's work."

For instance, our culture has traditionally described women as the "weaker sex." Nevertheless, perhaps because the two X chromosomes provide extra genetic protection, females have a lifelong biological advantage. Female fetuses are less likely to abort spontaneously or to die at birth. The approximately equal sex ratio at birth occurs because more males than females are conceived. Female children are less vulnerable to physical trauma. Adult women live longer (Maccoby, 1980:206–207).[5] In short, men tend to be stronger and women more durable (Huber, 1976). Our male-dominated society, understandably enough, values strength, not durability.

Feminists are wary of biological explanations of gender, and with good reason. "Theories" about people's biologically innate nature have often been used by conservative thinkers to rationalize and to justify inequality. Sociologists use the term *ideology* to refer to a set of ideas that functions to justify and defend the status quo (Mannheim, 1936). "Undesirable" Jewish characteristics provided the Nazis with a rationalization for their "final solution." Similarly, biological arguments have been used as ideology to keep women in their place. For example, in the late eighteenth and early nineteenth centuries, attempts were made to exclude women from British institutions of higher learning on the grounds that this experience would damage their health and reproductive capacities. Therefore, female intellectual development would be necessarily bought "at the price of a puny, enfeebled race" (Sayers, 1982:18). If "anatomy is destiny," then the traditional subordination of females to males is right and proper, and contemplation of alternatives to the gender status quo makes absolutely no sense. On the other hand, behavior patterns that are learned are arbitrary and, hence, replaceable with new behavior patterns.

The tendency for people to portray themselves in a favorable light by preferring certain theories over others may be human nature (Longino and Doell, 1983:207). What counts as "favorable light" and the linkage of self-esteem with certain explanations is culturally conditioned. Thus, in sixteenth-century Europe, individual resistance to the heliocentric account of the relationship between the earth and other heavenly bodies was related to the medieval idea that human uniqueness was signified by the earth's location at the center of a universe created by God. Nineteenth-century resistance to Darwinian evolutionary theory was "again a response to seeing human uniqueness threatened, this time by kinship with the non-rational and unenlightened apes." Today, protection of patriarchy has quite a lot to do with attempts to justify male social dominance by appealing to ostensibly innate differences between females and males. Although understanding the motivation for a theory's appeal is not the same thing as establishing its validity or invalidity, consumers are advised to be skeptical in defense of political knowledge.

Anthropology and the Relationship between Sex and Gender

Space limitations preclude an exhaustive inventory of approaches to the explanation of gender. Therefore, we will sample the approach sociologists find most relevant, namely the attempt by anthropologists to determine whether the gender arrangements of our own society are inevitable. Since the revival of the feminist movement, feminists have looked to anthropology for answers to these questions: "Were things always as they are today?" "When did it start?" (Rosaldo, 1980:391). The presence or absence of *cultural universals* in the anthropological record is taken to be evidence for or against a biological explanation. If a certain type of behavior is found in many cultures, despite other sorts of variation in cultural patterns, that behavior is assumed to be biologically determined, or at least linked in some way to physiology. If, however, cultural comparisons show inconsistency, if social arrangements are sometimes this way, and sometimes that, this cross-cultural inconsistency is interpreted as evidence for social causation. In previous sections, the latter meaning was given to temperamental variation in New Guinea (Mead, 1935) and to the berdache.

Two interrelated, and apparently universal aspects of the anthropological record are at the heart of the issue: the *universal asymmetry in cultural evaluation of the sexes* and *male dominance* (Lamphere, 1977; Rosaldo, 1974).[6] The first universal refers to the fact that if a particular area of activity is defined as exclusively or predominantly male, it is positively evaluated; if female, it is devalued. Mead (1935:302) recognized that despite the temperamental sex differences displayed in her New Guinea tribes, "the prestige values attach to the activities of men." The second universal is possibly a corollary of the first. Although women sometimes have a good deal of informal influence, "women are denied access to areas of public decision making open to men" (Lamphere, 1977:613).

> Male dominance is so widespread that it is virtually a human universal; societies in which women are consistently dominant do not exist and have never existed (Friedl, 1978:70).

Even the Iroquois, whose society was the closest approximation to the hypothetical form called a *matriarchate* that has ever existed, were not ruled by women (Martin and Voorhies, 1975:10). Iroquois women might install and depose their rulers, but the chiefs were men (Rosaldo, 1974:20).

Anthropologists have hypothesized that the ultimate source of the universal fact of gender inequality is the most important biological sex difference: women bear children and men do not (Sayers, 1982:7). However, it is the social inventions built upon this natural difference and the cultural meanings given to it that matter here. In pre-industrial societies, the division of labor erected upon biological sex meant that women were responsible for the domestic sphere, especially the feeding and care of children through their long period of helplessness and dependency. Men, by necessity, filled the more public roles of hunting, politics, military and religious activities, and handling the community's relations with outsiders (Rosaldo, 1974). This does not mean that women were unproductive. Women performed lighter tasks and those that kept them near home. Women are usually (but not invariably) responsible for such important activities as agriculture, cooking, and food gathering (Ambert, 1976:37ff).

Two polarities of personality are thought to have developed as a result of this division of labor. The pressures of socialization have encouraged women to develop domestic-sphere traits (feelings, communion with others, and nurturance), and men to develop task mastery, competitiveness and strong ego boundaries (Bardwick, 1979:177).

Anthropologist Briggs (1974:276) describes the separation of the public and private realms among contemporary Eskimo women and men:

> It is always a cause of excitement when visitors are seen approaching camp, and almost everyone who can walk runs out to watch; but women cluster near the tents or houses, while the men stand more boldly, further down the slope. When the sled or skidoo or boat has come to a stop, it is the men who flock to greet the arrivals. Women go to shake hands only if the person who has come is a close relative or a good friend; otherwise they go home again, make tea, and wait to be visited.

Women's inferiority had its social roots in the development of private property and the economic isolation of the nuclear family (Friedl, 1975). When class societies developed and goods were produced by exchange, rather than shared, women's child-care responsibilities rendered them economically dependent on men (Sayers, 1982:156). Men's public activities gave them a privileged access to resources which enhanced their power and provided disproportionate rewards. To return to the example of Eskimo households, "men make the decisions and women obey orders" (Friedl, 1975:43). Why? Traditionally, the men were responsible for all the hunting, moving as far from camp as necessary, while the women stayed in the camp, caring for the young children. The women were completely dependent on the men for their very survival. Movement in the public sphere gave men the opportunity to earn reputations as hunters and to establish trading relationships with outsiders. As hunters and traders, then, the men enjoyed opportunities for achievement, social prominence, and power from which the women were excluded. Nonetheless, the domestic sphere afforded Eskimo women various ways to exercise informal infuence (Friedl, 1975:40–41).

Gender asymmetry depends not only on who controls the material means of production, but on who dominates the means of symbolic production (Shapiro, 1981:122). The critical point here is not the biological inevitability of male dominance or the inherently superior nature of public versus domestic activities, but the key role played by beliefs. As dominant groups usually do, males propagated definitions of the situation that aggrandized themselves and their work. Subordinate groups, such as women, are wont to accept the dominant groups' definitions. Since culturally produced sets of meanings, rather than reproductive capabilities, which are at issue, the division of labor in contemporary society need not recapitulate the anthropological past. As human products, ideas are subject to revision (Richardson, 1981:186). The notion of male superiority, then, is open to question.

Moreover, "technology permits humans to transcend biology — people can fly although no one was born with wings" (Huber, 1976:2). Technology has made it possible for the average woman in industrialized nations to be pregnant only a few months of her life. In addition, such inventions as sterilization of milk, bottle feeding, and day-care centers have made the child-bearing function separable from the child-rearing function. The allocation of domestic tasks to women and public tasks to men can no longer be justified on biological grounds. In short, male dominance is universal but not inevitable (Richardson, 1981:188).

What is the current status of anthropological arguments about the origins of gender arrangements? Goffman's (1977:306) opinion is instructive:

> My position will be that the lesson that other
> societies . . . teach us has not yet been formulated
> soundly enough to provide us a warranted text to use for
> instructional purposes, and I propose to restrict myself to
> the here and now.

Similarly, anthropologist Rosaldo (1980:415) suggests that posing the question of origins, of "how did it begin," is an unproductive approach that too readily leads back to the "apparently primordial and unchanging facts of sexual physiology." That is, emphasizing "first causes" leads to insufficient appreciation of human arrangements as social creations. What matters is that gender inequality in contemporary Canadian society continues to rest upon unequal access to both material and symbolic resources (Armstrong and Armstrong, 1984; Smith, 1973).

Gender and Secondary Sex Characteristics

What can secondary sex characteristics tell us about the biological foundation of gender? First of all, they provide important cues for gender attribution of adults in everyday life (Kessler and McKenna, 1978:68). *Gender attribution* means labeling other people female or male. Genitals are the basis for the initial gender attribution which takes place at birth. However, genitals subsequently play a minimal role in this process because, in our society, they are concealed under clothing. Therefore, we rely upon such secondary traits as height, voice pitch, hip and breast size, and bodily hair to decide people's sex/gender. However, sociocultural factors influence which secondary traits are taken to be most relevant to gender. For example, in Canadian culture, but not European, femininity is marked by minimal body hair (Freimuth and Hornstein, 1982:524).

In addition, interpretation of secondary traits is related to the social construction of gender. In a culture such as ours that values sheer bigness, greater body size translates into status. Height and leadership in informal groups are modestly correlated (Gacsaly and Borges, 1979; Stogdill, 1974); male size and status are similarly related among, for example, executives, street-gang members, and athletes (Garn, 1966). The fact that the average Canadian woman is 93 percent as tall and 84 percent as heavy as the average Canadian man (Veevers and Adams, 1982) contributes to men's superiority. In her book, *Fat Is a Feminist Issue* (1978:62–63), Orbach argues that for some women, excess weight represents substance and strength. Being bigger and fatter is one way, albeit a deviant one, of feeling more powerful, more significant in a male-dominated society.

The gender role implications of strength are even clearer. The ability of males to help females with things that are heavy is an ingredient in the traditional sex division of labor (Goffman, 1977:320).

Transsexual Jan Morris (1974:149) remarks that she is no longer expected to carry heavy boxes. More important, however, is the implicit or actual physical threat that males present to females. The physical structure of male children gives them a significant initial advantage over female children. Later, direct physical force is not really necessary to maintain male status (Unger, 1978:502). As Goffman (1977:321) points out, "selective mating ensures that with almost no exceptions husbands are bigger than wives and boyfriends are bigger than their girlfriends." Actual battering or threat of battering is related to the domestic arrangements of many couples (Veevers and Adams, 1982). We return to the topic of gender and the body in Chapter 7.

To summarize, the connections between biology and gender are, for the most part, indirect and tenuous. In the main, "what we learn from looking at the interaction of biology and culture is that cultural beliefs about biological events imbue them with a significance greater than their physiological character" (Andersen, 1983:42). Height, weight, penis length, menstruation, menopause, aging, etc., though physiological facts, all take on somewhat different meanings in different cultures. In other words, even biological facts are socially constructed.[7] The biological differences between males and females are really quite insignificant in comparison with the immense gender differences erected upon this substructure. According to Goffman (1977:301–302),

> For these physical facts of life to have no appreciable
> social consequence would take a little organizing, but, at
> least by modern standards, not much. Industrial society
> can absorb new ethnic groups bearing raw cultural differ-
> ences, a year or so of isolating military service for young
> men, vast differences in educational level, business and
> employment cycles, the wartime absence of its adult
> males every generation, appreciable annual vacations,
> and countless other embarrassments to orderliness . . .
> For these very slight biological differences — compared to
> all other differences — to be identified as the grounds for
> the kind of social consequences felt to follow understand-
> ably from them requires a vast, integrated body of social
> beliefs and practices . . . .

Conclusions

Chapter 1 has focused upon gender as a dimension of social organization, rather than as a personal attribute. Male-female inequality and
power differentials constitute the most important dimension of gender.
The case of transsexuals as gender deviants was examined as the source
of information about the centrality and accomplishment of gender in
everyday life.

Biology has been used against women. Deterministic theories of various types have been employed to justify submissive and inferior feminine roles and to bolster the notion "that men are by nature better equipped to conduct the affairs of civilization . . ." (Hrdy, 1981:1). The biological contribution, if any, to gender is obviously a critical matter. However, to search for either biological *or* environmental causation of gender patterns, to pose the question as nature versus nurture, is a misleading and simplistic formulation of a complex question. In gender patterns, as in social behavior in general, both biology and environment are implicated. Biochemical and genetic factors set the stage, but culture and history provide the script for social life (Kunkel, 1977). The fact that socialization often emphasizes "natural" sex differences further complicates analysis. For example, our society provides more athletic facilities and opportunities for physically stronger males. Our interpretation of the evidence is that biology's influence upon gender is, for the most part, indirect. It occurs primarily through the way biology is interpreted.

We conclude that the experience of being male or female in Canadian society is fundamentally a social matter. Therefore, the learning of gender becomes the paramount consideration. We turn next to the sociology of knowledge as theoretical background for the study of gender socialization.

NOTES

1. "Gender" was previously a term used in connection with grammar. Possibly, its appeal to social scientists lay in the suggestion that the role differences between men and women are just as arbitrary as the assignment of gender in many languages. For example, in the French language, the sun is masculine and the moon feminine, while the German language reverses these gender assignments (Berger and Berger, 1984:54). Strictly speaking, however, Maccoby (1980:203) is correct when she points out that the gender/sex distinction "seems to prejudge important questions about the origins of sex-linked behavior."

2. Margaret Mead's biographer, Jane Howard (1984:141 ff.) argues that the Arapesh were considerably more aggressive than Mead admitted. For example, "an Arapesh man 'told Reo [Mead's husband] all about the nice brain soup which the warriors used to drink, brewed from the scooped-out brains of the enemy, although up to now they had been denying any touch of cannibalism' — a train of thought Mead did not pursue in her further writings . . ." (p. 145).

3. It is important to note that male-female inequality is not an isolated social fact. On the contrary, the gender inequality in a particular society must be understood in the context of the other patterns of inequality which obtain in that particular society (Lipman-Blumen, 1984; Shapiro, 1981).

4. Deaux's (1984:108) review of the psychological literature on sex differences concludes that "although additional evidence remains to be gathered, 5% may approximate the upper boundary for the explanatory power of subject-sex main effects in specific social and cognitive behaviors."

5. At times, men's greater physical vulnerability contributes to their higher social value. For example, nursing home workers observe that the few elderly men are much sought after by the more numerous elderly women (personal communication).

6. Some disagreement exists among anthropologists regarding universal sexual asymmetry (Atkinson, 1982:238). Leacock (1978) and Sacks (1979) pose counterarguments.
7. Gender is not the only biologically-based social status. Age, race, ethnicity, physical handicap, and physical size are other socially defined physical characteristics that can assume the importance of master statuses in our society (Williams, 1983:20).

2

The Sociology of Knowledge as Theoretical Foundation of Gender Socialization

Introduction

> *If social actors define persons as coming in two genders, then for sociologists that is what matters* (Matthews, 1982:32).

> *It should not prejudice my voice that I'm not born a man If I say something advantageous to the present situation.* (Aristophanes, *Lysistrata*, 413 B.C.)

Gender is a paradox — a fiction, without inherent meaning, yet immensely consequential for individual and society. The key to this conundrum is gender's status as a social fiction. A set of ideas becomes social fact when members of society agree that it is true and act as though it were true. In other words, "reality is *social*, and what we see 'out there' (and within ourselves) is developed in interaction with others" (Charon, 1979:36, emphasis in original).

For sociologists, the central question then becomes: How is the social reality of gender maintained?[1] A reasonably complete answer to this question will require this entire book. This chapter's task is to discuss the sociology of knowledge as theoretical foundation for the study of gender socialization. The sociology of knowledge concerns itself "with what people 'know' as 'reality' in their everyday . . . lives" and socialization with the internalization of social reality (Berger and Luckmann, 1966:15, 129). Before considering the topic of socialization (*how* gender ideas are learned), we turn our attention first to the ideas themselves. Of particular interest is the role of power in the social construction of gender.

The Sociology of Knowledge

The sociology of knowledge is a branch of sociology concerned with the "social location of ideas" (Berger, 1963:110), the "relation between thought and society" (Coser, 1968:428). Although some sociologists specialize in this area, its core ideas function as a "latent frame of reference" for thinking about many different sociological problems (Wolff, 1959:570). The sociology of knowledge is rooted in nineteenth-century European thought. The contributions of two men, Karl Marx (1818-1883) and Karl Mannheim (1893-1947), are important for our purposes.[2] Several propositions from the sociology of knowledge are helpful in understanding the social construction of gender.

Three Tenets of the Sociology of Knowledge

The first idea may be labelled the *existential conditioning of thought:* ". . . all knowledge and all ideas, although to different degrees, are 'bound to a location' within the social structure and the historical process" (Coser, 1968: 430). Karl Marx was primarily interested in a class analysis of society. His initial formulation linked ideas to the class position of their proponents and argued that intellectual activity was an expression of these class interests:

> The mode of production in material life determines the general character of the social, political and spiritual processes of life. *It is not the consciousness of men that determines their existence, but on the contrary their social existence determines their consciousness* (Marx, 1859/1913:11-12, emphasis added).

Later, Mannheim (1936) extended Marx's very important insight beyond its connection with social class to the proposition that *all* ideas are influenced by the social and historical situation from which they emerged (Coser, 1968:429). In short, the sociology of knowledge views thought as an "expression of social-historical circumstance" (Wolff, 1959:576).

The second tenet of the sociology of knowledge is the *ruling ideas proposition*. In *The German Ideology* (1947), Marx and his colleague, Friedrich Engels wrote:

> *The ideas of the ruling class are in every epoch the ruling ideas:* i.e. the class, which is the ruling material force of society, is at the same time its ruling intellectual force (p. 39, emphasis added).

Not only are ideas tied to class position, but some ideas are more influential than others. According to Marx and Engels (1947), the people who control the material means of production have the power to control the production and distribution of the ideas associated with politics, law, morality and religion. Moreover, these ideas serve to buttress the interests of the dominant class. To quote Berger and Luckmann

(1966:109) again, "He who has the bigger stick has the better chance of imposing his definitions of reality."

The third idea from the sociology of knowledge involves the concepts of *ideology* and *false consciousness*. In *Ideology and Utopia* (1936), Mannheim pursued Marx's analysis of ideas espoused by interest groups that serve to jusify the status quo:

> The particular conception of ideology is implied when the term denotes that we are skeptical of the ideas and representations advanced by our opponent. They are regarded as more or less conscious disguises of the real nature of a situation, the true recognition of which would not be in accord with his interests. These distortions range all the way from conscious lies to half-conscious and unwitting disguises; from calculated attempts to dupe others to self-deception (Mannheim, 1936:55-56).

Ideologies serve the powerful by presenting the powerless with a definition of reality that is false and yet orders their comprehension of the surrounding world. Here is where false consciousness comes in. When subordinate groups accept as valid and authoritative the ideology of dominant groups, they are engaging in false consciousness (Andersen, 1983:212-213). Put another way, false consciousness is "thought that is alienated from the real social being of the thinker" (Berger and Luckmann, 1966:6).

Three Potential Blind Alleys

Although the foregoing ideas have stimulated research and controversy, taken too literally or pushed too far, they can lead to intellectual blind alleys. For example, though "ideology" and "false consciousness" are useful concepts, especially in times of conflict, overuse can lead to suspicion and negativism. Interpreted rigidly, they lend themselves "to use as a rather crude tool for debunking all adverse thought" (Coser, 1968:429).

> The task of the sociology of knowledge is not to be the debunking or uncovering of socially produced distortions, but the systematic study of the social conditions of knowledge as such. Put simply, the central problem is the sociology of truth, not the sociology of error (Berger and Luckmann, 1966:12).

Similarly, the proposition of the existential conditioning of thought can lead to complete relativism of truth. If all ideas are mere reflections of social location, then any idea is as valid or invalid as any other idea. In this connection, Merton (1957:461) refers to "the peren-nial problem of the implications of existential influences upon knowledge for the epistemological status of that knowledge." Of the several solutions to this impasse that have been proposed, the one preferred here is this: the source of an idea does not logically predeter-mine the validity of that idea. Both are matters of empirical inquiry.

The third potential impediment to thought concerns the impli-cations of Marxian materialism for strategies of social change. Materialists emphasize the importance of satisfying the fundamental human requirements for food, clothing, and shelter. Therefore, for them, the mode of production has prime importance and intellectual activities are derivative. In other words, ideas are the ideological superstructure built upon an economic foundation (Armstrong and Armstrong, 1984: 150–151). Or, in the words of Marx and Engels (1947:15), "life is not determined by consciousness, but consciousness by life." There is a lesson in the materialist position for social movements trying to ameliorate the position of an underdog group, such as women. Seek to improve the disadvantaged group's economic situation. Don't bother about topdog's attitudes towards the underdog.[3] However, the contemporary position acknowledges that causality operates in both directions — ideas influence, as well as reflect social structure. "A sociological perspective on ideas recognizes that social reality is com-posed of both ideas and actual material conditions. Each has a tremen-dous influence on our lives" (Andersen, 1983:208). The relevance of this matter for the women's movement will be considered at the end of this chapter. The next item on our agenda is to ask, "What do the tenets of the sociology of knowledge have to do with femininity and masculinity?"

The Sociology of Knowledge and Gender Relations

The connection between the sociology of knowledge and gender is not spelled out in the writings of either Marx or Mannheim. However, in *The Origins of the Family, Private Property and the State* (1902), Marx's col-league Engels analyzed women's position relative to men's. He understood women's status to vary from society to society and epoch to epoch, depending upon prevailing economic and political relation-ships of the society (Sacks, 1974:207). Development of private property transformed women from equal members of society to subordinate wives. In the institution of bourgeois marriage, women exchanged their sexual and reproductive capacities for economic support. In private ser-vice to their husbands and families, they were excluded from public production.

As an economic theory, Marxism was androcentric. Women's situation was dealt with only tangentially. The liberation of women was dependent on the emancipation of the working class (Rowbotham, 1972:76). Here, the assumption was made "that history would take care of the 'woman question'; therefore, the issue [could] be ignored and the 'proper' focus of attention — class relations — be attended to" (Sydie, 1983:216). Similarly, MacKinnon (1982:520) writes,

> Marxist theory has traditionally attempted to comprehend
> all meaningful social variance in class terms. In this
> respect, sex parallels race and nation as an undigested
> but persistently salient challenge to the exclusivity — or
> even primacy — of class as social explanation (emphasis
> in original deleted).

So far as the sociology of knowledge is concerned, Marx concentrated on the biasing effects of social class on human knowledge.[4] Later, Mannheim (1936) extended Marx's list of the social groupings that shape our view of the world to include occupational, geographical, and national categories — but he totally ignored gender (Snyder, 1979:3). The task has fallen to contemporary scholars, especially Dorothy Smith (1974, 1975a, 1979, 1984), to work out the implications of the sociology of knowledge for gender relations.

In general, it may be said that the sociology of knowledge contributes valuable insight into the workings of gender in our society. For surely sex/gender challenges social class as a vital life-interest. The sociology of knowledge encourages a historical view on the construction of gender. There is no "universal" femininity or masculinity, but rather varying arrangements in different historical epochs. Even more important, it emphasizes large-scale social structures and the role of oppression in male-female relations. This perspective provides the theoretical backdrop, the broader picture for this book's detailed discussion of gender socialization. With the tenets of the sociology of knowledge in mind, it becomes impossible to understand socialization as a purely psychological process or to locate the source of gender troubles in people's heads.

The remainder of this chapter explores the relationship between the sociology of knowledge and gender relations. The next section adopts the stance of the sociology of knowledge to analyze what Steinem (1983a:349) calls "the injustice of dividing human nature into the false polarities of 'feminine' or 'masculine'..." Then, the connections are discussed between each of the three propositions of the sociology of knowledge and gender relations.

Gender as Taken-for-Granted Reality

In Chapter 1, we considered the "taken-for-granted assumption that there are in fact two gender categories into which it is important to sort all human beings" (Matthews, 1982:30). We concluded that this assumption magnifies minimal biological differences between the sexes. Further, we observed that gender can be equated with status and power differences and that it seems to be grounded in the reproductive abilities and the traditional sex-based division of labor between the public and domestic spheres.

These conclusions are fine as far as they go. However, they leave unanswered the important question: "How is gender as 'natural' reality accomplished?" Or rephrased slightly, "How is gender as hierarchy and gender as traditional division of labor sustained and perpetuated?" As Goffman (1977:302) points out:

> It is not . . . the social consequences of innate sex differences that must be explained, but the way in which these differences were (and are) put forward as a warrant for our social arrangements, and, most important of all, the *way in which the institutional workings of society ensured that this accounting would seem sound* (emphasis added).

Goffman (1977) goes on to suggest that "the chief consequence of the women's movement is not the direct improvement of the lot of women but the weakening of the doctrinal beliefs that heretofore have underpinned the sexual division of deserts and labor" (p. 302). In other words, the women's movement's questioning of the previously taken-for-granted ideas about gender was an extremely radical act. As we shall see, the sociology of knowledge helps to pinpoint the source and sustenance of traditional gender beliefs. Equally important, such an analysis identifies promising strategies for change. In Lipman-Blumen's (1984:198) opinion,

> Although some observers still find academic satisfaction in debating the origins of gender role differences, changing life conditions make the more central question not *"from* where?" but *"to* where?" in the decades ahead (emphasis in original).

The sociology of knowledge cultivates skepticism towards received "truths" such as the "naturalness" of gender. Warm-feeling-in-the-tummy ideas merit the same skepticism as those that provoke (mental) indigestion. Although it is infinitely more difficult to be skeptical about conventional wisdom we agree with than unpalatable ideas, all deserve an initial reaction of "Horsefeathers! How do you know that?" (Mackie, 1977a). In short, the sociology of knowledge encourages us to view gender as part of the *perceived* universe, rather than part of the universe (Matthews, 1982:31). Unfortunately, the women's movement had to occur before this lesson hit home.

Furthermore, the sociology of knowledge directs us to consider who benefits from sets of ideas. Mannheim's objective was "to trace . . . the specific connection between actual interest groups in society and the ideas and modes of thought which they espoused (Wolff, 1959:577)." That men are the intentional or unintentional beneficiaries of gender hierarchy and division of labor seems self-evident. Roxanne Dunbar (1970:479), an early women's liberation theoretician, argued, "All men enjoy male supremacy and take advantage of it to a greater or lesser degree depending on their position in the masculine hierarchy of power." During the early 1970s, the epithet "male chauvinist pig" (abbreviated M.C.P.) was frequently hurled at men. Men reacted with ridicule, anger, and confusion. At first, the "enlightened" male "responded to feminist assertions by donning sack cloth, sprinkling himself with ashes, and flagellating himself" (Goldberg, 1976:4).[5] Goldberg (1976:4–5) notes that many "well-intentioned writers on the male condition have also taken a basically guilt- and shame-oriented approach to the male, alternately scolding him, warning him, and preaching to him that he better change and not be a male chauvinist pig anymore."

Many feminists soon realized that women's oppression had more to do with large-scale social structures than the deliberate villainy of individual men. Dixon (1971:166), describing the women's movement in 1969, said, "A year ago the movement stressed male chauvinism and psychological oppression; now the emphasis is on understanding the economic and social roots of women's oppression . . . ." Commentators of both sexes came to understand that gender arrangements imprison men as well as women. Nevertheless, "the essential feminist insight" is that "the overall relationship between men and women is one involving domination or oppression" (Carrigan et al., 1985:552). Therefore, "the liberation of women must mean a *loss* of power for most men . . ." (p. 581, emphasis in original).

The Benefactors of Gender Arrangements

Feminists' attempts to understand the "economic and social roots of women's oppression" have, through the years, produced three theoretical positions on the question of who gains from gender: Traditional Marxism, Radical Feminism, and Socialist Feminism (Jaggar and Rothenberg, 1984; Wilson, 1982:35–48). Each theoretical position advocates somewhat different solutions to gender problems.

Traditional Marxism. Orthodox Marxists claim that women's oppression originated with the introduction of private property and the resulting class system. Following Marx, irreconcilable conflict between economic classes is regarded as the key to understanding both the shape of contemporary society and the desirable direction of social change. "Ultimately, women are oppressed, not by 'sexism,' not by men, but by capitalism" (Jaggar and Rothenberg, 1984:85).[6]

Women as a group are seen to be uniquely related to the means of production. One gender difference stems from the distinction in capitalist societies between commodity production (products created for exchange on the market) and the production of use-values (all things produced in the home). In capitalist societies, based on commodity production, housewives' unpaid efforts are not considered "real" work (Benston, 1969). Women's worth is seriously undermined by their position as "non-paid" "non-workers." Moreover, women's unpaid work in the home serves the capitalist system. To pay women for their efforts would mean a massive redistribution of wealth.

A second gender difference is women's status as a "reserve army" in the labor force (Connelly, 1978). "Reserve army" means that they are called into the labor force when needed (e.g., wartime) and sent home again when that need disappears. The cultural prescription that women belong in the home assures that the women will return to the home (Glazer, 1977). Moreover, capitalism employs women in low-wage sectors of the economy. Because in the past, they were usually part of a family unit, women "can often survive with less pay and disappear back into the home when they are fired or laid off" (Armstrong and Armstrong, 1978:137). The dominant class, then, benefits from women's work both inside and outside the home.

Women's disadvantaged position in the capitalist system can be quickly documented. According to United Nations statistics, women own less than one percent of the world's wealth (Spender, 1982:5). So far as Canada is concerned, corporations are in the hands of a small number of individuals, mostly British in origin. Clement (1975:266) reports that at the time of his study, 0.6 percent of the 946 persons in the Canadian corporate elite were women.

The traditional Marxist argues that the division of labor by sex is an inherent aspect of capitalism. Accordingly, women's liberation will come about through the overthrow of the capitalist system and its replacement with socialism. In a socialist system, women's economic dependency on men, and hence their subordination, would be abolished. Traditional Marxists assume that once women were economically independent, "remnants of the ancient prejudice against women would lose their plausibility and eventually disappear" (Jaggar and Rothenberg, 1984:86). Since capitalism is in the hands of a few men, and most men are alienated from their work, mere cogs in "impersonal machinery" (Sydie, 1983:202), most men will also benefit from capitalism's demise.

Radical Feminism. The more recent political perspective of Radical Feminism argues that the oppression of women is the fundamental oppression. Shulamith Firestone (1971:5), for example, warns against attempts "to squeeze feminism into an orthodox Marxist framework."

Women are seen to be oppressed by male domination in the private sphere, and only secondarily by class society. Indeed, radical feminists point to the oppression of women in non-capitalist societies.

Radical Feminism directs attention to the role played by sexuality and reproduction in keeping women down. By declaring that the "personal is political," women's sexuality is seen as an aspect of the power relations between the sexes (Shulman, 1980:590). A fundamental dichotomy exists between valued male production and devalued female reproduction (O'Brien, 1981). Lipman-Blumen (1984:22) elaborates on these points:

> In the private arena, the family as an institution . . .
> produces critical resources — the next generation, for
> one. But somehow these "means of reproduction" fail to
> bring women recognition, status, and power. Although
> women's biological contributions tend to entrap them,
> the resources contributed by women are still important.
> Otherwise, why the struggle for control over the means
> of reproduction — that is, women's reproductive capacity?
> Otherwise, why the serious policy debate about the right
> to contraceptive information and devices, as well as
> access to abortion? Otherwise, why are men willing to
> fight in court [and political and religious councils] to gain
> control over women's bodies and their sexual and repro-
> ductive functioning? In this case, folk wisdom gives us a
> clue to the meaning of social behavior. "Keep them bare-
> foot and pregnant" summarizes one strategy for sub-
> ordinating women.

Since Radical Feminists regard women's child-bearing function and subsequent dependence on men as the root of female oppression, in their opinion, only a biological revolution will free women (Firestone, 1971). Possibilities are extra-uterine reproduction or lesbianism. In general, Radical Feminists recommend, as a strategy of social change, separation from men in both domestic and economic spheres (Jaggar and Rothenberg, 1984:87, 219).

Socialist Feminism. The Socialist Feminist position accords with traditional Marxism that private property and class are central to an understanding of gender relations. However, the Radical Feminist insight of male dominance in the family is also incorporated into their perspective, and patriarchy joins capitalism as a source of women's oppression. The work of Kate Millett (1970) helped establish this view. See Sargent (1983) for a set of recent statements.

According to Smith (1983:316), we should "understand the inner life and work of the family and the personal relations of power between husband and wife as both situated in, and determined by, the general economic and political relations of a mode of production." She goes on (p. 323) to quote Nellie McClung's (1915/1972) account of the injustice suffered by farm women:

> I remember once attending the funeral of a woman who had been doing the work for a family of six children and three hired men, and she had not even a baby carriage to make her work lighter. When the last baby was three days old, just in threshing time, she died. Suddenly, and without warning, the power went off, and she quit without notice. The bereaved husband was the most astonished man in the world. He had never known Jane to do a thing like that before, and he could not get over it. In threshing time, too! (McClung, 1915/1972:114).

The death of the farmer's wife recalls to mind the argument made by Engels (1902) that the family is the basic unit of capitalist society and of female oppression. "The modern individual family is founded on the open or concealed domestic slavery of the wife, and modern society is a mass composed of these individual families as its molecules." Further, the first class oppression is that of the female sex by the male, "within the family, he (the man) is the bourgeois and the wife represents the proletariat" (Dunbar, 1970:486). Socialist Feminists hold that women's subordination in work in the home reinforces their subordination in the labor force. In the final analysis, "capitalism and patriarchy are mutually interdependent and reinforcing systems; women's liberation requires the abolition of both" (Jaggar and Rothenberg, 1984:89).

In general, then, we conclude that vested interests benefit from the perpetuation of patriarchy. Corporate capitalism benefits (Smith, 1973). Individual men benefit. As Pleck (1981b:235) points out, "men want power over women because it is in their rational self-interest to have it, to have the concrete benefits and privileges that power over women provides them." Nevertheless, it would be a mistake to see all men as agents of patriarchy to the same degree. The main beneficiaries of patriarchy are the white, affluent, heterosexual, well-educated males in capitalist advanced countries (Carrigan et al., 1985). "Patriarchy is a *dual* system, a system in which men oppress women, and in which men oppress themselves and each other" (Pleck, 1981b:241, emphasis in original). We turn now to a consideration of the implications for gender of the first tenet of the sociology of knowledge, the existential conditioning of thought.

Gender and the Existential Conditioning of Thought

The proposition of the sociology of knowledge that ideas are socially located finds expression in the sociology of gender relations as the subjective dimension of the *two-worlds metaphor* (Mackie, 1984a).[7] Daniels (1975:344), for example, points to "the contrasting world views of men and women." Smith (1974) speaks of the "world of men" and the "world of women" and argues that different locations in the social structure are associated with particularized boundaries of experience and thought patterns. Similarly, Bernard (1981) claims that "most human beings live in single-sex worlds, women in a female world and men in a male world," which differ "both subjectively and objectively" (p. 3). As Bernard's usage suggests, the two-worlds notion is a shorthand way of saying that the sexes' intellectual activity reflects distinctive social experiences. Linguists (e.g., Thorne and Henley, 1975) have identified gender differences in language use; language is the currency of thought. In other words, "language determines what we see and how we see it" (Bernard, 1981:375). Communication is at the heart of sociology's original conceptualization of social worlds: Shibutani (1962:136) wrote, "Each social world . . . is a culture area, the boundaries of which are set neither by territory nor formal group membership, but by the limits of effective communication" (emphasis in original deleted).

Specification of the content of thought is a very ambitious task. However, time, space, and causation appear to constitute the basic dimensions of reality (Zentner, 1982). Some female-male differences in the experience of these dimensions do seem to exist. For example, Steinem (1983a:173-175) writes of sex differences in the perception of *time*. She suggests that in contrast to the future orientation and career planning of middle-class men, women of all classes demonstrate a "stunning lack of career planning" (p. 173). They feel they must remain open and flexible in order to accommodate the needs and plans of husbands and children.

Sex differences in *space* use also reflect male superiority and female inferiority. (See Chapter 6.) "To be born a woman has been to be born, within an allotted and confined space, in the keeping of men" (MacKinnon, 1982:540). For instance, a traditional social control technique has been proscription of women's independent movement beyond their home (Fox, 1977). Although Canadian women are not formally confined, as are women in Arab-Muslim countries of the Middle East by the practice of purdah, feminist marches to "Reclaim the Night" protest women's intimidation through fear for their safety. (See Spring 1980 issue of *Signs* for discussion of gender and urban settings.)

So far as *causality* is concerned, women feel less in control of their own destiny than men (Maccoby and Jacklin, 1974:157). Since the degree of their autonomy is indeed more circumscribed, their sense of powerlessness seems reasonable. The foregoing illustrate sex differences in experiencing the parameters of reality.

ossible Etiology of Female and Male Worlds

What, specifically, are the sources of the "two worlds"? Most emphatically, the source is socialization, not biology. Within this context, several sources are implicated. First of all, Marx argued that thought is derived from the activities in which human beings engage. As we have seen, important differences do characterize male versus female activities:

Important!

> The segregation of women into the domestic unit performing their isolated household chores ensures that their consciousness differs from that of men. To the extent that women are also segregated into particular female jobs in the labour force, they will tend to develop a consciousness that is different from that of men (Armstrong and Armstrong, 1984:188).

Meg Luxton's *More Than a Labour of Love* (1980) describes the lives of working-class families in Flin Flon, a mining town in northern Manitoba. Her study distinguishes between the work of wage earners, based on economic relations, and the work of housewives, based on love relations. Quotations from first a miner and then a housewife provide a glimpse into the world of labor and the labor of love:

> I work hard, see. And it's not great work. And when I gets home I'm tired and fed up and I want to just rest till I feel better. I come home feeling sort of worn down and I need to loosen up and feel human again. At work there is always someone standing over and telling me I have to do this or that. Well, I don't want any more of that at home. I want to do what I want for a change. I want a chance to live when I'm off work (Luxton, 1980:45).

> Lots of people say what a housewife does isn't work. Well, it is work, and it's just like men's work only it isn't paid and it isn't supervised. But I have things I have to do at certain times. The main difference is, my work is regulated by his work. And whatever I have to do is somehow always overshadowed by the requirements of his work (Luxton, 1980:48).

It seems reasonable to hypothesize that differences in sexual and reproductive activities, as well as in productive activities, contribute to gender differences in consciousness. Stanley and Wise (1983:146) claim that "women *do* experience reality differently, just by having 'different' bodies, 'different' physical experiences, to name no others" (emphasis in original). How is one's consciousness influenced by having a vagina versus a penis? Does women's menstrual cycle and men's lack of same give women cyclical experience of time versus men's linear experience? How does size and strength affect consciousness? For example, does women's much greater vulnerability to rape intimidate them and undermine their courage?

Actor Dustin Hoffman offers his reason for playing the role of a woman in the 1983 film "Tootsie":

> . . . I really found myself wondering what it would be like to carry a baby. I wondered how many experiences I missed out on by being a man. I wondered how many experiences women missed out on by being a woman (St. David, 1983).

Having a penis apparently produced endless complications in the life of Julius Lester (1973:113):

> God, how I envied girls . . . Wherever *it* was on them, it didn't dangle between their legs like an elephant's trunk. No wonder boys talked about nothing but sex. That thing was always there. Every time we went to the john, there *it* was, twitching around like a little fat worm on a fishing hook. When we took baths, it floated in the water like a lazy fish and God forbid we should touch it! It sprang to life like lightning leaping from a cloud. I wished I could cut it off, or at least keep it tucked between my legs, as if it were a tail that had mistakenly attached to the wrong end. But I was helpless. It was there, with a life and mind of its own, having no other function than to embarrass me (emphases in original).

If gender differences in thought are in fact associated with bio-psychic sex differences, it is highly probable that it is the social interpretations of biology that count. As we saw in Chapter 1, sexual equipment and experiences are subject to cultural definition.

In general, the two-worlds metaphor labels distinctive aspects of female and male intellectual experience. The source of these differences is social experience in sexual, productive, and reproductive activities. As we shall see, power and hierarchy are overriding concerns. The two-worlds metaphor is a hypothesis that makes truth claims that require testing. For instance, is it true that female-male differences in thought prevail over class, age, ethnic, and regional differences? These are empirical questions. However, in addition to female bodies, all Canadian women are vulnerable to sexual objectification and rape. Most experience sex segregation and low pay at work and domestic power of men at home. Virtually all women do housework and have less leisure then men (Jaggar, 1986). Similar generalizations can be made about male anatomy and productive and reproductive labor. Meanwhile, we treat the two-worlds notion as a heuristic device for understanding gender relations. We turn now to one very important example of this metaphor.

Agentic and Communal Research Styles

The two-worlds proposition implies sex differences in the modes of thought of professionals at work. As one might suppose, feminists have been especially interested in this phenomenon within the academic profession. Carlson (1971, 1972) in psychology and Bernard (1973) in sociology have argued that fundamental differences exist in the ways women and men set about doing their research. Each sex has a preferred research style, with "agentic" methods being more congenial to male sociologists and "communal" methods being more congenial to female sociologists. "Agency tends to see variables, communion to see human beings" (Bernard, 1973:784). *Agentic research* is specified as preference for "hard" data, quantitative methods, laboratory experiments, social indicators, isolation and control of variables, and statistical tests of significance. Bernard explains why the agentic mode reflects machismo:

> The scientist using this approach creates his own controlled reality. He can manipulate it. He is master. He has power. He can add or subtract or combine variables. He can play with a simulated reality like an Olympian god. He can remain at a distance, safely invisible behind his shield, uninvolved. The communal approach is much humbler. It disavows control, for control spoils the results. Its value rests precisely on the absence of controls (Bernard, 1973:785).

Communal research, on the other hand, involves "soft" data, qualitative methods, empathetic understanding of the people being studied, case studies, autobiographies, observation of social behavior in situ, and no attempt to control variables, or even to talk in terms of variables. A positivistic view of social science, that is, one that stresses their similarity with the physical sciences, is not congenial to feminists.

An exploratory study carried out by the author (Mackie, 1985) asked, "Is the communal approach to research more characteristic of female sociologists and the agentic approach more characteristic of male sociologists?" In other words, was Bernard (1973) correct about hypothesized gender differences in style? This study also examined trends in research modes over time. If sociology has become less androcentric in recent years, such changes should be accompanied by acceptance of the communal research mode. Research articles in issues of five general-interest sociology journals in 1967, 1973, and 1981 and sociologists' publications in two inter-disciplinary women's studies journals were coded as being "agentic" or "communal."[8]

With regard to research mode employed, the analysis found that a gender difference does indeed exist in research orientation. When articles in the five sociology journals for the three time periods were combined, male-authored articles containing data were 89.7 percent agentic, compared with 71.2 percent of the female-authored articles (p. < .0005, one-tailed). Some 45 percent of women sociologists' articles versus 14.3 percent of men sociologists' articles in the two women's studies journals (from the time of their inception until 1981) were communal (p. < .025, one-tailed).

Gould (1980:467) argues that "female sociologists often find themselves torn between wanting to do a sociology of/for women that is challenging and critical, and wanting their work to be seen as legitimate by those who control the discipline." Evidently, the greater proportion of female sociologists' communal articles in the women's studies journals (versus the general sociology journals) indicates what female sociologists would *prefer* to do, as opposed to what they feel they *must* do to please editorial gatekeepers.

When trends in women's use of the communal mode were examined, an increase was registered between 1967 and 1973, and a decrease between 1973 and 1981. This pattern suggests the continuing power of male ruling ideas and the co-optation of women into the male-dominated discipline. These remarks take us to the next tenet of the sociology of knowledge.

Gender and the Ruling Ideas Proposition

Given the greater power and prestige accorded to males and male pursuits, it is hardly surprising that male and female intellectual worlds are unequal in status. If mental production is the privilege of the "ruling class," and men dominate women, then the authoritative perspective, the ideas that matter, obviously originate with men. In Smith's (1974:7) words, "the world as it is constituted by men stands in authority over that of women." This is partly what Simone de Beauvior (1949) meant when she described man as the Subject, the Absolute, and woman as the Other: "humanity is male and man defines woman not in herself but as relative to him . . ." (p. xvi). Finally, Spender (1985:1–2) gives emphatic expression to the ruling-ideas proposition in gender relations:

> Males, as the dominant sex, have only a *partial* view of
> the world and yet they are in a position to insist that
> their views and values are the *"real"* and *only* values; and
> they are in a position to impose their version on other
> human beings who do not share their experience. This is
> one of the crucial features of dominance; it is one of the
> characteristics of patriarchy, for it is the means by which
> one half of the human population is able to insist that
> the other half sees things its way. By this process alter-
> native views and values are suppressed and blocked.

Women's different experience is outlawed, is seen as
unintelligible, unreal, unfathomable. (Emphasis in
original.)

Social Circles and the Exclusion of Women

Women are excluded from the "social circles" of people whose experiences count, whose interpretations of these experiences have integrity.
"Men attend to and treat as significant what men say and have said"
(Smith, 1979:137). A year or so after "Tootsie" appeared, Barbra Strei-
sand directed and starred in the movie "Yentl," the story of a woman's
entry, through subterfuge, into the male world of sacred knowledge
of the Jewish scriptures, which was denied to women. Yentl is a turn-
of-the-century Polish girl who disguises herself as a boy in order to pursue Talmudic studies at a yeshiva.

We live in a society which still denigrates female intellect and
discounts female experience. What women say does not carry the
authority of male words. de Beauvoir (1949:xv) remarks:

In the midst of an abstract discussion it is vexing to hear
a man say: "You think thus and so because you are a
woman," but I know that my only defense is to reply: "I
think thus and so because it is true," thereby removing
my subjective self from the argument. It would be out of
the question to reply: "And you think the contrary
because you are a man," for it is understood that the fact
of being a man is no peculiarity.

Women's relative lack of intellectual authority is significant in
most societal institutions: the family, work, religion, politics, education, the arts, the mass media. So far as the arts are concerned, Virginia
Woolf (1928:51) wrote that Anonymous "was often a woman." Female
Victorian writers and even modern female painters have been forced
to assume masculine pseudonyms in order to have their work judged
on its own merit (Rosenberg and Fliegel, 1971). With a few exceptions,
men are the authority figures in Western religions — deacons, priests,
clergymen, bishops, cardinals, popes. Religious doctrine is male-
constructed. Only males may make ceremonial contact with the Deity.
In the Canadian broadcasting media, men predominate as newscasters,
announcers, advertising voice-overs, and other authority figures (Canadian Radio-television and Telecommunications Commission, 1982).
Tuchman (1978) aptly refers to the media's "symbolic annihilation of
women." (See Chapter 6.)

Women Professionals and the Ruling-Ideas Proposition

Female professionals often encounter "lay attitudes of distrust, based
on these perceptions of females as both the inferior and less intelligent

sex" (Theodore, 1971:9). Professional authority derives from a monopoly of knowledge beyond the public's ken (Wilensky, 1964). Therefore, denigration of female intellect strikes at the core of the client-professional relationship.

These comments apply to female academics. A male and female professor give identical lectures. Though students learn equally well from both, *his* ideas are accepted as more authoritative (Bernard, 1981:384). Her nail polish, clothes, voice tone, and personal life are objects of student gossip (Ambert and Symons Hitchman, 1976:136). Students' invocation of gender places female academics in a double bind:

> A social science professor remarks: "I feel as if I cannot win in the classroom. If I'm organized and 'professional' students perceive me as cold and rejecting. If I'm open and responsive and warm, I seem to be challenged and taken advantage of, perhaps considered not quite as bright" (Wikler, 1976, quoted in Martin, 1984:486–487).

Women's sexuality interferes with their authority claims ("soft body, soft mind" [Ellman, 1968:74]). According to Fasteau (1975:56), "most men cannot accept the fact that a sexy woman is also tough and competent." One of the few advantages women enjoy in aging and the perceived fading of sexuality that goes with it is the fact that the voice of the matriarch carries weight. The gray-haired professor knows what she is talking about! In this connection, American feminist writer Charlotte Perkins Gilman (1975:74) was discussing the age she would prefer to be, for life, with a group of girls. Most of them agreed on their current age, eighteen years. Gilman, however, chose fifty:

> "Why?" they demanded. "Because," I explained, "when I'm fifty, people will respect my opinions if they are ever going to and I shall not be too old to work" (Hunter Collective, 1983:586).

The "Long Silence"

The meaning of the ruling-ideas proposition for gender relations extends beyond the existence of two parallel intellectual worlds, one authoritative and one not. The metaphor of separate universes does not imply that women as well as men think the thoughts that matter especially to them and express their own ideas. Bernard (1981:11) says "the male world is not only segregative and exclusionary vis-à-vis the female world but is even, in varying degrees, positively hostile to it." Women have traditionally been " 'overlooked,' 'muted,' 'invisible': mere black holes in someone else's universe" (Ardener, 1975:25). In *A Room of One's Own*, Virgina Woolf (1928:45) contrasts women depicted in fiction written by men and women in real life:

> Imaginatively [woman] is of the highest importance;
> practically she is completely insignificant. She pervades
> poetry from cover to cover; she is all but absent from
> history. She dominates the lives of kings and conquerors
> in fiction; in fact she was the slave of any boy whose
> parents forced a ring upon her finger. Some of the most
> inspired words, some of the most profound thoughts in
> literature fall from her lips; in real life she could hardly
> read, could scarcely spell, and was the property of her
> husband.

Only recently have women begun to break their "long silence" (Rowbotham, 1973:30). Four complicated, interacting processes have been responsible for this silence.

"Voluntary" Silence. In the first instance, women have become "voluntarily" silent in mixed company. Convinced that they are less important than men, and have little worthwhile to say, women have let men do most of the the talking. Like good servants and good children, they have been "there," seen, but not heard. In a fortunate simile, Lofland (1975:144-145) compares the inconsequentiality of women to that of British servants in novels:

> By the "thereness" of women, I refer to a phenomenon
> rather similar to that of the portrayal of the servant in
> the classic British mystery story. Such persons seem
> always present. They glide in and out of rooms, pro-
> viding drinks and food. They are questioned by the
> police or private detective. Frequently they "discover" the
> body. Often they behave "suspiciously" enough to, at
> least momentarily, take center stage . . . And yet, despite,
> or perhaps in part because of, their omni-presence, they
> remain, by and large, merely part of the scene. They are
> continually perceived, but rarely perceivers. They are part
> of the furniture through which the plot moves. Essential
> to the set but largely irrelevant to the action. They are
> simply, there.

Women are not heard either because their voices are silent or because their conversation is not attended to. For example, P. Fishman's (1978) study of couples' recorded interaction (cited in Chapter 1) reported that men do the lion's share of the talking (and interrupting), and often choose the topics of conversation:

> Fishman's first impression: "At times I felt that all the
> women did was ask questions . . . I attended to my own
> speech and discovered the same pattern." In fact, the

women asked more than 70 percent of the questions.
Dustin Hoffman put this speech pattern to use in the
motion picture *Tootsie*, using the questioning intonation
frequently when impersonating a woman and rather less
frequently when acting unladylike (Pfeiffer, 1985:59).

"Edging Out" and "Taking Over." A second, related process which
has contributed to women's silence and invisibility involves the "edging
out" (Tuchman and Fortin, 1984) and "taking over" of their ideas by
the dominant sex. This process occurs both on the small stage of everyday interaction and the larger public forum of ideas. In both arenas,
women's intellectual accomplishments have been expropriated by men.
Sometimes women have fought this take-over. More often, they have
stood by and let it happen, or even actively colluded in the end result.
(The reasons for this behavior are considered in the discussion below
of false consciousness.)

An excellent account of the "edging out" of women and the
"taking over" of their good ideas in the micro-world is provided by
Smith's (1975a:365) description of West's (1973) unpublished master's
thesis. During tape recordings of conversations or formal meetings of
professionals of both sexes, West reported that,

> . . . a suggestion or point contributed by a woman may
> be ignored at its point of origin. When it is re-introduced
> at a later point by a man, it is then "recognized" and
> becomes part of the topic. Or if it is recognized at the
> time, it is re-attributed by the responder to another man
> (in the minutes of the meeting, it will appear as having
> been said by someone else). Or the next speaker after
> the woman may use a device such as "What Dorothy
> really means is . . ." . . .[This practice] is not simply im-
> posed by men upon women. Women participate in the
> ways in which they are silenced (Smith, 1975a:365).

At the societal level, the end-product of the "edging out/taking
over" process is recognized in the cliché, "men create culture and
women transmit it" (Tuchman, 1975:171). That is, men are perceived
to be the creators of great ideas and high culture, and women the
benefactors of genius and the "inculcators of art appreciation and social
graces, inspirers of men, civilizers of children within the context of the
home" (Tuchman, 1975:171). At best, women artists have been viewed
as amateur dabblers, deficient in originality (Sydie, 1980). Or traditional
women's work (e.g., patchwork quilts, china painting) has been labeled
craft, not art.

While it is true that men have produced the bulk of the intellectual innovation in art, science, and technology, the reasons are social
mechanisms, not women's intellectual inferiority. One broad structural

consideration is opportunity to create — appropriate schooling, social support of talent, and so on (Becker, 1981; Cole, 1979; Tuchman, 1975). To ask the rhetorical question, "Why have there been no great women artists?" is "an identification of renown with talent and a refusal to contemplate how much the social organization of training, production, and distribution influences who can become famous" (Tuchman and Fortin, 1984:74). Virginia Woolf put the matter succinctly. A woman has two requirements for creativity: money (economic independence) and a room of her own (solitude and freedom from demands of family and community) Rossi, 1973:624). These points receive further elaboration in Chapter 6.

At issue here are those occasions where women, individually or collectively, *have* had ideas, and their ideas have been expropriated by men. Here is one illustration of "taking over":

> Fame begets fame. Germaine Greer (1979) reminds us how this process operates in the case of works by artists who have died. Desiring to own, sell, or be associated with famous artists' works, dealers, curators, and critics may attribute the works of lesser artists to their more famous contemporaries. According to Greer, inasmuch as women have been classified historically as lesser, the best work in the *oeuvres* of women may have been slowly attributed to more famous artists — to men (Tuchman and Fortin, 1984:74).

At a more global level, the development of industrialism and capitalism resulted in the transfer of traditional women's skills and knowledge out of the household into industrial production (Smith, 1984). Today, we buy pork chops in plastic wrap and Sara Lee frozen cakes instead of home-processed food, and ready-made no-iron clothing and bedding instead of hand-sewn items. We purchase the services of dry cleaners, dressmakers, fast-food outlets, and restaurants.

> The traditional productive skills of women — textile manufacture, garment manufacture, food processing — passed into the factory system. Women of the working class might follow their old labor into the new industrial world, but they would no longer command the productive process. They would forget the old skills (Ehrenreich and English, 1978:10).

Similarly, women's traditional wisdom regarding herbs, healing, and childbirth was superseded by the "scientific" expertise of the male medical profession (Oakley, 1980). Indeed, healing by a woman became a crime which figured in the sixteenth-century European witch-hunts, in which millions of women were executed: "If a woman dare to cure *without having studied* she is a witch and must die" (Ehrenreich and English, 1978:35, emphasis in original). Among the "crimes" witches were accused of were providing contraception, performing abortions, and offering drugs to ease labor pains. The witch craze is a fascinating story in itself. (See Ben-Yehuda, 1980; Gray, 1979; Matalene, 1978.) However, for present purposes, the aspect to be emphasized is the edging out of women's medical knowledge by a rather primitive elite occupation which barred women from entry (Ehrenreich and English, 1978:29 ff.). This situation, as well as the historical processes mentioned earlier, have meant loss of gynocentric knowledge and an increasingly androcentric intellectual mode.

The "Losing" of Ideas. A third process responsible for women's silence and invisibility may be labeled the "losing of ideas." The ideas referred to are those that disturb the equanimity of the ruling class. Some of women's thoughts are disturbing simply because they suggest the possibility of an alternative perspective on the world. Other thoughts are viewed as subversive because they directly challenge male supremacy. In reaction, men "have dismissed and 'lost' those views which are not consistent with their own" (Spender, 1982:10).

Otherwise, how to account for the fact that a huge women's movement in the early decades of this century has all but disappeared? Spender (1982:4) says that in school, all she learned of the suffragette movement was that "a few unbalanced and foolish women had chained themselves to railings in the attempt to obtain the vote." Yet, later she discovered that in 1911 there had been twenty-one regular feminist periodicals in England, a women's press, and a feminist book store. Similarly, Rossi (1973:xi) began to search the written record, and found there was "a whole host of like-minded women" who had preceded her own generation. According to Spender (1982:13), ideas that constitute a political threat are censored and "lost," so that "every fifty years women have to reinvent the wheel." In brief, ". . . if they do not want to know, they will lose it" (Spender, 1982:11).

How do ideas get lost? The ruling-ideas proposition implies male gatekeepers who control knowledge. Unpublished ideas disappear when money cannot be found to publish them. Most women have been dependent on male financial resources. When irritating or foreign ideas do manage to appear in print, they fail to please the critics, who have traditionally been men (Lanser and Beck, 1979). Such ideas are not cited or quoted or anthologized or taught. Since women are outside the "social circle" of men whose ideas count for one another (Smith, 1975a), women's ideas often disappear into obscurity.

In 1963, Betty Friedan published *The Feminine Mystique,* a book instrumental in igniting the renewed women's movement. In that book, Friedan complained about the "problem that has no name." However, "the problem had been around for a few centuries and had even been

named before — but the name, and the namers, had been lost"
(Spender, 1982:724).

The Muteness of Women. The final cause of women's "long
silence" lies in the fact that women have become alienated from their
own experience, and hence, mute. Friedan (1963:18) wrote that women
complained, "I feel empty somehow . . ." or "I feel as if I don't exist."
Females raised in the shadow of the dominant male ideology think
about themselves and the world, to some extent at least, in male terms
and lack the ability to express themselves in their own idiom. In Smith's
(1975a:357) words, "For it is men who produce for women . . . the
means to think and image." Germaine Greer (1979:325) expresses the
result of this alienation for artists:

> For all artists the problem is one of finding one's own
> authenticity, of speaking in a language or imagery that is
> essentially one's own, but if one's self-image is dictated
> by one's relation to others and all one's activities are
> other-directed, it is simply not possible to find one's own
> voice.

Reality is constructed and perpetuated through symbols, and
through language as a specific set of symbols (Cicourel, 1970; Schutz,
1967; Whorf, 1949). Thus, to a considerable extent, what people think
and know and do is determined by the language categories at their
disposal. "Men have had the power to name, order, and classify while
also defining the rules of speaking which help keep women in their
place" (Jenkins and Kramarae, 1981:12). The English language, among
others, denigrates women while it asserts male superiority. In addition,
the language is inadequate for expressing the depth of female experience, which puts women at a disadvantage in understanding
themselves. For example, since males have had the "power to name,"
women's own sexual experience is often described in a misogynous
language of dirty jokes and offensive expressions for women (tramp,
piece of ass, pig, pussy). Women lack their own colloquial words for
vagina, for clitoris, for orgasm (Bernard, 1981:376 ff.). Popular culture
views women's speech as frivolous, unimportant:

> In the English language, we talk and we chat, we jabber
> and we chatter while men speak, proclaim and express
> concerns. In the French language, "elle parlote, babille,
> bavarde, jase, cause" while men "parlent, discourent,
> discutent" (Martel and Peterat, 1984:43).

In addition, the English language excludes and subsumes women
through generic masculine terms that are supposed to refer to people
in general: "he," "mankind," "man, the social animal," "men of good

will." (Or even, "Man, being a mammal, breast-feeds his young" [Martyna, 1980:489].) Bernard (1981:376) puts the whole issue very strongly. According to her, English is a "hostile language" that expresses the "misogyny of the male world."

As a consequence of women's thinking about themselves with male language and models, they are constrained to treat themselves "as looked at from outside, as other" (Smith, 1979:138). Imagine a group of young men and women sitting around a table in a tavern, drinking, talking, telling stories. A joke is told about the skillful seduction of a silly young thing. Both the women and men laugh. A few minutes later, an unknown woman walks past their table. The men exchange comments on the stranger's figure, while the women listen with interest. With the advent of the women's movement, women in situations like the above have been able to reflect on their experience and to realize the extent to which they identify with men and use men's eyes to look out at the world (Rowbotham, 1973:40). A Flin Flon, Manitoba woman describes the emotional experience of finding her own voice (Luxton, 1980:207):

> I cried the first I saw some women on TV talking about
> things that I'd felt. Before that I always thought it was
> just me but when I realized other women felt the same, I
> felt so good . . . I started reading everything I could get
> my hands on and talking to everyone.

The feminist critique of patriarchal language has been described as "wrenching back some word power" (Daly, 1978:9).

The Distribution of Ruling Ideas

The ruling-ideas proposition refers to the power of the dominant class to distribute as well as produce ideas. Mannheim (1936) wrote about the "social techniques" employed by dominant groups to reinforce their position. As noted above, men act as gatekeepers in the many societal institutions concerned with the distribution of social knowledge (Smith, 1975; Spender, 1985). The institutions promulgating gender ideas include the mass media, educational institutions from elementary school through university, church, political institutions, art, film and literature, law, medicine, and psychiatry. Canadians are bombarded by messages about gender from these institutions. For the most part, these messages are consistent and traditional (Mackie, 1983b).

The Mass Media and Ruling Ideas. The mass media have been described as "conductor[s] of ruling ideas par excellence" (Clement, 1975:274). A number of Canadian studies support the conclusion that the media reinforce gender hierarchy and gender traditionalism. For example, according to Clement (1975:332), very few women participate in media policy-making. In 1975, women represented only 3.8 percent of the Canadian media élite. More recently, the Canadian Radio-television and Telecommunications Commission (1982) published a critical report of gender stereotyping and representation of women in the broadcast media. Also, see Nugent, 1982. These concerns will be taken up in Chapter 6.

Academia and Ruling Ideas. Women have always been outside the academic social circles in charge of constructing knowledge. They have been excluded by formal admission policies and channeled into sex-typed fields. Where women have been present in our universities, they have been relatively few in number and lowly in status (Andersen, 1983:223–224). A brief discussion of the field of sociology serves to illustrate the ideological nature of academia.

Our discussion earlier in this chapter of agentic and communal research styles may have given the false impression that these modes co-exist comfortably within the discipline of sociology. Nevertheless, it should now be clear that male and female perspectives are *not* equal in status. Bernard (1973:785) observed that the agentic approach carries more academic prestige because "what men do is valued more highly than what women do." Indeed, prior to the women's movement, women were as invisible in sociology as elsewhere in society. Bernard (1973:781), among others, charged that the science of society is in actuality the male science of male society.

"The selective eye of sociology . . . has been blind to women for decades" (Epstein, 1981:149). The blindness of sociology (and the other social sciences[9]) extended from the research problems studied, to methodological and theoretical perspectives, to the teaching of sociology. Males "held 'normative power': the right to define what was appropriate, legitimate, important . . ." (Ward and Grant, 1985:143). Topics for study have been male-defined issues, which omitted women's experience entirely or misinterpreted that experience. Male sociologists focused their attention on social institutions and settings in which males predominate, such as the occupational, political, and legal systems. Where women were noticed at all, it was their connection to men that counted, e.g., as wives and prostitutes. Women took "the insubstantial form of ghosts, shadows or stereotyped characters" (Oakley, 1974:1). Pre-movement analyses of connections between the sexes (Parsons, 1954, 1955) emphasized complementarity. Little was said about power and tension between women and men (Carrigan et al., 1985:554).

With the notable exception of the pioneering work of Hacker (1951) and Komarovsky (1946), which went unappreciated at the time, pre-1970s sociology excluded the women's world. Until the women's movement, such topics as the following went unstudied: pregnancy, childbirth, and motherhood (Bernard, 1981; Chodorow, 1978; Oakley,

1980); women's domestic labor (Fox, 1980; Luxton, 1980); rape (Brownmiller, 1975); emotions (Hochschild, 1975, 1979, 1983); women's aging (Abu-Laban, 1980b, 1981); wife battering (Dobash and Dobash, 1979); women's medicine (Scully, 1980); widowhood (Lopata, 1973, 1984); women's role in cultural production (Tuchman, 1975; Sydie, 1980); gender and language (Spender, 1985); and obesity (Millman, 1980). This listing is but a sample of the new topics that have been explored and the researchers active in them. Obviously, the pre-feminist male view had been a "myopic view," which in omitting the concerns of half the world led to "skewed insights into human behavior" (Epstein, 1981:149).

As the ruling-ideas proposition would predict, sociological methods and theories have also been androcentric. In Smith's (1974:7) words, "how sociology is thought — its methods, conceptual schemes and theories — has been based on and built up within, the male social universe . . ." The aforementioned "machismo factor" labels women's exclusion from the research process as both agents and subjects of research. In recent years, scholars (Eichler, 1984; Eichler and Lapointe, 1985; Miles and Finn, 1982; Roberts, 1981; Stanley and Wise, 1983) have analyzed the ways in which sexism can enter the research process, from specification of concepts, to choice of research problem, gathering of data, to interpretation and publication of results. Men have been the traditional gatekeepers of academia (Smith, 1975a), reviewers of graduate thesis prospectuses, appraisers of proposals for research funding, editors of journals and books. Publishing is critical. As Spender (1981a:188) notes, "In a very fundamental sense, research which is not in print does not exist." The author's exploratory study (Mackie, 1985) of communal style, mentioned earlier, concluded that feminists' "rebellious constructions of the mind" (Berger, 1963:133) have not revolutionized mainstream sociology's methodology.

In the early 1970s, feminists also noticed defects in sociological theory. The theories designed to guide research and to explain social behavior were grounded in male experience and, therefore, omitted the female world. Rational, formal dimensions of social behavior were emphasized and the irrational, emotional, informal dimensions were overlooked. Even more disturbing, "scholarly" arguments were used to justify a sexist status quo (Oakley, 1974:28). For example, Parsons (1955) is accused of presenting a *Kinder, Kuche, Kirche* view of women's place, as though efficient societal operation demanded that women stay home and play their traditional role. Indeed, sociology's founding fathers have been called "sexists to a man" (Schwendinger and Schwendinger, 1971). Sociology's failure to deal meaningfully with half the members of society "throws a harsh light on the theoretical models that have shaped the profession for the past quarter-century" (Epstein, 1981:160). Too often, theoretical "sparks for the sociological imagination" have had to come from outside mainstream academic sociology (Gould,

1980:460). Recent assessments (Tancred-Sheriff, 1985; Stacey and Thorne, 1985; Ward and Grant, 1985) conclude that feminists have not yet had much impact on their discipline's theoretical constructions.

Sociology's previous insensitivity to gender and its neglect of women in research obviously affected the teaching of the discipline. Until the women's movement removed blinders, no one really noticed that students were being taught the sociology of male society. According to Nett (1981b:132), even the more recently published Canadian introductory sociology textbooks "perpetuate the exclusion and segregation of women . . . ." The introductory sociology course is the only formal exposure to the field that most university students will ever receive. Women's studies are certainly more visible in Canadian universities today than they were 15 or 20 years ago (Strong-Boag, 1983). However, in sociology, feminist ideas have become encapsulated in the specialty area of gender relations. Women sociologists are often left alone, with courses, textbooks, and conferences of their very own.

In general, women sociologists have been marginal members of their profession, caught between masculine and feminine worlds, but completely at ease in neither. Marginality offers the possibility of creativity, of intellectual appreciation of both worlds (Daniels, 1975:341).[10] However, too often completion of male-dominated social science training has taken away women sociologists' own voices:

> . . . women in more senior positions in the university do not ordinarily represent women's perspectives. They are those who have been passed through this very rigorous filter. They are those whose work and style of work and conduct have met the approval of judges who are largely men (Smith, 1975a:361).

Those women who have managed to retain their feminine perspective may suppress it in order to please male gatekeepers.

So far, sociology has resisted feminist transformation. "Feminist sociology . . . seems to have been both co-opted and ghettoized, while the discipline as a whole and its dominant paradigms have proceeded relatively unchanged" (Stacey and Thorne, 1985:302). Moreover, feminists in sociology have been less successful in reconstructing their discipline than have their sisters in history, anthropology, and literary criticism (Stacey and Thorne, 1985). One reason is the pluralist nature of sociology. Instead of orthodoxy, many competing theories co-exist, and intellectual battles need to be waged on several fronts.

A second basic reason why sociology resists feminist transformation is, of course, women's status in the discipline. Because women generally lack power and prestige, "the results of their labours are denigrated through mechanisms of privatization, ridicule and the male-defined aura of insignificance . . ." (Tancred-Sheriff, 1985:116). According to McCormack (1981:2), women "bear the burden of a pejorative stereotype which pictures them as lacking those unique qualities of mind which make for outstanding scientific achievement." For example, feminist analysis of sexist language meets hostility and ridicule (Blaubergs, 1980). Women are on the periphery of central specialty areas in sociology, and play leading roles only in specialities marginal to the discipline. Moreover, they are relatively few in number, especially as senior professors, department heads, deans, and editors of mainstream journals. For example, "the proportion of women holding full-time teaching posts in Canadian universities has risen marginally from 12.8% in the early 1970s to 16% in 1982–83 . . ." (Tancred-Sheriff, 1985:109). Only six of 44 Canadian and American sociology departments are chaired by women (Dill et al., 1983). Consequently, women lack "clout" in "what comes to count as scientific knowledge" (Collins, 1983:267). To some extent, "reality" is a function of the sheer number of voices in the chorus, crying that it is so (Festinger et al., 1956; Kanter, 1977).

Gender, Ideology, and False Consciousness

How do the concepts of ideology and false consciousness relate to gender? Recall that ideology refers to those ruling ideas that distort reality in order to justify current power arrangements. "False consciousness," on the other hand, labels the subordinate group's acceptance of ideology as valid and authoritative. In the context of gender, the major function of ideology is to rationalize the differences in the rewards and opportunities available to males and females. Moreover, the ideology must make these differences appear to be reasonable and natural, rather than arbitrary and unjust (Jaggar and Rothenberg, 1984:5). In short, ideology buttresses *patriarchy:* the domination of women by men, as a pervasive feature of gender relations in all kinds of societies (Smith, 1983:316).

The concepts of ideology and false consciousness have been implicit in our discussion up to this point of gender and the sociology of knowledge. However, our analysis can proceed a step further by suggesting answers to the question, "Why?" Why are men engaged in the production of ideology? Why are women submerged in false consciousness? Are men bad and women stupid? Lipman-Blumen (1984) has identified some basic sociological propositions that take us beyond such naive individualism.

Power, Ideology, and False Consciousness

Power is the crux of ideology and false consciousness. Gerth and Mills (1953:194) observe that "an adequate understanding of power relations

. . . involves a knowledge of the grounds on which a power holder claims obedience, and the terms in which the obedient feels an obligation to obey."[11] Whether sex differentials in power are seen to be rooted in the mode of production and/or reproduction depends on whether the analyst is a Traditional Marxist, Radical Feminist, or Socialist Feminist (see above). At the ideational rather than the materialist level, power may also be viewed as one solution to human feelings of existential helplessness and anxiety:

> Neither our fortune nor our fate is ultimately within our control. Uncertainty and awareness of the inability to control even one's own life and environment are the essence of the human condition (Lipman-Blumen, 1984:7).

Existential helplessness motivates many strategies, e.g., seeking certainty in religion. However, human beings seem to need more tangible security. The male strategy is to seek control over others. They feel strong and in control of their own lives if they can exert power over the even less powerful. Though women share this masculine strategy to some extent, e.g., their control over children, the feminine strategy has been to seek relief of their sense of helplessness by entrusting themselves to men and the institutions run by men (Lipman-Blumen, 1984:7).

Male power is grounded in institutions that amass resources and develop ideologies rationalizing the status quo. These ideologies, which stress male superiority, insist that women by nature lack the leadership qualities for dominance; that men are benevolent, omniscient, and predestined to rule; and that to deny male leadership is blasphemy (Lipman-Blumen, 1984:19). The core institution of patriarchy is the family. Religious institutions throughout history have taught male supremacy (Lipman-Blumen and Tickamyer, 1975:320). In recent centuries, science has become an important supporter of this ideology (Ehrenreich and English, 1978; Miles and Finn, 1982).

Male and Female Motives

Both sexes consider their condition "natural," the inevitable result of inborn biological differences and abilities. (See Chapter 1.) As Bem and Bem (1971:85) observe, "we are like the fish who is unaware that his [her] environment is wet." Indeed, research suggests that many Canadian women are oblivious to inequalities in the system and their own lack of power (Connelly and Christiansen-Ruffman, 1977).

Beyond "not knowing any better", what motives underlie male and female behavior? The male situation is, perhaps, the easier to explain. Despite the fact that power entails burdens, it is axiomatic in

AN OX NAMED MIKE

Nellie McClung (1873–1951) was a prominent campaigner for female suffrage in Western Canada, a member of the Women's Christian Temperance Union, and one of the first women elected to the Alberta Legislative Assembly. *In Times Like These* (1915/1972) is a feminist tract, portraying Canada as sorely in need of redemption by women, and the ideal Canada as Christian, rural, and dry (Strong-Boag, 1972). McClung's parable of Mike, the ox, shows good appreciation of the sociological axiom that "no group willingly relinquishes power . . . [but] cultivates and protects its own resources, while simultaneously seeking to devalue, deny, ignore, diminish, capture, or decimate the resources of the other" (Lipman-Blumen, 1984:8). McClung writes:

I remember when I was a little girl back on the farm in the Souris Valley, I used to water the cattle on Saturday mornings, drawing the water in an icy bucket with a windlass from a fairly deep well. We had one old white ox, called Mike, a patriarchal-looking old sinner, who never had enough, and who always had to be watered first. Usually I gave him what I thought he should have and then took him back to the stable and watered the others. But one day I was feeling real strong, and I resolved to give Mike all he could drink, even if it took every drop of water in the well. I must admit that I cherished a secret hope that he would kill himself drinking. I will not set down here in cold figures how many pails of water Mike drank — but I remember. At last he could not drink another drop, and stood shivering beside the trough, blowing the last mouthful out of his mouth like a bad child. I waited to see if he would die, or at least turn away and give the others a chance. The thirsty cattle came crowding around him, but old Mike, so full I am sure he felt he would never drink another drop of water again as long as he lived, deliberately and with difficulty put his two front feet over the trough and kept all the other cattle away. Years afterwards I had the pleasure of being present when a delegation waited upon the Government of one of the provinces of Canada, and presented many reasons for extending the franchise to women. One member of the Government rose and spoke for all his colleagues. He said in substance: "You can't have it — so long as I have anything to do with the affairs of this province — you shall not have it!"

Did your brain ever give a queer little twist, and suddenly you were conscious that the present mental process had taken place before? If you have ever had it, you will know what I mean, and if you haven't I cannot make you understand. I had that feeling then. I said to myself: "Where have I seen that face before?" Then, suddenly, I remembered, and in my heart I cried out: "Mike! — old friend, Mike! Dead these many years! Your bones lie buried under the fertile soil of the Souris Valley, but your soul goes marching on! Mike, old friend, I see you again — both feet in the trough!"

Source: Nellie McClung, *In Times Like These*. (1915/1972), pp. 57-58. Used with permission of the University of Toronto Press.

sociology that "no group willingly relinquishes power" (Lipman-Blumen, 1984:8). Accordingly, the dominant male group "cultivates and protects its own resources, while simultaneously seeking to devalue, deny, ignore, diminish, capture, or decimate the resources of the other" (Lipman-Blumen, 1984:8). Hence, male production of ideology. Ideology, instilled through socialization, is a more effective alternative than getting compliance through brute force (Lipman-Blumen and Tickamyer, 1975:320).

Five factors seem responsible for women's false consciousness. For one thing, women have traditionally been bound to men through sexuality, marriage, and procreation, and segregated from other women. These living arrangements have impeded women's understanding of their true interests. In the parallel case of racial inequality, the ghetto bred "an understanding of the dissimilarity between those inside and those outside its boundaries" (Lipman-Blumen, 1984:9).

Secondly, women have accepted certain "control myths" (Lipman-Blumen, 1984:9): that men are more knowledgeable and capable; that women are inferior; that men have women's interests at heart; that women can vicariously share in men's power, and so on. In Spender's (1982:6) words, the woman "usually comes to accept in part that the world is made for men and that her place within it, is as a subordinate — *for 'good' and 'sound' reasons*" (emphasis added).

Thirdly, women accept the status quo because the status quo pays off for some women, some of the time. According to Friedan (1963:160),

> A mystique does not compel its own acceptance. For the feminine mystique to have "brainwashed" [women] . . ., it *must have filled real needs* in those who seized on it for others and those who accepted it for themselves (emphasis added).

Patriarchal capitalism benefits middle-class women more than the poor, WASP women more than ethnic and racial minorities, the physically attractive more than the blemished, the young more than the old. In return for accepting as natural their subordinate status and curtailed opportunities, women are sometimes rewarded with affection, respect, and protection.

Too often, we underestimate the impact of class, race, ethnicity, and age upon both sexes' experience of gender. Take age as an example. Women (but not men) often grow more radical with age. Steinem (1983b:17) says of women:

> We tend to be conservative when we are young. We become less and less powerful as we go through the four big, radicalizing experiences of a woman's life: joining the

> labour force and discovering how it treats women; get-
> ting married and discovering it is not usually an equal
> partnership; having children and finding out who takes
> care of them and who does not; and aging.

Working-class women, especially those from stigmatized racial and ethnic groups, suffer greatly from the gender system. However, their lack of eduction makes it difficult for the feminist movement to reach them (Ambert, 1976:189).

Fourth, feminism has provoked a right-wing, authoritarian backlash.[12] "It is as if, at the height of the civil rights movement, a large percentage of blacks had suddenly organized to say: 'Wait a minute. We don't want equal rights. We like things just the way they are" (English, 1982, quoted in Caplan, 1985:351). This well-financed countermovement, spearheaded by fundamentalist Christian churches and the Moral Majority (in the United States), accuses feminists of destroying marriage and motherhood, legitimizing abortion, sponsor- ing homosexual marriage, attacking religion, sending female soldiers into combat, and sponsoring unisex toilets (Friedan, 1981; Steinem, 1983b; *Time Magazine*, July 12, 1982). They believe that financial dependence on men is "a safe, privileged, sheltered position for women" (Caplan, 1985:351). Dubinsky (1985) argues that the ideas of New Right women should not be dismissed as mere "false con- sciousness." Rather, their complaints have a materialist foundation that liberal feminism, with its emphasis on helping women "succeed" in a male-dominated world, has neglected:

> If feminism is for women who are slender, "intelligent"
> and upwardly mobile, and you are over forty, perhaps
> overweight and locked into a deadend job and/or
> marriage, then you are more likely to see feminism as a
> putdown than a sisterly call to arms (Ehrenreich, 1981,
> quoted by Dubinsky, 1985:40).

The anti-feminist countermovement has yet to reach its zenith in Canada.

Finally, a variety of social control mechanisms discourage women from questioning the validity of ruling ideas, for ideology is not impervious to skepticism. Spender's (1982:8) ambitious work documents that "for centuries women have been challenging men, and men have used punitive measures against them . . . ." Insubordinate women are punished with ridicule and dismissed as silly, stupid, or sick. Male intellectuals vilified early feminists (Rossi, 1973). Historians described the English suffragette movement as "a strange, melodramatic, and unlovely phenomenon" (Smith, 1957:689). Psychiatrists (Lundberg and Farnham, 1947:143) diagnosed feminism as "a deep illness." Mass media reporting trivialized the revived women's movement by labeling it "women's lib," focusing on a comic lunatic fringe of mythological bra burners,[13] and either sandwiching reports of movement issues between recipes and advice columns, or ignoring them altogether (Molotch, 1978). The control of deviants is not always subtle and indirect. Women have been imprisoned, force-fed, subjected to psychiatric ill-treatment and surgical abuse when they failed to accept prevailing gender norms (Ehrenreich and English, 1978; Schur, 1984).

In general, then, we conclude that the traditional gender arrangements continue because they are situated in power differences and sustained by ideology and false consciousness. The ideology is instilled through the socialization process, buttressed by most of the institutions of society (Hamilton, 1978:11), and reinforced through the micro-politics of interaction in everyday life.

The Sociology of Knowledge and the Women's Movement

As mentioned earlier in this chapter, the perspective of the sociology of knowledge on social change has serious implications for feminism as a social movement. At issue is the efficacy of ideas as agents of change. The orthodox Marxian position regards ideas as reflections of the social order, not determinants of social change. Many contemporary thinkers agree with Marx that altering ideas alone is not enough; women's power position cannot improve significantly without improvements in their material conditions (Armstrong and Armstrong, 1984; Spender, 1985:6). Jaggar and Rothenberg (1984:9) warn that "it would be a mistake to think that the main problem is ideological." Egalitarianism will come about only if radical changes occur in the structure of the family and the structure of the economy. Though Traditional Marxists, Radical Feminists, and Social Feminists all call for fundamental restructuring of societal institutions, their priorities vary between production and reproduction.

Nevertheless, feminist theorists tend to follow the modern sociology of knowledge[14] in refusing to dismiss the importance of ideas as causal agents and in accepting the dualistic assumption that social change results from the interaction of ideas *and* material factors (Kuklick, 1983:294). For instance, Lipman-Blumen and Tickamyer (1975:320) remark that "ideology . . . is a major underpinning of social structure, sometimes even preceding new structural changes." Similarly, Armstrong and Armstrong (1984:204) say that "equality between the sexes requires radical alterations in both the structures and ideas that perpetuate the division of labour by sex."

The most recent wave of the feminist movement itself illustrates the role of both material factors and ideas in producing social change. Changes in the economy, such as inflation and increased availability of service jobs that male workers do not want, drew women into the labor force (Harris, 1981). Altered material conditions encouraged feminist ideas. In other words, women did not flock to outside jobs *because* the women's movement stimulated their ambition. Work helps shape women's ideas about themselves and their milieu. Although the type of work women do has not changed extensively, their labor force participation has increased dramatically in the 1970s and 1980s (Armstrong and Armstrong, 1984:202–203). However, ideas too had causal significance.

The contemporary feminist movement in Canada officially began with the federal government's 1967 decision to establish a Royal Commission on the Status of Women in Canada (Morris, 1980). The Commission was to inquire into the situation of Canadian women and to "recommend what steps might be taken by the Federal Government to ensure for women equal opportunities with men in all aspects of Canadian society" (*Report of the Royal Commission on the Status of Women in Canada*, 1970:vii). Three years later, the Commission tabled its report, which contained 167 recommendations in the areas of the economy, education, the family, taxation, poverty, public life, immigration and citizenship, and criminal law. Prior to this political action, women's situation was not regarded as a social problem. However, the currents of intellectual thought in Canada, the United States and Western Europe, concerning equality of opportunity and human rights issues, were ripe for a reconsideration of women's rights. The economically prosperous 1960s was a decade of protest in the United States against the Vietnamese War, nuclear weaponry and the disadvantaged position of blacks, the poor and university students. The publication of Friedan's *The Feminine Mystique* led to the formation of the American National Organization of Women. As Spender (1982:720) documents, Friedan "did not burst onto the scene in 1963 without precedents." Women like Doris Lessing in *The Golden Notebook* (1962) and Rachel Carson in *Silent Spring* (1962) were already, in different ways, questioning society's value system. However, Friedan inspired a generation of accomplished feminist writers.

Ideas spilling northward across the border through media and personal contacts mingled with those of parallel, indigenous movements in this country (Morris, 1980). Women involved in these activist movements became aware of the subordinate position of their sex in organizations advocating freedom and equality for others. They were "only asked to do the cooking and cleaning, the licking of stamps, and the stuffing of envelopes...but never to advance their own ideas or become leaders themselves" (Marsden and Harvey, 1979:195). The Voice of Women (a "ban-the-bomb" organization) played a crucial role as a link between the New Left activist groups in Canada and elsewhere, and the mainstream, upper-middle-class women's organizations (Morris, 1980). It also served as a political training ground (Mackie, 1983b:292).

In terms of the sociology of knowledge, the women's movement saw a breakthrough of false consciousness and an emergence of gender consciousness, as women began to be a gender-for-themselves.[15] Marx (1963/1846–47) distinguished between a class-in-itself and a class-for-itself. Individuals in the former situation are objectively related to the means of production, but are unaware of their commonalities. The class-for-itself, on the other hand, is composed of people who share not only a common relationship to the means of production, but a class consciousness. Through struggle, the class-for-itself has thrown off false consciousness and developed an understanding of its own interests (Roy, 1984). Movements of liberation resemble the story of the Emperor and his fine clothes: "they make it possible for people to see the world in an enlarged perspective because they remove the covers and blinders that obscure knowledge and observation" (Millman and Kanter, 1975:vii). As Steinem (1983b:16) puts it, we have "seen things that we cannot now *unsee*."

THE EMPEROR'S NEW CLOTHES

Hans Christian Andersen's (1837) well-known story of "The Emperor's New Clothes" contributes to children's moral education on the subjects of vanity and gullibility and power in high places. However, the fairy tale also illustrates six lessons in the sociology of knowledge. This is so because the sociology of knowledge analyzes the processes by which reality is socially constructed (Berger and Luckmann, 1966:1).

Many years ago, there lived an Emperor who was interested in nothing but his clothes. One day, two rogues appeared at the court. They claimed the ability to weave beautiful garments that had the wonderful property of remaining invisible to incompetents and simpletons. Since the Emperor lusted after new clothes and wished to identify such weaklings in his court, he gave huge sums of money to the impostors. Everyone in the city soon knew of the wonderful properties of the cloth. Of course, the Emperor himself and his ministers admired the material they claimed to see on the empty looms. "Is not the work absolutely magnificent? What a splendid design! What glorious colors!"

The Emperor wore a new suit fashioned from this invisible material in a procession through the city. At first, his costume received extravagant compliments. "But the Emperor has nothing on at all!" said a little child. The child's comment was whispered throughout the crowd. At last, all the people cried out, "But he has nothing on at all!" The Emperor was vexed, for he knew that the people were right. But he thought the procession had to go on. The Lords of the Bedchamber took greater pains than ever to appear to hold up the train of the Emperor's costume, although in reality, there was no train to hold.

Hans Christian Andersen's story stimulates these sociological observations:

1. "If [people] define situations as real, they are real in their consequences" (Thomas and Thomas, 1928:572). That is, reality is subject to social definition. Even when this definition does not correspond to physical reality, it produces consequences with which people must cope.

2. Different locations in the social structure are associated with different ways of thinking. The Emperor, his ministers, the con men, and the child had different intellectual orientations towards the events.

3. "The ideas of the ruling class are...the ruling ideas" (Marx, 1947:39). Persons in positions of authority have the power to dictate what is so. "He who has the bigger stick has the better chance of imposing his definitions of reality" (Berger and Luckmann, 1966:109).

4. Social movements, such as the women's movement, have an impact on the public that is analogous to the child's cry, "The Emperor is naked!" Blinders are suddenly removed. "Like the onlookers in the Emperor's parade, we can see and plainly speak about things that have always been there, but that formerly were unacknowledged" (Millman and Kanter, 1975:vii).

5. There is power in numbers which can challenge other types of authority. If many of the ruled disagree with the ruling ideas, the validity of the ruling ideas can be shaken (Festinger et al., 1956:28).

6. Those with a stake in the old order resist new definitions of the situation. At the end of the story, the Emperor and the Lords of the Bedchamber persisted with the nude parade. Feminists should not expect their new insights to be immediately or universally acclaimed.

Through the feminist movement, women began to become a gender-for-themselves. Strictly speaking, we mean some women, not all women. False consciousness continues to characterize groups such as REAL Women. Feminists were now able to question the doctrine of male superiority, as well as the control myths supporting it. According to an active participant in the early days of the movement,

> The heart of the movement . . . rests in women's knowl-
> edge . . . that they are not inferior — not chicks, nor
> bunnies, nor quail, nor cows, nor bitches, nor ass, nor
> meat . . . . They know they are not animals or sexual
> objects or commodities (Dixon, 1971:177).

The movement permitted women to retrieve the experiences they had nearly lost in "male non-experience of them" (Rowbotham, 1973:37). Shulman (1980:594) describes this dimension of the women's movement:

> Those early [consciousness-raising] sessions were really
> fact-gathering sessions, research sessions on our feelings.
> We wanted to get at the truth about how women felt,
> how we viewed our lives, what was done to us, and how
> we functioned in the world. Not how we were *supposed*
> to feel but how we really did feel . . . .What made the
> discussions so powerful was the sense we had that a
> great floodlight had been turned onto the world, lighting
> up *all* our experience . . . (emphases in original).

Over time, the women's movement has developed a set of ideas that Mannheim (1936) would characterize as a "utopia." In contrast to ideology (which supports the status quo), a *utopia* is a complex of ideas held by a rising class/gender which looks to the future and calls into question the status quo. A utopia, in Mannheim's sense, is visionary but not an impossible dream.

> Only those orientations transcending reality will be
> referred to by us as utopian which, when they pass over
> into conduct, tend to shatter, either partially or wholly,
> the order of things prevailing at the time (Mannheim,
> 1936:192).

In the early years, the heart of the women's movement was the consciousness-raising groups, whose purpose was to develop an analysis of the society, as well as appropriate politics based on the experiences of being female (Polk, 1972:323–324). The feminist utopia, based on the value of gender equality, draws upon the writings of centuries of like-minded women (Rossi, 1973; Spender, 1982). The utopia of feminism "is premised on the belief that women suffer from oppressive inequalities in a number of areas and puts forward the ideal of a world in which the sexes would be equal" (Pierson and Prentice, 1982:37).[16]

Part of the process of becoming a gender-for-themselves involves an end to women's long silence. "The vast mass of human beings have [sic] always been mainly invisible to themselves . . . .Every mass political movement of the oppressed necessarily brings its own vision of itself into sight" (Rowbotham, 1973:27). "Bringing its own vision of itself into sight" has resulted in an explosion of ideas and activity. Language has been approached from a women's perspective which challenges sexist uses and structures. Feminist newspapers, periodicals, and publishers sprang up in Canada (Wolfe, 1982) and elsewhere. According to Strong-Boag (1983:94), "feminist scholarship in Canada is flourishing on a number [of], although not all, disciplinary fronts." For example, feminist historians have undertaken to retrieve women from obscurity and to develop a "fully human history" which takes "into account the experiences of both sexes" (Pierson and Prentice, 1982:43).

Women have come into focus for themselves through a thriving "women's culture," which encompasses art, poetry, literature, music. There has been renewed respect for traditional female wisdom concerning such matters as childbirth and childcare.

Because men's and women's roles interlock, feminist dissatisfaction has inevitably affected men. One result has been the production of much literature on the "male sex role" in the 1970s (Carrigan et al., 1985). Most of it, however, has concentrated on the restrictions, disadvantages and general penalties attached to being male. The feminist critique of the family was ignored. In other words, the source of the "masculine dilemma" has been psychologized. The "real self is seen as squashed, strained, or suppressed" by the demands of the male sex role (Carrigan et al., 1985:567). Disregarding the political implications of feminism meant that men could view the women's movement as a worthy parallel endeavor, rather than an assault on *them*. Exceptions, of course, exist, such as Fasteau (1974), Tolson (1977), and Komarovsky (1976).

The women's movement has certainly made men uncomfortable. In the 1980s, small numbers belonged to groups seeking equality for men who have lost custody of their children, self-help for their own violent behavior, or intellectual understanding of "the new man." The flavor of these groups has been therapeutic or concerned with self-improvement. Some, such as the fathers' rights groups, have been antifeminist (Carrigan et al., 1985:575). A minority of radical men has been willing to confront patriarchy (Snodgrass, 1977; Tolson, 1977).

The potential social base for a significant men's movement simply isn't there. Males experience psychological oppression from the gender socialization processes. Nevertheless, "they have not been economically or politically discriminated against because they are *men*" (Richardson, 1981:264, emphasis in original). The gender stratification system favors men as a group. Not many men would willingly forfeit the power, privileges, and resources that accrue to those at the top of the gender hierarchy.

The consciousness-raising aspects of the feminist movement have been accompanied by attempts to create the social structure envisioned in utopian ideals. Ideas are necessary, but not sufficient agents of change. As Steinem says,

> We accept the idea of equal pay; we don't have the
> reality of equal pay. We accept the idea of equal parent-
> hood; we don't have the possibility of equal parenthood
> as a real choice (Carter, 1984:205).

This movement effort focuses on influencing Canadian law and social policy. In 1981, thousands of women across the country successfully organized against opposition from the federal government to achieve recognition of legal equality of the sexes under the new Canadian Constitution (Kome, 1983). After April 1985, Section 15 of Canada's Charter of Rights and Freedoms became the basis for legal challenges to inequity in society's gender arrangements. Legal discrimination against women has decreased over the years. However, informal or customary injustices continue. Therefore, feminist groups across Canada are organized around such issues as reproductive freedom and control over own bodies; pornography and violence against women; provison of day care; pensions for housewives; rights of part-time workers; the rights of native Indian women; and equality in religious organizations. In addition, women have organized around the more general issues of nuclear disarmament and environmental concerns. Finally, structural changes have involved setting up special institutions for women, parallel to those in mainstream society. Examples include self-help medical clinics, media and cooperative day care.

Women's problems are far from being solved. The political and religious conservatism, as well as the economic hard times of the 1980s, threatens the feminist movement. The anti-feminist countermovement, referred to earlier, thrives in this atmosphere. For example REAL Women, a Toronto-based organization, champions traditional roles for the sexes and opposes equal pay for work of equal value, affirmative action programs, easier divorce, universal day care, abortion, and homosexuality (Riley, 1985). Despite the educational achievements of women (Buckland, 1985), a sizable gap exists in the employment opportunities of women and men (Calzavara, 1985). "In Canada today, there is still women's work and men's work; furthermore, women's work has changed little over the last fifty years" (Armstrong and Armstrong, 1984:201). The average income earned by Canadian women is 53 percent of the average earned by Canadian men (Statistics Canada, 1985:69). Outside work does not let women "off the hook." Many now carry household and child-care responsibilities on top of labor force participation. However, women are not economically independent. To survive, they must turn to those who control the resources: men. As Spender (1985:5) tells us, "for most women who want their supper there is the requirement that they must first sing."

Conclusions

This chapter has presented the core ideas of the sociology of knowledge as a general theoretical background for the discussion of gender socialization. When we come to see gender as a paradox — immensely consequential, yet fiction — we must ask how this social reality is maintained and perpetuated. If, as we argued in Chapter 1, male-female power symmetry is *not* erected upon significant biological distinctions, how is its existence to be explained? We ask, "Who benefits from traditional gender arrangements?" and conclude that gender hierarchy rests on male control of material and symbolic resources. The sociology of knowledge allows us to grasp both this duality of control and the means of change. Its Marxian origins make it impossible to forget the structural roots of gender. Its focus on thought points to the individual who comes to believe gender ideas.

The tenets of the sociology of knowledge and their connection to gender were outlined. First, the "existential conditioning of thought" proposition tells us that intellectual activity is a "reflection of the actor's bio-psychic and social life" (Remmling, 1973:3). This proposition finds expression in gender relations as the "two-worlds" metaphor. The "ruling-ideas" proposition in this context states that the ruling sex that controls material resources also has the ability to impose its world view on women. It is through the silence of women that the masculine version of reality is perpetuated (Spender, 1985). "Ideology" refers to those ruling ideas that distort reality in order to justify the political status quo. "False consciousness" labels the subordinate group's acceptance of ideology as valid and authoritative. An important example is the ideology of the "natural" differences between the sexes discussed in Chapter 1. To some extent, feminist politics are *cultural* politics (Tolson, 1977:18), which attack traditional gender ideology. However, they are also *structural* politics which seek a fair share of material resources.

In the chapters to follow, we begin to work on a smaller canvas as we consider how gender socialization is accomplished. In doing so, we attempt to interweave personal lives and social structure. On the one hand, an adequate treatment of gender socialization requires a fully drawn individual, not a caricatured hominoid. Feminist analysis, which is extremely informative concerning the structure and dynamics of patriarchy and capitalism, is a theory of adults that often takes men and women as "already-constituted categories" (Connell, 1985:262). Symbolic interactionism allows us to consider human beings, rather than categories, and directs us to attend to their knowledge of the world.[17]

On the other hand, grounding our explanation of gender socialization in the sociology of knowledge gives us some assurance that the whole question of social structure will not be "spirited away" (Carrigan et al., 1985:563). In this book, gender is defined as a basic element of social structure, not a collection of psychological traits. Societal division of labor is tied not to complementary personality dispositions (nor biology), but to male dominance. By registering the tension and power processes central to the social construction of gender, we avoid the voluntaristic psychologizing of the "sex role"/"socialization" tradition in society. Put another way, the achievement of equality between the sexes is not simply a matter of people "getting their heads straight" and thinking egalitarian thoughts. "Blaming the victim" (Ryan, 1971) for entertaining wrong-headed notions is an ineffective formula for action. Feminist utopias also require fundamental changes in underlying power arrangements.

NOTES

1. The question, "How is the social reality of gender maintained?" is more promising than the related query, "What is the origin of gender?" As pointed out in the discussion of anthropology and gender in Chapter 1, the pursuit of gender's origins turned out to be a false theoretical lead.
2. For simplicity's sake, both the early contributions of Emile Durkheim and Max Scheler and the work of more contemporary scholars are omitted from this discussion of the sociology of knowledge. See Coser (1968) or Berger and Luckmann (1966).
3. In *The German Ideology* (Marx and Engels, 1947:2), this parable is used to poke fun at Hegelian philosophers who believed in the primacy of ideas:
    Once upon a time an honest fellow had the idea that men were drowned in water only because they were possessed with the idea of gravity. If they were to knock this idea out of their heads, say by stating it to be a superstition, a religious idea, they would be sublimely proof against any danger from water. His whole life long he fought against the illusion of gravity, of whose harmful results all statistics brought him new and manifold evidence.
4. Sydie (1983:191–192) turns the sociology of knowledge back on itself and remarks that, "In many respects the Marxist tradition . . . proves to be as abstract and as 'masculine,' in its attention to the world of political and economic power, as the perspective it hoped to replace."
5. Goldberg (1976:4) cites the article "You've Come a Long Way, Buddy" (Farrell, 1971) to illustrate male guilt and self-hatred in the face of the women's liberation movement:
    The members of the men's liberation movement are . . . a kind of embarrassing vanguard, the first men anywhere on record to take a political stand based on the idea that what the women are saying is right — men are a bunch of lazy, selfish, horny, unhappy oppressors.
6. Armstrong and Armstrong (1984:177-178) quote Thorsell's (1967:162) remarks about Swedish women in the labor force: "Employers are not dissatisfied with the thought that some of the work force did not require promotion, accepted repetitive work and did not display overtly solidaristic leanings, etc." Armstrong and Armstrong go on to say, "There is no reason to suspect that Canadian employers are any more disturbed by the effects of the division of labour by sex."
7. Over the past decade, the "two worlds" of women and men have emerged as an implicit metaphor in the social scientific analysis of gender relations. For example, Millman and Kanter (1975:xiii, emphasis in original deleted) propose that "men and women may actually inhabit different social worlds . . ." Doyle (1983:163) states that "most American males see the world . . . in a very different way than most American females do." Greenglass (1982) named her book *A World of Difference: Gender Roles in Perspective.* Gilligan's (1982) *In a Different Voice* analyzes two "voices" or modes of thought about morality which she labels feminine and masculine. Bernard's *The Female World* (1981) is erected upon this metaphor. The sociological and ontological implications of the two-worlds proposition remain, for the most part, unexamined. Further, the proposition makes truth claims which must be tested. See Mackie (1984a) for a discussion of the relevance of this metaphor for the self-conception.
8. The analysis of research mode involved coding of these general-interest sociology journals: *The American Journal of Sociology, American Sociological Review, Pacific Sociological Review/Sociological Perspectives, Social Forces,* and *Sociological Quarterly.* In addition, the two interdisciplinary women's journals, *International Journal of Women's Studies* and *Signs* were coded. See Mackie (1985) for methodological details.

9. For example, in earlier years, anthropologists were advised by Evans Pritchard to "behave like a gentleman, keep off the women, take quinine daily and play it by ear" (quoted in Roberts, 1981:1).
10. The Social Sciences and Humanities Research Council of Canada, *On the Treatment of the Sexes in Research* (Eichler and Lapointe, 1985) advocates a "dual perspective" (or appreciation of the "two worlds") in research.
11. Of ideology in general, Gerth and Mills (1953:277) write: "Those in authority within institutions and social structures attempt to justify their rule by linking it, as if it were a necessary consequence, with moral symbols, sacred emblems, or legal formulae which are widely believed and deeply internalized. These central conceptions may refer to a god or gods, the "votes of the majority," the "will of the people," the "aristocracy of talents or wealth," to the "divine right of kings," or to the allegedly extraordinary endowment of the person of the ruler himself."
12. Phyllis Schlafly, opponent of the Equal Rights Amendment in the United States, is quoted as saying "the nuclear bomb is 'a marvelous gift that was given to our country by a wise God'" (*The Calgary Herald,* January 6, 1984:C7).
13. "On the occasion of a Miss America pageant, a marginal faction of young women threw their underwear into an Atlantic City, N.J. garbage can, attempting some clumsy metaphorical gesture, and grabbed headlines, air time and a disproportionate share of posterity . . . . (A note: no bras were actually burned that day. Not a single flame was lighted . . . .) 'Bra burners' was a convenient, slightly comic way of dismissing demands and resisting confrontations that had been deferred too long. Those women were a curiosity and thus a comfort to the opposition" (*Time Magazine,* July 12, 1982:17).
14. The recognition by contemporary scholars of the causal significance of both ideas and structural factors incorporates the theoretical insights of both Karl Marx and Max Weber. Weber's *The Protestant Ethic and the Spirit of Capitalism* (1930) is a test of the basic contention of Marxism that all cultural phenomena, including religion, are determined by the operation of economic forces. See Gerth and Mills (1953:298—305) for a discussion of the autonomy of ideas.
15. Similarly, Smith (1979:136) says, through the feminist writings of de Beauvoir, Friedan, Millett, and others, ". . . we became aware of the feminine mystique *as* a mystique which served to keep us in our places by invading our own consciousness as our beliefs, our values, our sense of morality, fitness, and obligation" (emphasis in original).
16. Pierson and Prentice (1982) refer to feminist "ideology" rather than "utopia," "partly because the term 'utopia' implies a value judgment unrealizable from the point of view of the upholder of the status quo" (p. 44). Although their point is well taken, the present author finds Mannheim's distinction useful.
17. In *The Structure of Sociological Theory* (1978:367), Turner says a key issue for symbolic interactionists is the range of their theory. Are the concepts and propositions of the perspective tied to the analysis of individuals and the micro-world? Or, does it have wider applicability to macro-social relations? Can interactionist theory inform social theory when it seeks to understand the full complexity of patterns of human organization?

CHAPTER **3**

The Fundamentals of Gender Socialization

Introduction

A popular line of children's books sold by the millions in supermarkets and drugstores included *When I Grow Up* (Vogel, 1968). A small boy and a small girl fantasize about the future:

> — He will be a baker, an icing expert. She will be the baker's wife.
> — He will be a mailman, delivering surprise packages. She looks, listens, says nothing.
> — He will be an explorer in the jungle, and will bring back a lion. She will curl the lion's mane in her beauty shop for animals.
> — He will be a policeman. She will wear a disguise and be his helper.
> — He will be a doctor. She will be a nurse.
> — He will be a fireman. She will be rescued by him.
> — He will be a deep-sea diver. She will be a mermaid and serve him tea and ice cream.
> — He will be an artist. She will be a singer. As he paints, three of the four people watching him are females. As she sings, all her admirers are birds.
> — He will be an astronaut and go the moon. She will be there, prepared to serve him moonburgers.
>
> (Source: Juanita H. Williams, *Psychology of Women.* Second Edition (1983). New York: W.W. Norton.
> Used with permission.)

Chapter 3 presents the fundamentals of gender socialization, beginning with the basic vocabulary of the socialization process. This section has a dual focus. We are concerned with the major concepts needed to analyze both socialization in general (the learning that neophytes do in order to become functioning members of society), and gender socialization in particular (the processes through which people learn to be feminine and masculine). Then, we turn to the content of gender socialization — gender-role attitudes, gender stereotypes, and occupational sex-typing. The last of these three topics asks whether small boys still fantasize about jobs that pay off in excitement and money, while small girls dream of being wives and helpers. The chapter ends with a consideration of the changing ideals of gender socialization. Among the questions raised are these: Why has androgyny fallen into disrepute? Is a gender-blind society possible?

The Parameters of Socialization

Childhood as Social Construct

What is a child? Are children "pure, bestial, innocent, corrupt" (Jenks, 1982:9)? "Little angels" or "little devils" (Synnott, 1983)? Are they priceless or worthless? How shall they be treated (Mackie, 1984b: 36 ff.)?

Childhood is a social construct. Within limits set by biology, society has great leeway in deciding what childhood is to be and how children are to be dealt with (Berger and Berger, 1975:62). In other words, the manner in which adults think of children, as well as the form of children's relationships with adults, alters from epoch to epoch (Jenks, 1982:25) and from culture to culture. In medieval European society, the concept of childhood simply did not exist (Ariès, 1962). That is, there seems to have been no awareness of the unique nature of children that distinguishes them from adults. The infant who was as yet too fragile to take part in adult life did not count. The high infant mortality rate of the time was partially responsible for this indifference to children. It was risky to get attached to a child who might die. As soon as the youngster could live without constant care, it was dressed as an adult and treated as a miniature adult.

Similarly, adolescence has not always and everywhere been recognized as a distinct stage of the life cycle (Gillis, 1974). The basis of adolescence is not puberty, but prolonged dependence on parents and increased education in specialized age-segregated institutions (Katz and Davey, 1978:S117). With increased life expectancy, society can now afford adolescence. When individuals had few years of life remaining after biological maturity was attained, precious years could not be spared preparing for adulthood (Rogers, 1981:12). Not too long ago, South Seas societies existed where girls were technically married at the age of seven or eight, moved to their husbands' household at ten or twelve, and gradually learned to perform the duties of a wife. Here, no social adolescence intervened between childhood and adulthood (Hunter Collective, 1983:144).

The treatment of children depends on the image society has of them. If children are priceless, they will be cherished. If worthless, they will be neglected, exploited, and abused (Lee, 1982:593). According to DeMause (1982:48),

> The history of childhood is a nightmare from which we
> have only recently begun to awaken. The further back in
> history one goes, the lower the level of child care, and
> the more likely children are to be killed, abandoned,
> beaten, terrorized, and sexually abused.

Childhood, as we know it today in Canadian society, is conceived of
as a special, valuable, and protected age. In twentieth-century North
America, there emerged the "economically worthless but emotionally
priceless" child (Zelizer, 1981). A great transformation in children's value
occurred as children's lives were gradually divorced from the
marketplace. The new emotional value of children is also related to this
century's falling birth and mortality rates. As family size declined, each
child became more precious. The state recognized children as "citizens
who have social rights, independent of their parents" (Lee, 1982:595).
In comparison with previous periods of history, socialization in contemporary Western society has taken on unique qualities of gentleness
and concern for all the needs of the child (Berger and Berger, 1975:64).
However, this is a generalization: "each generation, each social group,
every family and each individual develops different interpretations of
what a child is" (Denzin, 1979:38). Moreover, some youngsters still
receive harsh treatment.

Historian Eliane Silverman (1984:15–16) describes the construction of frontier childhood and female childhood in turn-of-the-century
Alberta:

> Childhood was the period of life most overladen with
> tradition, when parents hoped to form their children into
> the kind of adults they wanted them to be. Most often
> their vision of the grown-up child was based not on the
> world as it might be twenty years later, but on a
> nostalgic memory of the world as it had been during
> their own childhoods. In a frontier society, peopled by
> adults who had themselves broken radically from the
> past, the conservatism of childraising was more striking
> than it might appear in a traditional society . . . . Many
> adults of that first generation came to a frontier country
> not only to establish something new, but also to leave
> behind something old, something that didn't work for
> them, something too rigid and confining. They were
> often seeking autonomy, and yet they expected a tradi-
> tional relationship of obedience and authority with their
> children. They meant especially to teach girls to behave
> in ways that reached back into their own, their parents'
> and their grandparents' childhoods. For the most part,
> girls of all classes and ethnic backgrounds were
> supposed to learn obedience to their parents.
> However, the unconventional environment also exerted
> itself. The open land, for one thing, with its possibilities

for running wildly and freely, and seemingly eternally, offered girls a glimpse of something like freedom. The vagaries of crops, of weather, of institutions like schools open one term and closed the next, and of rapid growth, evoked the knowledge that life could be transitory and tenuous, and not well-rooted in the past. The understanding of hierarchy, of place, and of obedience was a bit harder to instill in frontier children than in children growing up in more settled places. Even as girls were absorbing the knowledge of roles appropriate to their gender, they also heard the whisper of the inappropriate.

(Source: Elaine Silverman, *The Last Best West: Women on the Alberta Frontier 1880-1939.* (1984, pp. 15-16). Used with permission of Eden Press.)

The point is the child's socialization experiences differ according to the interpretations of childhood in his/her historical period (Nett, 1981a). As well, interpretations vary in terms of particular families, region of the country, ethnic culture, and social class. Nevertheless, certain generalizations can be made about the contemporary socialization process.

The Nature of Socialization

Socialization is defined as the complex learning process through which individuals develop selfhood and acquire the knowledge, skills, and motivations required for participation in social life (Mackie, 1986b). This process is the link between individual and society and may be viewed from each of these two perspectives. From the point of view of the individual, interaction with other people is the means by which human potentialities are actualized. The newborn infant is utterly helpless. Though it has the potential for becoming human, it is not yet human. The infant's experience with other human beings is absolutely crucial for its survival as a physical being and its development as a social being. Effective socialization is as essential for the society as for the individual. The continuity of Canadian society requires that the thousands of new members born each year eventually learn to think, believe, and behave as Canadians. Each new generation must learn the society's culture. Social order demands self-discipline and control of impulses. However, socialization is also characterized by change. Social circumstances change, and as Silverman's (1984) account of frontier childhood makes clear, the current generation never duplicates the previous generation. Socialization begins with the individual "taking over" the world as it has been constituted by others. However, people rebel and innovate so that "the world, once 'taken over,' *may* be creatively modified or . . . even re-created" (Berger and Luckmann, 1966:130, emphasis in original).

Gender socialization, a sub-type of general socialization, involves the processes through which individuals learn to become feminine and masculine according to the expectations current in their society (Mackie, 1983b:83). In particular, individuals develop gender identity and learn gender norms. Especially important is the internalization of norms specifying gender inequality and gender division of labor. In Eichler's (1980:20) words, gender socialization "is the systematic teaching of a double standard." Gender socialization has been successful when the double standard seems "natural" to the people affected by it.

Primary and Secondary Socialization

Socialization is a lifelong process that begins with primary socialization, the basic induction into society which takes place in childhood and adolescence, and continues with secondary socialization. *Primary socialization* occurs in the micro-world of primary groups.[1] It involves the development of language and individual identity; the learning of cognitive skills and self-control; the internalization of moral standards and appropriate attitudes and interactions; an understanding of social roles. Gender identity, as well as a basic understanding of masculinity and femininity, is learned during primary socialization.

Primary socialization occurs in a crucible of highly charged emotional relationships with significant others. The child becomes emotionally attached to its care givers and these care givers, who control the rewards and punishments, are immensely powerful. As a consequence, these adults confront the child with their world. Their world becomes *the* world to the child:

> The child does not internalize the world of his significant others as one of many possible worlds. He internalizes it as *the* world, the only existent and only conceivable world. . . . However much the original sense of inevitability may be weakened in subsequent disenchantments, the recollection of a never-to-be-repeated certainty — the certainty of the first dawn of reality — still adheres to the first world of childhood (Berger and Luckmann, 1966:134-135).

Primary socialization not only introduces the child to a social world; it introduces the child to herself/himself (Berger and Berger, 1975:65). The child develops a self through the fundamental vehicle of socialization, namely, language. It would be almost impossible to exaggerate the importance of language in the development of human potentiality. The taken-for-granted world of meanings about males and females, including understanding of self as male or female, is formed in early childhood (Richer, 1984:167).

Secondary socialization is the social learning that occurs beyond the childhood and adolescent years. Since considerable secondary socialization takes place in the macro-world, the learning is usually less intense and more circumscribed than primary socialization. Nevertheless, the effects of secondary socialization on the individual can be quite profound.

Although primary socialization lays the foundation for later learning, it cannot prepare people for roles and situations that are either unforeseeable at the moment, or that lie far ahead in the future. For one thing, our age-graded society confronts individuals with new expectations as they move through the life cycle. Preparing for an occupation, marrying, bearing children, encountering middle age, and retiring all involve new gender lessons to be learned. Also, society changes and people must, therefore, equip themselves to cope with new situations. For example, the women's movement forced Canadians to deal with new notions about gender. Finally, some individuals meet new particularized situations, such as marital breakdown, chronic illness, geographical and social mobility, and widowhood, which may require further gender socialization.

Anticipatory Socialization and Resocialization

Two additional types of socialization cross-cut primary and secondary socialization. *Anticipatory socialization* is that which occurs in advance of actual role playing. This rehearsal for the future involves learning something about role requirements, both behaviors and attitudes, and visualizing oneself in the role (Mackie, 1986b). Children begin to practice being grown women and men long before they reach adulthood. Similarly, we think about being married, being parents, being workers before we actually assume these statuses.

Resocialization occurs when a new role or a new situation requires a person to replace established patterns of behavior and thought with new patterns (Campbell, 1975). Old behavior must be unlearned because it is incompatible, in some way, with new role demands. Resocialization is more characteristic of secondary socialization than of primary socialization. However, as youngsters mature, they too are expected to discard former behavior. A two-year-old boy may cry when he is frightened, but a twelve-year-old boy who climbs into his mother's lap and whimpers is thought to be odd (Mackie, 1986b). Canadian adolescents confront demands for new gender behavior. Gangling tomboys may suddenly be expected to be young ladies. The mid-life crisis is a recent social construction. After the landmark fortieth birthday, people are expected to "adjust to the end of romance, to empty nests, to lowered aspirations and expectations, even to 'middle-aged' spread" (Rose, 1979:278). Also, new social situations entail contradictions for adults. For example, the women's movement has resulted in redefinitions of the ways women and men relate to each other. Is it chivalrous or sexist to open doors for women (Walum, 1974)? How should the female electrician on the job site be treated?

Resocialization is sometimes painful and almost always confusing. Since established habits interfere with new learning, it is usually more difficult than primary socialization. Fortunately, the malleability of the self and the possibility of continuing personality change facilitate lifelong socialization experiences. Apparently, the "consequences of the events of early childhood are continually transformed by later experience, making the course of human development more open than many have believed" (Brim and Kagan, 1980:1). This capacity for change is often assisted by organizations, such as clubs for the divorced or widowed, that specialize in resocialization. As well, the local newsstand offers bibliotherapy for a variety of personal troubles.

Socialization as Reciprocal Process

Socialization is a two-way process that affects socializer as well as socializee. The child is not a "passive victim of socialization." Rather, she/he "resists it, participates in it, collaborates with it in varying degrees" (Berger and Berger, 1975:57). Both child and care givers are changed by the process. Just as the care givers socialize the child, the child socializes the care givers (Bell and Harper, 1977; Rheingold, 1969). This mutual influence extends from infancy, where the effect of an infant's cry on the mother is "all out of proportion to his age, size and accomplishments" (Rheingold, 1966, quoted in Peters, 1982:3), through adolescence, and into adulthood. In infancy, the child's demands and responses serve to teach the mother and father how to behave as parents. As the child matures, the parents become aware of new facets of mothering and fathering. Over the dinner table, a teenage girl explains to her parents that a boy can be her friend, without being her boyfriend. This conversation illustrates the fact that teenagers frequently teach their elders the latest nuances of gender.

Multiple Socialization Agencies

Socialization involves a number of different influences or agencies, operating in a variety of settings. Classic socialization theories, such as psychoanalytic theory, concentrated on the socialization link between child and parent, especially the mother. However, various social forces (e.g. employment of mothers outside the home, commuting, professionalization of child care) have operated to decrease the amount of parent-child interaction, and consequently to increase the child's involvement with an expanded set of socialization agents — peers, mass media, day-care centers, schools, community organizations (Gecas, 1981:177). In addition, people of all ages are socialized by the mass media — television, radio, records, tapes, books, newspapers, magazines. (See Chapter 6.) According to 1981 Statistics Canada figures reported by Eichler (1983:249), fewer than half of Canadian pre-school children are now cared for exclusively by their parents. In addition, mothers' recent involvement with activities outside the home has served to enhance the socialization efforts of other family members, especially fathers (see Lips, 1983). In general, the family is still the most important agent of primary socialization. No other agency rivals the family in terms of the intensity of emotions aroused or the scope of the power wielded. However, since the end of World War I, "experts" have presumed to inform Canadian parents concerning "proper" child rearing (Synnott, 1983:88).

"The 'widening world of childhood' spirals out from the parental home" (Clausen, 1968:132). At first, the child knows only the microworld of family, neighborhood, and perhaps, day-care center. However, socialization links the micro-world to the infinitely more complex macroworld beyond (Berger and Berger, 1975:69). Through its channeling function, the family mediates the macro-world for the child. That is, the family has the power to determine the child's exposure to particular schools, churches, and mass media programs, and to interpret for the child the meaning of these secondary influences. Therefore, the efforts of multiple socialization agencies tend to reinforce one another. This is especially true of gender socialization (Rickel and Grant, 1979). Nevertheless, agents may "specialize" in producing particular socialization outcomes. According to Richer (1983:123), peers may be especially effective in teaching children the invidious cultural distinctions between the sexes, and the superior value of males. Finally, agents may differ in importance to one sex versus the other. For example, the peer group appears to be more influential in the primary socialization of boys than of girls (Best, 1983).

Functions and Purposes of Socialization

Some outcomes of socialization are consciously sought while others are unintended. Helpful here is the distinction between *purpose* and *function*:

> A purpose is a goal that a person or group wants to accomplish; it is an "end-in-view." A function is a consequence, or effect, of action and interaction (Elkin and Handel, 1984:125).

Agency purposes and functions sometimes differ. A hypothetical parent may hold the gender-socialization purpose of exposing her young son and daughter to non-stereotyped views of their future occupational options. Therefore, she may consciously draw to their attention newspaper stories about female pilots and male dancers. However, this same woman may be visibly annoyed when her daughter sits with her legs apart and ignore her son's arrangement of limbs. In the first case, enlightened gender norms are the purpose of socialization, while in the second case, traditional gender norms are the function of socialization. Of course, functions and purposes often coincide. This outcome occurs more frequently in agencies that have a societal mandate to socialize (family, schools), than in those that do not (peer groups, mass media). Coincidence of functions and purposes pertains more to those areas of socialization that are understood to be important to the society (reading and writing; right and wrong) than to those areas that remain beneath the level of awareness (popular music). The section "Changing Gender-Socialization Ideals" later in this chapter indicates that since the advent of the women's movement, gender socialization has become both a more deliberate and more controversial topic.

Intra-societal Variations in Socialization

Although many values and norms are shared by all Canadians, differences are found by language, by region, by ethnic group, by religion, by social class, and by place of residence (urban or rural). These variations in social environment bring with them variations in the content of socialization. Social class will serve to illustrate the channeling influence of the family and intra-societal variation in gender socialization. A cross-national study of child-rearing values was carried out among French- and English-speaking Canadians (as well as parents in the United States, Japan, and six European countries). Working-class parents almost everywhere were more likely than middle-class parents to wish to maintain female-male distinctions (Lambert, Hamers and Frasure-Smith, 1980).

The Content of Gender Socialization

The "infant tumbles into a ready-made world" (McCall and Simmons, 1978:31) and must learn what is necessary to meet the expectations of this ongoing society. Gender constitutes an important part of this necessary knowledge. As Lambert (1971:2) points out, "beliefs about the roles of the sexes are threads running through the fabric of society, having multiple effects upon human institutions and themselves nourished and sustained by these institutions." Obviously, children must come to understand the place of gender in their society. This abstract, intellectual appreciation is an eventual product of pragmatic knowledge of their own gender behavior. In Professor Lambert's (1971:1) words,

> In acquiring images of the sexes, children are learning what is appropriate to the sexes. They develop ideas of what is right or proper for them as boys or girls to do, to believe, to aspire to, and ways to relate to others. They are learning about the social order, which in time will appear to them to be a natural social order in the sense that they will come to take it for granted as the framework within which they think and act.

Despite the foregoing, it would be a mistake to assume that Canadian youngsters encounter a uniform package of gender information. The family is not a passive agent of a monolithic culture. Instead, it "selects, adapts, modifies, and interprets" those aspects of the culture about which it is aware or concerned (McCall and Simmons, 1978:32). Also, gender socialization has recently become controversial. Some parents now advocate "unisex" training. Others (most) continue to urge differential socialization of girls and boys on the ground that adults of each sex will occupy quite different statuses.

The distinction between functions and purposes needs to be invoked. Day-to-day socialization is much less rational and deliberate than our discussion implies. Care givers not only transmit gender beliefs and norms as formal socialization lessons. They are, to some extent, prisoners of their own traditional gender socialization. A mother, who considers herself a feminist, discovers her young son experimenting with her makeup and high-heeled shoes. She shrieks at him in a voice that echoes in her ears as her own mother's voice. (When caretakers' deeds contradict their words, it is the action that makes the more telling impression.) The tendency of the family to follow what T.S. Eliot called an "antique drum" may be offset by the influence of such other agencies of gender socialization as the schools and the mass media, and by subsequent experiences during the lifelong process of socialization. Nevertheless, we repeat that "what is internalized through primary socialization retains much of its subjective reality, even when later learning overlays and contradicts it" (Laws and Schwartz, 1977:9, emphasis in original deleted).

In general, the content of gender socialization involves shared meanings of femininity and masculinity. Children learn the culturally appropriate ways of identifying and classifying males and females (including themselves), as well as the prevailing ideas about the relative prestige, qualities, and behavior of the sexes. As Chapter 2 suggested, the actual ingredients of femininity and masculinity, as social constructs, may derive from the needs of capitalism or patriarchy (Stanley and Wise, 1983:87). Be that as it may, the scripts for gender socialization encountered by neophytes include gender-role attitudes, gender stereotypes, and occupational sex-typing. Each of these topics will be discussed in turn.

Gender-role Attitudes

Societal attitudes are part of the message communicated to children regarding gender expectations. *Gender-role attitudes* may be defined as relatively enduring clusters of feelings, beliefs, and behavioral tendencies about the appropriate activities of women and men. Although attitudes are not synonymous with actions, they are often predispositions towards actions. The gender-role attitudes held by Canadians range from traditional to egalitarian, "from the view that women belong in

TABLE 3.1
Canadian Gender-Role Attitudes

Gallup Poll Question		TOTAL Sample Response
1. In your opinion, do women in Canada get as good a break as men or not? (1983)	Yes	47%
	No	53
2. In general do you think Canadian women dominate their husbands or do you think husbands dominate their wives? (1982)	Wives dominate	14%
	Husbands dominate	29
	Neither	51
	Don't Know	6
3. In your opinion should husbands be expected to share in the general housework or not? (1981)	Should	72%
	Should if wife works	17
	Should not	9
	No opinion	2
4. There are more married women—with families—in the working world than ever before. Do you think this has had a harmful effect on family life or not? (1982)	Yes, harmful	55%
	Not harmful	38
	Qualified	4
	Undecided	4
5. Do you think that married women should take a job outside the home if they have young children? (1982)	Yes	38%
	No	54
	Don't know	8
6. Do you think that married women should take a job outside the home if they have no young children? (1982)	Yes	87%
	No	8
	Don't know	5

7. Do you think women could run most businesses as well as men, or not? (1983)	Yes No Undecided	83% 12 4
8. If a woman has the same ability as a man, does she have as good a chance to become the executive of a company or not? (1983)	Yes No Undecided	44% 51 5
9. A suggestion has been made that, in this time of high unemployment, a married woman with a gainfully employed spouse should not be given equal opportunity in the job market. Do you agree or disagree with this? (1982)	Agree Disagree Undecided	25% 70 5
10. Recently the Canadian Catholics for Women's Ordination requested the Canadian Conference of Catholic Bishops to support and work toward the ordination of women. In your opinion would the ordination of women as Catholic priests strengthen or weaken Roman Catholicism in Canada or would it really have no effect? (1981)	Would strengthen Would weaken No real effect Don't know	24% 16 37 23
11. If in a National Leadership Convention, a federal political party chose a qualified woman as their leader, would you be more inclined to support that party, less inclined or would it not make any difference? (1983)	More inclined Less inclined No difference Don't know	11% 9 78 2
12. Would you favour or oppose recruiting every able-bodied young man in this country, when he reaches the age of 18 to spend one year in military training? (1983)	Would favour Would oppose No opinion	55% 41 5
13. And how about women, would you favour or oppose compulsory military training for one year for women at age 18? (1983)	Would favour Would oppose No opinion	37% 57 7

Source: Monica Boyd, *Canadian Attitudes Toward Women: Thirty Years of Change.* Women's Bureau, Labour Canada, Ottawa: 1984. Used with permission.

the home and are responsible for child-rearing, to the view that women and men should have equal access to identical positions and rewards" (Boyd, 1984:3).

Table 3-1 contains thirteen Gallup poll questions, taken from Boyd (1984),[2] which were asked of a national English-Canadian sample between 1981 and 1983. The topics covered by these questions illustrate, rather than exhaust, the universe of gender-role attitudes. In other words, particular studies merely sample Canadians' attitudes concerning this matter. In comparison with topics such as national politics, pollsters have asked relatively few gender-related questions over the years (Robinson, 1983:96).

In general, Table 3-1 informs us that Canadians continue to differentiate, to some extent, between the roles of men and the roles of women. As we might expect, attitudes concerning the domestic sphere tend to be more traditional than public-sphere attitudes. For example, 55 percent believe that working mothers have a harmful effect on family life (Q. 4). However, only 9 percent say a qualified female candidate for Prime Minister would reduce their support for a political party (Q. 11). The data shown in the table become more meaningful when they are compared with previous Gallup poll responses. In Boyd's (1984:23) words:

> Data collected from the Gallup polls during the past 30 years are a testimony of the enormous change which has occurred during the period with respect to women and women's issues. Yet, they also reveal a residue of earlier norms and practices.

To illustrate, only 13 percent of a 1970 sample (versus 38 percent in 1982) thought that married women with young children should take an outside job (Q. 5). Seventy-seven percent of the same 1970 sample felt that a childless married woman belonged in the labor force, versus 87 percent in 1982 (Q. 6). In 1971, 58 percent (versus 83 percent in 1983) felt women could run most businesses as well as men (Q. 7). In 1964, the Gallup poll asked, "If your party chose a woman as Federal Leader and if she was qualified for the job of Prime Minister, would you vote for her?" The 25 percent "No" response is considerably higher than the 9 percent who gave the traditional "Less inclined" reply to Question 11. Canadians are also more accepting of women lawyers, physicians, and ministers of religion. An increasing majority of Canadians support the principle of equal chances for employment and equal pay (Boyd, 1984:24). For example in 1965, 53 percent would give men first choice at scarce jobs, versus 25 percent in 1982 (Q. 9). The comparison of current and previous replies to Question 1 proved interesting. In 1971, 64 percent (versus 47 percent in 1983) said Canadian women get as good

a break as men. Apparently, women's-movement advocacy o
years has alerted the Canadian public to women's disadvi
position.

The sparse historical data we do have on Canadian gender-role
attitudes tend to agree with American studies, which report egalitarian
shifts over time (Cherlin and Walters, 1981; Thornton and Freedman,
1979; Thornton, Alwin and Camburn, 1983). This change is attributed
to such factors as public debate and media attention to gender, the growing labor force participation of women, higher education, and the
declining birth rate.

Some categories of Canadians are more liberal than others.
Studies show that women, younger age groups, and the better educated
hold more egalitarian gender attitudes than men, older groups, and
the poorly educated (Boyd, 1984:24; Gibbins, Ponting and Symons,
1978). The recent Boyd (1984) analysis of Gallup poll questions does
not report Francophone data. However, according to earlier studies
(Boyd, 1975; Gibbins, Ponting and Symons, 1978), though some of the
differences are small, there is a tendency for Francophones to be more
liberal than Anglophones about work issues and less liberal about
family-related issues.

Gender Stereotypes

Imagine a conversation with a friend who is describing two people
whom you have never met. One person is said to be gentle, sentimental, and cautious, while the other is described as adventurous, independent, and dominant. Would it be easier to picture one of these persons
as female and the other as male? If you visualize the first person as
female and the second as male, you have demonstrated your familia-
rity with gender stereotypes. What is more, you could be Canadian,
American, Dutch, Peruvian, Nigerian, Pakistani, or Japanese. Cross-
cultural research shows that citizens of 30 nations share similar general
beliefs about the sexes (Williams and Best, 1982).

A *stereotype* refers to those folk beliefs about the attributes
characterizing a social category on which there is substantial agreement
(Mackie, 1973). The term refers to beliefs shared by many individuals,
about traits that appropriately describe categories of people, such as
ethnic groups, old people, or university students. *Gender stereotypes* are
characteristics consensually assigned to females and males. Whereas
gender-role attitudes refer to people's ideas about the appropriate activities of women and men, gender stereotypes point to beliefs about
female and male "psychological makeup" (Williams and Best, 1982:15).

To social scientists, "stereotype" is not a dirty word. Stereotypes
are not, in themselves, "good" or "bad." They simply *are*. The categorization involved appears to be a necessary aspect of human cognition.

Our limited sensory apparatus cannot encode afresh each time, in detail, the multitude of stimuli rushing at us. Therefore, we place relevant stimuli into those categories designated as important from previous personal or cultural experience, and ignore the rest. Walter Lippmann (1922:59), the journalist who introduced the concept "stereotype" into the social science literature,[3] expressed the matter this way:

> Each of us lives and works on a small part of the earth's surface, moves in a small circle, and of these acquaintances knows only a few intimately . . . . Inevitably our opinions cover a bigger space, a longer reach of time, a greater number of things, than we can directly observe.

According to Lippmann, stereotypes, "pictures in our heads," compensate for the limitations of human perception and experience. Instead of trying to decipher the personality of every male or female passing through our lives, we resort to gender stereotypes. Indeed, we tend to view women and men as opposites: what is female is "not male," and vice versa (Deaux, 1985:68). Some stereotype traits are false, e.g., that women are talkative. Other traits may be truthful; however, like all generalizations, they do not take into account individual differences in the traits which occur within the sexes or the degree of overlap between the sexes (Williams and Best, 1982:16). For example, the male stereotype contains the trait "aggressive." In Chapter 1, we noted both the accuracy of this sex difference and the substantial female-male overlap. In short, "stereotypes both represent and distort reality" (Eagly and Steffen, 1984).

Because gender stereotypes capture folk beliefs about the nature of females and males generally, they are an important part of the cognitive environment of both children and their adult socializers. At an early age, children reveal considerable knowledge of them (Lambert, 1971; Williams and Best, 1982). Canadian researchers Edwards and Williams (1980:218) remark that despite the activities of the women's movement, gender stereotyping "continues to be a rather powerful social force." They go on to say:

> At a time when discriminatory treatment of men and women is seen, more and more, as unacceptable and, indeed, without justification, these data suggest that the more traditional views still permeate [Canadian] society (Edwards and Williams, 1980:218).

The study of pancultural gender stereotypes carried out by Williams and Best (1982) surpasses all previous research in this area. Their data cover adults and children in 30 countries, including Canada. Because of space limitations, our description of this important study will be confined to the research on children and emphasize Canadian findings. Research assistants gave children across the world these same instructions:

> What I have here are some pictures I would like to show you and some stories that go with each one. I want you to help me by pointing to the person in each picture that the story is about. Here, I'll show you what I mean (Williams and Best, 1982:154).

The "stories" were 32 very brief, three-sentence representations of gender stereotype traits (16 for each sex). For example, "One of these people is emotional. They cry when something good happens as well as when everything goes wrong. Which person is the emotional person?" Or, "One of these people is always pushing other people around and getting into fights. Which person gets into fights?" Accompanying these mini-stories were 32 pictures, each composed of a male and female figure in silhouette. After listening to each story, the child pointed to either the male or female figure. When two-thirds or more of the sample of children agreed that a "male-oriented" story characterized the male figure, or vice-versa, the trait (that is, the adult definition of the concept expressed in the story), was considered to be part of the children's stereotype.

Table 3-2 shows the stereotyped responses of the six-year-old and eight-year-old Nova Scotian children who participated in the Williams and Best (1982) pancultural research. In order to make the Canadian results more meaningful, the table also presents parallel findings from three other English-speaking countries (the United States, England, and Ireland). The data from these three countries are averaged and labeled "Amengire." Table 3-2 is based on the work of Edwards and Williams (1980), who carried out the Canadian segment of the project.

The Canadian children show an increasing awareness of the adult stereotypes over time. The six-year-olds knew 14 of the 32 adult-defined stereotype items. Although there are a few reversals, the older children were aware of 23 of the 32 items. The similarity of response between the Canadian and Amengire data is very high. Moreover, the cross-national data of Williams and Best (1982) show that similarities extend further afield to such countries as Brazil, Taiwan, and India. Cross-cultural similarity of gender imagery characterizes adults as well as children. The authors do not find their results surprising because cross-cultural similarities in gender-role behavior generally outweigh cross-cultural differences (Williams and Best, 1982:29).

The content of gender stereotypes reflects personality traits associated with the traditional gender division of labor between the domestic and public spheres. Note that the characteristics shown in

TABLE 3.2
The Gender Stereotypes of Canadian and Amengire Children

Stereotype Traits (Adult Definition)	Canadian Percentages		Amengire* Percentages	
	6-yr-olds	8-yr-olds	6-yr-olds	8-yr-olds
Female Traits				
appreciative	79	93	65	90
gentle	68	93	64	85
weak	64	93	63	88
soft-hearted, sentimental	61	89	75	90
emotional	64	89	75	85
excitable, high-strung	68	86	56	73
meek, mild	68	86	68	80
sophisticated, affected	75	79	67	90
affectionate	75	75	66	80
submissive, dependent	46	75	48	66
whiny, complaining	43	68	46	61
flirtatious, charming	61	61	56	57
rattlebrained, fickle	54	46	42	54
talkative	50	46	49	46
fussy, nagging	36	32	44	53
frivolous	43	21	35	23
Male Traits				
aggressive, assertive	82	100	82	94
strong, robust	86	96	88	98
coarse	79	96	73	86
cruel	82	93	79	91
loud	71	86	67	84
ambitious, enterprising	68	86	64	74
dominant, autocratic	82	82	67	80
disorderly	64	82	67	86
boastful	61	79	71	80
adventurous, daring	54	79	58	77
independent	57	79	66	84
severe, stern	75	68	69	67
confident, self-confident	54	57	51	50
steady, stable	46	43	37	33
jolly	39	39	50	48
logical, rational	46	25	49	42

Source: John R. Edwards and J. E. Williams, "Sex-trait stereotypes among young children and young adults: Canadian findings and cross-national comparisons." *Canadian Journal of Behavioral Science* 12(1980):210-220. Used with permission.
*Amengire figures are averages of data for American, English, and Irish children, originally reported in Best et al. (1977). The figures shown in Table 3-2 are taken from Edwards and Williams (1980).

Table 3-2 fall into a feminine–expressive cluster (gentle, adventurous, emotional) and a masculine-instrumental cluster (agressive, strong). Earlier research (Broverman et. al., 1972) found that the masculine traits were valued more highly than the feminine traits. Respondents of both sexes found masculinity to be more socially desirable than femininity.

It appears that social structure accounts for the content of stereotypes. Beliefs about gender develop, at least in part, from people's observations of women and men playing their traditional roles. For example, children are more likely to encounter women taking care of babies and men wielding authority in the workplace than the alternative combinations. Further, children are apt to believe that the characteristics thought to be necessary for child care (soft-hearted, affectionate) and for success in the labor force (dominance, objectivity) are typical of each sex. Therefore, fundamental change in the "pictures in people's heads" about men and women must await social change. In other words:

> Gender stereotypes . . . will not disappear until people
> divide social roles equally, that is, until child care and
> household responsibilities are shared equally by women
> and men and the responsibility to be employed outside
> the home is borne equally (Eagly and Steffen, 1984:752).

Traditional gender stereotypes, functioning as self-fulfilling prophecies, constitute an important impediment to social change. If women are assumed to be less competent, their performance may be judged less successful than it actually is. Or if women are assumed to be less competent, they may be given fewer opportunities to assert themselves (Wrightsman and Deaux, 1981:306).

Occupational Sex-typing

In 1974, sociologist Ann Beuf talked with three- to six-year-old children about work. Each child was asked, "What do you want to be when you grow up?" The boys seized upon adventurous careers: policeman, sports superstar, cowboy, and spy. The girls preferred quieter pastimes, especially nursing. Then the children were asked this hypothetical question: "If you were a boy (girl), what would you be when you grow up?" Several girls remarked that an opposite-sex occupation, such as doctor or milkman, was their *true*, but unrealizable ambition. One little girl "confided that what she really wanted to do when she grew up was fly like a bird. "But I'll never do it," she sighed, "because I'm not a boy." The girls had an answer to this hypothetical question. They *had* thought about what it would be like to be a boy. The boys, on the other hand, often regarded Professor Beuf with suspicion or astonishment. "That's a wierd question, you know" was a regular response. One boy sighed, "A girl? Oh, if I were a girl I'd have to grow up to be nothing." When the children did select particular occupations, in reply to both the realistic and hypothetical questions, about 70 percent of the choices were sex-typed.

Because work is such a vital part of life, the sex-typing of occupations is a central element of the societal script for femininity and masculinity learned by children. Many occupations have incumbents who are preponderately of one sex or the other. For example, in Canada, 99 percent of stenographers and typists and 95 percent of nurses are women, while 92 percent of dentists and 85 percent of lawyers and notaries are men (Armstrong and Armstrong, 1984). Women are much more occupationally segregated than men. Women tend to work in relatively few traditionally "female" jobs (e.g. clerical, health, teaching, and service occupations). Since women hold about 75 percent of all clerical jobs, the office has been described as a "female job ghetto" (Lowe, 1980). Although considerable publicity is given to female physicians, lawyers, dentists, and pharmacists, in 1981 each of these professions involved a tenth of one percent (or less) of all women workers (Armstrong and Armstrong, 1984). This sex-segregated occupational structure is, in part, responsible for the large differences between Canadian men and women with respect to income, job security, and opportunities for advancement (Boyd, 1984:18).

Occupational sex-typing, then, refers to the tendency to regard sex-segregated occupations as more appropriate for one sex or the other. Beliefs that men are better suited for certain occupations and women for others are buttressed by reference to gender stereotypes. Thus, women may be considered suited to nursing *because* they are nurturant and men to law *because* they are logical (Williams and Best, 1982). A person, such as the following woman welder, who crosses these traditional boundaries is frequently reminded of her deviance:

> I remember once when I was down in [a job] taking my test, they all . . . heard there was a woman down in the test room. They all left the job site when it was break time and came in to see me welding. They want to see either how good you're welding or they want to see if it looks like a woman welding or if it looks pink or if it's got frills on it. I don't know what they're looking for but they look at it all the time. You know. "I can't really believe you did this." And I say, "What did you want, bows?" (Armstrong and Armstrong, 1983:198).

Nemerowicz's book, *Children's Perceptions of Gender and Work Roles* (1979) sheds some light on the occupational views of children born since the advent of the women's movement. Nemerowicz asked second- and fourth-grade children to draw, first, a picture of a man working, then a picture of a woman working. The pictures were then labeled with the children's own descriptions. Eighty-six percent of the pictures showed men in activities usually associated with labor force participation. Men were shown engaged in construction, working with or driving cars, busy as firemen, policemen, garbage collectors, farmers. The most frequently-drawn activity for women was housekeeping (27 percent). Teacher, nurse, cashier, and secretary were the next most frequently depicted activities.

These children have noticed society's occupational sex segregation. They even have a "theory," based on biology and ignorance, to explain it. Interestingly, power is the essence of this "theory." Men are seen to be limited by their bodies from having babies, and by their ignorance from cooking and housekeeping. However, according to the children, men are capable of playing any social role (except mother) if they chose to obtain the information required by the role. On the other hand, women are thought to be more biologically constrained in the social roles they are able to play. Indeed, the youngsters believe women to be so weak and fragile that they avoid many work roles for fear of hurting themselves! Here is evidence of the children's underlying beliefs that social power is physically based, and that physical differences between the sexes necessitate distinctive social roles. Nemerowicz (1979:172) suggests a possible reason for the children's receptivity to these notions: "It may be . . . that children experience adult power, vis-à-vis children, as rooted in physical, coercive force, either actually or potentially."

Children's perceptions of the adult world describe their notions of "what is." What happens when they forecast their own future work, "what will be"? Nemerowicz's (1979) sample of children do not picture themselves engaged in the work roles they describe for same-sex adults. They anticipate work of a more prestigious nature! In comparison with the interviewees in Beuf's (1974) earlier study, these children seem more aware of the effects of the women's movement. Although their perceptions of their future are influenced by sex-typing, the girls are becoming more willing to challenge the sex-typing, and to choose jobs traditionally defined as masculine. (The actual future occupations of these girls is, of course, quite another matter.) Understandably, the boys show little interest in breaking into feminine occupations where rewards and prestige remain relatively low.

Returning again to the connection between physical strength and occupational requirements, the children studied by Nemerowicz (1979) have learned that work is not enjoyable. "It is rather, a burden, not without economic and power benefits, but a burden nonetheless" (p. 174). This burden is best borne by the strong, the male:

> There is a considerable amount of misperception, on the part of children, regarding the degree of physical difficulty, the degree of danger present, especially in fathers'

> jobs. Boys, however, get the idea that they will, as their
> bodies get stronger, be able to do the job without
> needing to fear the dangers. Girls are not as readily con-
> vinced that their bodies will provide them with what
> many occupational roles require (Nemerowicz, 1979:172).

Here, we have yet another iteration of the inferiority and superiority of female and male bodies respectively, which recalls the theme discussed in Chapter 2 of the physical body's relationship to the two-worlds phenomenon. The author concludes that taking the mystique out of adult roles would ease primary socialization. Her suggestion that "children should be assured that most roles can be learned by most people" (Nemerowicz, 1979:172) is sound advice.[4]

Changing Gender Socialization Ideals

Intellectuals, including social scientists, entertain strong opinions about the end-products of the process of gender socialization. These goals spell out the personality characteristics and behaviors to become eventually associated with one sex versus the other. The goals are buttressed by the assumption that appropriate gender socialization pays off in superior psychological adjustment. Here, we are dealing with purposes, rather than functions of socialization.

Canadian gender-socialization ideals are neither monolithic or static.[5] However, until the second wave of the feminist movement, traditional goals promulgated by male intellectuals prevailed. Over the last 25 years or so, these goals have been in flux, in response to changing gender arrangements in society. Feminist views have challenged male ruling ideas. Psychologist Sandra Bem (1974;1981;1983) has been particularly influential in articulating the implications of societal events for socialization goals. The positions taken by social scientists influence child-care experts, who, in turn, have some impact upon parents.

Three phases in intellectuals' thought about gender socialization can be distinguished.

Sex-typing

From the turn of the century on, science intruded into the rearing of children, especially middle-class children. Psychoanalytic theory, with its Oedipus and Electra complexes, was especially influential on social constructions of childhood (Synnott, 1983). Sex-typing was taken for granted by social scientists and laypersons alike as the goal of gender socialization.[6] Sex-typing and gender stereotyping are closely related constructs. As noted above, gender stereotypes are commonly held beliefs about the traits characterizing females and males. Sex-typing, on the other hand, holds that certain traits *should* characterize females and males. More particularly, *sex-typing* is "the prescription of different qualities, activities, and behaviors to females and males in the interest of socializing them for adult roles" (Williams, 1983:171). The sexes are regarded as quite distinctive. Moreover, femininity and masculinity are viewed as mirror images of one another (Spence, 1981:132). That is, just as female and male were traditionally viewed as biological opposites, clusters of feminine and masculine traits were seen as psychological opposites. More specifically, expressive traits and behaviors were prescribed for girls and instrumental traits and behaviors for boys:

> Men, in order to discharge their onerous instrumental role responsibilities properly, must be abundantly endowed with these self-assertive, goal-directed characteristics. Similarly, women must possess nurturant, interpersonally oriented characteristics to discharge their domestic, intrafamilial responsibilities (Spence, 1981:135).

Although some psychologists, Freudians, for example, viewed sex-typing as the natural unfolding of biology, learning psychologists saw the origin of sex-typing in the sex-differentiated practices of the socializing community (Bem, 1983:600). On the assumption that gender must be learned, society arranges for girls and boys to have different sets of socialization experiences, in order to prepare them for the distinctive adult roles they will play. Girls are exposed to dancing lessons and home economics classes; boys to athletics and shop courses. Private finishing school for girls and military school for boys exemplified such arrangements for wealthy children in past years.

As mentioned above, psychologists assumed that sex-typing was associated with superior psychological adjustment. The "normal" girl and woman were expected to be feminine, the "normal" boy and man to be masculine. Curiously, those who were considered experts at the time that sex-typing was the unquestioned standard failed to consider the possible negative impact of sex-typing on individuals (Garnets and Pleck, 1979:274). Traditional gender scripts set standards that some people, for a variety of reasons, cannot meet. For example, unattractive women, unsuccessful men, and homosexuals may be led to devalue themselves.

Given the proposition of existential conditioning of thought, we might expect a connection between social scientists' gender-socialization ideals and prevailing social conditions. Before the revival of the woman's movement, the traditional gender division of labor was pervasive and unquestioned. For instance, women's military participation in World War II did not challenge sex-typing. "The military retained a sexual division of labor and authority, excluded women from bearing arms, and paid them and their dependents less than men" (Silverman, 1982:516). North American gender definitions became even more orthodox in the decade or so following the war. Pleck (1981a:159) suggests that the immediate post-war period threatened the foundations of the traditional male role. Canadian and American soldiers had been on the winning side of a popular war. Their manhood seemed validated.

> How great, then, was their shock when, on returning home, they encountered wives and girlfriends who had acquired traditionally male jobs in war industries and new-found psychological independence from having to live without men; a job market transformed by wartime technological advances, requiring they obtain levels of training and education previously unprecedented; and postwar inflation making them less adequate as family providers (Pleck, 1981a:159).

The reserve army of working women, all along regarded as only temporary replacements for men, was sent packing from the factories. Married women were returned home, while the unmarried ones were channeled into traditionally female occupations (Pierson, 1977:145). The government dismantled the child-care facilities and withdrew its tax concessions to working wives. Now, women could earn only $250 a year without affecting their husbands' deductions (Phillips and Phillips, 1983:31). Federal civil service regulations restricted employment of married women (Archibald, 1979:17). Some of the women who unwillingly retreated from the labor force may have conveyed their discontent with their constricted lives to their daughters, who became the feminists of the 1970s (Silverman, 1982:517).

The intensely conservative 1950s accentuated the mystique of feminine fulfillment centering on home, husband, and "baby boom" kids (Friedan, 1963). Psychologists and child-care experts contributed to this imprisoning web of masculine ruling ideas. For instance, Bowlby's (1952) notion of "maternal deprivation" came to mean that mothers who failed to lavish 100 percent of their time and attention on their children produced neurotics and juvenile delinquents. Conveniently, Bowlby's ideas gained currency just after working women had been displaced by demobilized veterans (Laws, 1979:127). Similarly, sociologists, psychologists, and child-care specialists, no longer complacent that people's behavior would end up automatically matching their genitalia, now "became obsessed by the problem of 'socializing' children into their appropriate 'gender' or 'sex role'" (Ehrenreich and English, 1978:245). The assumption that sex-typing was essential for both smoothly functioning societies and well-adjusted individuals (Parsons, 1955) held undisputed until the advent of the feminist movement at the end of the 1960s. Prior to this collective rebellion, individual women who spoke out were belittled and abused for their personal failure to be happy (Spender, 1982:722).

Androgyny

In the latter half of the 1970s, androgyny, as a new gender-socialization goal, captured the imagination of social scientists. The publication of Bem's Sex Role Inventory (1974) scale to measure androgyny was a major influence upon this shift in social ideals. Bem's (1976:49) motive was explicitly ideological: ". . . my major purpose has always been a feminist one: to help free the human personality from the restricting prison of sex-role stereotyping . . . ."

While sex-typing demanded that the individual be either masculine or feminine, androgyny recommended being *both* masculine and feminine in relatively equal proportions. The term androgyny is derived from the Greek words for male and female physical characteristics. The notion of co-occurrence of feminine and masculine psychological elements is also an ancient one (Singer, 1976). In Greek mythology, Tiresias (who was somewhat more ambitious than the contemporary movie heroine, *Tootsie*) lived for seven years as a woman and seven years as a man in order to experience both sexes (Laws, 1979:308). Carl Jung's (1926) discussion of the *animus* (the male principle within the female) and the *anima* (the female principle within the male) originally introduced the idea of androgyny into psychology.[7] In *A Room of Her Own*, Virginia Woolf (1928:102) wrote:

> In each of us two powers preside, one male, one female, and in the man's brain, the man presides over the woman, and in the woman's brain, the woman predominates over the man. The normal and comfortable state of being is when the two live in harmony together, spiritually cooperating.

Today, social scientists define *androgyny* as the flexible integration of valued feminine (communal) and masculine (instrumental) traits. The androgynous ideal calls for people of both sexes to be, for example, assertive *and* compassionate, ambitious *and* sensitive to others' needs. The androgynous person is able to fire an inept employee, but to do so with an appreciation of that person's feelings. On the other hand, a person who is always competitive and aggressive at work, but very dependent and passive off the job, that is, a person who is unable to adjust his/her behavior to situational requirements, is neither integrated nor flexible (Basow, 1980:297). The term "androgynous" would not apply here. The androgynous person is comfortable exhibiting behaviors associated with either the female or male role, as appropriate to the requirements of the situation. Proponents of this new socialization ideal

(Bem, 1974) claimed that androgynous individuals were better adjusted and more socially effective than their sex-typed counterparts. However, research testing this claim has yielded equivocal results (Spence, 1981:138–139).[8]

The sociologist of knowledge would argue that chance cannot explain the elevation of the ancient concept of androgyny into the ideal personality pattern of the 1970s. Very few of the thousands of social science articles published each decade receive the enthusiastic reception accorded Bem's (1974) work. The intellectual resurrection of androgyny coincides with some very significant happenings in the "real" world. These events have slowly shifted the foundations of gender, namely, women's traditional role as homemaker and mother and men's traditional role as breadwinner (Pleck, 1981a: 159). Academics' changed views of socialization reflected these events.

For various economic reasons, such as inflation, a rising standard of living, and the expansion of service and clerical jobs understood to be "women's work," the labor force participation of women has risen dramatically since the 1950s. For example, the labor force participation of Canadian married women has increased fivefold since the post-World War II period (Lupri and Mills, 1983). Now, middle-class women joined their working-class sisters on the job. This change brought in its wake other developments: a falling birth rate, renegotiation of the old financial pact between women and men, and perhaps inevitably, the questioning of traditional gender norms (Ehrenreich, 1983:99). As women moved into the labor force, they encountered massive discrimination. Middle-class women's anger over mistreatment in the workplace and what Virginia Woolf described as "the cotton wool quality of daily life" in suburbia made them receptive to the feminist critique when it came (Berger and Berger, 1984:24).

According to Ehrenreich (1983:106 ff.), the androgynous vision took form in the decade of the 1960s. Protest against the Vietnam War highlighted the potential lethality of male aggressiveness. The counterculture flouted the "uptight," "straight" conventions of material success, marriage and career. Indeed, "the most shocking feature of the hippies . . . was that, with all the long hair, beads, and flowing makeshift costumes, 'you couldn't tell the boys from the girls' " (Ehrenreich, 1983:107). The Gay Liberation movement called into question conventional understandings of gender. The sixties was also marked by protest movements demanding just treatment for Indians, blacks, the poor, university students, and, eventually, women. The flowering of the feminist movement in the 1970s capped a series of events which had loosened the traditional links between biological sex and gender traits. Before too long, many men, responding to the feminist critique of gender roles, as well as other factors, rebelled against the breadwinner ethic and lifelong commitments to wives and children (Ehrenreich,

1983). Divorce rates skyrocketed. The ideal of androgynous socialization was one of many intellectual responses to these events.

By the mid-1980s, androgyny was still a mass-media fad. Though many parents were still offended, the novelty value of the gender-blurring sartorial styles of rock music idols Michael Jackson, Boy George, and Annie Lennox was beginning to wear off for the younger set. However, by the beginning of the eighties, feminist social scientists had become disillusioned with the concept. Psychologists criticized Bem's (1974) operationalization of masculinity, femininity and androgyny (Deaux, 1985:59). Now, androgyny was labeled a "transitional" concept, flawed but useful for setting the stage for the next socialization goal (Doyle, 1985:358).

Feminists criticized the androgyny ideal for four major, related reasons. First, as a new standard of personal adjustment, androgyny may set people up for failure by demanding the impossible (Hyde and Rosenberg, 1980). If everyone is expected to be both thoroughly expressive *and* thoroughly agentic, this new standard doubles the pressure of the traditional sex-typed socialization goal (Basow, 1980:299). "The individual now has not one but two potential sources of inadequacy with which to contend" (Bem, 1983:616). In these critics' opinion, androgyny failed to deliver its initial promise of better psychological adjustment.[9]

Second, androgyny has been called a "sexist myth in disguise" (Harris, 1974) because it ends up affirming the prestige and power of masculinity. Since our society rewards and admires masculine behavior, androgyny benefits women more than men (Pyke, 1980). With the possible exception of a few male pop idols, it is women who do most of the "gender-blending." For example, women buy books that instruct them how to behave and dress like men in corporate boardrooms. (Expressivity manuals for men have yet to appear on best seller lists.) Women buy the Calvin Klein line of jockey briefs and boxer shorts, complete with flies. (Lace teddies are *not* for sale in men's clothing departments [Finlayson, 1984:20].)

Third, and relatedly, androgyny does not eliminate gender stereotypes; it just combines them in new ways, rather like "John Travolta and Farrah Fawcett-Majors scotch-taped together" (Daly, quoted in Carrigan et al., 1985:567). In other words, androgyny continues to accept femininity and masculinity as meaningful personality components (Lott, 1981:178). To label one set of behaviors (e.g., self-reliant, ambitious, assertive, analytical) as masculine, and another set (e.g., affectionate, loyal, compassionate, gentle) as feminine, "is to obscure the essential humanness of the behaviors and to dull our appreciation of their fundamental teachability and modifiability" (Lott, 1981:172).

Fourth, as Bem (1976:59) herself predicted, the concept of androgyny contains the seeds of its own obsolescence. Androgyny implies the absence of gender role constraints or, expressed positively, the social conditions in which individuals can develop their full potential, regardless of their sex. Therefore, in a truly androgynous society, the concept of androgyny, "antithetically tied to the concepts of masculinity and femininity," simply would not exist (Eichler, 1980:69–70). In sum, androgyny is now appreciated as "a necessary step in the evolution of non-sexist thought" (Eichler, 1980:69).

Gender Transcendence

The current radical ideal looks beyond the combination of feminine and masculine traits in the personality, to a state where femininity and masculinity are transcended or superseded as ways of labeling and experiencing psychological traits and being well-adjusted human beings (Garnets and Pleck, 1979; Hefner, Rebecca and Oleshansky, 1975). The third criticism of androgyny, above, captures this idea. For gender-socialization experts (but not the general public), the goal has moved from *either/or* of sex-typing, to *both* of androgyny, to *neither* of gender transcendence. Doyle (1985:359) says that "although research into the transcendence of masculinity and femininity is still in its infancy," gender transcendence "may well be the research concept of the eighties and beyond."

The ideal of gender transcendence has profound implications for the way in which children are socialized. In a utopian society where gender has been superseded, each child would be taught that the meaning of girl/boy, female/male is exclusively biological. (See Figure 3-1.)

FIGURE 3-1
GENDER TRANSCENDENCE

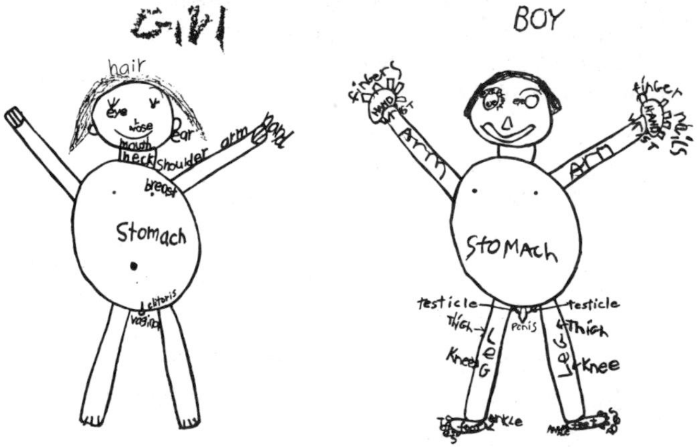

Source: Stephanie Waxman, *What Is A Girl? What Is A Boy?*
Toronto: The Women's Press, 1976. Used with permission.

The multitude of sociocultural elaborations on sex would disappear. Personality traits, interests, hobbies, toys, clothing, occupations, domestic division of labor — none would any longer be a function of sex (Bem, 1983).[10]

Stephanie Waxman's (1976) children's book, *What Is a Girl? What Is a Boy?* communicates clearly (and before its time) the concept of gender transcendence. The message is the centrality of sex and the reduced salience of gender. Photographs of children of both sexes and many races accompany the following excerpts:

—Some people say a girl is someone with long hair.	But Lucas has long hair. And he's a boy.
—Some people say a boy is someone with short hair.	But Mini has short hair. And she's a girl.
—Some people say a girl is someone with jewelry.	But David is wearing a necklace. And he's a boy.
—Some people say a boy is someone wearing pants.	But Keko is wearing pants. And she's a girl.
—Some people say a girl is someone with a girl's name.	Sam is usually a boy's name. But this Sam is a girl.
—Some people say a girl is someone who plays with dolls.	Burt Noah is taking care of his doll. And he's a boy.
—Some people say a boy is someone who doesn't cry.	But Eric is crying. And he's a boy.
—Then, what *is* a boy?	A boy is someone with a penis and testicles.
—And, what *is* a girl?	A girl is someone with a vagina and a clitoris.

(Source: Stephanie Waxman, *What Is A Girl? What Is A Boy?* Toronto: The Women's Press, 1976. Used with permission.)

Some psychologists (Williams, 1983) have located a non-sexist ideal of the healthy *person* in the work of Abraham Maslow (1954). Maslow believed that all human beings have needs and capacities, and that normal development consists in actualizing this basic nature. *Self-actualization,* or development of basic, inner natures to their fullest expression, occurs when an environment fostering growth is provided. Maslow studied living and historical examples of healthy personalities of both sexes. Williams (1983:380-381) has nicely summarized Maslow's ideal of the self-actualized person:

> What are the distinguishing features of the personalities of such actualized persons? They are realistically oriented, accepting themselves, other people, and the natural world for what they are. Their values are democratic, and they can identify readily with all kinds of people. They are at home in the world. They are spontaneous, open, and relatively free of neurotic defenses. Their appreciation of people and things is fresh rather than stereotyped. They have a child-like quality which lets them see and experience and feel as if each time is the first. They are problem-centered rather than self-centered. They are creative and resist conformity to the culture, transcending it rather than merely coping with it. Such self-actualized persons have a few deep relationships with certain important others. Emotionally self-sufficient, they strive for autonomy in their lives. They require privacy and enjoy solitude. With others, they are never exploitative, nor do they confuse means with ends. Their humor is philosophical, often at their own expense, rather than hostile.
>
> (Source: Juanita H. Williams, *Psychology of Women*. Second Edition (1983). New York: W.W. Norton. Used with permission.)

A tall order! However, the revival of Maslow's (1954) work suggests the possibility of a healthy personality independent of gender and emphasizes that valuable traits are human traits, with no gender label.

If the perspective of the sociology of knowledge is adopted and the underlying social conditions that foster ideas sought, what events correlate with feminist social scientists' disillusionment with androgyny and promotion of gender transcendence? Such comments are, of course, speculative. However, the latter, more radical feminist goal may well be the product of realization that obstacles to female-male equality are more formidable than they originally appeared. Ehrenreich and English (1978:319) comment on a decade's "progress" of the women's movement:

> . . . the world opening up to women today is not exactly the halcyon vista of "careers," options, relationships portrayed by our more positive-thinking feminist leaders. For every sexually successful single there must be a hundred unsuccessful, unslim, "unattractive" housewives. For every careerwoman, there are dozens of low-paid woman job-holders. For every divorce that frees a woman, there are others that throw women into poverty or loneliness. The alternative to the suffocation of domesticity turns out to be the old rationalist nightmare: a world dominated by the Market, socially atomized, bereft of "human" values.

Ehrenreich and English (1978:323) conclude that for women, ". . . there are no answers left but the most radical ones. We cannot assimilate into a masculinist society without doing violence to our own nature, which is, of course, *human* nature" (emphasis in original). Feminist psychologists (Greenglass, 1982:255) arrive at the same conclusion. The androgyny ideal ended up demonstrating that masculinity pays off, and therefore reinforced the grounds of women's subordination. The meaning of liberation for feminists is *not* becoming more like men. World events have hardened this viewpoint:

> The subjugation of women symbolized by gender is a paradigm of the power relationships upon which civilization is based. Men's attempts to control nature as they have controlled women have resulted in an environmental crisis of epic proportions. Men's attempts to dominate one another have brought the world to the brink of nuclear holocaust. If civilization is to survive, we desperately need a new way of looking at the world (Finlayson, 1984:21).

Is gender transcendence feasible as a "new way of looking at the world"? On the positive side, sex-typing is a learned phenomenon and hence, "neither inevitable nor unmodifiable" (Bem, 1983:603). As an *ideal*, the notion is attractive. Feminists agree with Bem (1983:609) that society's emphasis on the sex dichotomy is gratuitous. However, many social scientists are pessimistic about the possibility of transcending gender altogether. Gender transcendence implies a gender-blind society. As Spence (1981:146) points out:

> Whether one supports or rejects the proposal that, in an ideal society, the importance of gender should be minimized, the observation that in contemporary society gender is a central organizing principle in men's and women's images of themselves and in their construction of their social world is indisputable.

As we noted in Chapter 1, every known society is differentiated on the basis of sex. The origin of social structure based on sex appears to be the tie between sex and reproduction and lactation. According to sociologists' observations, differentiation, whether on the basis of sex, age, occupation, race, or ethnicity, is almost invariably accompanied by stratification (Eichler, 1980:71). Put another way, social organization almost never stops with arrangements for females to do this and males to do that. Instead, females and males form a status hierarchy: males enjoy more power, prestige, and material resources than do females. Moreover, societal arrangements built on sex and procreative lines immensely simplify social organization (Goffman, 1977:306). Although a gender-blind society is not impossible, it is improbable.

Conclusions

This chapter has reviewed the parameters of socialization and discussed gender-role attitudes, stereotypes, and occupational sex-typing as socialization content, as well as gender-socialization ideals. Social events of the 1960s and 1970s, especially the women's movement, provoked many social scientists and child-care experts to question sex-typing as a gender-socialization goal. Feminist opinion has greatly influenced the recent prescription of gender-socialization ideals. First androgyny, and now gender transcendence, have received considerable attention in feminist circles.

The experiences of psychologist Sandra Bem's son illustrates the gap between the gender-transcendence ideal and the realities of the contemporary context. Jeremy has been brought up with Waxman's (1976) *What Is a Girl? What Is a Boy?* One day, the four-year-old boy decided to wear barrettes in his hair when he went to nursery school:

> Several times that day, another little boy told Jeremy that he, Jeremy, must be a girl because "only girls wear barrettes." After trying to explain to this child that "wearing barrettes doesn't matter" and that "being a boy means having a penis and testicles," Jeremy finally pulled down his pants as a way of making his point more convincingly. The other child was not impressed. He simply said, "Everybody has a penis; only girls wear barrettes" (Bem, 1983:612).

The moral of this anecdote is that our society is not now gender-blind and is unlikely to be gender-blind in the foreseeable future. Although androgyny and gender transcendence are useful alternative goals, much contemporary gender socialization is still sex-typed. Even parents who consider themselves to be "liberated" do not wish to risk having their children become misfits in society as it is currently constituted (Katz, 1979:24). The next chapter reflects these facts.

NOTES

1. Cooley (1902) distinguished between primary groups and secondary groups. Primary groups are characterized by intimate, face-to-face association, and relatively intense emotional experiences. They encompass the entire person. Sociologists have described the primary group, e.g. the family and peer group, as the "nursery of human nature" and the "crucible of self and personhood." By contrast, experiences in secondary groups, e.g. the formal aspects of work organizations, are less intimate and intense and more segmented. That is, secondary groups are concerned with the individual in delimited statuses (employee, student), rather than the total person. Of course, primary relations often develop in the interstices of secondary groups. For example, student friendships thrive in the formal organization of the university.
2. The 13 items shown on Table 3.1 were chosen from the Gallup questions asked over a 30-year period, which have been analyzed by Boyd (1984). The questions were asked in the 1980s and measured an enduring attitude, rather than an ephemeral issue.

3. Lippmann (1922) invented a figurative usage for the word "stereotype," which up to then had referred exclusively to a metal plate used in printing.
4. An up-to-date Canadian replication of Nemerowicz's (1979) study of children's perceptions of work would be most welcome.
5. In Canada during the 1880s there emerged a primarily middle-class women's revolt against the uselessness of their dependent existence, the excesses of capitalism, and their exclusion from citizenship (Kealey, 1979). However, neither women's expanded experiences in the labor force nor the Suffrage Movement had much impact on sextyping. Women were "still 'primarily mothers of men'" (Vipond, 1977:124). According to Strong-Boag (1979:129), "the 'cult of domesticity' . . . overwhelmed war-weary Canadians by the 1920s. A renewed emphasis on family life and full-time mothering went hand in hand with a wave of Freudian-influenced popular psychology which emphasized sexuality and female irrationality."
6. The work of Biller (1971) and Lynn (1969) provide good examples of the taken-for-granted ideal of sex-typing.
7. However, Lott (1981:177), basing her remarks on Harris (1974), notes that Jung's propositions regarding androgyny did not lead him to espouse a position of gender equality. "Jung argued that while a man might either profit or suffer from the influence of his *anima* (feminine qualities), a woman must (should) deny her *animus* (masculine qualities) because otherwise she would make a poor lover, stop up her feelings, frighten men, or 'even become frigid' ."
8. High masculinity scores for men and women on both Bem's (1974) Sex Role Inventory and the Personal Attributes Questionnaire (Spence et al., 1975) are associated with indices of effective personal functioning. However, sex-typed women (those with high "feminine" scores on these scales) appear less well-adjusted than either androgynous or "masculine" women (Spence, 1981:139). Indeed, it appears that high masculinity scores on these scales are more strongly related to effective personal functioning and self-esteem than high androgyny scores per se (Basow, 1980:300).
9. Degree of psychological adjustment depends, to some extent, on the situation in which people must function (Greenglass, 1982:254). Much of the research referred to in note 8 above, where "masculinity" was found to be associated with mental health, was conducted on university students. The university environment emphasizes achievement, competition, and ambition. Therefore, rewards accrue to those who possess such "masculine" characteristics. However, sex-typed individuals who find themselves in settings that demand sex-typed behavior may show good adjustment. Hoffman and Fidell (1979) reported stereotypically feminine middle-class women with full-time responsibility for home and children to be well-adjusted. Their masculine and androgynous counterparts were, however, more likely to be in the labor force and deriving satisfaction from their outside employment.
10. Bem (1983) refers to children for whom the salience of gender has been reduced drastically as "gender-aschematic children." "Schema, according to cognitive psychologists, are cognitive structures consisting of networks of associations that serve to organize and guide the interpretation of information. Every human society, Bem observes, teaches its members a diverse network of associations linked to concepts of "masculinity" and "femininity." The stress that society places on the importance of gender turns this network into cognitive schema that lead the individual to organize and process diverse kinds of information in gender terms, including information about the self" (Spence, 1981:139). According to Bem's (1981) research, gender is a more central schema for some people than others. The "schema" concept is discussed further in Chapter 4 of this book.

4

Symbolic Interactionism and Gender Socialization in Childhood

Introduction

I can't remember the crash, just the lights. And when I opened my eyes again there were more lights, shining right in my face . . . . I was going to start hollering really loud but then the one I'd decided must be the doctor said something that got my attention. "Hold him still now. I'm going to try to stitch that hand and he isn't going to like it."

That should have made me completely hysterical but for some reason it calmed me down instead. All I could think of was how proud my mom was going to be when she found out I didn't make a fuss. "Cowboys don't cry," was what she'd always say when I got banged up somehow. And since there was nothing in the world I wanted so much as to be a cowboy like my dad, you can bet I listened to her. She was always really proud of me when I didn't cry over little things.

It turned out that this wasn't a little thing. My right hand had gone through the windshield and it was cut up so bad that I've still got the scar . . . .

It seemed like that doctor was taking forever but Mom still didn't come. Then, when he was almost finished with me, there was a knock on the door. I sighed with relief. I knew it was going to be Mom out there. She'd come in and put her arms around me and everything would be okay.

A nurse opened the door. But it wasn't Mom who came in. It was Dad. He was sort of limping and he had a piece of tape above his eye but outside of that he didn't seem to be hurt much. I was sure glad to see him . . . .

"Where's Mom? Dad, where is she? I want to see my mom!" I must have yelled it pretty loud because suddenly everything went dead quiet and everybody in that Emergency Room was looking at us.

For a minute, Dad just stood there, staring at me with that empty, helpless look on his face. Then, finally, he said in a voice that didn't even sound like him, "Your mom can't come, Shane."

"Why not?" I whispered, and I didn't sound like me, either.

Dad's voice didn't change. It was still flat and lifeless but the words burned into me like he was shouting them at the top of his voice. "Cause she's dead."

The silence in that room hung like a heavy fog and there, right in the middle of it, were Dad and I, staring at each other but not really even seeing each other. Maybe the fog was too thick.

Finally, Dad seemed to sort of break loose. He took a step toward me and kind of held out his arms and I thought, "He's gonna hold me. Dad's gonna put his arms around me and hold me and somehow we're gonna make it 'cause we still got each other . . . ."

"Oh, Shane, I . . ." he started, and his voice sounded more real. I thought he was going to cry but that was all right because if he cried, I could cry, too. But, suddenly, halfway through that sentence and halfway through that step, he stopped and turned away. I heard him take a deep breath and swallow hard. "Shane, I got some things to take care of. I'll be back in a little while," he said in that empty voice again. He was almost running when he went out the door.

(From *Cowboys Don't Cry* by Marilyn Halvorston. © 1984 Irwin Publishing Inc. Used by permission of the Publishers.)

This chapter returns to the question, "How is the social reality of gender maintained?" However, this time, the matter is examined at the social-psychological level of everyday experience. Understanding of gender as a social-psychological problem is sought through the theoretical perspective of symbolic interactionism. As we shall see, interactionist ideas are generally compatible with those of the sociology of knowledge (Berger and Luckmann, 1966; Ropers, 1973). The macro-level tenets and implications of the sociology of knowledge discussed in Chapter 2 serve to frame our treatment of the micro-level processes of gender socialization.

Berger and Berger (1975:8) tell us that the sociologist must be constantly aware of the "two-fold manifestation" of society, the microscopic and the macro-scopic:

. . . in our experience of society, we simultaneously inhabit different worlds. First of all, crucially and continuously, we inhabit the *micro-world* of our immediate experience with others in face-to-face relations. Beyond that, with varying degrees of significance and continuity, we inhabit a *macro-world* consisting of much larger structures and involving us in relations with others that are mostly abstract, anonymous and remote. Both worlds are essential to our experience of society, and (with the exception of early childhood, when the micro-world is all we know) each world depends upon the other for its meaning to us. (Emphasis in original.)

The children's story *Cowboys Don't Cry* (Halvorson, 1984) depicts a fictional boy, Shane, possessed of self-consciousness; aware of his relationships with others (and the responsibilities and rights entailed by these relationships); knowledgeable about his particular corner of Canada; equipped with skills that range from table manners to arithmetic to handling horses; concerned with behaving appropriately as a boy today and a grown man in the future. Neither storybook children nor real-life children are born with all this knowledge of themselves or their social and physical milieus. Rather, they acquire it through socialization, "a process involving interaction between 'old hands' and new recruits" (Laws, 1979:240). As traditional gender socialization progresses, female and male knowledge of the micro-world and macro-world mentioned above becomes increasingly divergent.

Chapter 4 deals with the mechanisms of gender socialization. Exactly *how* does society's script for femininity and masculinity get inside the child? *How* do little boys learn to be cowboys who don't cry? *How* do little girls turn into mothers who comfort would-be cowboys? At issue is the development of gender identity and the learning of gender norms in childhood. A conceptual tool is needed to tackle this problem. That tool is the theoretical framework of symbolic inter-actionism. Therefore, our discussion of gender socialization must be delayed briefly in order to explain what symbolic interactionism is all about.

Symbolic Interactionism

What are theories? What good are they, anyway? Theoretical guidance is needed to make sense of the problem of gender. It won't do simply to collect observations about how gender seems to operate in our society and let the "facts" speak for themselves. The "facts" never speak for themselves. Instead, they are always interpreted within some theoretical framework (Lauer and Handel, 1983:7–8). For one thing, observations must be systematically organized if they are to tell us anything mean-ingful about the world. The "data from the world of observation must be enmeshed in a web of ideas if there is to be a significant scientific yield" (Deutsch and Krauss, 1965:vii). In addition, theory guides research by leading to predictions about events not yet observed (Shaw and Costanzo, 1982:9).

The status of theory in the social sciences differs somewhat from that in the sciences generally. In the latter case, a *theory* is defined as "a set of logically related hypotheses specifying expected relationships among variables, based on concepts describing selected aspects of the world and assumptions about the way it works, and open to falsifica-tion from evidence drawn from the world" (Stryker, 1980:8). Theory, in this sense, serves as a model for the social sciences. However, Jonathan Turner (1978:13) tells us that

> . . . most sociological theory constitutes a verbal "image of society" rather than a rigorously constructed set of theoretical statements organized into a logically coherent format. Thus, a great deal of so-called theory is really a general "perspective" or "orientation" for looking at various features of the social world which, if all goes well, can be eventually translated into true scientific theory.

For this reason, symbolic interactionism is really a theoretical framework, perspective, or orientation. However, for simplicity's sake, it will hereafter be referred to as a "theory." Symbolic interactionism comes closest to being theory in the technical sense when it deals with the problem of socialization (Stryker, 1980:8).

If only one theory commanded sociologists' allegiance, the study of gender relations would be relatively straightforward. However, theories, like the "facts" of gender they attempt to explain, are social constructions. Both are the outcome of a web of social practices. Fortunately (or unfortunately, depending upon one's outlook and energy level), there exist an abundance of alternative theoretical perspectives. Although it might by psychologically comforting if one "true" view of gender carried absolute authority, grappling with a variety of ideas offers intellectual challenge. Even more important, the sociology of gender relations is at an early stage of development; no one theory holds all the answers. Therefore, alternative perspectives fill gaps left by symbolic interactionism. Accordingly, the theoretical analyses of gender socialization presented in this book feature symbolic interactionism, augmented by ideas drawn from the cognitive developmental, social learning, and psychoanalytic traditions.[1]

The Central Tenets of Symbolic Interactionism

A history of the ideas central to symbolic interactionism begins with the Scottish moral philosophers of the eighteenth century, such as David Hume and Adam Smith, and continues with the American pragmatic philosophers of the late nineteenth and early twentieth centuries — William James, John Dewey, and especially George Herbert Mead. Sociologists Charles Horton Cooley, W.I. Thomas, and Max Weber were important contributors from the same period of time (Stryker, 1980:4). Contemporary refinements to the perspective have been made by many sociologists, notably Herbert Blumer, Manford Kuhn, and Erving Goffman. Although a complete roster of symbolic interactionists would be about as interesting to read as a telephone directory, their names do serve to emphasize that the construction of a theoretical orientation involves many thinkers, over a long period of time. Nevertheless,

> . . . interactionalism stands in debt to the genius of one man, George Herbert Mead . . . Mead borrowed ideas from others, and combined them with his own insights, to produce a synthesis which stands as the base for modern interactionism (J. Turner, 1978:312).

Despite the fact that there is no one orthodox version of what symbolic interactionism really means (Stryker, 1981:26), a consensus exists that the perspective embraces this core set of assumptions:

1. Symbolic interactionists emphasize the distinction between *homo sapiens* and lower animals.[2] Consequently, analysis focuses "upon the experiences of people as social persons rather than upon the physical and organic facts about people as animal organisms" (Gerth and Mills, 1953:3).

2. According to the interactionist position, distinctively human behavior is symbolic behavior. Animals and humans are qualitatively different largely because humans have the capacity to use much more complex language. The term *symbol* indicates that people do not typically respond directly to stimuli, but assign meanings to stimuli, and act on the basis of these meanings. These meanings are shared social definitions, socially derived through interaction with others (Manis and Meltzer, 1978:6).

3. Symbolic interactionists argue that the essence of the sociologist's task is analysis of the social or group bases of human behavior (Haas and Shaffir, 1978:3). Human groups take the form of people engaged in *social interaction*; that is, taking "account of the actions of one another as they form their own action" (Blumer, 1969b:10). Interaction is symbolic in the sense that it occurs through people's interpretation of the symbols that others convey. Role-taking is the basic mechanism by which interaction occurs (J. Turner, 1978:328). *Role-taking* (taking the role of the other) means "imaginatively assuming the position or point of view of another person" (Lindesmith and Strauss, 1968:282).

4. Symbolic interactionists view individual and society as two sides of the same coin. One cannot possibly exist without the other. On the one hand, society is composed of people in interaction. On the other, *homo sapiens* is not born human, but becomes capable of distinctively human conduct only through association with others (Manis and Meltzer, 1978:6). In short, "social structure creates social persons who (re)create social structures who . . . ad infinitum" (Stryker, 1980:53). However, the foregoing does *not* imply that society, or the social groups composing it, invariably has a benign influence upon the individual

(Hewitt, 1984:74). For example, many people chafe under the strictures of gender requirements.

5. The construction of human behavior occurs, in part, through *definitions of the situation*. Though there is some physical reality "out there,"[3] people respond not directly to this "objective reality," but to a symbolic interpretation of that reality (Charon, 1979:36–37). In other words, definitions of the situation intervene between situations and people's reactions to them: "an interpretation, or point of view, and eventually a policy and a behavior pattern" (Thomas, 1937:18). Definitions of the situation may be personal (idiosyncratic) or cultural (standard meanings of events embedded in the community's culture, and learned through socialization) (Stebbins, 1967). Gender stereotypes are one example of the latter. Finally, "if [people] define situations as real, they are real in their consequences" (Thomas and Thomas, 1928:572). Witness the ramifications of the assumption that women and men *are* opposite sexes!

6. Though the place of power in an interactionist framework is the subject of controversy (Stryker, 1980:146 ff.), many contemporary interactionists (Stryker, 1980; Thomas, Franks and Calonico, 1978) acknowledge power's key role in social relationships. Haas and Shaffir (1978:7–8), for example, remark that power "is a constant and impressively direct element in our everyday interactions." Power differentials distinguish individual from individual, and group from group.

7. Symbolic interactionism involves a set of assumptions about human nature that are implied in the above tenets. Human beings are social beings. They are symbol-creating, symbol-using creatures, who have, to a considerable extent, become liberated from biological programming (J. Turner, 1978:327). They actively shape their own behavior, rather than passively responding to external stimuli:

> Human behavior is an elaborate process of interpreting, choosing, and rejecting possible lines of action. This process cannot be understood in terms of mechanical responses to external stimuli . . . . Human beings are, at least in part, participants in creating their own destinies (Manis and Meltzer, 1978:8).

Humans possess minds (they interact with themselves), and selves (they are objects to themselves). The fact that individuals are conscious *and* self-conscious gives them the capacity to shape their own behavior. The formation of self is a crucial aspect of the socialization process (Manis and Meltzer, 1978:165).

8. In science, theoretical statements are created to be proven wrong. Theoretical ideas "must be tested against the facts of the world" (J. Turner, 1978:11). Each theoretical orientation has somewhat different

methodological notions concerning the nature of this confrontation between its hypotheses and the facts of the world. The chief methodological tenet of symbolic interactionism holds that sociologists should not confine themselves to behavioristic or external reporting of human behavior, but should examine the meaning the behavior has for the actors. In other words, the investigator should take the role of the people being studied, in order to determine how they define their situations and how their situations are jointly constructed (Manis and Meltzer, 1978:8-9). Although participant observation and the feminine communal mode (see Chapter 2) is the preferred research style, "nearly all methods and techniques are represented in one form or another" (Maines, 1981:473).[4]

The Congeniality of the Symbolic Interactionist Perspective

There are three reasons why symbolic interactionism has been chosen as the guiding theoretical orientation for this book. Interactionism's appeal lies, first of all, in its long-standing focus on socialization and its sophisticated treatment of this topic. As Ishwaran (1979:5) notes, "It is the symbolic interactionists who have provided the main impetus of the sociological enthusiasm with child development or 'development of human nature.'" Learning to be feminine or masculine is the chief concern of this book.

The second source of the appeal of symbolic interactionism is the interest it shares with the sociology of knowledge in the production, transformation, and maintenance of meaning (Maines, 1981:463). This perspective fits well with our view of gender as social product. Moreover, it accommodates scholars who believe that traditional gender definitions should change. In the words of Yoels and Karp (1978:31):

> From the interactionist perspective, society exists through
> the symbolic communication occurring between persons.
> *Since . . . there is no inherent meaning in an object, it is*
> *always possible for persons, through their symbolic activity, to*
> *re-define objects in ways that challenge pre-existent definitions*
> *of reality* (emphasis added).

Put another way, "people transform themselves and their worlds as they engage in social dialogue" (Stone and Farberman, 1970:v).

Finally, symbolic interactionism lends itself to the task at hand because it is a theoretical perspective with the potential of bridging social structure and person (Stryker, 1980:53). Reciprocity of person and social structure is an important tenet of interactionism. The primary goal of this book is to develop a conceptual framework for the explanation of gender socialization. Socialization is a social psychological problem; the focus is upon the individual in social context. However, our understanding of gender socialization would be inadequate if macro-sociological factors, especially the power structure underlying the process, were ignored. Maines (1977:235) claims that the symbolic interactionist perspective

> does not exclude or deny the existence of phenomena such as social class, bureaucracy, social institutions, power structures, international relations, or social stratification, which are usually included in considerations of social organization and social structure.

Despite the congeniality of interactionism to this book's aims, no theory is perfect. This perspective, like all others, has gaps and deficiencies. Some aspects of gender socialization are handled better by other theoretical traditions. When necessary, symbolic interactionism will be supplemented with insights drawn from elsewhere. For example, Mead's (1934) framework of childhood socialization is a rational, cognitive theory, which fails to come to grips with emotions and the unconscious (Meltzer et al., 1975:84). Selected ideas from psychoanalytic theory (Chodorow, 1978; Lynn, 1959;1969) supplement Mead's framework. Symbolic interactionism suffers from a masculine bias. Gilligan's (1982) work provides some remedy at the chapter's end. As a social psychological theory, symbolic interactionism tends to be ahistorical, apolitical, and non-economic (Meltzer et al., 1975:97). As a result, its concepts do not deal adequately with the mechanisms and dynamics of social change (Gould and Kern-Daniels, 1977:185). Though our socialization focus precludes thoroughgoing analysis of these large-scale matters, recognition of their parameters is provided by the sociology of knowledge, which was considered at length in Chapter 2.

The Sociology of Knowledge and Symbolic Interactionism

How do symbolic interactionism and the sociology of knowledge fit together? What similarities and differences exist between these two general frames of reference? The sociology of knowledge is not an inclusive theoretical perspective of the same order of abstraction and generality as symbolic interactionism (or Marxian conflict theory, from which most ideas of the sociology of knowledge derive). Rather, the sociology of knowledge is best viewed as a few powerful ideas that have proven useful for thinking about many different sociological problems (Wolff, 1959:570). Also, symbolic interactionism and the sociology of knowledge spring from different philosophical and national roots. To borrow Huston's (1983:396) metaphor, although the two perspectives "do have fundamentally different roots somewhat like two trees growing on opposite sides of a road," they have grown closer together with time. Now, "their branches reach across to meet one another." In the present context, it can be said that while the two traditions have enough in common to make them compatible orientations for one book, they have sufficient complementary differences to avoid redundancy.

Most important for present purposes, both perspectives focus upon thought and its social linkages. The sociology of knowledge "attempts to draw the line from the thought to the thinker to his [her] social world" (Berger, 1963:111). Similarly, symbolic interactionism is preoccupied with these six questions: (1) What is meaning?; (2) How does personal life take on meaning?; (3) How does meaning persist?; (4) How is meaning transformed?; (5) How is meaning lost?; (6) How is meaning regained? (Stone and Farberman, 1970:1). Both perspectives posit a dialectic between individual and society (Berger and Luckmann, 1966:194).

The two approaches, however, have different explanations for the emergence of "reality." For interactionists, meaning is jointly constructed by interacting individuals. Alternatively, meaning derives from an inherited, socially constructed, cultural residue. Although Mannheim (1936:31) did write that "knowing is fundamentally collective knowing," sociologists of knowledge tend to emphasize the subcultural, institutional, and socio-historical context of thought. The critical difference is the delimited *situational* focus of the interactionists versus the *social structural* emphasis of sociologists of knowledge. Berger and Luckmann (1966:193-194) note:

> The failure to make the connection between Meadian social psychology and the sociology of knowledge, on the part of the symbolic-interactionists, is of course related to the limited "diffusion" of the sociology of knowledge in America, but its more important theoretical foundation is to be sought in the fact that both Mead himself and his later followers did not develop an adequate concept of social structure.

Because sociologists of knowledge recognize the importance of hierarchy in social life, their treatment of social structure is superior to symbolic interactionists' endeavors. Sociologists of knowledge contend that "the essential structure of society has a materialistic base which is lodged in massive and powerful social institutions, namely, political, military, and economic institutions" (Maines, 1981:462).

As mentioned above, theoretical perspectives often compensate one another's strengths and weaknesses. Such is the case here. Symbolic interactionists counterbalance the more adequately drawn picture of social structure by sociologists of knowledge with their own more sensitive portrayal of the individual. Interactionists view people as rational, creative beings who enjoy a measure of autonomy. By contrast, the nature of individual subjectivity is not developed systematically in Marxism, the theoretical source of the sociology of knowledge (Ropers, 1973). Indeed, Marxism assumes nothing happens to people before they get their first jobs (Jaggar, 1986). Sociologists of knowledge have a more deterministic image of the individual (Wolff, 1959:581). Although the Marxist tradition and its offshoot, the sociology of knowledge, convey a general concern about human suffering, the largely irrational individual is a dupe of societal forces. According to Fromm (1961:20-21), Marx "believed that most of what men consciously think is 'false' consciousness, is ideology and rationalization; that the true mainsprings of man's actions are unconscious to him."[5] Men (and women) smarten up considerably with the coming of class (and gender) consciousness.

Relatedly, symbolic interactionism is better prepared than Marxism and the sociology of knowledge to see things from research subjects' point of view, to avoid imposing intellectuals' predetermined definition of *their* situation. For example, full-time housewives may be labeled as "oppressed proletariat" and whatever contentment they derive as "false consciousness." Symbolic interactionists understand that sociologists' theories may not exhaust *their* reality. They take people at their word. Sociologists of knowledge, on the other hand, recognize the possibility of self-deception.

The basic compatibility of Mead and Marx, key contributors to interactionism and the sociology of knowledge, is nicely summed up by Anderson (1971:viii), quoted in Ropers (1973):

> At first glance, the juxtaposition of Marx and Mead may strike [scholars] as an anomaly. But as I hope the reader will gather, Marx the social structuralist and Mead the social psychologist can indeed "shake hands" in sociology. Both believe in man as a maker of society and history and share the conviction that free men in life-nourishing groups can build progressively more humane and more just social institutions.

Contemporary scholars, operating in the traditions of Mead and Marx, also believe in woman as "maker of society and history" and as perpetrator of social change. To summarize, the sociology of knowledge and symbolic interactionism, taken together, facilitate an integrated understanding "of the relationship between structural features of our highly organized society and the interpersonal development of sociosexual arrangements" (Gould and Kern-Daniels, 1977:185).

The Timetable of Gender Socialization

Every Canadian child learns society's rules of correspondence between sex and gender, as they pertain to self, others, and relations between self and others. The fundamentals of gender socialization are mastered suprisingly early. Preparatory gender learning begins in the first weeks and months of life (Cahill, 1980:126). The child's interaction with care givers begins immediately after birth and thereafter "every succeeding exchange between the child and the mother can be viewed as an instance of socialization" (Lindesmith et al., 1977:313). The groundwork for both gender identity and language is well established between eighteen months and three years (Huston, 1983:407). The age ceiling for sex/gender reassignment procedures for hermaphrodites is generally thought to be one-and-a half years (Money and Ehrhardt, 1972:13). After that, a child already convinced of one gender identity has trouble accepting the other. For this reason, gender relations specialists watch with great interest the case of former Siamese twins, Win and Lin (Chapter 1).

Between three and eight years, children's understanding of gender is greatly elaborated. By the age of three, youngsters show pronounced sex-typing of play activities and interests, and classify themselves, others, and toys according to gender appropriateness. Between three and seven, they show understanding of gender stereotypes and occupational sex-typing and increasingly prefer same-sex peers. Behavioral enactment of subtle personality traits associated with gender occurs somewhat later (Huston, 1983:406–407). Though children's *awareness* of societal stereotypes increases with age well into adolescence, their *acceptance* of stereotypes is "immutable, inflexible, or morally right" appears to decline during middle childhood and adolescence (Huston, 1983:403). Youngsters are concurrently learning about sexuality and relating to members of the other sex.

Children arrive at kindergarten with their ideas about gender already well-established. Richer's (1983) report of "girl germs" in the Ottawa kindergarten (described in Chapter 1) indicates very early acceptance of male superiority by both sexes. Moreover, gender identity is "very solidly entrenched" at this age (Richer, 1979:198). Raphaela Best (1983:59) describes kindergarten registration day of soon-to-be five-year-olds:

> For this special occasion the girls were wearing frilly dresses and polished Mary Jane shoes and had carefully curled hair. They walked proudly and rewarded adults who praised them for their appearance with a pleased smile. "I got this dress for Easter," said one little girl to the teacher who interviewed her. Little boys in long pants, shirts with collars, and, often, bow ties, tried hard to appear manly and masterful. "I'm exceptionally bright," said one of them to the teacher who was interviewing him.

Although these American kids knew next to nothing about reading, writing, and arithmetic, their gender socialization lessons were already well prepared.

Primary gender socialization continues into the teenage years. The volatile period of adolescence is marked by pressure to solve the problems of "Who am I?" and "What shall I become?" At age seventeen, poet Sylvia Plath wrote this passage in her diary:

> There will come a time when I must face myself at last.
> Even now I dread the big choices which loom up in my
> life — what college? what career? I am afraid. I feel
> uncertain. What is best for me? What do I want? I do not
> know (Lifshin, 1982:91).

As adolescents mature into creatures with sharp sexual urges, femininity/masculinity becomes an increasingly important identity. Moreover, the decisions they make at this time carry lifelong consequences, and these decisions are made within the context of society's gender expectations (Mackie, 1979:147).

The gender learning begun in childhood and adolescence is refined, qualified, and rechanneled throughout the life cycle. The secondary socialization and resocialization processes involved will be discussed in Chapter 5. Although every phase of gender socialization deserves close attention, the critical stage is early childhood, "where the taken-for-granted world of meanings about males and females is initially formed" (Richer, 1984:167).

Symbolic Interactionist Views of Self and Identity

Symbolic interactionists argue that the shaping of the self lies at the heart of primary socialization (Stryker, 1981:14). For them, "gender development is one aspect of self development" (Cahill, 1980:123). Therefore, the general pattern of self-development must be considered and the concepts involved specified before turning to the special problem of gender development. Contemporary interactionist analysis rests on the pioneering work of Mead (1934) and Cooley (1902).

The Meaning of "Self"

The newborn infant does not come equipped with a self. Although the infant is born with the physiological potential to reach this goal eventually, the self is acquired, not innate. Mead defined the *self* as that which is an object to oneself. In other words, the self is reflexive. To have a self is to have the ability to think about oneself, to evaluate oneself, and to act socially toward oneself. For most of us, the self is the most fascinating object in the world. We devote considerable time to self-contemplation. We have a high (or low) level of self-esteem. When we congratulate ourselves for an honest act or chastise ourselves for a piece of stupidity, we are acting toward ourselves. It is important to realize that the self is a communicative process, not a "thing." The self is not a substantive entity that dwells behind the eyes or under the heart. Rather, it consists of the processes of thinking and acting toward oneself (Mackie, 1986b).

Acquiring a Self: Basic Assumptions

How does the self become an object to itself? Although this question will be considered in detail in the next section, three key assumptions about self-development will be presented here. First, the ability to act towards oneself as object depends upon the acquisition of language. Thinking (mind), self-reference, and connection to the external world of people and physical things all become possible with language. Language is the way society "gets into" children and transforms them into moral beings. In short, language is the primary vehicle of socialization.

Second, the self is social: it emerges out of interaction with significant others. *Significant others* are socialization agents who are emotionally important to the child, such as the parents. Cooley (1902) used the metaphor of the *looking-glass self* to illustrate his point that children acquire a self through adopting other people's attitudes towards them.

> As we see . . . our face, figure, and dress in the glass,
> and are interested in them because they are ours, and
> pleased or otherwise with them according to as they do
> or do not answer to what we should like them to be; so
> in imagination we perceive in another's mind some
> thought of our appearance, manners, aims, deeds,
> character, friends, and so on, and are variously affected
> by it.
> A self-idea of this sort seems to have three principal
> elements: the imagination of our appearance to the other
> person; the imagination of his judgment of that appear-
> ance; and some sort of self-feeling such as pride or
> mortification (Cooley, 1902:184).

In other words, children's selves reflect interpretations of others' appraisals of what kind of person they are. These interpretations may or may not be accurate. Mead's (1934) more sophisticated ideas about self-development incorporate Cooley's insights.

Third, both language and acquisition of a self require role-taking. In order to communicate with another person, it is necessary to take the role of the other, to adopt the other's point of view about what is being said. Suppose you greet me Monday morning by asking, "How are you?" Before I can properly reply, I have to put myself in your shoes and decide whether you really want to hear all about my physical and psychological well-being or whether you are merely being polite. In the first case, I will tell you at great length how I am feeling. In the second, I will answer, "Fine, thank you" (Mackie, 1986b).

The development of the self requires this ability to take the role of the other, which is a fundamental aspect of language use. Because the self is social, the child must be able to adopt the perspective of other people toward herself or himself. Having a self means viewing yourself through the eyes of other people.

In the child's early years, self-development involves taking the role of significant others. Eventually, the child is able to take the role of what Mead (1934) called the *generalized other* — the generalized standpoint of society as a whole. The generalized other "is not a concrete, specific other person, but an abstract other — one's conception of the ideal expectations to which one is subject" (Hewitt, 1984:84). Instead of a child thinking, "Mom says I mustn't cry when I don't get my own way," the more mature youngster can now think, "*They* say boys mustn't cry." In a complex society such as Canada, there is not just one generalized other, but many. While some norms and values represent the perspective of society as a whole, others are more particularized. The concept *reference group* incorporates the notion that the individual may take the role of many groups (Hewitt, 1984:84). A reference group is defined as "that group whose perspective constitutes the frame of reference of the actor" (Shibutani, 1955). Reference groups need not be membership groups. Also, the source of the perspective is sometimes a reference individual, rather than a group.

The "I" and the "Me"

Mead's (1934) self encompasses both a socially defined aspect and a spontaneous, creative aspect. The *Me* represents internalized societal attitudes and expectations. The *I*, on the other hand, is the acting, unique, unfettered self. Unlike the battling Id, Ego, and Super-ego in psychoanalytic theory, the "I" and "Me" collaborate. The "I" provides individuality and initiative for behavior, while the "Me" provides direction for this behavior, according to the dictates of society. Remember, though, that the self is a process and that "I" and "Me" are phases of that process, states of consciousness, not concrete entities.[6]

The "I" – "Me" distinction points to an important feature of the symbolic interactionist view of the relation between individual and society. "Human conduct is novel as well as routine, innovative as well as conforming" (Hewitt, 1984:74). The self is composed not only of the pliant "Me," but the nonconforming "I." Here is a fictional father's conversation with his grown son about gender socialization that apparently did not "take:"

> "You were the scrawniest baby I've ever seen in my life. For the first three months you cried without stopping. It's a wonder that didn't drive your poor mother absolutely crazy. Then you grew up to be the scaredy-cattest kid in the neighborhood. I used to think sometimes you caught it from your mother.
> "You were afraid of the dark. You were afraid of loud noises; you used to hold your fingers in your ears at baseball games and you'd stuff cotton in them on the Fourth of July. You were afraid to ride a bike, to roller-skate, even to swim. I don't think you learned swimming till you were over thirteen years old.
> "And you were afraid of all the other kids on the block. You'd come running home with some little kid half your size chasing you. That's how you learned to run, running away from everybody.
> "I was sure you'd never learn to take care of yourself; that you'd live with us all your life. I remember being so embarrassed because you were one of the world's worst baseball players.
> "And you grew so fast, early. For a while, when you were about ten or twelve, you were a head taller than anybody in your class. This made it worse. Little kids would take turns beating up on you so they could say they licked the big sissy down the block. Summers, you spent your time hiding in the cellar, on the porch reading or later fooling around with your birds. Sometimes I look at you now and I can't believe it's the same person."
>
> (From *Dad* by William Wharton. Copyright © 1981 by William Wharton. Reprinted by permission of Alfred A. Knopf, Inc.)

Stages of Self-development

According to Mead (1934), the genesis of the self occurs through three sequential stages, in which each phase makes possible the one that follows.

1. During the *Preparatory Stage*,[7] the child is on the verge of being able to take the role of the other (Meltzer, 1978:18). He/she imitates the behavior of significant others, but has no real understanding of this behavior, e.g. a small boy babbling into his Fisher-Price car-shaped toy telephone. During the Preparatory Stage, the child begins to acquire the necessary linguistic skills, including a name, to differentiate self from other objects in the environment. Role playing is incipient.

2. In the *Play Stage*, the child begins actual role playing. The little girl pretends she is a mother or supermarket cashier or the Cookie Monster. What is important here is that the child is demonstrating the

ability to adopt the mother's role (as one example), and to act back on herself from the perspective of this role. In pretending that she is the mother admiring her imaginary child's pretty dress, the little girl is placing herself in her own mother's shoes and reacting to her own behavior. This type of play indicates that the self is forming. However, according to Mead, the self at this stage lacks integration. Because the child is capable of taking the role of only one person at a time, the reflected view of the self is a series of fragmentary views of significant others.

3. A coherent self develops during the *Game Stage*, when the child becomes capable of taking a number of roles simultaneously. Mead used the game of baseball to explain this process. (Note Mead's choice of a masculine game as analytic device.) Playing baseball requires the ability to adopt several roles at the same time. Being a catcher involves understanding the roles of pitcher, shortstop, opposing team member up to bat, and so on. The events in a particular game must be understood from all of these various perspectives. The child manages this task by forming a composite role out of all the particularized roles. In other words, the child now views herself or himself from the perspective of the generalized other.

Although symbolic interactionists do not fix specific age levels to the above phases (Denzin, 1972), the research findings of developmental psychologists establish appropriate age parameters. The Preparatory Stage covers roughly the first two years of life, the Play Stage the intervening period until the child enters school, and the Game Stage from age six or seven until puberty. Nevertheless, because of individual, subcultural, and cultural variability, these age ranges should not be taken too literally.

Identity

Contemporary analysts have elaborated upon Mead's (1934) "self" to produce the concept of "identity." The "Me" aspect of the self reflects society. (Recall the looking-glass self.) Since modern society is exceedingly complex, interactionists regard the self as differentiated into *identities* (Stryker, 1981:23). Put another way, identities are "sub-units of the global concept of self" (Burke, 1980:18, original emphasis deleted). More specifically, identities are internalized positional designations. *Position* refers to any socially recognized category of actors (boy, mother, farmer, Presbyterian). *Role,* the linking concept between personality and social structure, refers to the behavioral expectations attached to position (what boys, mothers, farmers, Presbyterians are supposed to do) (Stryker, 1980:57). Goffman (1971:189) says:

> By "social identity," I mean the broad social
> categories . . . to which an individual can belong and be

seen as belonging: age-grade, sex, class, regiment, and so forth.

The individual's placement in these categories simultaneously involves self-identification and identification by other people. Possessing a given identity means that the person is situated by himself/herself and by others in those social terms (Stone, 1962:93).

Significant Others' Stance Towards the Child

Already Socialized Care Givers

The child's acquisition of gender identity requires interaction with significant others. Therefore, it's worth knowing what is on the minds of these significant others. As well-socialized adults, gender matters a great deal to them. They come to child rearing, equipped with gender stereotypes and gender role attitudes. According to research, these views come into play very soon after gender attribution is made of their newborn child. Rubin et al. (1974) interviewed 30 pairs of parents at a Boston hospital within 24 hours of the birth of their first child. Fifteen of the couples had daughters and fifteen had sons. Infant girls were described by the parents as "softer," "finer-featured," "littler," and "prettier," boys as "bigger," "stronger," "firmer," and "more alert." Although males are generally slightly longer and heavier at birth (Barfield, 1976), the hospital records showed that these particular male and female infants did not differ whatsoever in birth length, weight, or health. Throughout childhood, it is the fathers who are most concerned about the sex appropriateness of their children's behavior (Maccoby, 1980:240).

Care givers also come to child rearing handicapped with what Mannheim (1952) called the *problem of generations*.[8] By this, he meant that a generation constitutes a social location, like a social class. Individuals who have shared the same experiences during their formative years, throughout life share characteristics and distinctive thoughtways which demarcate them from other generations. As illustrated by Silverman's (1984) description of frontier childhood, the parental generation's gender notions lag somewhat behind cultural developments. Traditionalism in the socialization process occurs partly because as older persons, the socialization agents find it difficult to revise basic values to which they became committed in their earlier years (Davis, 1940). The "problem of generations" accounts for some of the discrepancy between purposes and functions noted earlier in this chapter. It is one reason why socialization does not always proceed smoothly, why children rebel.

Child-care Experts

Care givers are not left alone to face child rearing. Since the emergence of a "scientific" approach to child raising at the end of World War I (Synnott, 1983:88), Canadian parents have been deluged with magazine and newspaper columns and child-care manuals. Parents have been intimidated by these experts who "contrasted their superior professionalism with parental amateurism." They claimed that the Canadian home was the "most mismanaged and bungled of all human industries" and that Canadian women raised their children "by a rule of thumb that hadn't altered since Abraham was a child" (Strong-Boag, 1982:161). The rapid rise of the child expert is another example of the "takeover" of women's knowledge described in Chapter 2. According to Ehrenreich and English (1978:184–185):

> . . . the child-raising science which developed was a masculinist science, framed at an increasing distance from women and children themselves. It was a science which drew more and more on the judgments and studies of the experts, less and less on the experience of mothers — until . . . it comes to see the mothers not only as the major agents of child development but also as the major *obstacles* to it (emphasis in original).

Dr. Spock's *Baby and Child Care* was originally published in 1946, revised several times, and the best-selling new title since 1895, when best-seller lists began. Spock (1976) explained that the fourth edition attempted to eliminate sexist biases:

> I always assumed that the parent taking the greater share of the care of young children (and of the home) would be the mother, whether or not she wanted an outside career. Yet it's this almost universal assumption that leads to women feeling a much greater compulsion than men to sacrifice a part of their careers in order that the children will be well cared for. Now I recognize that the father's responsibility is as great as the mother's.

In the mid-1980s, experienced women joined professional child-care experts in offering advice. In her book, *What Did I Do Wrong? Mothers, Children, Guilt* (1985), Lynn Caine answers "Probably, less than you think." Fredelle Maynard's *The Child Care Crisis* (1985) is less reassuring, especially for women who must work outside the home. Maynard believes mothers should stay home for the first three years of their children's life. She warns against sexual abuse, hepatitis and neglect of individuality in day-care centers. We know that experts' books are bought by many parents. However, we do not really know how much of their advice is actually heeded.

The Initial State of the Child

The child begins life oblivious to the social world into which it has been born. However, this bundle of potentialities does have the capability to develop language, self, and gender identity. Simply by being human, a strong need emerges before too long to make sense of its cognitive environment. Therefore, the child is an active agent in its own gender development (Cahill, 1980:130). In a sense, the self-motivated child socializes itself.

The world comes to be understood through the development of *schema*, cognitive structures that aid in the processing of information. Since gender is salient in our culture, gender eventually serves as an important schema for understanding self and society. In other words, self mirrors society. Nevertheless, children do not conceptualize reality, including gender, in the same way adults do. Some years must pass before the young person shares with adults the same rules for constructing meaning (Kessler and McKenna, 1978:82, 96). These ideas are drawn from the work of cognitive developmental theorists (Piaget, 1928; Kohlberg, 1966).

The Development of Gender Identity

The development of gender identity is traced below in terms of Mead's (1934) stages of selfhood. Gender learning has been described as "the single most potent and long-lasting aspect of the socialization process" (Katz, 1979:4). However, keep in mind that there are other dimensions of primary socialization, such as the development of morality and self-control. Also, the "stages" and "phases" of socialization are themselves social constructions or tools for understanding gender development. Therefore, they should not be reified.

The Preparatory Stage

The Acquisition of Language and Self. Although the infant's adult socializers place it in a gender class at birth, some time must pass before the child is aware of itself or its gender. At first, the baby has no conception of what belongs to its body and what does not:

> At six or eight months he has certainly formed no clear notion of himself. He does not even know the boundaries of his own body. Each hand wandering over the bedspread for things which can be brought into the mouth discovers the other hand and each triumphantly lifts the other into his mouth; he draws his thumb from his mouth to wave it at a stranger, then cries because the

> thumb has gone away. He pulls at his toes until they
> hurt and does not know what is wrong (Murphy et al.,
> 1937, quoted in Lindesmith et al., 1977:315-316).

Language, self, and social awareness are all acquired concurrently. Language provides names for self, others, and environmental objects. Names permit the child both to differentiate itself from other objects and to participate in group life. It is almost impossible to exaggerate the import of language. Since the structure and content of language semantically derogate women (Schulz, 1975), language itself has a subtle, but profound effect on the child's eventual comprehension of gender.

Let's begin at the beginning with an infant who lacks language. Though experts find it difficult to establish how the child obtains its earliest symbols, some "initiative" seems required of the child: "parents imitate the noises and sounds of their very young children in greater degree than these children imitate the noises and sounds of parents" (Stone, 1962:105). Through babbling, the infant accidently hits on a word-like sound ("ma-ma"). Impressed care givers imitate the word. Through repetition, the sound becomes a significant symbol in parent-child interaction. Gradually, the child learns to imitate adult sounds and to associate sounds with sensations. The child has made two momentous discoveries: things have names; *he* or *she* has a name (Hewitt, 1984:96-97)!

Names are extremely important. Even before the child's birth, parental speculations on its sex are usually linked with the choice of a name (Wolfenstein, 1968:268-269). A name individualizes the infant and classifies it by gender. That is, baptizing a child "Karen Jill" simultaneously separates this infant from other infants and indicates its femaleness. According to Sherif (1982:378), "the earliest self-identification with a gender label may be no more complicated than accepting one's own name." Later, the child may be subtly influenced by the gender connotations of names:

> Male names tend to be short, hard-hitting, and explosive
> e.g., Bret, Lance, Mark, Craig, Bruce, etc. When the
> given name is multisyllabic (e.g., Benjamin, Joshua,
> William, Thomas), the nickname tends to imply hardness
> and energy (e.g., Ben, Josh, Bill, Tom, etc.). Female
> names, on the other hand, are longer, more melodic, and
> softer (e.g., Deborah, Caroline, Jessica, Christina) and
> easily succumb to the diminutive *ie*-ending form (e.g.,
> Debbie, Cary, Jessie, Christy). And although feminization
> of male names (e.g., Fredericka, Roberta, Alexandra) is
> not uncommon, the inverse rarely occurs (Richardson,
> 1981:46).

(See Rickel and Anderson, 1981.) By repeatedly asking, "What's that? What's that?," the child learns the names of things. Care givers answer, "That's a cat. That's a chair. That's Daddy." The child's own name allows differentiation of self from all other objects in the environment. At some primitive level, the child reasons: "That is a cat. That is a chair. I am Oliver."

> By hearing his name repeatedly the child gradually sees himself as a distinct and recurrent point of reference. The name acquires significance for him in the second year of life. With it comes awareness of independent status in the social group (Allport, 1961:115).

The appearance of pronouns in the child's vocabulary also suggests a growing awareness of self-as-a-distinct object (Denzin, 1972:307). "I" and "mine" versus "you" and "yours" indicates awareness of boundaries.

As the next step in the genesis of self, children learn not only that "things have names" but "names have things" (Lindesmith et al., 1977:289). In other words, children come to appreciate the characteristics of objects, including themselves. A kitten is a soft, four-legged creature with a miaow and a tail. A fire is red, hot, and dangerous. Oliver is a fat, little butterball, who hates spinach, whines sometimes, but is a very good boy. Later on, mastering the "things of names" also entails learning the meaning of abstract terms, whose meaning cannot be grasped by pointing to an example in the environment (e.g. God, playing fair, being ladylike).

Care Givers' Differential Treatment of Girls and Boys. Four steps may be isolated in the formation of gender identity (Cahill, 1980):

(1) Care givers define female and male infants differently.
(2) Care givers act differently towards female and male babies.
(3) Care givers use sex-designating labels ("girl," "boy") with gender distinctive interaction with the child.
(4) Children respond to themselves as significant others respond to them (the "looking-glass self").

As a result, a child learns, for example, that he is a boy, that boys are valuable, tough, and so on, and that gender is a matter of consequence in Canadian society.

Many studies show that parents hold gender-stereotyped perceptions, expectations, and values for their children (Huston, 1983:429). (See Rubin et al., 1974, described above.) As a result, they treat their daughters and sons differently (Block, 1978). For example, through clothing choice, parents announce their child's gender. Stone (1962:105-106) observes that

> . . . dressing the child in blue invests the child with
> masculinity; in pink, with femininity. In this way, the
> responses of the world toward the child are differentially
> mobilized. The world handles the pink-clad child and the
> blue-clad child differently. The pink-clad child is *identified*
> differently. It is "darling," "beautiful," "sweet," or
> "graceful;" the blue-clad child is "handsome," "strong,"
> or "agile." (Emphasis in original.)

Unisex baby clothing has become more common since Stone made his remarks in 1962. Nevertheless, stores still contain racks of clothing easily identified as masculine or feminine, and few people have the courage to present a newborn boy with pink clothing.

Middle-class parents are apt to decorate rooms to match their infant's sex. A female infant's room is more likely to be decorated in pink, with soft ruffles, or flowers. Soft-bodied stuffed animals, kittens and lambs, watch over her as she sleeps. "Thus, the experience of being a female infant includes a physical environment that is generally 'softer' in terms of colors, objects, and handling . . ." (Katz, 1979:13).

Do parents *interact* differently with their female and male children? Although there appear to be few consistent behavioral differences between infants during the early months of life (Maccoby and Jacklin, 1974), more verbalization is directed towards boys. During the second year of life, parents interact more with girls. The girls are encouraged to spend more time touching and staying near mothers, while boys are left alone more and punished more (Huston, 1983; Lewis, 1972). Sex-typed parental treatment is summarized by Bronfenbrenner (1961:260):

> With sons, socialization seems to focus primarily on
> directing and constraining the boys' impact on the
> environment. With daughters, the aim is rather to protect
> the girl from the impact of the environment. The boy is
> being prepared to mold his world, the girl to be molded
> by it.

As children mature, care givers attend to traits central to gender stereotypes. They encourage "appropriate" gender traits and punish "inappropriate" traits (Williams and Best, 1982:18). The child hears such expressions, as, "You're a pretty girl," or "That's a big boy," associated with this different behavior. These expressions "serve as signs leading to self-identity much as a name does" (Hartley, 1964:5).[9]

As Lewis (1972:56), notes, "what the parent does to the infant, the infant is likely to do back." In other words, the child views herself/himself through the eyes of significant others. Gender matters greatly to care givers. Now, gender also matters to the child. Nonetheless, at the end of the Preparatory Stage, the child's grasp of gender is still quite amorphous.

The Play Stage

As Stone (1962:104) observes, "prior to entering the stage of play, . . . the child must have acquired a rudimentary language at least." This stage begins at approximately three years and ends with entry to grade school. During the Play Stage, the child's greater linguistic and role-taking capabilities result in further self-development. In Mead's (1934) terms, facility with language makes possible the internalized "I" – "Me" dialogue that is the process of the self. So far as gender identity is concerned, "progress" of two sorts is made. The gender schema — the meaning of girl/boy as an organizing concept — becomes more sophisticated. Moreover, this cognitive development is accompanied by enhanced competence in gender expression (Cahill, 1980), and consequently, increased sex differences in behavior (Katz, 1979).

The idea of play was used metaphorically by Mead (1934) to indicate that the child's playful taking the role of significant others resulted in the incorporation of the perspectives of these others into the "Me." Contemporary socialization experts also regard children's play as a very serious matter (Stone, 1970). Denzin (1975:475) asserts that "play constitutes the most important interactional experiences of the young child." As a result, "play, both solitary and conjoint, is the most important mechanism in the learning of gender expression" (Cahill, 1980:32). Play mirrors societal organization. Children learn that adult females and males play different roles (mother, father) with distinctive expressive styles (warm mother, authoritative father).

Imperfect Gender Schema. The child enters the Play Stage able to categorize self and other as boy or girl and showing preference for either "boy" or "girl" toys and activities. The child, in effect, thinks "I am a girl. Therefore, I want to do girl things" (Kohlberg, 1966:89). This knowledge helps children to comprehend the world and motivates them to seek further understanding. However, youngsters this age do not yet interpret gender in the same way adults do. For one thing, they do not regard gender as a constant. A little girl may talk about being a Daddy when she grows up. A nursery school teacher reported that the favorite joke of her three-year-old charges involved gender change:

> Saying to a girl, "You're a boy," and to a boy, "You're a girl," represented the height of wit for these three-year-olds. It was a particularly good joke when the boy who had started it one day said to the teacher: "You're a boy" (Wolfenstein, 1968:268).

Joking reassignment of names also plays on the uncertainty of gender identity. The child says to Billy, "You're Carol," and to Carol, "You're Billy." Both feel threatened and affirm their own name. "No, I'm Billy. I'm a *boy!*" (Wolfenstein, 1968:270).

Children's unsophisticated views of gender are also reflected in the criteria they employ to differentiate the sexes. They cite clothing, hair length, and urination posture in gender attribution. Even towards the end of the Play Stage, genitals and sexuality are confusing to them. Lindesmith et al. (1977) tell the story of their five-year-old acquaintance who attended a party at which children of both sexes bathed in the nude. "When asked how many boys and how many girls were at the party, she answered: 'I couldn't tell because they had their clothes off'" (p. 374). Similarly, Richmond-Abbott (1983:104–105) relates the following incident:

> At one family gathering at which the author was present, a five-year-old boy had just been told by his parents that boys had penises and that girls did not and this was the way you told one from the other. [Notice that the child has *not* been told that girls have vaginas.] He went around the room of fully clothed adults and tested his new knowledge by pointing to each one in turn and saying, "You are a boy, so you have a penis; you are a girl in a skirt, so you don't have one." He waited until each person gave the answer that told him he was right, and when he had made the full circuit of the room, he walked off satisfied. Later, the mother confessed that he was still not sure of the permanence of these characteristics. He had told her that afternoon, "When you grow up, you can be a boy and ride a bicycle like daddy."

By the age of five or six years, children learn gender constancy (Katz, 1979:15). They achieve this understanding at the same time they appreciate the constancy of objects, e.g. that a kite doesn't shrink when it gets farther away (Richmond-Abbott, 1983:105). As mentioned in Chapter 3, children have a good knowledge of gender stereotypes by six to eight years. Solitary and group play both contribute to this gender learning.

Toys. Sex-typed playthings provide children with raw material for fantasy role playing. Up to age two, children receive many of the same toys (teddy bears, blocks, educational toys). However, during the Play Stage, care givers' choice of toys reinforces their gender expectations. Rheingold and Cook (1975) inventoried the bedrooms of middle-class children and concluded that parents provided different environments for girls and boys. Boys' rooms contained more vehicles, sports equipment, art material, construction and military toys. Their rooms contained toys of more categories. Indeed, research shows that boys are given better, more expensive toys (Sutton-Smith, 1979:237). Rheingold and Cook (1975) found that girls' rooms contained more dolls and miniature domestic equipment.

Sex-typed toys, especially those promoted on TV (Ruble et al., 1981), facilitate traditional gender role playing. "Boy toys . . . encourage rougher play, activity, creativity, mastery, and curiosity; girl toys, on the other hand, encourage passivity, observation, simple behaviour and solitary play" (Ambert, 1976:71). The boy, equipped with lego blocks, chemistry set, and computerized robots, imagining himself as construction worker, scientist, or spaceman, acts toward himself as a male in many adult statuses. The girl, nurturing her Cabbage Patch or Strawberry Shortcake doll, is the perpetual mommy. Indeed, a girl spends more years playing with her dolls than her mother spends with her babies (Rossi [1964], cited in Richardson [1981:57]).[10] In general, preschool girls' play shows more "home-centered affiliative interests," involving dolls, while boys' play shows more "villainous danger-centered interests," involving vehicles and guns (Sutton-Smith, 1979:239). As a male university student remarked, "I had 'action figures' when I was a kid. G.I. Joe killed Ken almost every day." Here, we see the split between domestic and public spheres. These generalizations do not, of course, hold for all households. For example, children in mixed-sex families will be exposed to more other-sex toys.

Chapter 6 discusses the role of television and storybooks in gender socialization.

Considerable research shows that children actively *prefer* "sex-appropriate" toys. They don't simply play with the sex-typed toys that care givers provide. By nursery-school age, boys placed in a situation where many toys are available will choose toy cars, trucks, and airplanes. Girls choose dolls, domestic equipment, and crayons (Maccoby, 1980:212). Same-sex bias is also involved. For example, Katz and Zalk (1974) found that little girls invariably preferred girl dolls to boy dolls, and attributed positive characteristics to girl dolls and negative ones to boy dolls. Laws (1979:248-249) cites research that found boys avoided an attractive but "sex-inappropriate" toy to a greater degree than girls did, especially when the experimenter was present, and that boys showed more reluctance to play the role of a girl in a "pretend" telephone conversation. Similarly, a Canadian study (Berger and Gold, 1976) of problem-solving performance in young children reported that boys have a greater need to separate themselves from opposite-sex activities than do girls. Dichotomization apparently plays an important role in gender learning. In the words of Katz (1979:14),

> Children categorize themselves not only in terms of what
> they are but in terms of what they are not. If girls are
> good, then boys must be bad. If girl dolls are pretty,
> then boy dolls must be ugly.

Despite the similarity of the sexes and the physical inaccuracy of referring to the "opposite sex," children learn as a *social* fact that male equals not-female, and vice versa.

Same-sex Play. Do girls and boys play in different ways (Maccoby, 1980:212-217)? For the first two years of life, their play patterns are similar. However, in the third year, children show strong preference for same-sex playmates. (Richer [1984] observed the emergence of same-sex preference a year later.) One interesting study (Jacklin and Maccoby, 1978) placed previously unacquainted 33-month-old children in a playroom. Adult observers could not identify the sex of these children, who all wore pants and T-shirts. However, the babies themselves somehow "knew" and directed more social behavior towards playmates of the same sex.[11] Apparently, very young boys do "something" that makes other babies wary. Other male babies find this "something" exciting and their tendency to withdraw is counterbalanced with positive attraction. The girls are less interested and retreat (Maccoby, 1980:215).

The strength of these same-sex choices is shown by a study of pre-school teachers' attempts to shift children in the direction of more mixed-sex play. Serbin et al. (1977) first observed children engaged in spontaneous, same-sex play. Then, for a ten-day period, teachers reinforced play with an other-sex child with extra approval and attention. Cross-sex play increased steadily during this ten-day period. However, when the reinforcement was discontinued, the children soon returned to their earlier sex-segregated choices (Maccoby, 1980:214).

Gender-differentiated Play. The play of young girls and boys differs qualitatively. Boys engage in much more friendly rough-and-tumble and aggressive play than girls. Struggle for dominance also occurs more frequently in boys' play groups (Maccoby, 1980:216). Social play involves negotiation: What shall we play? How shall we play it? Striking sex differences exist in how these negotiations are carried out. Boys shout, quarrel, and make "facial gestures" (heads up, chins thrust out). Girls avoid physical power tactics and resort to exclusion ("You can't play with us!") (Sutton-Smith, 1979:241-242).

Gender Roles in Play. These questions are critical from the symbolic interactionist perspective: when children are left alone, do they actually adopt gender roles spontaneously? If so, do they play sex-appropriate roles, or do children of both sexes adopt female and male roles equally often? Answers to these queries are provided by Greif's (1976) observational study of same-sex and mixed-sex pairs of pre-school children, engaged in free play in a room well stocked with toys.

Greif (1976) concluded that gender role playing appears spontaneously in a free play situation. Children three-and-a-half to four-and-a-half years old spent 5 percent of their time playing gender roles. For children aged four-and-a-half to five-and-a-half, the amount of gender play increased sharply to 22 percent. Moreover, the roles adopted were mostly sex-appropriate. Popular roles for boys were father, son, husband. Mother, daughter, wife and baby were played exclusively by females. The children were aware of the complementarity of roles.

For example, one four-and-a-half year old girl interrupted her house-cleaning activities to say to her male playmate, "Don't forget to take your lunch, husband" (p. 387). Likely because these children already grasped the greater power and prestige of male roles, most role reversals involved little girls who wanted to play male roles:

> In one case, an aggressive five-year-old girl persisted in labelling her male playmate "mother." He was quite upset, and kept protesting that he wasn't mother, but was father. His playmate reluctantly relinquished the role of father only when he threatened to tell on her if she continued calling him mother (Greif, 1976:390)!

According to informal reports of 1980s play, familial roles are still spontaneously adopted. However, some change may be occurring in the content of the roles. For example, miniature "fathers" are now more interested in tending "babies."

From the symbolic interactionist point of view, the Play Stage serves two socialization functions (Stone, 1970:546-549). Through the drama of play (nurse, cowboy, creature from outer space), the child gets "outside" herself/himself and comprehends self from another perspective. In addition, some play serves as a vehicle for anticipatory socialization as children rehearse roles (pupil, parent, spouse) they will encounter later in life. During the Play Stage, youngsters experience in fantasy both the self as gendered being and the gender-based social organization of adult society. This emphasis on gender is inevitable because, as Stone (1970:552) points out, "much of the drama of childhood replicates the interaction of the larger society in which it occurs."

The Game Stage

Mead (1934) used the game as metaphor to explain the emergence of an integrated self.[12] In contrast to the unstructured, *ad hoc* nature of play, games involve rules. This more sophisticated, rule-bounded activity requires assuming simultaneously the perspectives of several others.

> The child first comes to understand the meaning of a rule — that a rule must be obeyed by all — in a game with others where, if the rules are broken, the game does not function (Coleman, 1976:460).

Analogously, the well-socialized individual comprehends the necessity of obeying societal norms. The looking-glass self (the "Me") now reflects the attitudes of the generalized other. Growing up and participating in games both require more complicated role-playing and role-taking skills. Indeed, many games simulate complex societal activities, such as war (chess, checkers) and commerce (Monopoly). Competition and contest epitomize the game.

The Game Stage (approximately age seven years to puberty) marks important developments in gender socialization. During this phase, girls and boys encounter increasingly divergent expectations from reference persons and groups. Peers and teachers join family members as authorities. Boys and girls have different friendship patterns and different forms of game playing. Consequently, they acquire different sorts of social skills that may well have implications for their later adult behavior. Of overriding importance is the fact that peer activities reinforce the notion that males are superior to females.

Familial Influence. Research in North America and Europe consistently reports these parental differences in gender-relevant socialization (Huston, 1983:430-431). Males, more than females, are encouraged to compete, taught not to cry or express feelings, threatened with punishment, and pressured to conform socially. Females exceed males in receiving affection and trust, and having parents who keep track of their whereabouts and worry about them. Parents have higher expectations for their boys' long-range educational achievement. Parents allow their boys more geographical mobility and more freedom from adult supervision than they do their girls. For example, employed Canadian mothers more often leave their sons than their daughters unsupervised after school (Gold and Andres, 1978). Parents interrupt their girls' speech more often than their boys' (Greif, 1979, cited by Weitzman, 1979:6). Interruptions provide a clear index of perceived power and status. Finally, though little research has been done in this area, it appears that siblings socialize one another.

The School Teacher's Influence. Teachers reinforce the traditional gender norms children learn in the family and neighborhood (Weitzman, 1979:39). Richer's (1979) observational study of Ottawa kindergarten classes shows how the teacher emphasized the gender schema. The teacher found gender to be a practical means to organize the children. For example, children lined up by gender to move from one activity to another — trips to the library, the gymnasium, retrieving food from their lockers, preparing to go home. Also, gender was used to motivate participation: "The girls are ready, the boys are not," or "Who can do it the fastest, the boys or the girls?" During coordination exercises, commands were given by gender: "Boys, put your fingers on your nose; girls, put your hands on your laps; boys, touch your toes." When someone slipped up here, the teacher's admonishment sometimes took this form: "Are you a girl? I thought all along you were a boy." Richer (1979) tells us that such situations left the child squirming with embarrassment. Likely, part of the reason was loss of status associated with his "demotion" from boy to girl. Nevertheless, many studies conclude that teachers prefer "feminine" qualities and behavior, e.g. passive obedience. As a consequence, boys receive more disapproval and scolding from their teachers than girls (Huston, 1983:439), and girls, therefore, find elementary school a more congenial place. Best (1983:61) observed that

> . . . when the boys eagerly ran outside to play, the girls fought among themselves for the "privilege" of staying indoors and helping the teacher . . . . They did such "feminine" tasks as clapping erasers, cleaning art corners and sinks, and straightening up book cases and cupboards. The teacher rewarded the girls by praising them lavishly and admitting that she didn't know what she'd do without them.

Richer (1984) concurs. He suggests that

> . . . as school progresses, boys are increasingly forced to *confront* the school as a group; the boys thereby differentiate themselves both from the school and from the girls, who exhibit considerably greater compatibility with the social demands of public education (p. 177, emphasis in original).

Play and Games. Three preliminary points need to be made. First, most children's play is sex-segregated (Richer, 1984). Same-sex play, which begins early, continues to characterize the seven- to thirteen-year-old children of concern here. Second, following Mead (1934), all children in this age range are considered to be in the Game Stage. However, strictly speaking, boys are more frequently engaged in games and girls in play. Third, children of both sexes evaluate boys' activities and boys more positively than girls activities and girls' (Richer, 1984:167). These remarks are expanded below.

The rare cross-sex play that does occur tends to be immature courtship activity. According to researchers (Richer, 1984; Sutton-Smith, 1979), the most common type is a chasing game, in which girls chase boys and kiss them when they are caught. Richer (1984:168) describes the Ontario "kissing girls" game:

> The game . . . involves any number of girls chasing any number of boys. If the boy is caught a kiss can be given by one or several girls. In a variant of this, several boys might themselves catch one of their number and bring the typically wildly resisting boy to the girls to be kissed. Indeed, the boys often assist in this process by holding their peer down so that he can more easily meet his fate. (The image evoked is that of a sacrificial offering.)

Boys rarely chase girls, and when they do bother, it is to push or pull hair rather than to kiss. According to Richer (1984:169), the game of the seductive chase reinforces traditional gender patterns. This is so both because it demonstrates the greater desirability of males, and because it suggests implicitly that the main impetus for cross-sex interaction is sexual activity.

Despite some evidence that sex differences have lessened in the last thirty years the sex-segregated play of girls and boys takes quite different forms (Eder and Hallinan, 1978; Lever, 1976 and 1978). Girls play indoors more than boys. Girls' activities tend to be private (played behind closed doors), while that of boys is more public. Girls' indoor play is quieter and more restricted in body movement. Girls prefer smaller groups, often a dyad of best friends; boys congregate in larger groups. The size of the play group is influenced by the type of game preferred, as well as the indoor-outdoor setting. Girls prefer activities like tag, hopscotch, jumping rope, Barbie dolls, and conversation. Boys, on the other hand, prefer team sports. The group size has several implications. The larger number of participants needed encourages boys' groups to expand to include newcomers. In contrast, the girls, who tend to engage in more intimate behavior than boys (telling secrets, for example) protect their groups against newcomers. Girls' groups tend to be more age-homogeneous, perhaps because only age-mates can be best friends. But boys' games require many participants. When age peers are scarce, younger children are allowed to join in. "You're better off with a little kid in the outfield than no one at all" (Lever, 1976:480). Finally, boys' larger groups involve hierarchy and dominance behavior (Maccoby and Jacklin, 1974).

In general, girls play and boys game. Boys tend to play competitive games, involving teams of interdependent players with definite and differing roles and specific rules. Hockey is a good example. Such games require coordination of effort and continuous negotiation of rules. Girls prefer turn-taking activities, where each girl skips or bounces a ball. Because of the turn-taking, girls spend considerable time as an audience watching the performer. In contrast, boys all tend to play at the same time (Sutton-Smith, 1979:244). Girls' activities involve indirect competition between individuals, rather than teams. Indeed, girls are less likely to compete at all. Girls prefer to ride bikes, boys to race them. Bodily strength and bodily contact are irrelevant in girls' games. Girls' games provide fewer opportunities for dispute. When a quarrel does break out, girls rarely quarrel over rule interpretation, as boys do. Instead, the game breaks up and the girls go home (Lever, 1976).

Girls participate in predominantly male games more than boys play in girls' games. Boys are likely to need an extra team member from time to time. Also, girls gain prestige from associating with the more highly valued male activities. Boys, on the other hand, are punished for "sissy" behavior. Consequently, when boys do play girls' games, they display *role distance* (Goffman, 1961b). They are there, not as serious role players, but as buffoons or teases, to annoy the girls. However, girls playing boys' games do so as serious participants (Lever, 1976:481).

Finally, the ambience of boys' and girls' play differs. Boys impose a *machismo* code on one another (Best, 1983:22). Be first. Be tough. Defy authority. Don't be a sissy or crybaby. Keep your distance from females of all ages. For example, Firestone (1978:100) writes:

> It is not uncommon anywhere in Newfoundland to see a
> pair of boys facing each other with rocks, alternately
> throwing, and dodging. These duels can themselves be
> seen as the development of an ability to meet attack with
> composure and expectation that one's own hostility will
> be met in the same way.

According to Best (1983:88), "after the almost painful picture of the boys' world and its impact on the rejected boys, entering the girls' world was like moving from a dark and fearful forest into a sunny valley." Not pressured to be "instant women," pre-pubertal girls tend to be adult-oriented, nurturant and affectionate.

Adult Implications of Childhood Games. Boys and girls acquire different sorts of social skills from their childhood games that may well have implications for their sex-differentiated behavior in adulthood.

Girls learn the type of interpersonal skills required by small, intimate groups, such as sensitivity to others' feelings, the ability to disclose information about themselves, and to show affection. Girls learn to converse, to be imaginative, and empathetic. Girls get to know the best friend and her moods so well that "through non-verbal cues alone, a girl understands whether her playmate is hurt, sad, happy, bored . . ." (Lever, 1976:484). Girls learn to be an appreciative audience, while boys learn to take the stage. Boys learn to coordinate their actions, to cope with impersonal rules, to work for collective as well as individual goals, to negotiate, to deal with competition and criticism.

> Boys must learn to "depersonalize the attack." Not only
> do they learn to compete against friends, they also learn
> to cooperate with teammates whom they may or may not
> like personally (Lever, 1976:485).

Both boys and girls acquire a very strong impression of the sex hierarchy.

It seems reasonable to suppose that this childhood learning serves as anticipatory socialization for the "two worlds" of adulthood. Childhood play equips adult females to deal with people in primary group settings, like the family, but not in secondary group settings where power is wielded and the business of the world conducted (Lever,

1978:482). Boys' games, particularly team sports, provide a learning environment for the cultivation of skills later demanded by bureaucratic work organizations. However, a *macho* boyhood may handicap the expressivity of men in intimate settings. Sutton-Smith (1979:243–244) rephrases the above ideas in terms of sex differences in power. He remarks that one sex can be

> seen as having access to the combat for society's rewards and able to use all its talents in an aggressive way toward that end. The other sex is then seen as learning power restrictions, restrictions on body, on movements, on competition; learning to proceed rather by ritual and in solitary or dyadic setting.

The lessons learned from both male and female play would be valuable to both sexes in adulthood. However, given the present structure of Canadian society, there is no doubt that childhood play handicaps the girls more than the boys.

Symbolic Interactionism as Masculine Perspective

We have used the symbolic interactionist theory of self-development to trace the emergence of gender identity through infancy and early childhood (where the family is the supreme socialization agent) through middle childhood (where the peer group becomes all-important). Female and male children stand poised on the brink of adolescence, characterized by distinctive interpersonal orientations. The girls are concerned with their relationships with others, with communality. The boys are already well-schooled in the skills of instrumentality. Although both sexes understand the "theory" of gender (social norms and stereotypes), each is somewhat mystified and intimidated by the other sex. Sex-segregated play has permitted contrived fictions about the other sex to survive untested.

Does "different" necessarily imply superiority in the case of males and inferiority in the case of females? In the minds of pre-women's movement theorists it certainly did. As the sociology of knowledge would predict, masculine bias colors the reasoning of George Herbert Mead and subsequent symbolic interactionists.[13] Because of these masculine blinders, Mead and his disciples did not have a great deal to say about the experiences of girls and women. However, the chain of their reasoning is unmistakable. Boys emerge from the Game Stage with the ability to take the role of the generalized other, to comprehend the abstractions of social relationships. Girls, on the other hand, have become more and more proficient in taking the role of significant others. In Meadian terms, by not moving on to the level of the generalized other, girls fail the task of the Game Stage. They end up with a self-image lacking in integration and a particularized perspective of themselves and the community. If maleness is accepted as the norm, the female orientation is deficient. Moreover, since the "Me" is internalized societal norms, i.e. conscience, the female sense of morality is defective. Finally, impersonality, competition and power are the rules of the marketplace. Women, lacking instrumental skills, are simply incapacitated for the action that counts.

Gilligan on Moral Development

In 1982, Carol Gilligan published *In a Different Voice,* which argues that the feminine orientation is a *different,* not an inferior, mode of thought. Though psychologist Gilligan doesn't cite Marx or Mannheim, her perspective accords with the sociology of knowledge and the "two worlds" proposition. However, her work has been criticized for sex-typing and paucity of supporting data. (See Kerber et al., 1986.)

Gilligan's (1982:10) work builds upon Lever's (1976) observation (noted earlier) that, "rather than elaborating the rules for resolving disputes, girls subordinated the continuation of the game to the continuation of the relationship." Connectedness with others is all-important to girls and women. Ruptured relationships, power, and aggression all deeply threaten them. Males, on the other hand, see the world in terms of autonomy, hierarchy, and conflict. Intimacy threatens them.[14] Gilligan hypothesizes a different type of morality for each sex. According to her, female morality is the morality of the "web," that is, a morality that emphasizes fulfillment of responsibilities of individuals connecting with one another. In comparison, masculine morality is analogous to a "ladder." In the latter case, morality consists of a hierarchy of fundamental rights and freedoms that regulate the behavior of independent, competitive individuals. Females, then, have different, but not less mature, constructions of moral problems.

The sex differences in moral thought hypothesized by Gilligan are produced by children's early experiences with female caretakers. Girls learn femininity through attachment to the mother, the primary care giver and model in childhood. Boys, however, learn masculinity through separation from the mother figure (Chodorow, 1974; Lynn, 1959, 1969). An episode from Dr. Benjamin Spock's biography illustrates the role of peers and games in male youth's separation from the mother.

> At Yale, [Spock] took up crew and rowed his way to a gold medal in the 1924 *Chariots of Fire* Olympics. The victory was "of enormous importance," he says, converting an over-protected mama's boy into a confident young man (Leo, 1985:67).

Throughout life, "male gender identity is threatened by intimacy while female gender identity is threatened by separation" (Gilligan, 1982:8). Only from a male vantage point does females' sense of connection to others become construed as failure to develop. Both caring and doing are admirable qualities.

The Outcome of Childhood Gender Socialization Experiences

Gender socialization, play, and games extend beyond childhood into the adolescent and adult years. However, it is useful to pause and compare female and male products of the childhood years. Also, we need to correct possible misinterpretations of our discussion to this point. Symbolic interactionism does not convey the conflict, frustration, and pain that often surround gender socialization. Since gender is a moral fact, it often arouses considerable emotionality in both socialization agents and recipients. Psychoanalytic theory handles these dimensions better than symbolic interactionism.

Girls realize early that they are second-class human beings. Because masculinity is more prestigious, and male activities more interesting, girls adhere less rigidly to gender stereotypes (Lambert, 1971) and sex-typed interests than do boys (Huston, 1983:104). An elderly Alberta woman still resents the injustice of her traditional upbringing:

> We had a cabin up in Banff that my grandfather had
> built. All our friends from here would come to visit us,
> and there'd be stacks of dishes. I would be told to go and
> help the hired girl; the boys would never. Or I'd have to
> set the table. "Why can't the boys set the table?" Or the
> boys would be allowed to go somewhere that I wasn't
> allowed to go. I wasn't allowed to have a bicycle, and I
> was so mad . . . . I guess I was expected to sit and play
> the piano, or embroider, or knit, or some damn thing. I
> resisted all along. I should have been a boy (Silverman,
> 1984:28).

Many girls, then and now, pass their childhood as harum-scarum tomboys. Indeed, Hyde et al. (1977) report that 51 percent of an adult women sample claimed to have been tomboys in their childhood. To make things even more confusing, girls are often socialized in a contradictory fashion (Weitzman, 1979:81). Sometimes, they are reinforced for the masculine behavior rewarded by our society, e.g. being athletic or smart. Sometimes, the axe falls when they fail to be demure and ladylike.

More socialization costs lie in the future. Although Canadian girls thrive in elementary school, they "receive less family encouragement to pursue higher education than do boys, but such encouragement, it turns out, is especially critical for girls" (Turrittin et al., 1983). Trained to achieve vicariously through males, girls learn to set aside their own needs and ambitions to help others (Lipman-Blumen, 1984:66). For these and other reasons, females tend to end up in low-skill, low-paying, dead-end jobs. Parents' greater chaperonage of girls is designed to protect them from adult male strangers. However, children "kept under close surveillance may also miss opportunities to develop a sense of their own competence and may incorporate their care givers' fears of venturing out into the wider world" (Huston, 1983:431). Chodorow (1978:212) argues that daughters' "insufficiently individuated sense of self" and separation from others is a lifelong problem.

Part of the pain of being born male comes from the demand to be little men, to be emotionally and physically tough, to compete, to be independent, before boys are developmentally capable of these accomplishments. Boys' uncertainty about what masculinity is all about compounds the problem. The relative absence of the father and the overwhelming presence of the mother arouses anxiety in boys,

> an anxiety which frequently expresses itself in overstraining to be masculine, in virtual panic at being caught doing anything traditionally defined as feminine, and in hostility toward anything even hinting at "femininity," including females themselves (Hartley, 1959:458).

Because of the greater availability of the mother (as well as female substitute care givers) during early childhood, little girls more easily develop their gender identity through imitation and positive reinforcement. However, little boys must shift from their initial identification with the mother to masculine identification.[15]

Unlike girls, boys must learn through abstractly piecing together the intellectual problem of the meaning of masculinity (Lynn, 1959, 1969). The feminized school environment is little help. Learning comes from peers, from mass media, and from punishment for displays of feminine behavior. Masculine behavior is rarely defined positively as something the boy *should* do. One reason is that the male gender role is "so strongly defined in terms of work and sexuality, both of which are usually hidden from the eyes of children" (Colwill, 1982). Instead, undesirable feminine behavior is indicated negatively as something he should *not* do (Hartley, 1959). For example, in toy-choice experiments, boys will avoid playing with lipstick, mirrors, hair ribbons, purses, or nail polish. However, they act as though they are curious about these objects, but must not play with them when anyone is watching

(Maccoby, 1980:238). As a consequence of these childhood experiences, adult males remain anxious about their gender and somewhat hostile towards females and homosexuals. Nevertheless, males learn to prefer the more inflexible, but more prestigious masculine role to the devalued feminine one.

Finally, our discussion of childhood socialization may have given the false impression that people are completely molded by the norms and values of their society (Wrong, 1961). Children are not all identical products turned out by an omnipotent socialization factory. For one thing, human beings possess the ability to question and to innovate. Mead acknowledged the spontaneous, creative "I," as well as the socialized "Me." Individuals make roles, as well as take them. Further, although nearly everyone is socialized within the family, the actual content of socialization varies from family to family. Growing up in a working-class (versus a middle-class) family; in British Columbia versus Quebec; in a one-parent family versus one where both parents are present; these variables and many others make any account of uniform socialization a fiction. By necessity or choice, some of these family experiences blur gender distinctions. Says Lambert (1971:31):

> If sex is a basis of differentiation of each person's duties
> and rights within the family, then we suppose children's
> attitudes toward the sexes will reflect this fact. And if sex
> is unimportant as a basis of role assignment in the
> family, then children will think in "modern" or non-
> differentiated ways. Thus, we make the assumption that
> mind is a derivative of social structure, in this case,
> family structure. We make the further assumption that
> children extrapolate from these experiences to the world
> in general.

Some children are raised in homes where parents take a conscious stance against traditionalism. Sex-typing is neither approved nor modelled and care givers have the courage to risk producing misfits in a sex-typed society. Anthropologist Margaret Mead received early training from her sociologist mother:

> She used to take me to weddings all over South Jersey.
> . . . Most of the women were dabbing tears out of their
> eyes; my mother was always busy taking notes (Howard,
> 1984:22).

However, as the 1990s approach, the evidence does not suggest that substantial numbers of parents are embracing gender transcendence as a goal.

Conclusions

Chapter 4 has applied the principles of Meadian social psychology to the question of the development of gender identity. In directing our attention to such social phenomena as names, the looking-glass self, and childhood play, symbolic interactionism contributes substantially to our understanding of the emergence of femininity and masculinity. Since symbolic interactionism provides sociology's theoretical treatment par excellence of the problems of socialization, it is not surprising that this should be so. However, the symbolic interactionist inference of the underdeveloped feminine "Me" is questioned from the perspective of the sociology of knowledge, and of Gilligan's (1982) work. The rational, conflict-free socialization depicted by the interactionist framework is contradicted by psychoanalytic notions. In an ideal world, both sexes would benefit from the orientation and skills of the other. However, so far as this imperfect world is concerned, females who emerge from childhood without instrumental, achievement skills are "socialized for weakness" (Bernard, 1973:779).

In the next chapter, we return to the themes of gender socialization and content. We focus upon the gender learning of adolescents and the gender resocialization of people later in the life cycle. Symbolic interactionism and the sociology of knowledge continue to provide theoretical guidance.

NOTES

1. Symbolic interactionism is a theoretical perspective in both social psychology and general sociology. Other theoretical orientations in general sociology are structural functionalism, the conflict approach, and ethnomethodology. The last two perspectives are implicated in discussions of the sociology of knowledge in this book.
2. Stryker (1981:28) observes: "Symbolic interactionists have traditionally asserted the uniqueness of the human species, premising their argument on the presumably unique capacities of humans and the emergence of self. That these presumably unique aspects of humans are indeed unique is severely challenged by recent work with chimpanzees. Apart from undergirding an extreme form of denial of the relevance of work on non-human animals for understanding human behavior, however, it is difficult to see what is gained from the assertion of human uniqueness."
3. Symbolic interactionism has been criticized for insufficient attention to the factual underpinnings of definitions of the situation. For instance, the late Donald Ball (1969:5) advised that "if an actor puts his head in a guillotine because he thinks he will get a haircut, the fact that he may lose his head instead is not strictly of interest from this standpoint [symbolic interactionism]."
4. Glaser and Strauss (1967) call for the discovery of "grounded theory" as a way of bridging theory and research. Grounded theory is generated inductively through systematic data gathering, rather than deductively from *a priori* assumptions.
5. Not everyone would agree with Fromm (1961) that the Marxian man/woman is irrational. According to Ropers (1973:43), "Marx saw man as basically a rational purposive producer . . . ."
6. Hewitt's (1984:72) comment may make clearer the "I" – "Me" distinction. "Perhaps the most important (and often misunderstood) of Mead's insights into the self is to be found in his well-known distinction between the 'I' and 'Me.' These personal pronouns...are labels for the two phases of the self as a process. 'I' designates the 'subject' phase of the process, in which people respond as acting subjects to objects or to the

particular or generalized others in their situations. 'Me' labels the 'object' phase of the process, in which people respond to themselves as objects in their situation."

7. The Preparatory Stage was not explicitly named by Mead himself. However, recent scholars have inferred this stage from fragments of Mead's essays (Meltzer, 1978:18).

8. To Mannheim, the critical factor in the "problem of generations" was the common experience of the age-group, not age *per se*. "The fact of belonging to the same generation or age-group and that of belonging to the same class, have this in common, that both endow the individuals sharing in them with a common location in the social and historical process, and thereby limit them to a specific range of potential experiences, predisposing them for a certain characteristic mode of thought and experience, and a characteristic type of historically relevant action" (Mannheim, 1952:291).

9. Although the symbolic interactionist account of gender identity formation asserts that learning takes place, it does not tell us *how* children learn. To understand the mechanisms of learning, we need to consult the social learning theoretical tradition in social psychology.

10. An early *Ms.* magazine article on toys complained about dolls "that frug, burp, cry, wink, and tell time" and asked cynically, "when will they fake orgasms?" (Lyon, 1972:55).

11. Katz (1979:12) reports research that indicates that infants younger than a year make discriminative responses between female and male adults. Cues appear to be voice pitch, handling differences, and odor. As Katz remarks, "infants apparently acquire rudimentary concepts about gender long before they know much else about the world."

12. Cognitive developmentalist Jean Piaget (1932/1965) studied the game of marbles to determine how children develop morality. As Lever (1976:479) points out, Piaget "mentions almost as an afterthought that he did not find a single girls' game that has elaborate an organization of rule as the boys' game of marbles."

13. Freud and Piaget joined Mead in equating child development with male development. Piaget (1932/1965:77) considered that girls' relative disinterest in the elaboration of rules meant that moral development "is far less developed in little girls than in little boys." (See Note 12 above.) Similarly, Freud held that women's anatomical inferiority, their regretable lack of a penis, led to ethical inferiority. Freud said: "I cannot escape the notion (though I hesitate to give it expression) that for women the level of what is ethically normal is different from what it is to men. Their super-ego is never so inexorable, so impersonal, so independent of its emotional origins as we require it to be in men" (quoted in Weyant, 1979:361). This position can, of course, be put to empirical test. Are there sex differences in moral behavior?

14. Although Gilligan (1982) talks about feminine and masculine "voices," she does not claim that these modes of thought are sexually dimorphic. She cautions the reader that "this association is not absolute, and the contrasts between male and female voices are presented . . . to highlight a distinction between the two modes of thought and to focus a problem of interpretation rather than to represent a generalization about either sex" (p. 2).

15. Psychoanalytic theory emphasizes the child's identification with the same-sex parent and relationships with the opposite-sex parent as central mechanisms of gender socialization. Sex-typing and appropriate gender identity are assumed to be necessary for psychological well-being.

5

Gender Socialization in Adolescence and Adulthood

Introduction

> One week after my husband's death I was alone with my children. It takes about the same length of time to be left alone with a new baby to bring up. In the latter case, nerves are offset by joy and anticipation. In the silence following the frenzied activity of funeral arrangements and people dropping in, the sad fact begins to sink in: life will never be the same again. You are definitely alone. With a lot to learn. As one friend put it: it took me twenty years to learn to live with my husband; I wasn't going to unlearn overnight. Neither will you (Wylie, 1982:14).

Gender socialization extends, with variable intensity, from infancy to old age. Although primary socialization lays the foundation for later learning, it cannot completely prepare people for adulthood. For one thing, definitions of the situation alter as a result of economic, technological and demographic trends, and social movements. For another, our age-graded society confronts individuals with new expectations as they move through life. Becoming an adolescent, choosing an occupation, marrying, bearing children, encountering middle age, retiring, and dying all involve new lessons to be learned. All of these experiences impinge differently on females and males. Betty Lou Wylie's (1982) previous years had not prepared her for widowhood. If she had died first, her husband would not have faced identical socialization challenges. Both the "two worlds" of gender and male-female power differentials continue to the grave.

Overview of Post-childhood Socialization

Chapter 5 begins with primary gender socialization in adolescence. "Adolescence" may be variously defined (Rogers, 1981:6ff). Physically, it is the span of life "between the obvious onset of puberty and the completion of bone growth" (Konopka, 1973:292). Chronologically, it is the period between 12 and 18 or 19 years. Socially, *adolescence* is both a rehearsal for adulthood (a period of anticipatory socialization), and a stage in its own right, with a distinctive subculture (Elkin and Handel, 1984:258). Although physical adolescence is as old as the human race, adolescence as a social status is a nineteenth-century invention of Western culture. (See Chapter 3.)

The volatile period of adolescence is marked by pressure to solve the problems of "Who am I?" and "What shall I become?" As youngsters mature into creatures with sexual urges, masculinity/femininity becomes an increasingly central component of identity. The salience of gender is also reinforced from without. Teenagers, especially girls, are exposed to more complex and more precisely defined norms of sex-appropriate behavior than are young children. Decisions are made within the context of societal gender expectations. Many of them carry lifelong consequences (Mackie, 1983b:115–116).

When does adolescence end and adulthood begin? We define *adult socialization* somewhat arbitrarily as socialization occurring after the completion of general education, whether secondary school, college or university (Mortimer and Simmons, 1978:422). From maturity to old age, adult socialization is concerned, directly or indirectly, with sexuality, family, and work. Male ruling ideas define all three areas.

In this chapter as in the last, we follow the symbolic interactionist dictum that people learn who they are and how they ought to behave in interaction with significant others. Our analysis continues to be guided by Mead's (1934) conviction that the emergence of the self through social interaction constitutes the basic socialization process (Bush and Simmons, 1981:140).[1] Since adult socialization is typified by acquisition of role–specific knowledge (Berger and Luckmann, 1966:138), and gender is a feature of self clearly tied to roles, role analysis — role acquisition, role transition, role loss — is central to our discussion. During early adulthood, new roles of paid worker, spouse, and parent are taken on. Late adulthood involves role loss as people retire, spouses depart through divorce or death, and children reach their own adulthood (Sales, 1978:158). We shall be concerned both with the different meaning of these experiences for females and males and the impact of masculine superiority and ruling ideas.

Throughout the chapter, we acknowledge the interactionist tenet that people are active participants in their own socialization,

> . . . that socializees constantly create new meanings,
> develop their own understandings and definitions of the
> situation, and structure ambiguous social settings to meet
> their goals and solve common problems . . . (Mortimer
> and Simmons, 1978:430; emphasis in original deleted).

Voluntarily childless couples, single-by-choice mothers, live-in companions, blended families, female-headed families, gay relationships, lesbian mothers, lifelong singles, and communal families are all examples of recently created meanings of the family. Berger and Luckmann (1966:137) tell us that "socialization is never total and never finished." Though gender socialization continues into old age (albeit at lessened intensity), humans retain some capacity to resist the societal script, to play things their way. All the world may well be a stage. Shakespeare to the contrary, men and women are not *merely* players. Nevertheless, the scriptwriters and stars tend to be men.

Adolescent Gender Socialization

The Challenge of Adolescence

Adolescence has been both romanticized as a period of irresponsible frivolity and deplored as a time of inevitable distress and conflict. Results of a national survey of Canadian teenagers (Bibby and Poster-ski, 1985) contradict the first view. In the words of a sixteen-year-old Ontario girl:

> Teens are expected to feel happy about themselves while enjoying their "carefree" years. These years I find are hard, trying, and painful — it's basically growing up and coming to terms with the fact that you're now almost an adult and can't depend on any one (Bibby and Posterski, 1985:51).

According to official records for 1982, some 1,300 Canadian teenagers killed themselves. Moreover, it is estimated that between 30 and 100 attempts occur for every "successful" suicide (Bibby and Posterski, 1985:69). Although authorities no longer regard "storm and stress" as the hallmark of adolescence,[2] most agree that the years spent in the "uneasy biological borderland between childhood and adulthood" (Berger and Berger, 1984:5) are fraught with challenge. In her famous diary, Anne Frank (1952:41) recorded the exasperation produced by the marginality of this age:

> My treatment varies so much. One day Anne is so sensible and is allowed to know everything; and the next day I hear that Anne is just a silly little goat who doesn't know anything at all and imagines that she's learned a wonderful lot from books. I'm not a baby or a spoiled darling any more, to be laughed at, whatever she does. I have my own views, plans, and ideas, though I can't put them into words yet.

The question "Who am I?" takes on special urgency in adolescence.[3] Pubescent changes (a body growth rate equal to that of early childhood and the new addition of genital maturity) disturb the sense of self established in childhood. The adolescents' task is to re-establish identity: to refine "a sense of who they are and what makes them different from everybody else" (Santrock, 1984:425). Gender identity, an understanding of oneself as a sexually and socially mature male or female, is a fundamental component of this refined identity. Developing a mature gender identity means coming to terms with these issues: physical sexual maturity; relationships with the other sex; future options with regard to vocation and marriage (Katz, 1979:20).

Socialization to function as an adolescent and the anticipatory socialization for adulthood involves learning values, motivations, skills and roles. This learning occurs in interaction with significant others who provide the mirror for the adolescent version of the self. The family remains influential where values and beliefs and future goals and educational aspirations are at stake. However, in matters of current lifestyle (fashion, music, social activities), friends take precedence over family (Davies and Kandel, 1981). Obviously, "the stronger the bonds between parents and children, the more central the parents will be as significant others" (Acock, 1984:160).[4] The sections that follow consider first, gender differences in the identity problems of adolescence, and then, the three issues outlined above as parameters for adolescent socialization in Canadian society.

Gender Differences in the Adolescent Search for Identity

For both sexes, the peak of gender role differentiation occurs in adolescence and early adulthood, "the ages during which the sexes meet for pairing purposes" (Ambert, 1976:81). At no other point in the life cycle are pressures as strong for the female to be feminine and the male masculine. Changes in youngsters' identities occur when significant others fail to validate the old "childish" self-concepts in appropriate ways. However, adolescents too dwell in separate gender worlds; the search for gender identity differs somewhat by sex. Teenagers who do not fit gender stereotypes, physically, sexually, or temperamentally, suffer. However, the indices of pain vary by sex. Childhood emotional disorders are more common in boys than girls. Emotional problems among females increase as they pass from childhood to adulthood. In adolescence, the sex ratio is nearly equal. Although the female suicide attempt rate is the higher, male teenagers succeed in killing themselves more often. More females become anorexic or bulimic. Males have more trouble with alcohol (Al-Issa, 1982). Three major gender socialization differences may be identified: discontinuity; devaluation; and being versus doing.

Discontinuity. More discontinuity exists between girls' gender socialization in childhood and adolescence. During childhood, the male role is the more inflexible. In childhood, young girls are allowed to dress and act like boys. A great many are tomboys (Hyde et al., 1977).[5]

Adolescence usually brings new pressure upon girls to define themselves as gendered persons. When Maria Campbell was a child in northern Saskatchewan, her tomboy activities were reinforced:

> Reward came whenever Daddy would say [to her
> brothers] "Dammit you boys! Maria can do it and she's a
> girl! Can't you do it at least half as good? If you can't, I'll
> send you in with the old ladies and get her to help me!"
> (Campbell, 1973:34).

However, with adolescence came new expectations for this young Métis woman. Maria had a crush on Harold, an older "man" of seventeen. She thought he, too, was interested until this accidental meeting took place:

> [Harold] introduced me to his girlfriend and said, "This
> is Maria. She's the girl I was telling Mom I'd love to have
> for a little sister. She can ride, hunt, shoot and do
> anything a grown guy can do. She's Dannie's daughter." I
> didn't stop to say hello but raced upstairs. I was com-
> pletely heart-broken and swore I would never have
> anything to do with men again. Mom had warned me
> that men liked dainty ladies, not girls who ran wild and
> dressed like boys (Campbell, 1973:95-96).

By comparison, boys, from childhood on, experience unrelenting pressure to be masculine.

Devaluation. Our society's devaluation of females is a second reason for gender differences in adolescent socialization. In Chodorow's (1971:286) words, the "tragedy" of woman's socialization is that her basic identity is "clearly devalued in the society in which she lives." Initially, girls are brought up in the feminine world, where mothers and teachers are powerful and prestigious (Chodorow, 1971:282). With adolescence comes an implicit awareness of society's denigration of females.

Journalist Michele Landsberg (1982:205) describes the initiation rites of a middle-class Toronto high school in which her thirteen-year-old daughter was "invited" to participate:

> The instructions for the initiation were drawn up by the
> school's female gym teachers and sent home on mimeo-
> graphed paper. It seemed that only grade nine girls, not
> boys, had to take part. The girls were to dress up as
> babies, carry rattles, wear diapers over their clothes, and
> crawl around the cafeteria floor saying "goo-goo" as they
> went. As the event transpired, it was an ideal opportu-
> nity for the watching boys to snicker, loll about, and

> pinch girls' rumps as they crawled by. Girls who refused
> to participate were, according to one youngster I spoke
> to, made to go out on the sports field, wear a sign on
> their chest saying "SUCK," and practise that old chestnut
> of an exercise known as "I must, I must, develop my
> bust."

Landsberg's daughter stayed home.

Despite such experiences, only a small minority of young people perceive the inequality of women as an urgent problem (Bibby and Posterski, 1985:152). Young women are at the peak of their power. Most will not fully comprehend the meaning of female subordination until they encounter some of the radicalizing events – abortion, marriage, childbirth, jobs – which sensitize them to gender inequality.

Being versus Doing. A third gender difference in the adolescent search for gender identity may be labeled "being versus doing" (Chodorow, 1971). Let's take the male situation first. Males have to *do* something in order to earn and re-earn masculinity. These five male gender norms specify these expectations (Doyle, 1985:91):

(1) *Antifeminine norm.* Males are admonished never to act in ways that may be interpreted as feminine. If females are stereotyped as emotional, dependent, and nonassertive, males must be the opposite to prove themselves manly.

(2) *Success norm.* Males must strive to outdo others in countless ways, including work, sports, amassing money and/or possessions, drinking, etc.

(3) *Aggressive norm.* Down through the centuries, males have been expected to fight for what they consider right.

(4) *Sexual norm.* Males are defined as the initiators of sex. For many males, sexual conquest is the strongest proof of manhood.

(5) *Self-reliant norm.* Males are supposed to be tough, cool, unflappable. Therefore, they feel pressure to act as if they are in control of themselves and whatever situations they find themselves in.

By contrast, females have traditionally learned two main norms: the "marriage mandate" and the "motherhood mandate" (Doyle, 1985:88). Although most teenagers of both sexes say they plan to work and marry (Bibby and Posterski, 1985), being wives and mothers still takes priority in female self-identification. Girls tend to *voice* the ethic of achievement, but to *plan* marriage (Denmark and Goodfield, 1978:376). In other words, females' gender identity ultimately depends on "being," while males' depends on "doing." Therefore, "our culture puts real pressure on girls to postpone their identity settlements so that they may easily adapt to the requirements of the men they will marry" (Douvan, 1969). For this reason, Sheehy (1974:65) speaks of young women's "complete-me marriages." Though family and symbolic agencies convey these norms, peers are particularly influential significant others.

Adolescent Sexuality and Peer Relationships

Early Adolescence. Youngsters twelve to fifteen years of age must cope with both social and sexual implications of puberty. The peer group is extremely influential in this process. As in childhood, its influence tends to be conservative. Gender-stereotyped behavior is emphasized (Greenglass, 1982:72). Especially for boys, peer acceptance is contingent upon acting out traditional features of male roles, such as being tough and being cool, in exaggerated ways (Doyle, 1983:105). Same-sex friends help teenagers to differentiate themselves from their families. They serve as a comparison group to interpret one's own physical changes (Katz, 1979:18). New roles and new experiences require experimentation. The peer group can provide "a receptive and enthusiastic audience for the testing of ideas that adults might find tiresome or presumptuous" (Bell, 1981:47).

Long before puberty, children are surrounded by allusions to sex – television, movies, billboards, magazine covers. They pick up knowledge and attitudes in their own homes about bodily functions, nudity, modesty, and reproduction:

> "I'm not supposed to talk about people being pregnant."
> Alice folded her hands in her lap and pinched her lips
> together . . . . Mrs. Wendleken [Alice's mother] didn't
> even want cats to have kittens or birds to lay eggs, and
> she wouldn't let Alice play with anybody who had two
> rabbits (Robinson, 1972:42).

The shocking incidence of incest and child abuse (Badgley, 1984) means that many children experience violent sexual initiation. For the majority, however, the peer group remains the key socializer in matters sexual. Sources of information and misinformation include conversation, "dirty" jokes, and experimentation (Laws and Schwartz, 1977:39).

Signs of sexual maturity at puberty precipitate adult gender-identity development. Other people notice sprouting breasts and chin fuzz and respond to the adolescent as a sexual being. A stranger whistling on the street, a mother advising on her daughter's new capacity to become pregnant, boys' locker room teasing — experiences like these crystallize gender-role development. Adult expectations appropriate for a child give way to those of a soon-to-be adult. Girls are being transformed into sex objects.

As the two-worlds hypothesis suggests, female and male socialization differ. Girls first experience sex objectification:

> At puberty, the adolescent's body is getting away from
> her, it is no longer the straightforward expression of her
> individuality; it becomes foreign to her; and at the same
> time *she becomes for others a thing;* on the street men

> follow her with their eyes and comment on her anatomy
> (de Beauvoir, 1949:28, emphasis in original).

Boys begin to understand their sexuality as expression of power and anti-feminism. They worry about being a "fairy" or a "fag" (Whitehurst and Booth, 1980:64). The fact that males' puberty starts a year later than girls' increases their concern. Youngsters of both sexes are obsessed with their bodies. However, boys' more frequent and more social experience of masturbation makes discovery of their sexuality more open. Male definitions of sexuality prevail as girls behave passively and males aggressively (Wilson et al., 1977:269).

Late Adolescence. Heterosexual partners are key significant others in the gender-identity development of youngsters 15 or 16 to 19 years (Katz, 1979:19). Platonic friendships can be very important. The adolescent boy and girl can test emerging adult maleness and femaleness against each other in a "safe" (non-sexual) environment (Brenton, 1974:163). A female friend can be particularly useful to the male. Since male competitiveness discourages disclosure of anxieties and weaknesses to other males, female friends can serve as safe confidents (Chafetz, 1974:165).

Non-platonic heterosexual social arrangements vary from casual co-presence at cabarets, parties, and dances, to "going out" or "dating" (to use the old-fashioned sociological term). Fifty percent of Bibby and Posterski's (1985:32) national sample of Canadian teenagers reported deriving "a great deal" of enjoyment from dating. Dating, especially in its early stages, is still patterned according to traditional gender stereotypes, with the male initiating most dates and taking most of the risk of rejection (Allgeier, 1981; Green and Sandos, 1980). However, the female is freer to make the first move in a flirtation and to take more responsibility in established relationships (McCormick and Jesser, 1983).

Dating tends to reinforce the sex-typed socialization of earlier years. The first important romantic relationship may represent the crossroad where the young woman volunteers for "second place" and accepts male definitions of her situation. Carol Gilligan (quoted in Van Gelder, 1984:101) suggests:

> . . . . adolescent girls often operate on the assumption
> that disagreement is a disaster. They so fear isolation that
> they believe that if men were to see them as they really
> are, they would turn away. The temptation is to become
> interested in the way the boy experiences the world,
> and . . . to "float" in the relationship: you know, "Tell
> me what you want me to be and I'll be it."

The gendered nature of the dating situation becomes even more distinct when its sexual aspects is considered.

Peer norms clearly support sexual activity. Bibby and Posterski (1985:77) report that while "80% of the country's young people hold that premarital sex is all right when people *love* each other, more than 50% feel relations are also acceptable within a few dates when individuals *like* each other" (emphasis in original). Since these peer group norms often conflict with parental norms, heterosexual peers become increasingly important definers of self and the world. A female university student, quoted by Herold (1984:20), said:

> After having intercourse for the first time I felt that what
> I had done was wrong for it went against my religion
> and my parents' views, but at the same time felt the
> need to secure my boyfriend's love.

This more profound shift in significant others which occurs in late adolescence is an inevitable step in socialization, as teenagers strive to disentangle themselves from the parental nest (Zellman and Goodchilds, 1983:50). However, sex highlights the unequal power structure of dating relationships: the expectation that the male initiates sex (and may, on occasion, use force to get what he wants), and the female is responsible for the outcome (Zellman and Goodchilds, 1983:55). Sexual negotiations occurs much earlier in dating relationships of the 1980s versus the 1950s.

Exploration of adolescent sensuality generally occurs with a partner of the opposite sex. However, when it does occur with a same-sex partner, adolescence becomes an extremely trying period of life (Herold, 1984:36). The fact that homosexuals are the "number one target" of Canadian teenage humor is indicative of the strong peer pressure to be seen as "normal," i.e. heterosexual (Bibby and Posterski, 1985:84). This scorn for homosexuality also suggests the precarious state of gender identity in adolescent "normals."

Sexuality has different meanings for late adolescent females and males: love versus conquest. Young Canadian females are more likely to require a love relationship as a prerequisite for premarital sex. More males, on the other hand, are interested in sex solely for physical pleasure (Herold, 1984:11):

> Among the male folklore is the idea that in later
> adolescence boys can suffer real physical damage if their
> hormonal urges toward sexual expression are thwarted.
> Some boys prevail on the sympathies of girls to "help"
> them. Of course, part of the female socialization scripting
> *is* to be helpful to males and to be sympathetic to their
> problems; that the problem is very much a fabrication
> attests to the power of definitions and socialization
> responses (Whitehurst and Booth, 1980:65).

The double standard still lives on in the minds of young men (White-hurst and Booth, 1980:66). While many sexual adventures are considered normal and proper for themselves, it is the female's responsibility to act as the "gatekeeper" who sets limits on sexual activity (Herold, 1984:16).

Though heterosexual relations assume great importance in late adolescence, same-sex peers still wield a powerful influence. This influence operates differently for females and males. The female peer group approves good looks, clothes, and popularity with the boys. According to Greenglass (1982:73), "while pressure on girls for early marriage is now decreasing, there is still considerably more pressure on adolescent girls to establish heterosexual relationships than to pursue a career." Girls with weak career ambitions sometimes look to motherhood as a shortcut to adult status (Herold, 1984:128). The male peer group, on the other hand, emphasizes sports, future job or career preparation, and girls as the means to explore their sexuality (Greenglass, 1982:74).

Future Options

Paradoxically, adolescence is characterized by both short-term hedonism and future-orientation. While pleasure seeking and immediate gratification through music, clothes, partying, alcohol, and drugs play a prominent role, there is concern, greater than any other period of the lifecourse, with the present as preparation for the years to come (Campbell, 1975:34). Such questions as, "What are you going to do after high school?"; "Are you going to university?"; "Just how serious are you about that boy?" (Campbell, 1969:825) become more urgent with each passing year of high school. Personal plans must be made in the shadow of high unemployment and divorce rates and possible nuclear war. A Quebec girl told Bibby and Posterski (1985:159): "Teenagers today are scared. With unemployment, the economy, divorce and the world's peace situation — we all wonder what will happen."

As experts point out, late adolescence is a watershed period where often irreversible decisions are made concerning the timing of education, work, marriage, and child bearing (Huston-Stein and Higgins-Trenk, 1977:50). However, it is moot whether, at this point in their socialization careers, adolescents really have the freedom to chart their own destinies. (Sociologists of knowledge adopt a more deterministic position than their symbolic interactionist colleagues.) Young women are channelled into expressive, vicarious achievement roles and young men into instrumental, direct achievement roles (Lipman-Blumen and Tickamyer, 1975:305). This channelling involves internal and external barriers. The internal barriers, which operate at the psychological level, are gender traits produced by nearly two decades of socialization:

THE SOCIAL CONSTRUCTION OF SEXUALITY

Sexuality, like gender, is a social construction (Laws and Schwartz, 1977). Biological facts, such as hormones, do not cause human sexuality. Instead, sexual behavior is mediated by meanings.

Social constructions of sexuality change over time. Take masturbation. In turn-of-the-century Canada, a best-selling sex manual, little more than an anti-masturbation tract, began by suggesting that "self-abuse" could be learned innocently enough by sliding down bannisters and wearing tight clothes, or not so innocently from other children (Bliss, 1974). However begun, the "solitary vice" rapidly led to grim consequences:

> The health declines. The eyes lose their lustre. The skin becomes sallow. The muscles become flabby. There is an unnatural languor. Every little effort is followed by weariness. There is a great indifference to exertion . . . . [The victim] complains of pain in the back; of headache and dizziness. The hands become cold and clammy. The digestion becomes poor, the appetite fitful. The heart palpitates. He sits in a stooping posture, becomes hollow-chested, and the entire body, instead of enlarging into a strong, manly frame, becomes wasted, and many signs give promise of early decline and death . . . . If the body is naturally strong, the mind may give way first, and in extreme cases imbecility and insanity may, and often do come as the inevitable result (Sylvanus Stall, *What a Young Boy Ought to Know,* 1897:104-105, quoted in Bliss, 1974:327-328).

In the 1920s, Canadian author Max Braithwaite was given a similar book called *The Solitary Vice,* which he says

> . . . scared the bejesus clear out of me. I still get horrible feelings of guilt and fear, and my brow starts to sweat, just thinking about it . . . . Of all the good things my father did for me — and he did plenty — he came close to wiping them all out by placing that awful book in my hands" (Braithwaite, 1969:147).

Interpretations of sexuality vary with social location, e.g. generation and gender. "Where adolescent sexual behavior has been described as 'behavior in search of meaning,' in marriage or other adult committed relationships, it may well be that where sexuality is concerned, meaning is in search of behavior" (Miller and Fowlkes, 1980:790). Parents and their teenage children define sexuality differently. Researchers Bibby and Posterski (1985:77) quote an Alberta sixteen-year-old: "This is 1984, wake up mom. Everyone has sexual relations."

The meanings of sexuality for females and males are not equivalent. For example, masturbation plays an earlier role in male sexuality. Beginning at an early age, girls (but not boys) fear being hurt by sex (Best, 1983:122). Rape has been described as "a kind of terrorism which generally limits the freedom of women and makes women dependents on men"

(Griffin, 1971:35). Herold et al. (1979) report that only 18 percent of a sample of women university students never worried about being the victim of sexual offenses, such as rape, exhibitionism, being followed, and obscene phone calls. While girls worry about the size of their breasts, boys worry about the size of their penises. A fifteen-year-old writes to a newspaper advice column:

> I'm in a normal Grade 10 class and after gym when I shower all the other guys laugh at me. My penis is so small it is only about half as long as my baby finger. I've even thought about getting a sex change when I'm older, just to get rid of my small penis (*The Calgary Herald*, May 26, 1985).

Ann Landers asked her women readers to respond to this question: "Would you be content to be held close and treated tenderly, and forget about 'the act'?" More than 90,000 women replied, and 72 percent said they far preferred being hugged and treated tenderly by men to having sexual intercourse with them (*The Calgary Herald*, January 16, 1985). Men, presumably, would have answered differently.

The powerful in society impose their construction of sexuality on the less powerful. More often than not, the less powerful segments of society adopt the perspectives of the more powerful as their own. Parents feel it is their responsibility to impose their standards of sexuality upon their children. Similarly, institutions such as the law and the church have traditionally held views on sex matters that fit their own purposes (Laws and Schwartz, 1977:1). Positions on homosexuality, contraception, and abortion have been part of both law and religious teachings in this country. The manual on masturbation quoted above was distributed by the Methodist Church in the early 1900s. In many cases, males have had the power to define sexuality for both sexes. Social constructions are embedded in language and sexual intercourse, for example, is named from the male perspective:

> All the vulgar linguistic emphasis is placed upon the *poking* element, *fucking, screwing, rooting, shagging* are all acts performed upon the passive female: the names for the penis are all *tool* names" (Greer, 1971:32, emphasis in original).

A man and a woman share the same bed, but he "screws" while she "makes love."

Interpretations of male authorities have overridden women's subjective experiences of sexuality. Sigmund Freud wrote of the

> momentous discovery which it is the lot of little girls to make. They notice the penis of a brother or a playmate, strikingly visible and of large proportions, at once recognize it as the superior counterpart of their own small and inconspicuous organ, and from that time forward fall a victim to penis-envy (Freud, 1927, reprinted in Unger and Denmark, 1975:131).

The Freudian dogma of the vaginal orgasm (versus the clitoral orgasm) held until 1966 when Masters and Johnson published *Human Sexual Response* (Laws and Schwartz, 1977:15). Gynecological texts are a primary professional socialization agent for our society's official specialists on women. Several years after the publication of the findings of Kinsey et al. (1953) and Masters and Johnson (1966), a number of gynecological texts claimed that the male sex drive was stronger than that of the female; that the female was interested in sex for procreation more than for recreation. A few called most women "frigid," and called the vaginal orgasm the "mature" response (Scully and Bart, 1973).

Many other examples exist of the ruling-ideas phenomenon in the area of human sexuality. Homosexuality has been an emotionally charged political and legal issue in Canada. Many regard homosexuals as sick people, despite the fact that since 1974 the American Psychiatric Association no longer considers homosexuality to be an illness (Herold, 1984:38). Menopausal women have been regarded as "has-beens" on the grounds of their inadequacy for male purposes, i.e. physical attractiveness and fertility (Laws and Schwartz, 1977:69). Members of our society find abhorrent the idea that old people are capable of sexual activity. Posner (1975) suggests that though there are many jokes about dirty old men, the idea of "a sexy old woman is so horrendous that it is even difficult to joke about!" (p. 471).

The sexual scripts for female and male behavior are changing in the 1980s:

> Considering that human physiology never really changes, it's truly remarkable how often sexual mores *do*. In the late Sixties and well into the Seventies the rule seemed to be that if a man and a woman were destined to become lovers, they did so at the earliest reasonable opportunity. These days, for better or worse, people seem to be a tad more circumspect . . . . In the 1980s a date is not just a prelude to the inevitable; it is an opportunity, rather, to be charming and charmed, persuasive and persuaded, seductive and just possibly seduced (Shames, 1984:254).

Kinsey reports that more reliable contraception, hippie and liberation movements encouraged the sexual revolution of the 1960s and 1970s. Herpes and AIDS have recently scared people into being a "tad more circumspect." As well, feminists have reconsidered the wisdom of sexual liberation. (See Chapter 7.)

non-competitiveness, passivity, and the need for connection and intimacy with others in females and their opposites in males. External or structural barriers involve discriminatory policies, sex-typing of occupations (and the high school courses leading to them), presence or absence of role models, peer group and family pressures.

Education has been a crucial external barrier to women's equality. In the words of Lipman-Blumen (1984:134–135):

> Education is a radicalizing force. Beginning with its most
> basic ingredient, literacy, education fosters radicalism by
> enabling the less powerful to read and spread dissent.
> Education thus threatens the power establishment, whose
> power is enhanced by its control over knowledge . . . .
> Education, the potential equalizer and radicalizer,
> everywhere has been less available to women.

For this reason, such early feminists as Mary Wollstonecraft and John Stuart Mill believed that education could set women free (Rossi, 1973:3). Throughout the world, women are still educationally disadvantaged; 60 percent of the globe's illiterates are women (Finn et al., 1979). In modern Canada, external barriers still exist. However, they are the less formidable problems of counselor bias, stereotyping of mathematics and science courses as masculine endeavors, and so on.

At the verbal level, female and male plans for the future are similar. Both sexes contemplate a university education, a job, a marriage and children (Bibby and Posterski, 1985:167). The occupational plans that young women articulate appear to reflect the influence of the women's movement. The domestic dreams of both sexes are traditional. Both sexes prefer traditional domestic arrangements to innovations modelled by some of their elders. For instance, a Calgary, Alberta male high school student recently told an interviewer:

> I just think of my personal future and how it's going to
> be and really the things that just come to mind are hav-
> ing lots of money, shiny cars, a big house, a nice dog
> and a goldfish (Boras, 1985).

However, when the situation is examined more closely, the effects of internal and external constraints are discernible. Priorities begin to diverge more sharply for female and male adolescents. Many girls have confused images of the future and they are unable to formulate realistic plans for their lives (Press, 1985). Although they have been exposed to both the ideal of occupational achievement and their eventual destiny in marriage and family roles, the girl is apt to hold her future in abeyance until the right young man comes along. The adolescent boy has his problems, but role conflict between work versus family destiny is not one of them. According to a Toronto high school guidance counselor:

> Even [in the 1980s], most girls' unspoken thought still is
> that sometime in their 20s they'll meet a nice man who'll
> look after them for the rest of their days. A teen-age boy,
> after all, has expected to support his family ever since he
> rolled his first truck through a make-believe construction
> site. Yet the average girl still thinks she will work only
> until a mortgage is paid or a baby born — just as her
> mother probably did (*Chatelaine*, October, 1983).

In late adolescence, girls' earlier academic success has been reversed. When science and mathematics courses become optional, females are more likely than males to avoid them (Scott, 1981). This step, in part, explains why science, engineering, and technology remain male-dominated professions (Sheinin, 1981).[7] As girls approach the age for actual labor-market entry, they lower their aspirations and revise their career goals toward more traditional choices (Miller and Garrison, 1982). Proportionately fewer girls continue their education beyond high school (Hunter, 1981). As the less-valued sex, females receive less family support to continue their schooling, and such encouragement is especially critical for girls (Turrittin et al., 1983). Statistics Canada (1985:xiii) reports that in 1982-83, women constituted 51 percent of all university students, up from 37 percent in 1970-71. However, university women were overrepresented in part-time studies and underrepresented in graduate programs. Moreover, women in post-secondary education remain concentrated in traditionally female fields of study, e.g. education, nursing, and social work. Despite earlier lofty ambitions, most Canadian women end up in female job ghettos (Armstrong and Armstrong, 1984).

Male preparation for the future is no less constrained by gender scripts. Young men's occupational ambitions are higher than those of young women. Work is a major ingredient of masculine self-esteem. Males are expected to spend a lifetime in the labor force. As Lowe and Krahn (1984:1) point out, the work ethic is the subjective underpinning of the capitalist economic system. Although male job plans are not sabotaged by dreams of settling down with Mrs. Right and producing babies, obstacles also impede their life course. The majority abandon earlier hopes for university education or technical training (Bibby and Posterski, 1985:161), presumably for economic reasons. For many, the threat of long-term, perhaps permanent unemployment is very real. Given the centrality of work in our society's definition of masculinity, it's hard to grow up when there isn't enough worthwhile work to do.[8] A national study of adolescent aspirations (Baker, 1985:165) concluded that "we need to search for more effective ways of sensitizing these young people to the realities of their future without dampening their spirits or lowering their aspirations."

Gender Socialization in Adulthood

In adulthood, as in childhood and adolescence, the problem of socialization is bringing the individual to internalize societal definitions. The male influence upon these definitions remains the overriding fact. However, the content of socialization lessons shifts with time. The primary socialization of childhood and adolescence teaches language, self-concept, moral standards, and the general knowledge and skills relevant to many societal roles. By comparison, secondary socialization focuses on role-specific knowledge (Brim, 1968:186). New roles are encountered, continuing roles are re-defined, some roles are lost. Many of these role transitions demand alterations in gender norms and gender identity.

According to the symbolic interactionist framework, the childhood socialization experiences outlined in Chapter 4 provide a prototype for adult learning (Stryker, 1964:141). The self is defined through interaction. The meaning and requirements of adult roles are learned through role taking. People come to categorize themselves as others categorize them. Significant others interpret the generalized other's view of gender. However, in adulthood, a myriad of less significant others functions as a "chorus" in this regard (Berger and Luckmann, 1966:151). Impetus for adult change often comes from the individuals themselves, seeking to become more acceptable in their own eyes (Brim, 1968:189). Humans respond not to the environment as physically given, but to the environment mediated through symbolic processes. Since they can produce their "own" symbols, they can be self-stimulating (Stryker, 1964:135). Nevertheless, these symbols reflect patriarchal attitudes. (See Chapter 6.)

How much can the self change during secondary socialization? Symbolic interactionists reject the Freudian view that development stops in childhood. As Strauss (1969:43) put it, "human careers . . . have always an unfinished character, a certain indeterminacy of outcome." The role demands and maturational changes of adulthood result in alterations, generally but not necessarily "fine tuning" to the basic self formed in childhood and adolescence. Nonetheless, primary socialization channels and sets limits for secondary socialization. The latter "must deal with an already formed self and an already internalized world" (Berger and Luckmann, 1966:140).

Gender Differences in Secondary Socialization

There are at least six interrelated ways in which secondary socialization differs by gender. Therefore, being a female in the labor force, a wife, mother, divorcee, widow, or elderly woman is not the same as being a man in the labor force, a husband, father, divorced male, widower, or old man.

First, societal scripts give adult women and men different life priorities. When these ruling ideas are obeyed, women end up preoccupied with intimacy, relationships, and the domestic sphere, and men with achievement, instrumental values, and the public sphere.

Second, the power differential between men and women results in dissimilar socialization experiences. It is almost impossible to exaggerate the importance of power.

Third, the asynchrony of the timetables for women's and men's lives means that what seem at first to be very similar role transitions are actually phenomenologically divergent. For example, a man can father a child well into late middle age, even old age. A woman cannot (Rossi, 1980:29). Therefore, women must decide whether to bear a child before time runs out.

Fourth, biological aging has different meanings in male and female biographies. Women find themselves doubly stigmatized in the last stage of their life cycle, but all along, they have lived under a "double standard of aging" (Bell, 1970).

Fifth, women's longer and more complex lives provide them with greater opportunity than men for role transitions (Riley, 1985:338). This difference, in turn, increases the possibility for women to become entangled in role strain.

Finally, since gender socialization in childhood and adolescence were far from identical for females and males, and subsequent socialization builds upon this foundation, their secondary socialization necessarily differs.

The above points will be elaborated as discussion moves from gender socialization in early adulthood to middle adulthood and old age.

Gender Socialization in Young Adulthood

The majority of young adults in Canadian society face three gender-relevant tasks: finding a mate or partner and developing a relationship with that person; having children and parenting them; and establishing work competence (Katz, 1979:21). In working out solutions to these problems, contemporary young people have more leeway in timing and alternative forms than did previous generations. Marriage, children, and serious vocational commitment may all be delayed, or avoided entirely. Some people repeat stages several times in their lifetimes. The mate may be a "long-term" live-in relationship or a legal spouse. (Since cohabitors look to the family for a model, researchers [Newcomb, 1982:146] find little difference between marriage and cohabitation in the way roles are performed.) Children may be delayed, adopted, or blended in stepfamilies. Single-person and single-parent households are becoming more common. Though we recognize this variation in form and timing, for simplicity's sake, we concentrate on the modal patterns.

Significant gender socialization experiences generally occur in primary relationships within the family and work institutions. Therefore, the main business of this chapter is with the micro-world. However, it is important to emphasize that this interaction is structurally situated. In Smith's (1983:316) words, "the inner life and work of the family and the personal relations of power between husband and wife" are "products of how family relations are organized by and in economic and political relations of capitalism." In short, the means of production in the society condition the home and work roles of both sexes.

According to symbolic interactionism, a common thread runs through mating, parenting, and working. Positions such as wife, father, secretary are socially recognized categories. Attaching a positional designation to a person organizes other people's behavior towards this person. Labeling a woman a "wife," for example, means others respond to her on the basis of scripted expectations. By viewing herself in the "looking glass" of others' attitudes, especially those whose positions interlock with her own (husband, mother-in-law), the woman comes to define herself according to the same script. Her conformity is not, of course guaranteed. Humans have the capacity to innovate, to rebel, and to seek alternative role partners and "looking glasses."

Mating

Love. In North America, nearly everyone expects to fall in love eventually. Our society is one of the few to portray romantic love as the basis for marriage (Walster and Walster, 1978:40). When signs of bodily arousal — light-headedness, rapid heartbeat, queasy stomach, inability to concentrate — are experienced in a context in which their cause can be attributed to another person, they are defined as "love." (In other circumstances, these same bodily symptoms are interpreted as anxiety, anger, excitement, or euphoria [Gagnon and Greenblat, 1982:133].) Moreover, the experience of "love" varies by gender. In dating relationships, women are more likely than men to report symptoms of love, such as "floating on a cloud" (Peplau, 1983:242). Different styles of love are preferred, with women favoring emotional closeness and verbal expression, and men preferring to give instrumental help and sex and to share physical activities. Since women are allowed dominion over such expressive matters, only their style of love is recognized as "love" in our society (Cancian, 1985).

Timetables. Though love is not property of the young, their "social clock" (Neugarten and Datan, 1974:62) establishes an appropriate time to settle down.

> Within six months before and after our graduation from school, all but one of my friends got married. I don't think it could be that everybody met the right girl by coincidence. There must have been an element of its being the right time . . . (Sheehy, 1974:101).

The biological clock is a greater influence on the courtship timetable of the woman, who according to the traditional script, must find a mate while she is still nubile and maximally attractive. A minority of both sexes, subjected to contrary social pressures, manages to ignore traditional scripts and remain single (Darling, 1977).

Most Canadians select mates with similar socioeconomic and ethnic backgrounds (Ramu, 1983). Within this context, the *marriage gradient* (Bernard, 1972) prevails. Women marry somewhat older, taller, more financially secure, and experienced men. Since men with these attributes have more power and resources than their brides, the marriage gradient contributes to the non-egalitarian nature of marriage (Baker and Bakker, 1980:554).

Power. Power is an important property of both courtship and marriage. Indeed, marriage has been described as "the primary political experience in which most of us engage as adults" (Brandt, 1984:232).[9] Two points about the operation of power in dyads need to be made (Sprecher, 1985). First, power resides in control of resources. Physical strength, status outside the relationship, money, love, sex are all resources whose control leads to power. Usually, the bases for power differ for females and males. Men are more likely to control money, status, and brute force, and women, sex. Second, power in dyads resides in one partner's dependence upon the other. Dependence may be financial or emotional. It hinges, to some extent, on the existence of alternatives to this particular relationship. The "principle of less interest" (Waller, 1937; Turner, 1970) explains some of the dynamics of dyadic relationships. According to this principle, the dyad partner who cares less about the quality of the relationship, or whether the relationship continues at all, enjoys an advantage over the other. The man is the partner of less interest in traditional relationships.

Women are especially powerful in the courtship stage. Traditionally, they have traded their beauty, sexuality, and fecundity for male-controlled resources, such as status and protection (Sprecher 1985:459). Never again do women feel so cherished. According to a major study of American couples, things soon change:

> During the excitement of courtship a man takes time
> away from his work and other interests to lavish it upon
> her. Courtship is usually a time for sharing activities,
> intense conversations, and emotional intimacy. The
> experience can confirm a woman's romantic hopes of
> what a companionate relationship will be like. After their
> marriage, or when they move in together, men soon
> return to their previous routines, occupying themselves
> with the mundane but necessary task of making a living
> (Blumstein and Schwartz, 1983:176).

Singles Bar. The action in a singles bar illustrates some of the classic power plays involved in courtship (Cloyd, 1976). Being in this setting communicates peoples' status as potential mates. Women and men operate under a somewhat different *modus operandi:* she signals availability through body language and eye contact; he then initiates an encounter (and risks rejection). If she rejects his advances or no men approach her all evening, failure is highly visible. Face-saving strategies must be worked out (Goffman, 1967). The rejected male may mutter to other males that the women present are all "losers." The rejected female may deny she is in the market for a man and pretend to be totally engrossed in conversation with her same-sex friend (Berk, 1977).

The bar's closing time forces a couple, who have been drinking, talking, and dancing, to make a decision whether to continue or to terminate the relationship. The male generally presses for immediate sex, the female for a future date. Cloyd (1976:308-309) relates this overheard dialogue between a persistent male and a female who manages to fend off his advances.

Male:	You're a lot of fun to be with. Has your friend found herself a friend too?
Female:	No, I saw her over at the bar a little while ago. I imagine she is waiting for me.
Male:	Oh, why don't you tell her that I'm going to drive you home?
Female:	No . . . I'd like to, but I have driven her, so I'm sort of responsible for getting her home.
Male:	Well, how about if I follow you and after you have dropped her off, we can go somewhere. Does she live very far from here?
Female:	Yeah, she lives clear across town. Besides, it's getting kind of late. I'd like to — maybe I'll see you here next week.
Male:	No, I don't come here that often. What's your phone number? I'll call you tomorrow.
Female:	We have just moved into a new apartment and don't have a phone yet. But I'll probably be here next week. If you're around, we might get together then.
Male:	Oh, okay. We'll see you around. Take care.

As the above dialogue suggests, courting roles entail complicated ploys. Playing them convincingly requires socialization. Despite more liberal gender and sexual norms, "the sexual politics of courtship may be especially resistant to change because couples beginning to court often engage in posing — the tendency to fall back on those gender roles that are stereotypically appropriate or safe . . ." (McCormick and Jesser 1983:71). As well, newly acquainted pairs may mis-read one another's intentions. For instance, males may misperceive females' friendliness as sexual interest (Abbey, 1982). This failure to take the role of the other may be a factor in "date rape."

Marriage

The newly married assume the statuses of wife and husband. When others act toward them as persons so categorized in our society, they begin to understand themselves in the same way. Their role playing is also guided by their store of gender stereotypes and family memories. Definitions of family life vary by social class and ethnicity. Working-class families hold more traditional views of gender than the middle class (Lambert, 1971; Romer and Cherry, 1980; Swatos and McCauley, 1984). "Ethnic" families, i.e. those unassimilated to the North American ethos, tend to exhibit intensified forms of patriarchy (Cassin and Griffith, 1981:110). Indeed, gender, ethnicity, and class are interrelated statuses (Juteau-Lee and Roberts, 1981).

"Recipe knowledge" (Berger and Luckmann, 1966:65) provides couples with a preliminary understanding of marriage. Role taking is supplemented by negotiated role making. Negotiations involve such matters as household duties, sex, kin, and recreation. Men may find their socialization for marriage more difficult than women. In childhood and adolescence, boys learn emotional distance from females, independence of action, and desire for adventure. Marriage demands resocialization, unlearning of established patterns. However, female socialization for marriage begins in childhood (Baker and Bakker, 1980:551).

Marriage as Reality Construction. Sociologists of knowledge Berger and Kellner (1970) view marriage as a dramatic act which causes reality to be reconstructed for its participants. Husband becomes for wife, and wife for husband the significant other *par excellence,* the "nearest and most decisive coinhabitant of the world" (p. 12). Pre-existing relationships are re-assessed in accordance with this "drastic shift" of marriage. Changes occur in partners' self-conceptions. It is primarily through conversation that the symbolic world is reconstructed:

> Each partner ongoingly contributes his conceptions of
> reality, which are then *talked through,* usually not once
> but many times . . . . In the marital conversation a world
> is not only built, but it is also kept in a state of repair
> and ongoingly refurnished (Berger and Kellner, 1970:15).

Although Berger and Kellner do not say so, the husband is the more influential partner in this reconstruction. Certainly, the couple's life style (place of residence, daily rhythms, friendships, possessions) is typically determined by his occupation (Lopata, 1973:409).

Marriage as Power Arena. The "two worlds" of gender override the shared reality of marriage discussed above. Husbands' and wives' productive and reproductive experiences are sufficiently distinctive to produce and reinforce separate worlds. In Bernard's (1972:15) words, "there are two marriages . . . in every marital union, his and hers. And his . . . is better than hers." Women's loss in marriage is symbolized by her traditional name change. Witness this Letter to the Editor regarding Maureen McTeer and Joe Clark (in 1986, Minister of External Affairs):

> With regard to the article in your magazine about Joe Clark's wife, Maureen . . ., no doubt many people, myself included, are thinking that it is high time that she started to call herself by her *proper* name — Mrs. Joe Clark! This would be of considerable advantage to Clark's political career, apart from the fact that it is the *natural* thing for a woman who loves a man sufficiently to marry him to take his name (Maclean's, March 21, 1983).

The crux of the matter is economics and power:

> The relative power of husband and wife in the family depends largely on their respective anchorage in the occupational system, since that system is the main determinant of status and privilege (Coser and Coser, 1974:90).

This is why feminists have attacked the family as a deeply flawed institution. Dixon (1971:170), for example, claims that the "institution of marriage is the chief vehicle for the perpetuation of the oppression of women; it is through the role of wife that the subjugation of women is maintained." Sometimes this control is physical. An estimated one in ten Canadian women who are married or in live-in relationships with men is battered (Propper, 1984:106). According to a study of Ontario family court records, only 5 percent of spousal assault cases involve husbands. Injuries here are less severe (Kincaid, 1982).

So far as economics is concerned, the twentieth-century North American economy is based on the principle of the family wage (Ehrenreich, 1983:7-8). The "breadwinner ethic" has required men to become wage earners and to share their wages with their wives and dependents. The assumption is made that when women work, they are already supported by men and can therefore be paid less than men. As a result, women have traditionally been interested in "landing" a man, while men have resisted becoming "the lifelong support of the female unemployed" (Ehrenreich, 1983:3). Money being a resource, wives' generally inferior economic position renders them less powerful. Smith (1973:17-18) makes the point very clearly:

> The underlying determination of the relations between
> men and women is this relation to the economic struc-
> ture whereby the relation of wife to husband mimics the
> relation of husband to capitalist. She works for him
> because he owns the means of production upon which
> she depends.

The woman's economic dependence is increased if she is a full-time housewife, with small children and separated from the public sphere which her husband interprets for her. Economically dependent, a stranger in the public sphere, she learns through interaction how to be powerless. Meanwhile, he learns how to be the powerful partner. Mira, a character in Marilyn French's novel, *The Women's Room* (1977:247), summarizes the rules of marriage from the wife's perspective:

> She had been presented with a set of terms: your func-
> tion is to marry, raise children, and if you can, keep your
> husband. If you follow these rules (smile, diet, smile,
> don't nag, smile, cook, smile, clean) you will keep him.

Parenting

Producing (or adopting) children and parenting them is the second task of young adulthood. As mentioned in Chapter 3, the reciprocal process of gender socialization affects parents as well as child. Here, our focus is upon parenthood as a source of gender learning for *caretakers*. The impact of parental roles upon self occurs through internalizing others' responses to positional designations of mother and father. As well, gender-relevant behaviors are learned in interaction with role partners, including the child. Given the radical feminist emphasis on reproduction (Chapter 2), we consider parenting to be an important reason for the divergence between the "two worlds" of women and men. Because of space limitations, our attention is confined to the modal pattern of the heterosexual couple with one or two children. Our interest here is the young family. Though adolescent and adult children continue to be socialization agents for their parents, this influence occurs in subsequent phases of the life cycle.

Parenting has a more profound impact on the lives of women than men. Think about the connotations of our language for parenting:

> The meaning of "fatherhood" remains tangential, elusive.
> To "father" a child suggests above all to beget, to provide
> the sperm which fertilizes the ovum. To "mother" a child
> implies a continuing presence, lasting at least nine
> months, more often for years (Rich, 1976:xiv).

In our society, as in most others, women not only bear children, but take primary responsibility for parenting their own and other people's children (Chodorow, 1978). This arbitrary association between child bearing and child rearing is fostered "by a powerful social belief that having children is 'natural' for women . . ., that mothers make the best rearers of their children" (Luxton, 1980:81). Feminists have come to understand motherhood as a female experience shaped by male expectations and structures, indeed, as the linchpin of patriarchy (Rich, 1976). For this and other reasons, parenthood has been undergoing redefinition. Decline in fertility, voluntary childlessness (Veevers, 1979), separation of parenting from marriage by single-by-choice mothers, and fathers-for-custody groups are all indications of this redefinition.

Child Rearing. Parenting as differential gender socialization experiences for women and men begins with the contemplation of a child. The "motherhood mystique" teaches that a woman must experience maternity in order to find feminine self-actualization and true happiness.

> "The woman who has not had a child," said H.L.
> Mencken, "remains incomplete, ill at ease, and more
> than a little ridiculous. She is in the position of a man
> who has never stood in battle; she has missed the most
> colossal experience of her sex" (*Esquire*, June 1984, Vol.
> 101, p. 141).

Knowing their fertility ends with menopause puts time pressure on the decision to have a child. This decision may be complicated by the fact that the prime child-bearing years are the same years needed to establish a career. Men face neither sex nor gender constraints.

Empirical studies support the proposition of the sociology of knowledge that reproduction has differential effects on women's and men's thoughts. Lips' (1983) Manitoba study of first-time expectant parents found that the experience was a more profound one for pregnant women than for their husbands. Significantly more women rated child bearing as important to femininity than men rated it as important to masculinity. In other words, the "motherhood mystique" is still operative. Moreover, these mothers-to-be believed that their husbands had a stronger investment in the impending parenthood than was actually the case.

A British study (Rossan, 1984) also affirmed the impact of maternity on the woman. Changes in her body and its functioning alter her self-conceptions. After the baby is born, her relations with significant others shift. For example, many new mothers spend little time alone with their husbands. Discussions with their spouses are almost exclusively concerned with the baby. Occupational identity and job concerns recede. These women now seek out as friends other mothers of small babies and see childless friends less. In sum, child bearing socializes both parents. However, women are more deeply affected than men.

The entrance of an infant into a marriage accentuates traditional gender roles. The division of labor in the home becomes more sex-segregated, especially in working-class homes (Lamb, 1978). Following gender scripts, men and women display distinctive attitudes toward parenting (LaRossa and LaRossa [1981], described in Rossi [1984]).

Fathers distance[10] themselves from the parental role, especially before the child can walk and talk. "The men act clumsy when handling the baby and show less skill than they actually possess when in company" (Rossi, 1984:7). The women, by contrast, tend to embrace the mother role, "submerging themselves in the role and trying to act more skillfully than they in fact feel" (p. 7). The fact that second-time fathers behave the same way suggests that role distance has more to do with gender attitude than lack of experience.

The nature of paternal versus maternal interaction with young children both reflects and reinforces traditional gender roles. Women's responses tend to be nurturant and expressive; they hold babies to care for them and soothe them. By contrast, fathers handle babies in order to play with them and have difficulty comforting infants. The masculine instrumental response is illustrated by the remarks of Stuart, a history professor. When the interviewer suggests that Stuart doesn't seem to interact much with his son, Stuart explains:

> Uh, not on a continuous basis . . . . I mean, I give him a bottle; he's just learning to hold it up for himself now. I continually will teach him things or try to: how to hold his bottle, how to get it if it's fallen over to one side . . . . Right now I am trying to teach him how to roll over . . . he should know by now, but he's got this funny way. He tries to roll over with his arms stuck straight out . . . . Also, I will interact with him . . . by trying out new toys (Rossi, 1984:7).

Impact on Women's Status. In addition to calcifying gender roles through the division of labor, parenting exacerbates woman's dependency and subordination. This is especially the case for women who withdraw from the labor force with the birth of a child and become economically, socially, and emotionally dependent on their husbands. Of all the factors that may deter a wife from seeking paid employment, the presence of pre-school children is the most important (Lowe and Krahn, 1985:3). As Lips (1981:143) points out, "there seems to be more than a little truth in the old saying that the best way to control a woman is to 'keep her barefoot and pregnant' . . . ."

The accentuation of women's powerlessness that often accompanies parenthood explains the anti-natalism of the early stage of the new feminist movement. It also explains why access to contraception and abortion have been important issues. Feminist Adrienne Rich (1976:292) wrote: "The repossession by women of our bodies will bring far more essential change to human society than the seizing of the means of production by workers." (See Chapter 7.) In recent years, marked decline in the number of children born, decrease in unwanted births, delayed child bearing, shorter time periods of active mothering, outside employment of mothers, alternative structures for mothering such as day-care centers, have all helped to shift the balance of power in women's favor (Gerson et al., 1984).

Working

Establishing themselves occupationally is the third major task young adults face. As mentioned in Chapter 2, distinctive work experiences are considered by sociologists of knowledge to be a central determinant of the "two worlds" of men and women. Symbolic interactionists agree. As Everett Hughes (1958:7) put it, "a man's work is as good a clue as any to the course of his life, and to his social being and identity." From the interactionist perspective, occupational socialization consists of "learning the ropes," substituting realism for idealism (in the case of the professions), developing an appropriate definition of the work situation, and investing the self in the occupational role (Mortimer and Simmons, 1978:442-443). Here, attention is confined to gender-relevant aspects of this process.

Three generalizations guide our discussion of occupational socialization. First, it is important to distinguish between structural characteristics of the work setting and individual attitudes and motives as explanations for the work behavior of women and men, and to recognize the limitations of the latter. Opportunity structures, internal labor markets, dominance structures, and sex ratios are examples of structural variables (Kanter, 1977b). As Kanter (1976:416) points out, "if women sometimes have lower aspirations, lesser involvement with work, and greater concern with peer group relations — so do men in positions of limited or blocked mobility." In short, to say that women lack ambition because that's the way they were socialized is a true but incomplete statement.

Second, work and family roles are interrelated. How individuals function in either of these spheres is affected by their involvement in the other (Pleck, 1977). As we shall see, many work-family interrelationships are the product of gender constructions.

Third, as a consequence of their simultaneous involvement in work and family, women and men are subject to various types of *role strain*, i.e., "felt difficulty in fulfilling role obligations" (Goode, 1960). Women's greater family responsibility increases their potential role strain. Men's lesser role strain is one reason for Bernard's (1972) thesis that men benefit more than women from the institution of marriage. Until fairly recently, men were able to keep separate their work and family roles (Miller and Garrison, 1982). However, the women's movement and changing economic arrangements have exacerbated the strain for both sexes. Our analysis of work socialization focuses first on women, then on men.

Women's Work Situation. Young women about to undergo occupational socialization face a role conflict between the traditional goal of family and undemanding job and the liberated goal of serious career commitment (Komarovsky, 1946). Countervailing influences impinging upon them make this role strain almost inevitable. On the one hand, gender stereotypes and occupational sex-typing point young women toward traditional goals. In many cases, their own juvenile work experience actualizes the social script. According to White and Brinkerhoff (1981), children's job opportunities at home and in the community are every bit as sex-segregated as their parents' work. Girls baby sit and clean house; boys have more and better paying opportunities outside the home doing yard work and manual labor (Greenberger and Steinberg, 1981; 1983). On the other hand, the educational system rewards achievement and competition by both sexes, and feminist ideals have been widely publicized. In most cases, traditionalism wins. As a result, gender constitutes a more formidable barrier to women's occupational achievement than lack of resources, academic ability or socioeconomic background (Marini and Greenberger, 1978).

Consider the situation of the woman who "chooses"[11] the traditional path and either abandons career efforts or postpones them until her children (real or imaginary) are grown. A Saskatchewan baby sitter and housekeeper told Armstrong and Armstrong (1983:26):

> I guess when I was younger, I thought it was just temporary; I'd be getting married . . . . Not that I couldn't have gone on. I should have furthered my education but by the time I got around to realizing I wasn't to be married, I figured it was too late and so I didn't do anything about it.

In 1981, the top five women's occupations were secretary, bookkeeper, salesperson, teller, and waitress (Armstrong and Armstrong, 1983). Women's work in the labor force is characterized by role strain of other sorts. The workplace is organized according to male rules. Hierarchy, success striving, and above all, denigration of relationships are alien to women (Gilligan, 1982; Sassen, 1980).

Women's work often entails the transplantion of traditional gender norms from home to job. The secretary is often described as an "office wife" (Kanter, 1977a:69-103). Paid or unpaid, women scrub floors, serve food, sort laundry, teach children, care for the sick, make clothes, wash hair and answer the telephone (Armstrong and Armstrong, 1984:54). Although not much effort is needed to learn these ropes, jobs are now performed according to masculine rules. Both white- and blue-collar jobs entail subordination to male bosses, lower pay, and often sexual harassment and poor working conditions. As women become aware of such egalitarian innovations as the Canadian Charter of Rights, the female work situation is bound to produce role strain.

Increasing numbers, but small proportions, of women now embark on professional careers. Though the professions involved are usually sex-typed ones, such as nursing and school teaching (Armstrong and Armstrong, 1984:36), our discussion is confined to the extreme case of women in "masculine" professions. For a minority of women, such factors as privileged class position, parental encouragement, non-traditional role models, playing competitive sports and male sponsorship within work organizations (Symons, 1981) tip the scale in favor of non-traditional, challenging work.

Women in male-dominated professions also experience role strain. For one thing, maleness is the norm and femininity is denigrated. A Canadian woman in a senior management position said:

> We were born women and we should bloody well not be putting ourselves down for it. And we shouldn't be trying to change it. We shouldn't be trying to become like men, although we can learn from them. I think that we can use our femininity in a very practical sense (Symons, 1981:349).

Some rebel against the masculine work ethic and argue that "equality should not mean equal ulcers, equal cardiac failures . . ." (Berger and Berger, 1984:28). Others knuckle under to the masculine ruling ideas. There are additional problems. As noted in Chapter 2, women are often excluded from colleague circles where decisions are made, knowledge and favors exchanged, and loneliness assuaged. Fellow practitioners are a source of professional identity and useful information. This collegial function is crucial for incompletely socialized neophytes. As Becker (1972) tells us, "A School Is a Lousy Place to Learn Anything." Finally, professional women still meet out-and-out prejudice on the job (Miller and Garrison, 1982:254).

Attempting to combine work and family roles often leaves women "hopping on one foot and then the other" (Harper, 1985:781). This type of role strain is more serious for career women than for women with jobs. One strategy is to remain unmarried (or to get divorced). The late Judy LaMarsh, Minister of National Health and Welfare and Secretary of State for five years, told an interviewer:

"I've never had it in my mind that I was going to raise
children and be a housewife. Not because I have anything against it; I have to keep my own house and I like
to cook and design interiors — but I don't want to pick
up wet socks and towels and clean off babies' bottoms. It
just doesn't interest me at all. Some people have a very
loving nature, and to do those things are signs of love
and it fulfills them to do it. I'd rather not do it if I can
avoid it. I was engaged for about three days when I was
a law student to a naval officer because I thought it
would be such a gas that he would only be around one
month of the year." Her priorities have always been clear.
"It would be completely unfair to have a husband," she
said in 1964, "and to have him tagging around after a
cabinet minister" (Robertson, 1975:15-16).

Because our culture has not yet routinized the articulation of
demanding work, marital, and parental roles (Coser and Rokoff,
1971:539), professional women with families must *ad hoc* their own
"juggling acts." For example, Toronto lawyer Jane Pepino

. . . has never taken more than a week's maternity leave
but calls bonding a top priority. So after each birth, she
brought her baby back to work and nursed on demand
in the office. "If Drew cried while clients were with me,"
she recalls, "I'd give them a choice: adjourn for 20
minutes or carry on while I nursed. Most of the time, we
carried on. Those older men were quite heartwarmed"
(R. Maynard, 1985:141).

Such women risk being altercast as Superwomen. Gloria Steinem is
quoted as follows:

No feminist ever said we should be Superwomen . . . .
No one has any right to expect us to be. The Superwoman was the response of a reluctant society saying,
"Okay, you can be a lawyer or a carpenter if you want to,
but only if you keep preparing three meals a day, taking
care of the kids, and, in general, if you don't disturb the
order of things as they were" (Carter, 1984:205).

Gender inequality continues to characterize the division of labor in
Canadian households (Clark and Harvey, 1978; Meissner et al., 1975;
Lupri and Mills, 1987). Whether or not married women work outside
the home, they still carry major responsibility for housework and
children.[12] On top of this, many wives are expected to participate as
unpaid hostesses, typists, bookkeepers, etc. in their husband's job so
that his job really amounts to a "two-person career" (Papanek, 1973).
A classic example is the Protestant minister and his wife.

Married women with paid work commonly experience the type of role strain called *role overload* — the constraint of coping with inordinate demands on one's time and energy (Mackie, 1976). Such overload is a major reason why many women turn to unchallenging work and part-time work, and show interrupted career patterns and low commitment to professional jobs (Coser and Rokoff, 1971). Nevertheless, research (Spreitzer et al., 1979) suggests that the benefits of multiple roles outweigh the costs. A large repertoire of roles provides a buffer against failure, enriches the personality, and enhances the self-concept (Sieber, 1974).

> Role requirements give purpose, meaning, direction, and guidance to one's life. Up to a certain point, the greater the number of identities held, the stronger one's sense of meaningful, guided existence. The more identities, the more "existential security," so to speak (Thoits, 1983:175).

Indeed, human energy seems to be a sociocultural variable, not a biological constant. Energy is abundant and expandable, not scarce:

> Abundant energy is "found" for anything to which we are highly committed, and we often feel more energetic after having done it; also, we tend to "find" little energy for anything to which we are uncommitted, and doing these things leaves us feeling spent, drained, or exhausted (Marks, 1977:927).

Finally, about half of Canadian married women are full-time housewives, a role characterized by its own brands of strain. Women receive neither pay nor status for doing housework. Until recently, their activity was not even defined as work. Eichler (1978:53) considered it "one of the great achievements of the feminist movement that unpaid labour has been at least partially recognized for what it is, namely labour." The indeterminant nature of the role, its ambiguity, creates role strain, especially for new housewives (Lopata, 1971:152). In large part, housewifery is a role one constructs for oneself. Many women complain about the loneliness, monotony, and social devaluation of their work (Mackie, 1976). Housewives were stung by the criticism of early feminists, who "shared the prevailing male contempt for women's domestic efforts" and described housework as a form of "indoor loitering" (Ehrenreich, 1983:100).

Men's Work Situation. Work is central to male consciousness. According to the traditional script, "it is well-nigh impossible to be a man without having an occupation, and how much of a man and what kind of a man one is are measured largely by the nature of the occupation and the success with which it is pursued" (Turner, 1970:225). Male occupational socialization is no less constricted by gender norms and family considerations than women's. However, men's less complex working lives produce fewer types of role strain.

The young man's occupational "choice" is also influenced by juvenile job experience, gender stereotypes, and occupational sex-typing. Although men have more occupations to choose from, they must stick to the traditional script. The option of full-time house-husband is generally unavailable. Besides, few men would "allow themselves to be placed in such a powerless situation" (Baker and Bakker, 1980:554). While most men's jobs are now, in theory, open to women, and women gain prestige from doing them, the tiny minority of men who do aspire to women's work lose status and place their masculinity on the line. Sociologist Mary Dietz (1981:9) says, "the usual response when I tell people that my son is a ballet dancer is 'How nice' and a rapid change of subject." According to her, the public typifies danseurs as "effeminate, and latent or overt homosexuals" (p. 26). Next to the injunction "don't be like a girl," no other feature of the male gender is as important as the edict to succeed (Doyle, 1983:163). In Coach Vince Lombardi's words, "Winning isn't everything. It's the only thing." Work sustains the masculine identity, as work sustains life itself. Therefore, when circumstances force young men to scale down their ambitions (and Bibby and Posterski [1985] found that most do), the result is role strain. According to Rinehart (1975:10) most Canadian jobs fail to satisfy many of the needs and aspirations of the individuals who hold them. The outcome is alienated labor. "Each day men sell little pieces of themselves in order to try to buy them back each night and weekend with the coin of 'fun'" (Mills, 1951:237).

Since the Industrial Revolution, the masculine success ethic has been tied to the breadwinner role in the nuclear family (Doyle, 1983:163). Men were able to define meaningless and onerous jobs as worthwhile through "priding themselves on the hard work and personal sacrifice they are making to be breadwinners for their families" (Pleck, 1981b:242). The traditional bargain between breadwinner and dependent wife acknowledged that husbands gave work higher priority than family. Therefore, family demands were not allowed to impinge on husbands' work. The reverse, however, was acceptable (Pleck, 1977:423).

Linking work and masculinity often backfires. Unemployment, for example, becomes defined as a flaw in the man, not the economy. Especially important, wives' increased labor force participation is producing role strain for many husbands (Bernard, 1981b). Twenty years ago, some men tried to preserve their power in the home by keeping their wives out of the work force. ("No wife of mine will ever work.") Now that two paychecks are a necessity for many families, husbands feel threatened if their wives' work rivals theirs in income or prestige. Wives now have resources to challenge their husbands' power.

As a result of the above role strains, and such other factors as recognition that overwork invites heart attacks, and ideas from the women's movement, some males are beginning to question their commitment to marriage and the breadwinner's role (Ehrenreich, 1983). Our discussion of middle adulthood will return to this matter.

Parting

Though most Canadians intend to marry for life, an increasing number of marriages end in separation or divorce, when the reality constructed in the marriage has become unsatisfactory for at least one partner (Frank, 1979:171). Since the median duration of marriage before divorce was 9.9 years in 1980 (Vital Statistics, Vol. 11: Table 16), and some time elapses between the death of the marriage and actual divorce, "parting" is dealt with here as a problem of young adulthood. However, marriages fail at all stages of the life cycle. Loss of marital roles has a profound impact on the self-conception. Moreover, the learning required to come to terms with marital dissolution varies for females and males.

Explaining why the Canadian divorce rate has risen steadily since liberalization of the divorce legislation in 1968 and why even greater numbers of people are separated (McVey and Robinson, 1981) is beyond the scope of this book. However, such factors as the increased earning capacity and labor force participation of women, their higher educational attainment, declining fertility, and questioning of traditional gender norms have all contributed to the redefinition of marriage and enhanced acceptability of divorce (Becker, 1981). Thoughts of divorce entertained by both spouses increase with the wife's work experience and decrease with the presence of young children (Huber and Spitze, 1980).

Just as there are "his" and "her" marriages, there are "his" and "her" divorces (Baker, 1984). Just as marriage was the fulcrum for the construction of reality (Berger and Kellner, 1970), the end of marriage sees life arrangements become unstuck. Significant others are cast aside: "partners once seen as symbols of youth, beauty, and trust are regarded as threatening, ugly, and untrustworthy . . ." (Peters, 1983:283). The former spouses are propelled into a host of new problems and experiences which differ by sex. As previous solutions unravel, most face all over again the tasks of economic/work arrangements, parenting, and new relationships with the other sex.

The economic implications of separation and divorce are quite different for husband and wife. The end of marriage often spells downward economic mobility, even poverty, for the women involved (Boyd, 1977). There are a number of reasons for this state of affairs. Women generally earn less than men. Moreover, divorced and separated women suffer from the widespread perception that men are the chief bread-

winners and women merely secondary earners. Also, women returning to the labor market after some years of full-time housewifery are
unlikely to be well-trained. The situation may be further exacerbated
by the cost of child care while the woman works, by reduced or non-
existent credit rating (Boyd, 1977:48), and by the likelihood of ex-
husbands defaulting on support payments (Baker, 1983:291). All in all,
the wife faces sterner resocialization lessons in the economic area.

When couples split, the meaning and experience of parenthood
changes. (See Schlesinger, 1985.) The mother, who is usually custodial
parent, must learn to raise children alone and on diminished financial
resources. The father, on the other hand, frequently joins the legion
of Uncle Dads, with no meaningful role in his children's lives beyond
visiting privileges.

> If the weather was nice, I would walk [my children]
> down to a nearby park to play Horse with a spongy
> basketball, or take them to the zoo, where I would see
> other Uncle Dads doing weekend duty. We could
> distinguish each other from the regular, full-time dads
> because they were allowed to look bored (Smith, 1985).

The movement in support of joint custody is growing (Roman and
Haddad, 1978), especially among well-educated fathers. Single-parent
families, joint-custody and blended-family constellations of step- and
natural parents and children all require extensive resocialization. All
these novel situations demand role making ("How does a step-mom
prove herself as a parent to a fifteen-year-old boy?") and negotiation
of relationships ("How does a divorced man relate to his ex-wife in a
joint-custody situation? To his former in-laws?")

Since three-quarters of the divorced eventually remarry (McKie
et al., 1983:233), the majority of divorced people again date, court, and
establish partnerships. Most divorcees do not reject marriage *per se*. Men
find marriage a congenial state (Bernard, 1972) and are quicker to
remarry (Baker, 1984). Beyond intangible attractions, women in financial need are more likely to remarry (Peters, 1983:297).

Second-time around dating and mating involve many of the
challenges discussed earlier in this chapter, plus some new ones. If a
decade or so has elapsed since they last were on the dating scene, they
feel foolish and out of practice. The very terms "dating," "boyfriend,"
"girlfriend" sound juvenile when one's own children are onlookers.
Second marriages too are different propositions. They are contracted
with personal knowledge of marital impermanence and failure, in the
shadow of fractured relationships with previous significant others.
Despite commonalities, gender again makes a difference. Four-fifths
of divorced men, but only two-thirds of divorced women, ever remarry
(Ambert, 1980:189). Divorced men initiate dating more easily and are

more likely than their female counterparts to describe themselves as "elated and free" after divorce (Hetherington et al., 1979). Women are more likely to experience a decrease in self-esteem and community status after divorce (Schlesinger, 1970).

Supply and demand associated with the marriage gradient is one reason why remarriage is easier for men. It has been customary for women to find an older partner. Mid-1980s marriages of such celebrities as Mary Tyler Moore and Olivia Newton-John to younger men were well publicized. However, given the role of age in reinforcing male power, such December-May arrangements remain an anomaly. Much younger women are considered suitable partners for divorced men and they are more plentiful. Marriages between age-discrepant partners pose unique problems, such as non-matching generational memories, disagreement over the desirability of producing offspring, and different retirement ages (Ambert and Baker, 1984:100).

Gender Socialization in Middle Adulthood

The "middle-age crisis" and "middle-age crazy" of pop psychology and Hollywood fame are recent social inventions. Before the early 1970s, the middle years were simply a way station between youth and old age. Suddenly, the "big four-oh" birthday has become charged with significance, and a mid-life crisis a self-fulfilling prophecy. Social labels are applied to people who reach milestone birthdays. What happened? For one thing, the experience of aging has been affected by biological and cultural changes over previous decades: increased life expectancy, effective contraception, shorter child-bearing and child-rearing phases in family life, growing concern for egalitarian relationships between women and men inside and outside the family (Rubin, 1979:226). Added to these factors are heightened visibility of the aged as a segment of society and harbinger of the future, and the growth of introspective narcissism (Lasch, 1979) as aftermath of the social movements of the 1960s. As well, it was not until the mid-1970s that psychologists began to publish developmental studies of adults (Brim, 1976). Works like Levinson's *The Seasons of a Man's Life* (1978) and Sheehy's *Passages* (1974) captured the public's fancy as intellectual frames of reference for understanding middle age.

Crisis or Transition?

Experts agree that middle age involves inescapable challenges, that people are likely to undergo personality change as a result of mid-life "growing pains" (Brim, 1976:8). However, the word "transition" is more accurate than "crisis." According to Brim (1976:8), crises (that is, rapid and substantial personality shifts and radical dislocation of previous frameworks for living) occur only for individuals who encounter multiple, simultaneous demands for personality change. He concludes that such pop-culture renderings of life stages as the "male mid-life crisis" are as creditable as astrology and tea-leaf reading (p. 7). The transition has been associated with various ages (40-50, 44-47, even 35-60). Since significant middle-of-life events occur at different ages for different people (Rossi, 1980:13), it is the definition of the situation that counts. [13]

To the extent that the mid-life transition is a product of the human condition, commonalities exist between female and male experiences. However, divergencies also occur. Most important, men's transition currently focuses on work, women's on family. An accurate assessment of women's situation is only beginning to emerge. Before feminist social science studies, e.g. Rubin (1979), female middle age was defined by male experts who assumed biological determinism of feminine behavior (Barnett and Baruch, 1978:190). We discuss first the commonalities, then the divergencies of mid-life experiences.

Mid-life Experiences Common to Both Sexes

Some mid-life conditions are human conditions. Middle age is a social interpretation of chronological time. Life is now restructured in terms of "time-left-to-live rather than time-since-birth" (Neugarten, 1968:97). One's own eventual death becomes a certainty. Aging and death of parents removes the buffering generation between self and death. The body signals youth's end. Hormone production drops. Hair thins and grays. Midriffs thicken. Faces wrinkle. Bifocals and dentures loom. Heart attacks threaten. Stressful changes in family life occur, including children who have "contracted" a particularly difficult case of adolescence (Smith, 1985) or left home, death or dependency of parents, and mid-life transitions of spouses. These situations all present problems for socialization or resocialization.

Women and men exhibit some common reactions. Above all, neither sex wholeheartedly welcomes the arrival of middle age in a youth-oriented society (Broschart, 1978:259). Mid-life experiences provoke introspection, stocktaking, self-evaluation. Achievements are reviewed in the light of previous goals. Sometimes, the assessment produces a sense of despair and failure. Even when individuals deem themselves successful, experiences of mortality, aging bodies, and diminishing opportunities must be handled. Almost inevitably, people ask themselves, "What am I going to do with the time that remains?" Aspirations are revised and life-area involvements are shifted with "now or never" urgency. "We only go around once, so why should I stick with this dull job or mediocre marriage?" The hedonistic self-indulgence that sometimes occurs (Brim 1976; Mortimer and Simmons, 1978) has become the hallmark of the mid-life crisis in popular culture. In the 1980 movie "Middle-Age Crazy," Bruce Dern trades in his wife for a football club cheerleader and his Oldsmobile stationwagon for a Porsche, and lives to regret it. In "Kramer vs. Kramer" (1979), Meryl Streep abandons Dustin Hoffman and child to satisfy her vocational ambitions. Despite these similarities, women and men interpret mid-life problems in terms of their gender scripts. We turn first to the more highly publicized male version.

Gender Differences in Mid-life Experience

Men's Reactions. Since masculine gender norms emphasize work, it makes sense that male stocktaking focuses upon occupational achievement. Mid-life feelings of failure at work can have diverse outcomes: substitution of lesser, more attainable life goals, career changes, or enhanced interest in a new or continuing family (Mortimer and Simmons, 1978:443). The spectre of heart attacks motivates reactions that vary from sudden enthusiasm for physical fitness to loss of interest in being a "success machine" (Ehrenreich, 1983).

Substantial numbers of men shift their major investments from work to family. As Rossi (1980:11) observes, this alteration of life priorities implies that during "all the long years of early marriage and family formation, they were largely passive spectators in the home setting." Men's new interest in the family may be ill timed. As husbands become more affiliative, their wives, who are becoming more agentic and independent, may be looking beyond the home for satisfaction (Lowenthal et al., 1975). This shift in gender orientation is one reason for the vulnerability of mid-life marriages.

Women's Reactions. Masculine ruling ideas define women in terms of value to men, as sex partners, child bearers, and child rearers. Females' social currency thus depends on attractive, fecund bodies. (See Chapter 7.) Middle age takes away these resources. Bell (1979:75) speaks of the double standard of aging, the "truism of our culture that . . . the inevitable physical symptoms of aging make women sexually unattractive much earlier than men." Power and money age well!

In view of the foregoing, it is hardly surprising that male experts, perceiving women as bodies, baby-making machines, and mothers, have painted a black portrait of women's mid-life difficulties. Feminist research has begun to refute male views (Posner, 1979).[14] From the male perspective, menopause became the "death of the woman in the woman" (Ehrenreich and English, 1978:111). One male "expert" described menopause as "castration" and the sufferer of this "living decay" as "no longer a woman but a neuter" (Wilson, 1966). Nonetheless, research (Neugarten et al., 1968:200) reports many women to be delighted to be done with "menstruation and its attendant annoyances . . . ."

Similarly, "experts" labeled children's leave-taking the "empty nest syndrome" and linked it with depression in middle-aged women. Presumably, the basis for this male definition of the situation was "the belief that a woman is little more than the builder of the nest and the nurturer of the young . . ." (Rubin, 1979:14). In actual fact, almost all the women studied by Rubin responded to the departure of their children "with a decided sense of relief" (p. 15). The "empty nest syndrome" turns out to be "pious fiction" and considerably less burdensome than either young children (Gerson et al., 1984) or the grown children of the 1980s who won't leave home (Foote, 1982).

What, then, is the nature of women's mid-life transition? Loss of family roles and functions does precipitate self-evaluation. Full-time housewives often look beyond the home and family for an answer to "What next?" One of Rubin's (1979:211) respondents said:

> Yesterday I was picking up some clothes to put them in
> the washer, and suddenly I realized that I was doing the
> same work now that I was doing twenty-nine years ago
> when I first got married. *It's like never growing up.*
> (Emphasis in original.)

Some women toy with the idea of divorce. Some carry through (Rabkin, 1985). Many women return to the labor force or to higher education where occupational socialization the second time around can be a tough proposition. Reflecting on their biographies can be a radicalizing experience for women past the age when gender pays off. Mid-life mothers, sometimes less traditional about gender than their own daughters, may serve as role models for non-traditional role combinations (Bernard, 1975).

What about middle-aged women who have had outside jobs all along? A woman with any level of job is less vulnerable to crisis than one whose interests have been submerged in husband and children (Cumming et al., 1975). Since both job and family are salient for women with high commitment to their outside work, the mid-life transition of career women partakes of those of both full-time housewives and men:

> No matter if she works outside the home as well as in it,
> no matter how important her work or how successful she
> may be at it, the tasks by which she is defined, judged,
> and validated are those of the family; therefore, those are
> the ones by which she measures herself . . . (Rubin,
> 1979:110).

As the mid-life transition draws to a close, women and men become more similar. Their social roles become less distinctive and personality traits less stereotyped. For example, women become more aggressive and less sentimental, while men become less aggressive and more affiliative and nurturant (Neugarten and Garron, 1965). Couples who stay together require resocialization in order to adapt to each other's new attitudes and extra-familial roles. Husbands whose wives have just ventured into the public sphere must relinquish their lifelong monopoly on reporting the world to their wives (Wax, 1979:193). Spouses must redefine the "marital roles of husband and wife as they reemerge as separate roles after the long confusion they have had with parental roles" (Brim, 1968:213). Perhaps most important, they must deal with the shift in the balance of power in the wife's favor. Post-parental marriage can be a "golden period" of shared activities and decreased concern over economic survival (Brim, 1968).

Gender Socialization for Aging

Age, like gender, is a social construct erected upon a biological base. No consensus exists as to when people in our society pass from middle-age status to elderly. Events such as the retirement dinner, the first pension check, the first grandchild, or the sixty-fifth birthday do not necessarily change personal or social identity from middle-aged to old (Matthews, 1979:58). Gerontologists, however, distinguish between the "young-old" and "old-old" (Neugarten, 1974), with the first cutting point at 65 and the second at 74 or 75. It is members of the older category who manifest the problems of aging — poverty, ill-health, social isolation (Hess, 1985:321).

If the timing of old age is somewhat variable, its low status is abundantly clear. Old age is a stigmatized status in this youth-oriented society (Goffman, 1963). However, because everyone who is lucky enough to live will eventually grow old, old age is a little different from other stigmas. Regarding old people as "not quite human" is not as comfortable as viewing people with one leg as "not quite human" (Matthews, 1979:61).

The changing physical, economic, and social conditions associated with aging require socialization for people of both sexes (Rosow, 1974). However, aging is especially difficult for women. The inequities that accrue to women from living under male ruling ideas appear to crystallize in old age (Abu-Laban, 1981:85-86). To be old and female has been described as the "double whammy" (Posner, 1980). Women, who all along have lived under the double standard of aging, are doubly stigmatized in the last stage of their life cycle.

From the symbolic interactionist perspective, the key feature of aging is progressive role loss or role exits. In youth and middle age, the loss of one social position is generally accompanied by entry into another. For example, people leave school and acquire jobs. They divorce and remarry. In old age, exits are not followed by re-entrances. The terms "retirement" and "widowhood" designate the permanent loss of two crucial social roles (Blau, 1970:615). Despite the greatly expanded ranks of the aged, too few roles have so far been institutionalized to foster their continuing contributions to society. "Older women in particular . . . are in the end the ones most often left alone to create new roles for themselves" (Riley, 1985:339).[15] However, women seem on the average to weather role transitions better than men (Riley, 1985:338). Since involvement in social roles supports identity, including gender identity, this cumulative role shedding has serious consequences for old people's views of themselves as feminine and masculine persons. The blurring of gender roles that began in the middle years is accelerated when child rearing (and often, marriage) is over, and the distinction between paid and unpaid work is set aside (Riley, 1985:343). As the traditional gender division of labor disappears, the elderly become more androgynous. We place women and their losses at the forefront of our discussion.

Loss of Spouse

Old women are more likely than old men to be widowed and to live alone. In 1981, 76 percent of men 65 years and over were married, but only 40 percent of older women. Only 14 percent of men were widowed, compared to 49 percent of women (Novak, 1985:49). An estimated 36 percent of elderly women live alone, compared to 14 percent of men (Statistics Canada, 1984). Marriage is protection against institutionalization. Widowed women are less likely than widowed men to remarry. Women's greater life expectancy results in a shortage of eligible men. The fact that the traditional direction of age differences between bride and groom is even greater with second marriages means women in second marriages face an increased probability of widowhood and a longer period of single survivorship (Abu-Laban, 1981:90).

For both sexes, widowhood is the greatest shock in old age (Novak, 1985:49). Indeed, widowhood is the single most disruptive crisis of all the life cycle transitions (Haas-Hawkings et al., 1985). The degree of trauma depends, of course, on such variables as the state of the marital relationship, the stage of the marriage, and the manner of death. Young "off-time" widows appear to suffer more traumatic effects than older widows (Glick et al., 1974), possibly because people go through a "rehearsal for widowhood" (Neugarten, 1968) as they grow older and watch their friends go through the death of a spouse (Lopata, 1984:5). However, despite such anticipatory socialization, the task before the bereaved person is enormous. In addition to "grief work"

(Lindemann, 1944), the widow must learn (or delegate) her husband's instrumental skills, e.g. handling the car, the furnace, the bankbook. For the male, widowhood magnifies the socio-emotional disadvantages of masculinity. He has lost his closest confidante; he is less likely to seek emotional support from his own sex; he lacks homemaking skills; and he is at high risk in terms of suicide potential, morbidity, and mortality rates. The rapidity of male remarriage may indicate an "acute and devastating need for interpersonal support" (Abu-Laban, 1980b:204).

If, as Berger and Kellner (1970) argue, wife and husband reconstruct reality, including themselves upon marriage, then widowhood requires that that reality and self be reconstructed yet again (Lopata, 1984). For example, the death of a spouse often means the loss of the only person who shared one's adult history and memories. Perhaps, one begins to think of oneself as truly old when no one is left who remembers one as young. No longer being part of a couple is a serious matter in an androcentric world. For women, loss of a man and movement into the company of other women may be interpreted as a drop in status (Abu-Laban, 1980a:129). Suttee, the Hindu practice of burying the widow alive with her deceased husband or burning her on his funeral pyre, was an extreme expression of the conviction that a woman without a man had no place in society (Stein, 1978).

Loss of Financial Security

Lack of money is a very serious problem faced by the elderly. The vision of retirement as a time for couples to cultivate leisure pursuits and travel the globe must be reconciled with deteriorating finances. Income drops by about one-half at the time of retirement (Abu-Laban, 1980a:127). Shortage of money affects nearly every aspect of life, including shelter, nutrition, and health. Elderly widows are especially likely to be poor. In 1982, their average income was $10,000, 72 percent of the average for unattached elderly males (Statistics Canada, 1985:66). Skid row is no longer the exclusive domain of men (Ross, 1982). (See Tindale [1980] for a discussion of homeless men.)

Elderly women are poor because they devoted their lives to their families without pay and believed they would always be taken care of. "When they become widows, as they almost inevitably must under our present marriage customs, the vast majority find that the promised security does not exist" (Dulude, 1978:95). Women of that generation were socialized to believe that they needed little education or job training. Those who were in the labor force worked for low pay or part-time, which gave access to low pensions, or (the more typical case) for small firms without pension plans at all (Novak, 1985:148). In the end, women's lifelong preoccupation with the family fails to pay off.

Loss of Work

Most of the public and political debate on aging has been framed in terms of masculine ruling ideas. Attention has been focused on the trauma of male retirement. Consequently, both the most serious problems of elderly women, such as poverty and isolation (Hess, 1985), and women's adjustment to retirement (Burwell, 1984) have been neglected. However, given the different meaning that work has had in men's and women's lives, sex differences in retirement experiences might be expected. Specifically, since males derive personal identity and social worth from their work, one would expect their retirement to represent a more serious role loss for them (Blau, 1973). Simone de Beauvoir (1970:295) describes Ernest Hemingway's attitude toward retirement:

> Hemingway said that the worst death for anyone was the loss of what formed the centre of his life and made him what he really was. Retirement was the most loathsome word in the language. Whether we chose it or whether we were compelled by fate, retiring, giving up one's calling — the calling that made us what we were — was the same as going down to the grave.

Like housewives, retired workers "in a society in which money determines value" engage in use-value activities outside the money economy — home care, hobbies, volunteer work. In this type of society, activity not worth money is considered valueless (Hochschild, 1975a:564). This type of logic leads to the expectation that workers resist retirement and are unhappy after retirement occurs. Surprisingly, research provides only qualified support to both the hypothesis of male retirement trauma and the hypothesis of sex differences. Each will be discussed briefly in turn.

According to research, most people stop working as soon as it is financially feasible to do so, and most of these "young-olds" adjust to it with little trouble (Novak, 1985:169). For instance, Atchley's (1982) sample members of both sexes found that retirement turned out to be better than they had expected. Indeed, life satisfaction improved slightly after retirement. The belief that retirement increases mortality and people die shortly after retirement is not true (Parker, 1982:119). Social class is an important variable here that operates somewhat differently for men than women. Working-class men, those who do not own or control the means of production, and who have had low work satisfaction, are pleased to retire. Their life satisfaction has come from family and leisure roles and it is to these roles that they now turn. "Being the man of the house" has depended less on work outside it and more directly on being a husband and father (Hochschild, 1975a). By contrast, middle-class and professional men, with control over their work, have enjoyed their work and wish to continue. However, they realign themselves to leisure occupations that resemble work. The middle class has more resources to cope with the loss of work and their morale is higher. Generally, retired people continue with the same non-work activities, rather than taking up new roles (Parker, 1982). For all men, health and income are the factors that count in retirement adjustment.

Retirement does not emasculate or devastate. Why? These possibilities suggest themselves. Adjustment may be aided by anticipatory socialization in the last years of paid work that stresses the negative aspects of the job and the positive experiences that lie ahead. Reference group support likely operates — one's friends are also retiring and retired; collective socialization can have profound effects (Becker, 1970:589). Perhaps, masculine gender identity is sufficiently invested in alternate leisure and family roles. Relatedly, retirement is a continuation of the androgynizing move, begun in middle age, away from work and toward relationships as the source of male identity. Finally, Becker's (1970:586) concept of *situational adjustment* seems to be involved:

> One of the most common mechanisms in the development of the person in adulthood is the process of situational adjustment. . . . If he has a strong desire to continue, the ability to assess accurately what is required, and can deliver the required performance, *the individual turns himself into the kind of person the situation demands.* (Emphasis added.)

Men learn to be retired by learning the definitions of the situation that pertain to the retired role. What they formerly considered to be peripheral leisure activities must now be seen not only as satisfying but also significant (Parker, 1983:71). Since retirement is institutionalized, expected, the "right thing" to do, the man can attribute this withdrawal from the occupational role to society, not personal failure (Riley et al., 1969:966).

With a few exceptions, the retirement of women from the labor force is similar to men's. Income and health are central to the adjustment of both sexes (Burwell, 1984). However, being married is associated with retirement adjustment for women but not men (Atchley, 1982). And social class operates differently. Women with lower occupational status and unmarried women plan to delay retirement for economic reasons (Atchley, 1982). Burwell (1984) cites Atchley and Corbett's (1977) intriguing finding that retirement comes for many career women before they feel they have achieved their professional goals. Such women were late-starters in careers (because of time out for child rearing) and time ran out for them. Finally, women who have been full-time housewives do not retire in the usual sense of the term. However, if still married, they will be affected by their husband's retirement (Parker, 1982:120). The reversal of power differential begun with the mid-life transition is accentuated in old age.[16] The retired husband, who has lost his occupationally derived advantages, may now be a twenty-four-hour-a-day nuisance in his wife's domestic domain.

The current generation of elderly Canadians is a product of traditional gender socialization and unique historical experiences. Demographic and technological developments suggest that aging in the future will be a different proposition. For example, with increasing proportions of older people in our population, the cult of youth should fade so that growing old will no longer be the *faux pas* it used to be (Neugarten, as interviewed by E. Hall [1980]). The electronic revolution in the organization of work currently under way should reduce work's cardinal importance in the definition of masculinity. New economic arrangements may mean old people in the future need not contend with poverty. However, as Abu-Laban (1981:96) warns, though "the lot of older women would be improved as a concomitant to improvements in the lot of the old in general, prophecies of 'deliverance' for older women, *as women*, are not assured" (emphasis in original). Only the disappearance of patriarchy can lift the stigma of femininity.

Conclusions

Chapter 5 employed symbolic interactionist and sociology of knowledge perspectives to trace the development of gender identity from adolescence, through early and middle adulthood to old age. The body of the chapter concentrated on the cross-cutting of two critical diffuse statuses (gender, age) by which societies categorize all individuals. Three broad generalizations and a caveat may be drawn from this chapter. First, being born female as opposed to being born male deeply influences the nature and quality of experiences throughout the life-course. Male ruling ideas affect females from cradle to grave. Second, differentiation by gender peaks in adolescence and early adulthood, and declines thereafter into old age. Third, taken-for-granted ideas about normal human development, i.e. age stereotypes, defining what is possible, acceptable, desirable at various points in the life cycle, are linked in the public's mind with masculine-defined gender stereotypes. The normative force of these expectations contributes substantially to the "reality" they describe. To some extent, cultural knowledge about how women and men age operates as self-fulfilling prophecy, producing or reinforcing the patterns it presumes (Dannefer, 1984:107-108). If the feminist goal of gender transcendence were to be realized, and the cultural elaborations upon sex stripped away, socialization from infancy to old age would be dramatically altered.

Our caveat warns against accepting the content of Chapter 5 as the complete and literal truth regarding gender socialization from adolescence to old age. Instead, our discussion should be viewed as the best answer that can be offered under present circumstances. For various reasons, the analysis is a necessary oversimplification of the actual realities of gender socialization. No previous work has dealt theoretically with gender socialization over the entire life course. Like all first attempts, this one is somewhat unsophisticated. Also, space limitations have made it necessary to concentrate on the "main street" of gender socialization, and to mention briefly or ignore altogether the "side streets" and "narrow pathways." Finally, because gender socialization in adolescence and adulthood has received considerably less research attention than childhood, empirical data are needed to test and to refine many of the ideas presented in this chapter.

NOTES

1. Bush and Simmons (1981:140) note that "although Mead does not really discuss how the self may continue to evolve throughout a lifetime, his theory strongly implies the potential for such development."

2. G. Stanley Hall, the author of the first scientific work on adolescence (1904), viewed it as a period of inevitable *Sturm und Drang*. Margaret Mead's study of adolescents on the island of Samoa, *Coming of Age in Samoa* (1928), led psychologists to reject the belief that stress and conflict in adolescence is inevitable and universal (Santrock, 1984:23). However, Derek Freeman, *Margaret Mead and Samoa* (1983) has reopened the debate. Freeman attempts to refute Mead's claim that adolescence in Samoa is or was an untroubled time.

3. There is some overlap between symbolic interactionist ideas and the well-known work of Erik Erikson (1963, 1968). Erikson, writing in the psychoanalytic tradition, characterized the primary challenge of adolescence as "identity versus role confusion," the forging of an identity that can envision adult commitments. However, Gilligan (1979:437) asks, "But about whom is Erikson talking? Once again it turns out to be the male child." The female "holds her identity in abeyance as she prepares to attract the man by whose name she will be defined, the man who will rescue her from emptiness and loneliness by filling 'the inner space'" (p. 437).

4. No Canadian data have been systematically gathered to show how parents view adolescents in general or their own children in particular. However, Bibby and Posterski (1985:7) note that some parents dealing with their recalcitrant teenagers feel young people "aren't quite human," that "they are working not with a 'generation gap' but a 'species gap.'" Acock (1984:160) describes an American study, Miller et al. (1983), which reported that half the fathers and mothers have a negative attitude toward teenagers in general and stereotype them as "lazy," "rebellious" and so on. One in four of the parents held a negative attitude toward their own adolescent children. Results such as these are one reason why the adolescent peer group is so influential.

5. Santrock (1984:462) notes that "most studies of gender deviance *have included only boys* who are diagnosed as gender deviant when they play almost exclusively with feminine sex-typed toys, dress up in female clothes, choose girls rather than boys as playmates, engage in female role playing, fantasize about being girls, and express themselves with feminine gestures . . ." (emphasis added). Girls in our society are allowed more flexibility in dress, play activities, and interests.

6. Canadian humorist Max Braithwaite (1969:143) describes his sex education in the 1920s "the last decade when sex was still under a rock," as follows: "We learned about sex in the gutter, and as far as I'm concerned that's the best place to learn it. One thing about being instructed in the pleasures and hazards of sex by our peers was that they, at least, were honest. They may have been a bit mixed up here and there on some of the more technical points, but no other kid would ever deliberately lie to me regarding such matters, which is more than I can say for the adults."

7. See Kimball (1981) for a thoroughgoing analysis of why biological theories fail to explain the differential participation rates of women and men in the sciences. She points out that the sex differences in participation in scientific fields is very large, incomparison with the very small (but statistically significant) sex differences in mathematical and visual/spatial abilities.

8. Thirty years ago, Paul Goodman (1956:17) wrote: "It's hard to grow up when there isn't enough man's work. There is 'nearly full employment' (with highly significant exceptions), but there get to be fewer jobs that are necessary or unquestionably useful; that require energy and draw on some of one's best capabilities; and that can be done keeping one's honor and dignity."

9. In sociology, the economic perspective of marriage is emphasized by structuralists (those who emphasize the family's relationship to the means of production and its position in the stratification system). Structuralists and sociologists of knowledge share the same Marxian roots. However, symbolic interactionists view marriage (as all social relationships) as fundamentally symbolic (Nett, 1978).

10. *Role distance*, a concept originated by Goffman (1961b), may be defined as the individual's desire to dissociate herself/himself from some or all of the expectations of a particular role because these role obligations threaten the self-concept. The inclination to role distance tends to be stimulated by the presence of an audience, who the actor feels may denigrate her/him for enacting the expectations. Role distance is not refusal to play the role, but rather an adaptive strategy, whereby the performer can more or less fulfill his/her role obligations while maintaining self-respect (Stebbins, 1975:133).

11. The terms "choose" and "decision" connote freedom of action which is often unavailable. The process may be one of drift and reaction to circumstances and opportunities.

12. Hartmann (1981:385) summarizes the research on household division of labor:

> First, the vast majority of time spent on housework is spent by the wife, about 70 percent on the average, with both the husband and the children providing about 15 percent on average. Second, the wife is largely responsible for child care. The wife takes on the excess burden of housework in those families where there are very young or very many children; the husband's contribution to housework remains about the same whatever the family size or the age of the youngest child. It is the wife who, with respect to housework at least, does all of the adjusting to the family life cycle. Third, the woman who also works for wages (and she does so usually, we know, out of economic necessity) finds that her husband spends very little more time on housework on average than the husband whose wife is not a wage worker. Fourth, the wife spends perhaps eight hours per work in additional housework on account of the husband. And fifth, the wife spends, on average, a minimum of forty hours a week maintaining the house and husband if she does not work for wages and a minimum of thirty hours per week if she does.

In Hartmann's opinion, the time spent on housework can be fruitfully used as a measure of power relations in the home. For an opinion contrary to Hartmann's, see Valadez and Clignet (1984).

13. With regard to the generality of midlife crises, Rossi (1980:14) remarks that so far, research on middle age in North America is based on a particular cohort of people, with direct or indirect experience of the Depression. Mortimer and Simmons (1978:444) suggest that it may be more likely to occur in high level professionals and managers, with high work involvement, clearly recognized timetables for gauging success, and numerous occasions for self-evaluation.

14. On the March 17, 1984 edition of the CBC radio program "Quirks and Quarks," Dr. Anne Voda remarked that feminist scholarship depicts the menopause as a normal process rather than a disease. However, she went on to say that "the focus of the feminist scholarship has been in some ways to invalidate the experience as a real physiological event for women . . . and my research has validated at least the hot flash as a real experience . . . ." According to Burwell (1984:197), research may help us to reject two prevalent but contradictory views of the menopausal woman: either

she is in the grip of a disease caused by estrogen deficiency, or suffering from symptoms that are "all in the head."

15. Role-loss theorists such as Blau (1973) have been criticized for taking the "victim" approach by focusing on loss and neglecting opportunities for role-making which continue to be available throughout the life course (Marshall, 1980:84).

16. According to Freedman (1979, cited in Bernard [1981a:174], in ten cultures around the world, women in the older age brackets tend to become more "outspoken and assertive," whereas men become "more passive and giving with age."

6

Symbols and the Production of Gender

Introduction

> Symbols are the stuff out of which cultures and societies are made.
> *(Zetterberg, 1965:1)*

> Words are not, of course, the same as their referents. The word tree cannot yield shade.
> *(Gusfield and Michalowicz, 1984:419)*

> . . . a patriarchal society is organized so that the belief in male supremacy 'comes true'.
> *(Spender, 1985:1)*

Human beings live in an environment expanded to include the symbolic as well as the purely physical (Hewitt, 1984:27). A symbol is something that stands for something else. The word "tree" stands for tall, live, leafy structures. The color "red" means stop and "green," go. Money symbolizes buying power (Firth, 1973:26). Gender is a complex of symbols, built upon biological sex, dealing with the attributes, the rights and duties, and relative prestige of females and males in Canadian society. Language thus contains codifications of what boys and girls, men and women are and what they shall do — that is, it represents the *social* reality of gender (Zetterberg, 1965:2). Chapter 6 focuses upon symbols as one answer to the question, "How is gender as taken-for-granted reality accomplished?"

Women have been excluded historically from the production of culture. The English language has been literally "man made." Men have controlled language, and it has worked in their favor. Women "remain 'outsiders,' borrowers of the language" (Spender, 1985:x, 12). Furthermore, women have been on the margins of the social circles where knowledge is created. As a result, "male-stream thought" (O'Brien, 1979:100) either misrepresents women's experience or omits it altogether. Gender itself is defined from the masculine perspective. The powerful use language "to define, label, evaluate, and rank-order" (Lipman-Blumen, 1984:75).

For children, this male-dominated symbolic world is *given*. Their self-imagery and consciousness are shaped through language, the major socialization vehicle. To a considerable extent, what people think and know is structured by the language categories at their disposal (Whorf, 1949). Since language and gender are linked in many complex ways, children's linguistic lessons are also lessons in gender relations. The process continues into adolescence and adulthood through exposure to symbolic forms (popular music, advertising, pornography) that derogate women or render them invisible. With the coming of the women's movement, this androcentric symbolic order is no longer opaque. Its socially constructed and incomplete nature is beginning to be understood and masculine domination challenged. Symbolic modes' more representative of women's experience are being created.

Classification of Symbols

Symbols may be classified as mediated or unmediated, popular or high culture, and disseminated by mass media or limited circulation. These distinctions will organize this chapter's consideration of gender symbolism. *Mediation* refers to the intervention of packagers, gatekeepers or distributors. Our discussion begins with the unmediated symbolic portrayals of gender in language, non-verbal communication, and humor. Pornography and children's literature are examples of mediated symbols treated later in the chapter. In general, mediation enhances male power. This is so because men "control what enters the discourse by occupying the positions which do the work of gatekeeping and the positions from which people and their 'mental products' are evaluated" (Smith, 1975a:357).

Mediated symbolic forms may be classified as either *popular culture* or *high culture*. As the term suggests, popular culture implies popularity: items are purchased or witnessed by many people, are widely enjoyed, and are used as a resource for conversation (Fine, 1977). Usually, profit-minded entrepreneurs produce and distribute these symbols (Gans, 1966:552). Examples of popular culture treated in this chapter are TV sit-coms, rock music, and video games. High culture, on the other hand, evokes standards of esthetic excellence and refers to symbolic forms produced primarily for their intrinsic worth, such as opera, drama, classical music, and the like. Graphic art has been chosen for treatment here.

The popular culture-high culture distinction is somewhat arbitrary. Cultural products are subject to "esthetic mobility"; some works, considered popular but esthetically worthless when produced, have been subsequently elevated to high esthetic rank (Peterson, 1977:389). Women's needlework and the music of the Beatles are cases in point. Instances of downward esthetic mobility also occur. The work of many nineteenth-century painters, distinguished in their day, has been passed over by succeeding generations (Sydie, 1980:172). In the past, both popular and high culture have been androcentric. Both are now being influenced by feminist ideas.

Cultural meanings do not simply enter people's heads in some mystical way, "thereafter to direct their interpretations of experience and monitor their behavior" (Grayson, 1983:391). Therefore, sociologists focus on the means by which symbols are disseminated. The *mass media* are impersonal communication sources, such as records, books, magazines, and television, which reach large audiences. Although all such symbols are mediated, they may be either popular or high culture. For example, TV presentations of rock videos and symphony concerts are popular and high culture, respectively. Mass dissemination of gender imagery may be contrasted with more personal and limited circulation sources, such as conversation among friends, sermons from the pulpit, and classroom lectures.

Canadians' dependence on the mass media for information and entertainment makes their presentation of gender a matter of great importance. In general, the media tend to be sexist (Tuchman, 1979:533 ff.). For one thing, few women hold responsible positions in media industries. Moreover, it is hard for those who do to resist ideas and attitudes that disparage women (Tuchman, 1979:535). Successful female professionals are those who have satisfied the criteria of male gate-keepers (Smith 1975a:367). Secondly, sexism is profitable to advertisers and, derivatively, to the media. Thirdly, the media are sexist because they mirror cultural notions about gender, and in turn, shape and strengthen societal norms (Albrecht, 1954).

As the above discussion emphasizes, sociologists do not conceptualize symbols as free-floating entities detached from social context. The interactionist tenet that the world is a world of meanings does not imply "that it is a world of ideas *alone*" (Marshall, 1978–79:356; emphasis added). Rather, symbols and social structure are interdependent. Cultural forms have human origins in social interaction. In turn, social interaction proceeds by means of symbols. It is the business of the sociologist of knowledge to relate symbols and symbolic productions to their sociocultural milieux. Our emphasis here is on male ruling ideas.

Our first topic is the fundamental relationship between gender and unmediated symbols: verbal language, non-verbal language, and humor. We turn then to selected examples of mediated symbols as they operate in the gender socialization of children, adolescents, and adults. Though space limitations preclude an exhaustive treatment, examples of popular and high culture, as well as mass media and face-to-face dissemination, are represented.

Unmediated Symbols

Verbal Language

Language is an immensely significant factor in the accomplishment of gender as "natural" reality. The experience of a stable reality *out there* is fostered by language, the first institution encountered by the individual biographically, indeed, *the* fundamental institution of society. Language has the quality of *historicity* — it existed before the individual was born. Language is experienced as *external* reality, not the idiosyncratic creation of its users: it is there and it must be learned. Language *objectifies* reality. It firms up and stabilizes the incessant flux of experience into meaningful entities and relationships. Language is an *all-encompassing* reality. Almost everything the person experiences is structured on the basis of the underlying and systematic reality of language, "filtered through it, organized by it, expanded by it or, conversely, banished through it into oblivion . . ." (Berger and Berger, 1975:76). Language has *moral authority*. There is correct and incorrect English. Whether the individual likes it or not, the canons of language must be obeyed. In sum, language provides society's most powerful hold over us (Berger and Berger, 1975:75–81).

Historically, women have been excluded from the public arena and consequently, from the production of language and culture (Spender, 1985:52). Therefore, language ignores and derogates women. As a result,

> all words — regardless of their origin — which are
> associated with females acquire negative connotations,
> because this is a fundamental semantic "rule" in a
> society which constructs male supremacy (Spender,
> 1985:18).

The "semantic derogation of women" (Schulz, 1975) both constructs and confirms female inferiority. As children learn their language, they also learn something about women's place and men's place.

The Semantics and Syntax of Sexism

Sexism in the structure of the English language has three features: females are ignored, defined from the male perspective, and deprecated (Henley et al., 1985).

Ignoring Women. In the English language, the masculine is the unmarked form and all people are male until proven otherwise (Spender, 1985:20). Language excludes and subsumes women through generic masculine terms. Some grammaticists claim that "man," and "his" also imply "woman," "she" and "her." However, research (MacKay, 1980; Schneider and Hacker, 1973) indicates that words such as "man" and "he" trigger male imagery almost exclusively. Religious symbolism has been described as a "paradigmatic case of the male naming of the world" (Spender, 1985:165). God is father, judge, shepherd, king. The socialization lesson here is that females don't matter.

Defining Women from the Masculine Perspective. The masculine power to name has resulted in women being defined in relation to males and secondary to them (Henley et al., 1985:170). For example, women are labeled for men's convenience. Upon marriage, the woman traditionally loses her own surname, adopts her husband's, and becomes "Mrs." in all but the most personal contexts. When the sexes are linguistically grouped, females are the second sex: "boys and girls," "husbands and wives," "his and hers." Henley et al., (1985:171) argue that "this order is not coincidental, but was urged in the sixteenth century as a proper way of putting the worthier party first." Occupational titles also establish males as primary, females as secondary. When women move beyond their traditional sphere, special markers are needed — female physician, lady pilot. As children learn language, they also learn that women are adjuncts to men.

Deprecating Women. Finally, language depreciates women. For example, language defines women as sex objects. One study (Stanley, 1973) identified 220 words for sexually promiscuous females and only 20 for sexually promiscuous males. Women are labeled "nympho," "hooker," "tramp," "whore" and "slut." Sexual labels for men carry more positive associations, reflecting, perhaps, the morality of machismo: "Casanova," "Don Juan," "letch," "stud." Moreover, masculine connotations tend to be strong and positive, while feminine connotations are negative, weak or trivial. Over time, words such as "king," "prince," "lord" have maintained their elevated meanings, while similar words "queen," "madam" and "dame" have acquired debased meanings (Henley et al., 1985:171). Compare the connotations of taking defeat "like a man" versus taking defeat "like a woman." Labeling a woman "mannish" is less insulting than labeling a man "womanish."

Then there are "praise him/blame her" pairs of words. He is a "bachelor" (romantic, eligible, free), she is a "spinster" or "old maid" (poor thing!). He is a "chef" and expert, while she is merely a "cook." He is a "master" of all he surveys, she is a "mistress," sexual property. She "chattered," he "discussed." She "nagged," he "reminded." She "bitched," he "complained." She is "scatterbrained," he is "forgetful." She has "wrinkles," he has "character lines" (Eakins and Eakins, 1978:125–134).

While individual examples of sexism in language may seem trivial, their combined impact is profound when we remember that people's perceptions of the world are linked closely to their language.

"The group which has the power to ordain the structure of language, thought and reality has the potential to create a world in which they are the central figures . . ." (Spender, 1985:143). As a consequence, males come to understand themselves as powerful and important. Women, by contrast, learn to view themselves from outside, as inferior Other. Moreover, women lack the language needed to encompass adequately their own experiences. Language is political, and men's control of women is intimately tied to their control of symbolic forms (Jenkins and Kramarae, 1981:13).

Conversational Procedures to Accomplish Power

Conversation serves as a mechanism for reifying certain versions of reality at the expense of others, and therefore, as a tool of domination (Molotch and Boden, 1985:273). Men make and enforce the rules for both sexes.

Stereotypes portray women as talkative. They gossip. They natter about trivialities. Certainly, they violate men's expectation of their silence. Nevertheless, study after study reports that men speak more often and at greater length than women (Henley et al., 1985:173, 177). Women do not gossip more than men (Levin and Arluke, 1985). Men also speak louder than women (Kramer et al., 1978:639), and their lower-pitched voices are more highly valued.

> Men with high-pitched voices may be taken for women in phone conversations (and treated accordingly), disregarded in group conversations and ridiculed behind their backs. But female newscasters with lower pitch are preferred and are hired; since lower pitch is associated with males, who have more authority in our society, it carries more authority in a female also (Henley et al., 1985:174).

Women are more polite than men (Lakoff, 1975):

The woman: "Oh dear, you've put the peanut butter in the refrigerator again, haven't you?"
The man: "Shit, you've put the damn peanut butter in the fridge again."

Females' more circumspect speech signals their subordination. Inferiors *should* be more polite. Men are more profane and vulgar. "Oh fudge! My hair is on fire!" is a recognizable caricature of women's speech. Swearing and sex talk among men can function to intimidate or exclude women (Coyne et al., 1978). Feminists study the ways women "have been 'protected' from obscenity, yet made the object of much of it" (Jenkins and Kramarae, 1981:11).

The conversational division of labor reflects and reinforces gender. In addition to talking more than women, men interrupt them more. Interruptions serve "as a projection on the speaker's part that he or she is worthy of more attention — has more of value to say and less to learn — than the other party (Kollock et al., 1985:35). West and Zimmerman (1977) found similar patterns of interruption between adults and children and males and females, suggesting that the differences are tied to status. As mentioned in Chapter 1, women accept greater responsibility for keeping conversation going (suggesting topics, asking questions), while men often use minimal responses ("uh-huh," umm") or *non sequitors* as a lazy way of filling a turn or showing lack of interest in what women have to say (P. Fishman, 1978). Dominance is not the only motive. In *The Male Machine,* Fasteau (1975) attributes "blankness" in conversation with his wife to fear that spontaneous talk would reveal "unacceptable feelings," such as vulnerability or failure to "measure up" to the masculine ideal. We return to the role of language in the politics of gender at the end of this chapter.

Non-verbal Communication

Although language is our major mode of communication, humans have other ways of sending messages to one another. Staring, winking, smiling, shrugging are all well-recognized means of "speaking." According to one study, non-verbal communication carries four times the "conversational" weight of verbal messages when both are used in communication (Argyle et al., 1970).

Though females and males are more alike than different in their non-verbal behavior (Birdwhistell, 1970), those learned sex differences that do exist have two functions. First, they serve to communicate "I am female" or "I am male," in Goffman's (1976) words, to display gender. Because of the innate similarity of the sexes, elaborate codes have developed which allow others to determine our sex without inspecting our genitals. Differences in appearance, in walking, arrangement of limbs while seated, smoking cigarettes, etc. make one's gender visible and salient (Pearson, 1985:265). Second, non-verbal cues indicate status and power. Henley et al. (1985:179) argue that the subtle nature of non-verbal communication, compared with speech, renders it "a perfect avenue for the unconscious manipulation of others." They go on to say:

> Nonverbal behavior is of particular importance for women, because their socialization to docility and passivity makes them likely targets for subtle forms of social control, and their close contact with men — for example as wives and secretaries — entails frequent verbal and nonverbal interaction with those in power. Additionally,

women have been found to be more sensitive than men
to nonverbal cues, perhaps because their survival
depends upon it (Henley et al., 1985:179).

Chapter 7 returns to the topic of gender display and appearance. Here, we focus upon five major types of non-verbal signals of status inequalities (Henley, 1977). Children, in learning the subtle canons of body language, have their notions about male superiority-female inferiority reinforced.

Gaze

Women engage in more eye contact than men (Exline et al., 1974). They look at one another more and hold eye contact longer with each other than men do with men (Eakins and Eakins, 1978:150). Contrary to cultural myths, women also gaze more at men than vice versa. In status-differentiated groups, the high-status person typically receives the most visual attention. Thus, the low-status person "looks to" the high-status person for direction or approval (Lamb, 1981). Also, people do more looking when they are listening to another speak. As noted above, men in mixed-sex groups do more talking than women.

Smiling

Women smile and laugh more than men, whether or not they are happy or amused (Frances, 1979). Since the traditional feminine role calls for affiliative social behavior, women may smile more to meet social obligations than to express genuine warmth or friendliness. Feminists have interpreted the smile as a gesture of submission. Firestone (1971) called the smile "the child/woman equivalent of the shuffle; it indicates acquiescence of the victim to his own oppression."

Demeanor

Goffman (1967:77) defines *demeanor* as "that element of the individual's ceremonial behavior typically conveyed through deportment, dress and bearing." Females show more circumspection in their demeanor, a less casual posture and bearing than do males (Eakins and Eakins, 1978:159 ff.). Men tend to keep their legs apart at a ten- to fifteen-degree angle; women keep their knees together. The torso lean of the male in conversation is farther back and more relaxed than the female's. In general, women's bodily demeanor is more restrained and restricted than men's. Once again, a status explanation seems in order: "Among nonequals in status, superordinates can indulge in a casualness and relative unconcern with body comportment that subordinates are not permitted" (Eakins and Eakins, 1978:159).

Touching

Touching is a gesture of dominance and acquiescence to the touch a corresponding gesture of submission.

> Just as the boss can put a hand on the worker, the master on the servant, the teacher on the student, the business executive on the secretary, so men more frequently put their hands on women, despite folk mythology to the contrary (Henley et al., 1975:181).

Touching is the non-verbal equivalent to first-naming. When both are used reciprocally, they indicate solidarity or intimacy; when used non-reciprocally, they indicate status (Henley, 1985:194). Females also experience more same sex touching than males. Apart from formal hand-shaking and locker-room swatting, male touching of other males carries homosexual connotations (Deaux, 1976:65).

Personal Space

In comparison with women, men command more personal space. Men prefer greater standing and sitting distances between themselves than do women. They expansively dominate the space around them — they sprawl, they sit with legs spread out, they pace a room, they gesture extravagantly. By contrast, women condense or compress. They keep legs crossed, elbows at sides, move around the room or stage less when speaking in public, maintain a more erect posture, and seem to be trying to take up as little space as possible (Henley, 1977). Sex differences in space communicate dominance and submission. Higher-status people command more space. They have larger houses, cars, offices, desks. Inferiors own less space, and their personal space is more readily breached by others (Eakins and Eakins, 1978:169–171). People of both sexes are more willing to intrude upon a woman than upon a man (Unger, 1978:477).

     In summary, important gender socialization lessons are conveyed by the "silent language" (Hall, 1959). This is so for the simple reason that most of these lessons remain below the level of conscious awareness.

Humor

Humor is "a distinctly human achievement: among living things only human beings laugh" (Wolfenstein, 1954:11). Our society especially values humor. Ninety-four percent of the subjects in one study (Allport, 1961) claimed their own sense of humor to be equal to, or above, average. Humor comes in many forms: satire, irony, black or gallows humor, ethnic jokes, sex jokes, puns, slips of the tongue, spoonerisms, riddles, anecdotes, limericks, practical jokes.

The essence of humor, why something is funny, defies simple explanation (Davis and Farina, 1970). According to symbolic interactionists, however, humor depends on the "resources of language." This is true in the superficial sense that words and sentences are frequently used to create humor, and in the deeper sense, that humor "presupposes a common universe of discourse and shared experiences" (Lindesmith et al., 1977:165–166). Secondly, they stress that humor's meaning is sustained in interaction.

> To laugh in the company of others presupposes a minimum of common "definitions of the situation." Those who refuse to join in common laughter are frowned upon, they are "bad sports"; on the other hand, if an invitation to laugh is not accepted by the group, the incipient humorist feels "out of place." In laughter one must share and share alike (Coser, 1959:172).

Below we discuss several gender-relevant (and unmediated) functions of humor in interaction.[1]

Communicating Attitudes

Humor communicates attitudes, including attitudes towards other people. The ambiguous nature of humor allows people to convey feelings without being held accountable for them (Sanford and Eder, 1984). Because humor is playful, they can communicate the message and "then take it back if need be by saying 'it was only a joke'" (Kane et al., 1977:13). Jokes provide an unobtrusive measure of public opinion, since jokes have to be relevant to be funny.

There is an anti-female bias in North American humor that reflects and reinforces women's inferior status in society (Cantor, 1976: McGhee, 1979; Zimbardo and Meadow, 1974):

> Judge: "You are charged with throwing your wife out of the window."
> Robinson: "I did it without thinking, sir."
> Judge: "Yes, but don't you see how dangerous it might be for anyone passing at the time?"

Palmore's (1971) content analysis of jokes about aging found that those dealing with aging women were more negative than those dealing with aging men. "Old maids" were variously defined as "a lemon that has never been squeezed"; "a woman who is always looking under her bed in the hope of finding a burglar" (p. 184). There were no "old bachelor" jokes.

Since "in jokes" are related to social worlds (Lindesmith et al., 1977:168), women and men find different things funny. Males appreciate aggressive humor more than females do (Groch, 1974), while the reverse holds true for absurd humor (Brodzinsky et al., 1981; Terry and Ertel, 1974). Men find sexual humor funnier than do women (Brodzinsky et al., 1981; Groch, 1974). These observations bring us to the next generalization about humor as social behavior.

Ingroup/Outgroup Relationships

Laughing at the outgroup serves to strengthen the bonds of the ingroup. *We* share common attitudes. *Their* difference provokes *our* laughter. For example, an observational study of American adolescent girls during their lunch periods found that jokes about male genitals served to communicate intimacy, solidarity, and female superiority. "Why is a chicken so ugly?" "Because it's got a pecker right between its eyes" (Sanford and Eder, 1984:237).

Ingroup humor, such as ethnic jokes, is generally kept from outgroup targets. Women's humor satirizing men is usually told behind male backs. In mixed groups, women often adopt a self-deprecatory humor (Walker, 1981). The point is illustrated by the mediated humor of early Joan Rivers, who joked about her life as a fat kid. "I was my own buddy at camp . . .," "In my class picture, I was the entire front row" (Israel, 1984:112). However, males have not hesitated to communicate to women humor disparaging women. The fact that women purportedly found it funny (Cantor, 1976) brings us to the last social function of humor.

Humor, Power and Status

In everyday interaction, humor often becomes a vehicle for demonstrating superior status or power. Groups of males who engage in contests to "do one better" often use humor in a competitive way (Sanford and Eder, 1984). The humorous insults exchanged by young boys in the black ghetto game, "playing the dozens," is an excellent example:

— Your family is so poor the rats and roaches eat lunch out.

— Your house is so small the roaches walk single file.

— Your mama sent her picture to the lonely hearts club, and they sent it back and said "We ain't that lonely!"

> — I walked in your house and your family was running
> around the table. I said, "Why you doin' that?" Your
> mama say, "First one drops, we eat" (Kochman,
> 1969:33).

The boy who gets off the most insults wins.

An early field study sheds light on humor as power and status play. Coser (1960) recorded instances of humor and laughter in the staff meetings of a mental hospital over a three-month period. She found that higher-status people (e.g., psychiatrists) were much more likely to make jokes than lower-status people (e.g., paramedicals). A witticism was never directed at anyone present of higher rank. Even though a considerable number of women were at the meetings (including two female psychiatrists), men made 99 out of the 103 jokes. Nevertheless, the women often laughed harder. Laughter can be a form of ingratiation: the higher the status of the joketeller, the "more likely the same joke, story or pun is to evoke laughter from the audience" (Kane et al., 1977:16).

This sex division of humor-related behavior is simply another aspect the sex division of interactive work discussed earlier. In our society, a man with a good sense of humor is someone who tells good jokes. A woman with a good sense of humor is someone who laughs at men's jokes (Eakins and Eakins, 1978:77). Indeed, this behavior pattern of male clown and female admirer begins to appear in the early elementary school years.

> It is not clear at this point whether parents and other
> socializing agents begin actively encouraging humor in
> boys and discouraging it in girls at this age, or whether
> each sex simply begins adopting the patterns of behavior
> they see in the adults around them (McGhee, 1979:201).

Humor initiation appears to be associated with other traditionally masculine traits — aggressiveness and dominance (McGhee, 1979:187). Female attempts to be funny may meet with male disapproval, especially where female wit can be interpreted as subversion of male authority (Eakins and Eakins, 1978:77). Women's tendency to self-disparaging humor is clearly tied to their lower status. The probability of jokes at the expense of others increases with increased status (McGhee, 1979:186). Coser (1960) found that only 7 percent of the senior staff jokes were directed at themselves, while 36 percent of junior staff's jokes were self-depreciating.

With the advent of the women's liberation movement, humor that denigrates women is no longer appreciated (McGhee, 1979:199), and self-deprecatory female humor is going out of style. Perhaps this shift is responsible for the accusation that feminists lack a sense of humor (Walker, 1981).

Mediated Symbols

The next section of this chapter considers a selection of symbolic sources of gender socialization that have been packaged for consumption. The processing is generally done by male gatekeepers, according to masculine rules. We begin with gender symbols consumed by children and consider storybooks and television. Then, we turn to popular music and video parlors, whose main consumers are adolescents. Finally, we deal with mediated symbols designed for adult consumption. Graphic art is a unique case, where the symbols are high culture and are disseminated face-to-face, rather than by mass media. This section then concludes with a discussion of erotica and pornography. These age divisions are, of course, somewhat arbitrary; people of all ages listen to rock music and enjoy television.

Children's Storybooks

> Once upon a time, a baby named X was born. This baby
> was named X so that nobody could tell whether it was a
> boy or a girl. Its parents could tell, of course, but they
> couldn't tell anybody else (Gould, 1972:74).

Storybooks teach as they entertain. Stories "have always been a means of perpetuating the fundamental cultural values and myths" (Weitzman et al., 1972:1148). Words and illustrations impress gender images on the minds of children. It is difficult, if not impossible, to gauge the impact of children's literature in isolation from other socialization sources. However, many authorities view children's books as reflections of societal values (McClelland, 1961) and active socializers (Pyke, 1975:53) which influence later behavior. As Madsen (1979:221) points out, "stories leave indelible impressions on a young child who does not have the mental maturity to distinguish clearly between fantasy and reality." An old German cautionary tale described

> a bad girl who raced with boys [and] broke her leg. Her
> pantaloon and leg broke off in one piece like china, with
> a jagged edge. She was carried home on a shutter. A
> grieved parent carried the leg (McNulty, 1982:176).

A modern child is unlikely to take this story literally. However, with some notable recent exceptions, contemporary plots continue to perpetuate stereotyped imagery. It is reasonable to suppose that these symbols make an early contribution to the "natural" reality of gender.

Fairy Tales

Fairy tales originated in patriarchal European societies before the invention of the printing press. Retold, rewritten, refilmed, they remain popular today. In general, the imagery of females is not flattering. Snow White and Sleeping Beauty are passive heroines who "awaken from their sleep not to conquer the world but to marry the prince" (Gilligan, 1979:438). Snow White serves the seven dwarfs. Cinderella sweeps the ashes. Cinderella and her stepsisters compete for the attentions of the Prince. The stepsisters industriously lop off their toes and heels so as to fit into a glass slipper that was never intended for them anyway (Laws, 1979:233–234).

A few fairy-tale heroines show some spunk. Little Red Riding Hood bests the Wolf. Gretel shoves the wicked witch into the oven. However, most of the strong, clever women in fairy tales are fearsome characters, often old and ugly. Witches and sorceresses place spells on men. The wicked stepmother — the embodiment of evil — has no male counterpart (Hunter Collective, 1983:28–29).

Examples of males with undesirable characteristics can also be found in fairy tales. Jack in *Jack and the Beanstalk* does not appear too bright when he sells the family cow for a handful of beans. The Giant in the same story is cruel. Several husbands are ridiculously dominated by their wives (Madsen, 1979:215). At his wife's insistence, the father of Hansel and Gretel loses his children in the forest. However, according to numerous studies,

> there are literally hundreds of stories that portray boys in positive situations, thereby overshadowing their small amount of negative images in comparison. They are few in number in proportion to the many negative female images portrayed in children's books. It is, therefore, the sexist patterns pertaining to the female that are so prevalent in children's literature of which we need to be especially conscious (Madsen, 1979:216).

Storybooks in the 1970s

During the 1970s, the women's movement motivated reexamination of children's literature as a conservative source of gender socialization. As well, feminists inspired such stories as Gould's "Story of X," excerpted at the beginning of this section. Several critical studies were published. Weitzman et al. (1972) found that both prize-winning picture books and the Little Golden Book best-sellers numerically underrepresented females in the titles, central characters, illustrations, and stories. Most children's books were about boys, men, and male animals. However, both sexes were stereotyped: "boys are active while girls are passive;

boys lead and rescue others, while girls follow and serve others" (Weitzman et al., 1972:1125). Occupational roles were varied and creative for males, limited to domesticity for females. While male friendship bonds were stressed, only rarely were females shown working or playing together. Pyke's (1975) survey of 150 children's books reported that females are not shown to work outside the home: the "perennial apron is their trademark and is worn even by female squirrels" (p. 68). Females were rarely seen reading. The typical family scene showed Daddy reading the newspaper while Mommy served. Women were not shown behind the wheel of a car.

> Boys in these stories climb trees and fish and roll in the
> leaves and skate. Girls watch, fall down, and get dizzy
> (Bem and Bem, 1984:14).

Storybooks' physical representation of people was often faulty. Little boys were pictured as significantly taller than girls of the same age. While males were all ages, women were either young mothers or grannies (Madsen, 1979).

These storybooks conditioned males to heroic behavior (Madsen, 1979). Boys were exposed to masculine models who were intellectually curious, in control of situations, and generally successful. However, open expression of such normal emotions as fear, frustration, or affection was seldom allowed male characters. In general, children's books of the 1970s taught that males are more highly valued than females.

Storybooks in the 1980s

> *When Mama gets home*
> *Too late for a meal*
> *How will the cubs*
> *And Papa Bear feel?*
> (Source: Berenstain and Berenstain, *The Berenstain Bears
> and Mama's New Job*, 1984. Used with permission
> of Random House Inc.)

As feminist criticism was disseminated, publishers, editors, writers, illustrators, librarians had their "consciousness raised" along with the rest of the population (Reinstein, 1984). Are the storybooks of the 1980s more sensitive to gender? Unfortunately, no recent research has examined a representative sampling of books. However, sex-typed offerings are still available in children's sections of bookstores and libraries. Traditional fairy tales remain popular. A beautifully illustrated version of Hans Christian Andersen's *The Little Mermaid* sold well during the 1984 Christmas season.

> In Andersen's story, the little mermaid falls in love with a
> prince and exchanges her voice for human legs, only to
> stand mutely by as the prince jilts her for a human
> princess. In desperation, the land-bound mermaid throws
> herself into the sea and turns to foam (Tousley, 1985).

The almost exclusively male fantasy world of Dr. Seuss continues to sell well: *The Cat in the Hat, The Fox in Socks, The Grinch Who Stole Christmas* and other central characters, whether people, animals, or machines, are nearly all masculine (Bem and Bem, 1984:13).

Nevertheless, children's shelves also contain storybooks that challenge gender stereotypes. A few are old favorites. The feminist collection *Free to Be You and Me* remains in print. Lindgren's *Pippi Longstocking* is an adventurous girl, so strong she could lift a horse if she wanted to. Isadora's *Max* is a crack baseball player who discovers that his sister's ballet class is a great way to warm up for a home run. Stinson's *Red is Best* features a little girl obsessed with the the color red. Among other advantages, red mittens make better snowballs and red socks jump higher. In Munsch's *The Paper Bag Princess,* the heroine rescues Prince Ronald from the dragon, "only to discover that he is a hypercritical dandy who objects to her singed clothes and battle scars" (Ross, 1983:44). In the end, she calls him a "bum" and they don't get married. Excellent books are there. However, in the mid-1980s department stores and chain bookstores were swamped by commercial "non-books," featuring Strawberry Shortcake, Care Bears, and Cabbage Patch Dolls.

Television for Older Children

With only slight exaggeration, the cliché, "the more things change, the more they remain the same" summarizes the history of gender symbolism in television. In the 1950s and 1960s, sit-coms featured ideal (American) families with dizzy mothers ("I Love Lucy"), incompetent fathers ("Ozzie and Harriet"), and nice kids ("Leave It to Beaver"). Cowboys ("Gunsmoke") and private eyes ("77 Sunset Strip") were macho men. In order to function as competent adults, women apparently required mystical powers; however, the heroines of "Bewitched" and "I Dream of Jeannie" confined their supernatural shenanigans to the domestic sphere.

The 1970s brought the women's movement and brand-new programming formulae. Ralph Cramden's "You wanna take a trip to the moon, Alice?" treatment of his wife ("The Honeymooners") was replaced by single mothers ("One Day at a Time"), divorce ("Rhoda"), and sex ("Soap"). A few programs portrayed assertive women ("Maude") and expressive men (M.A.S.H.), but well-rounded human beings were a distinct minority. Some sit-coms moved into the workplace ("Mary

Tyler Moore"), where decorative career women concentrated on solving interpersonal, rather than work problems. Iron men continued to solve crimes ("Mannix," "Kojack").

So far, the 1980s has provided more sex and glamor ("Dynasty"), more violence ("The A-Team"), and more silly adults ("Three's Company"). With some exceptions ("The Cosby Show"), women are still scatterbrained ninnies or Christmas tree ornaments and men ineffectual creatures or violent animals. Cartoons feature a lady Smurf in high heels and "dumb-as-a-post" Fred Flintstone. Saturday morning advertisements for Masters of The Universe and Fitness Freak Barbie are even more sex-typed. Systematic reviews of the media, e.g. the Canadian Radio-television and Telecommunications Commission (1982), agree with this impressionistic survey that television is a major contributor to gender stereotype.

The Importance of Television

Television is *not* just another mass medium. Unlike such other media as radio, movies, or magazines which are used selectively, TV is used "by practically all the people . . . practically all the time" (Gerbner, 1978:47). This means that "enormous, otherwise heterogeneous audiences are attending ritualistically and relatively nonselectively to the same basic, repetitive messages" (Morgan and Rothschild, 1983:34). For this reason, television has been characterized as a "community of discourse" with functions comparable to those of a language: "It integrates and controls; it provides common elements for strangers to use when they meet and creates strictures for what can be noticed or said" (Tuchman, 1979:540). Therefore, television plays a particularly vital role in the construction of gender. It is a key resource of meanings and a significant constraint on the range and direction of gender definitions.

Though television serves as a universal curriculum (Gerbner and Gross, 1976), its impact on children has been cause for alarm. Television "crowds out" other uses of time (Condry and Keith, 1983), especially the time spent by earlier generations in reading and game-playing. Being part of this community of discourse now contributes a vital dimension of peer socialization. Being television-wise brings prestige on the playground (Ellis, 1983). Children discuss what they have seen on television and enact the roles of TV characters in their fantasy play (Fouts, 1980). Moreover, children under the age of eight cannot distinguish TV commercials from programming, and cannot explain the selling interest of commercials (Liebert et al, 1982). As Schuetz and Sprafkin (1978:69) point out, commercials "are produced specifically to attract and persuade, with every effort made to make them appear credible." Research shows that children who are frequent TV watchers are more likely to accept both gender stereotyping and occupational sex-typing (Liebert et al., 1982:167).

Gender Imagery in TV Programming

Television programming is "a dramatic demonstration of power held mostly in the hands of white, middle-class males in the prime of life" (Morgan and Rothschild, 1983:35). Males dominate the television screen (Canadian Radio-television and Telecommunications Commission, 1982). Females are underrepresented in prime-time adventures, situation comedies, and even cartoons (which include fewer female than male "anthropomorphized foxes or pussycats" [Pyke and Stewart, 1974]). According to Tuchman (1979), this "symbolic annihilation" of women captures the powerless position of women in society.

The presentation of the sexes is unbalanced in function as well as numbers. The makeup of the TV labor force has consistently shown little relationship to the real-life employment patterns of women (Dominick, 1979). Women are most often portrayed as economically dependent housewives and mothers (CRTC, 1982:4). Men are represented as occupying a disproportionately high percentage of the work force, a great diversity of occupations, and higher-status jobs. "This demographic under-representation and misrepresentation is an indication of 'who counts' in society" (Wilson, 1981).

Among the recommendations of the Canadian Task Force on Sex-role Stereotypes in the Broadcast Media CRTC (1982:29–35), are the following:

— Broadcasting should include a wide variety of images reflecting the diversity of women in our culture. This includes women of all ages, women of differing ethnic groups, and women of differing physical appearance.

— Women should be presented in a more balanced and realistic way in terms of their occupations and activities in contemporary society.

— Women should not be presented as either excessively concerned with youth and beauty or neurotically afraid of aging.

— Women should not be used as sexual stimuli or lures, or as attention-getting, but otherwise irrelevant, objects.

— Women should be more adequately represented as news readers, reporters, and hosts. "In news and current affairs programming, women are seldom presented as experts; women's opinions are not sought as often as men's" (p. 5).

— A balance of female and male perspectives should be represented in stories, issues, topics, and images, as well as in writing, editing, directing, and producing.

The Task Force concluded:

> Stereotyped images of women and girls are reinforced
> and perpetuated, and to some extent even seemingly
> legitimized, by the mass dissemination of these images in
> broadcasting. Such images constitute a limiting or nar-
> rowing of women's, men's, and children's perceptions of
> themselves and their roles in society (CRTC, 1982:3).

Portrayal of Gender in Advertising

> "Barbara . . . Barbara . . . you up?"
> "I'm up now."
>
> The insomniac husband finally succeeds in awakening
> his sleeping wife, who dutifully trots to the bathroom to
> get his Brand X medicine. Dosed up, the husband drifts
> off to sleep, leaving the wife staring into space, wide
> awake.

This Sucrets ad illustrates several concerns about advertising's picture
of men and women (CRTC, 1982:21). Both sexes are stereotyped. Neither
the helpless, inconsiderate, controlling husband, nor the obedient, nurturing wife captures the changing roles of men and women in today's
society. The voice-over (the off-stage voice of authority) completing the
hard sell is male. Despite feminist complaints, the ad continues to run.

These complaints began nearly 20 years ago. The Royal Commission on the Status of Women in Canada (1970) accused the media
of perpetuating stereotyping of both sexes. It was especially critical of
the "degrading, moronic" depiction of women in advertisements, and
argued that although men as well as women are stereotyped, "the
results may be more damaging for women since advertising encourages
feminine dependency by urging women not to act but to be passive,
not to really achieve but to live out their aspirations in the imagination
and in dreams." A study sponsored by the Canadian Council on the
Status of Women (Courtney and Whipple, 1978:13) concluded "that
women are portrayed in extremely limited roles" and that this portrayal
"has not changed significantly in the 1970s." The fact that in 1982 the
CRTC registered similar concern is a commentary on the powerlessness
of women in our society.

Changing economic and demographic patterns in the 1980s
have resulted in some changes in advertisers' image of the women likely
to sell their products (DeVries, 1984). Superwomen (young, pretty
Chartered Accountants) joined the mommies in pink-checked aprons
fretting over "ring around the collar." For several reasons, this trend
failed to mollify feminist critics. Most women are not executives or professionals. Moreover, the women were often shown in poses and acti-

vities that suggest a frivolous attitude towards work. Though men are shown more often with children or in the kitchen, they still instruct females in their realm or act the buffoon. In the last few years, the Superwoman image has been softened by the revival of romance and femininity. For advertisers this has been an invitation to continue to use women's bodies to sell products, to push cosmetics, to tell women they should look "better" than their age. Advertisers have managed to twist the messages of the women's movement to their own advantage (Warren, 1978) — for example, the Virginia Slims cigarettes slogan, "You've come a long way, baby!" The "New Woman is the same old Dumb Dora — physically, mentally and morally weak, but oh so willing to please her man" (Zwarun, 1982b). She is still presented as finding satisfaction "principally through the embrace of commodities" (Berman, 1981:54). Men continue to prevail as the voice of authority (Knill et al., 1981).

Advertising expert Michael Schudson (1984) describes advertising as a "distinctive and central symbolic structure" (p. 210) that caters to the "modern passion for goods" (p. 129). He goes on to say:

> Advertising . . . surrounds us and enters into us, so that when we speak we may speak in or with reference to the language of advertising and when we see we may see through schemata that advertising has made salient for us (Schudson, 1984, 210).

Because ads are designed to sell to target audiences, they use social types or demographic categories, and not particular persons, to dramatize their goods. For example, Robert Young did not play himself in the Sanka ads, but a "Father Knows Best"/"Marcus Welby, M.D." mature, cheerful, sensible character. For this reason, advertising reproduces and exaggerates social inequalities, including gender. In short, television "recharges and extends [gender] definitions and images . . . and keeps them circulating as part of the common stock of taken-for-granted knowledge" (Murdock, 1974:209). To adults, ads are irritants and intrusions. To children, they represent the Generalized Other.

Popular Music for Adolescents

Popular music is a "potent sociopolitical tool" (Denisoff and Peterson, 1972). Its messages appeal simultaneously to the intellect with lyrics and to the emotions with melody and rhythm. Rock music is currently the most important cultural expression of popular music. In Canada, rock music accounts for 80 percent of all records sold (Harding and Nett, 1984:62). More records are purchased by teenagers than any other age group (Marks, 1979:335). Music replaces television as adolescents' top leisure activity. While TV is structured and packaged largely by middle-aged adults in the mainstream of society, much of the music that youths listen to "is created by individuals close to their own age who stand apart and may be at odds with adult society" (Larson and Kubey, 1983:14). Although the adolescent audience for pop music is not homogeneous (Tanner, 1981), rock music was the favorite of more than three-quarters of the Canadian teenagers surveyed by Bibby and Posterski (1985:36). In 1984, an estimated 1,500 youngsters witnessed Boy George's four-minute passage through Mirabel, the Quebec airport. A 15-year-old, who played truant to see him, said "I've never loved anyone like I love him, I swear to God" (*The Calgary Herald*, March 29, 1984). The lyrics, rhythms, and harmonics of rock provide raw material for youth to draw upon in learning gender roles and composing gender identities (Larson and Kubey, 1983:15). How does rock portray gender relations? According to experts (Harding and Nett, 1984:60), rock music is "probably the most blatantly misogynistic and aggressive form of music currently listened to."[2]

Women as Producers of Popular Music

As our discussion in Chapter 2 would predict, the rock music industry is male-dominated. Recording industry executives and producers, broadcasting industry station managers, program directors, and disc jockeys are predominantly men (Harding and Nett, 1984). The majority of the audience for rock music is male, with young women favoring more conventional forms of pop music (Tanner, 1981).

Until quite recently, rock cultural heroes were male. At the beginning of rock, in the 1950s, the music was performed exclusively by men. Bill Haley, with his "Rock Around the Clock" (1955) was the first white musician to bring rock 'n' roll to the adolescent masses. A few black women in groups such as the Supremes succeeded in the early 1960s. However, in the 1960s, women musicians were relegated to the backstream by the invasion of the Beatles and the Rolling Stones from Britain. Raunchy lyrics and electric instruments (which women did not play) edged women out of rock. During that era, women such as Joni Mitchell and Joan Baez were prominent in asexual folk music. In the 1970s, such women performers as Janis Joplin and Gracie Slick re-entered the mainstream fronting for male bands (Harding and Nett, 1984:63). However, "their messages concerning the emerging female were lost among the crowd of male performers" (Marks, 1979:353). In the mid-1980s, a few women — Cyndi Lauper, Madonna, Tina Turner, Pat Benatar — had hits on the charts (Miller et al., 1985). However, their presence has done little to mitigate the "knee-jerk misogyny" of the rock scene.

The masculine-style rock performance has been described as "an insistent, repetitive power trip to keep the audience awed, obedient, and flat on its back" (Weisstein and Blaisdell, 1972:27):

The lights are out on the audiences because, after all, who wants to see *them*. The lights are undulating on the musicians. There they are. There's the star singer, wailing and grinding ass to show us what we should want. And then there are the other musicians with some other *schtick* designed for audience adoration. And they're coming on cool and savage, contemptuous of the audience and then indifferent to it, working themselves up, getting off on their power over us. The hostility level's rising, and the sound level is unbearable, and by the end of the performance the audience is ecstatically defeated, depleted, deafened, detumescent. The ceremony of the masculine power is complete (Weisstein and Blaisdell, 1972:26).

Rock Music's Depiction of Women

The sexist nature of rock music symbolism is understandable. Rock music has mainly been the expression of the problems and fantasies of young male performers tailored for male audiences. Its degradation of women has been recognized for some time.

The worst picture of women appears in the music of the Rolling Stones, where sexual exploitation reaches unique heights. A woman is a "Stupid Girl" who should be kept "Under My Thumb," a "Honky Tonk Woman" who gives a man "Satisfaction." In "Yesterday's Papers," where women are equated with newspapers, the dehumanization is carried to an extreme. Who wants yesterday's papers, the song arrogantly demands, who wants yesterday's girl? The answer: Nobody. Once used, a woman is as valuable as an old newspaper, presumably good only for wrapping garbage (Meade, 1972:174).

According to a content analysis carried out by Harding and Nett (1984) basic attitudes in rock lyrics have persisted over the decades. These lyrics define women in terms of their biological relationships to men, and cast them into either the erotic role or the nurturing role. The erotic image, the more prominent of the two, depicts women as sexual servicers of men. "Woman's place is . . . between the sheets" (p. 65). Women must be controlled and dominated by men, not only for male benefit, but for their own good:

Violence is rampant. A woman's head will roll if she doesn't get out of his sight (Ted Nugent, *Heads Will Roll*) or on one of his bad days she will find his axe on her, but only after *she* has fetched it (Pink Floyd, *One of My Turns*) (Harding and Nett, 1984:65).

The less frequent nurturing image describes women as tender and pure and appeals to young males.

The album covers in which rock is packaged are even more erotic than the lyrics (Harding and Nett, 1984). Journalist Michele Landsberg describes the album covers of middle-of-the-road rock music available in Toronto's Sam the Record Man:

> The album jackets sum it all up: women holding champagne bottles between their legs; half-naked women in chains; wet-lipped women; parts of women; a woman with a wad of bubblegum being pulled off her naked breast; a naked, headless woman holding a TV set in front of her torso (the record is called *The Tube*); a woman's crotch menaced by a huge hairy spider. Acres of the stuff (Landsberg, 1982:209).

Women do not fare much better in rock videos:

> [Men] get to play a wide range of fantasy roles, from heroes to clowns. But women? All too often — especially as supporting characters in the videos of male singers — they're played as bimbos. Dressed in fishnet and leather they drape themselves over car hoods, snarl like tigers, undress in silhouette behind window shades . . . . Most rock videos give free rein to the cheesiest imagery of women as playthings (Barol, 1985:54).

In recent years, some new themes in popular music have been added. Punk rock features androgyny. David Bowie with his makeup and dyed hair created a sexually ambiguous image (Hebdige, 1979:60). New Wave music was used by both sexes to attack one another. "Both sexes strut around in torn shirts and jeans, leather clothing, and accessories such as paper clips, swastikas, dog chains, and razor blade earrings" (Marks, 1979:360). The celebration of rape and murder in the music of such groups as Twisted Sister and Mötley Crüe is truly frightening. A few women arists have taken central stage. However, Cyndi Lauper's 1984 "Girls Just Want To Have Fun" was light years away from Helen Reddy's 1975 feminist anthem, 'I Am Woman." Lauper is saying girls don't take life seriously. They are hedonistic creatures without ambition (Niels Reinholdt, personal communication). In summary, popular music conveys sexist imagery to its adolescent audiences.

Video Arcades, Computers and Adolescents

The symbolic environment which symbolic interactionists see as defining and embracing human life is rapidly becoming an electronic environment (Ellis, 1983). Young people, surrounded by bedroom TV sets, Walkman cassette players, and video movies, are at the center of this emerging technological revolution. Video arcades and computers are important examples of this phenomenon. In video games, symbols of balls with large mouths eat symbols of ghosts. Symbols of spacecraft attack symbols of alien invaders (Ellis, 1983:9). Computers are instructed by BASIC, FORTRAN IV, COBOL and other machine languages. Computers are not analogous with television.

> Television is something you watch. Video games are
> something you do, something you do in your head, a
> world that you enter, . . . and, to a certain extent, they
> are something you "become" (Turkle, 1984:67).

It would be almost impossible to exaggerate the importance of computers, "the most powerful yet of the artifacts of this inventive century" (Condry and Keith, 1983:88). In 1983, *Time* magazine chose the computer instead of naming a Man or Woman of the year. At the societal level, computers have brought about extensive and fundamental changes in work, education, science, and recreation. According to Sherry Turkle's *The Second Self: Computers and the Human Spirit* (1984), computers may also be changing how people think. Users whose involvement is intense begin to approach the world in terms of systems logic and describe themselves in terms of computer language. Emotional problems become "bugs" in their "master program," and psychotherapy is "debugging" or "reprogramming." "Hardwire," "buffer," "default solutions" are among the computer metaphors (Turkle, 1984:17).

Video games elicit mixed reactions. On the one hand, adults fear the degree and intensity of their children's engagement with them. "It's eerie when their playmates are machines" (Turkle, 1984:14). Social commentators are concerned about the malicious, violent content of some games. For example,

> . . . one in which the player assumes the role of an
> arsonist, and attempts to burn down a building without
> getting caught; one in which the player attempts to run
> down simulated players on the highway for points; and
> one in which the player assumes the role of a character
> (General Custer) who attempts to rape an Indian woman
> tied to a stake (Condry and Keith, 1983:104).

They worry that "zap the enemy—blow them up" games may make it easier for children to accept real violence (Ford, 1983). Video arcades, with their bluish light and space-age noises, are compared with pool halls and condemned as the "latest seducer of the young" (Panelas, 1983:52). By 1982, more money, quarter by quarter, was being spent on video games than on movies and records combined (Turkle, 1984:65).

On the other hand, the value of video games (along with micro-computers in schools) as socialization into the computer culture is acknowledged. Though youngsters' intense involvement with video games has been described as an "addiction," it is certainly not a "mindless addiction." In deciphering the logic of the game, in achieving a meeting of mind and computer program, children are learning how to interact with computers (Turkle, 1984:68).

Gender Differences in Involvement with Computer Symbols

Females and males differ somewhat in both frequency and quality of involvement with computers. Bibby and Posterski (1985:40) asked a national sample of Canadian teenagers about their leisure activities. Twenty percent of the males and 7 percent of the females said they went very often to video arcades. Seventeen percent of the males versus 7 percent of the females often played video games at home. Even in school, computers appeal less to females (Condry and Keith, 1983:106).

At least three reasons explain this difference. Video arcades are mainly a masculine milieu (Panelas, 1983:62). Video parlors provide a social and cultural space, free from surveillance of adult authorities, where teenagers can meet peers, relieve boredom, practice adult routines, and rank their relative prowess in game-playing. Competition and control are important to males. "You walk out of the arcade and it's a different world. Nothing you can control" (Turkle, 1984:72). Girls feel less at home in this masculine subculture.

Secondly, the violent fantasy of most video games appeals less to females than males (Condry and Keith, 1983:106). There is a third reason older girls, at least, are less likely to be computer-oriented. Computers are usually introduced into schools in mathematics programs where girls have a history of low expectations (Van Gelder, 1985:91). Steps are now being considered to make computers in the school setting more congenial to girls. The machines can be used in language and arts classes as easily as in mathematics classes. In addition, some unisex educational software is being designed. For example, the "Voyage of the Mimi" series includes a module that lets children apply math and map-reading skills to rescue a whale caught in a fish net (Van Gelder, 1985:91).

Gender differences also exist in attitudes towards computers. As implied above, females are more likely to be "technophobes," to be fearful of computer technology. As well, many girls "show disinterest or even marked dislike for *what computers do,* period" (Van Gelder, 1985:90, emphasis in original). More interesting is Turkle's (1984) identification (following Gilligan, 1982) of masculine and feminine styles of computing. The masculine style approaches the world as something that can be brought under control. Computers are mastered and manipulated in traditional ways taught in computer courses. "Hard" masters are overwhelmingly male. "Hackers [usually male] use their mastery over the machine to build a culture of prowess that defines itself in terms of winning over ever more complex systems" (Turkle, 1984:20). The "soft" feminine style is more intuitive and interactive. It involves relating to the computer as self rather than other. "Soft" masters are more likely to see the world as something they adjust to rather than control. Shelley, a graduate student in computing science, illustrates the feminine style:

> My father was an electrician and he had all of these
> machines around. All of these wires, all of this stuff.
> And he taught my brothers all about it. But all I
> remember him telling me was, "Don't touch it, you'll get
> a shock." I hate machines. But I don't think of computers
> as machines. I think of moving pieces of language
> around. Not like making a poem, the way you would
> usually think of moving language around, more like
> making a piece of language sculpture (Turkle, 1984:117).

As yet, "hard" mastery is the prestigious way to relate to computers.
Increasingly, modern life requires computer literacy. Women conditioned to doubt their aptitude for mathematics and computing science will pay a large price:

> Computer technology is increasing employment opportu-
> nities in the occupations where women are least repre-
> sented; on the other hand, it is diminishing employment
> opportunities in the clerical occupations and in the
> related administrative and supervisory positions which
> women were using as career ladders (Menzies, 1984:292).

The relationship of female and male children with computers is a microcosm for the larger world of relations between gender and science. Women are left outside of science, which is usually defined in terms of "hard" mastery (Turkle, 1984:118).

Graphic Art: High-Culture Symbols for Adults

> Women painters, like women poets, women novelists,
> women musicians, women politicians, women prisoners,
> have been lesser men. They have gone far in imitation,
> but have not had the initiative or the ability to blaze new
> paths for themselves (Bulliet, 1927; quoted by Mitchell,
> 1978:68).

AN OFFICE OF HER OWN

The solution to my life occurred to me one evening while I was ironing a shirt. It was simple but audacious. I went into the living room where my husband was watching television and I said, "I think I ought to have an office."

It sounded fantastic, even to me. What do I want an office for? I have a house; it is pleasant and roomy and has a view of the sea; it provides appropriate places for eating and sleeping, and having baths and conversations with one's friends. Also I have a garden; there is no lack of space.

No. But here comes the disclosure which is not easy for me: I am a writer. That does not sound right. Too presumptuous, phony, or at least unconvincing. Try again. I write. Is that better? I *try* to write. That makes it worse. Hypocritical humility. Well then? . . .

A house is all right for a man to work in. He brings his work into the house, a place is cleared for it; the house rearranges itself as best it can around him. Everybody recognizes that his work exists. He is not expected to answer the telephone, to find things that are lost, to see why the children are crying, or feed the cat. He can shut his door. Imagine (I said) a mother shutting her door, and the children knowing she is behind it; why, the very thought of it is outrageous to them. A woman who sits staring into space, into a country that is not her husband's or her children's is likewise known to be an offense against nature. So a house is not the same for a woman. She is not someone who walks into the house to make use of it, and will walk out again. She is the house; there is no separation possible.

Source: Alice Munro, "The Office," *The Dance of the Happy Shades*, 1968. Used with the permission of McGraw-Hill Ryerson Limited.

Bulliet was not the first or the last critic to ask, "Why have there been no great woman artists?" or to frame a reply in terms of women's inferiority. Obviously, "there are no great women artists because women are incapable of greatness" (Nochlin, 1971:480). The essence of this argument is the assumption of individual genius, the Great Artist,

> . . . bearing within his person since birth a mysterious
> essence, rather like the golden nugget in Mrs. Grass's
> chicken soup, called genius or talent, which must always
> out, no matter how unlikely or unpromising the cir-
> cumstances (Nochlin, 1971:489).

As you may recall from Chapter 2, the sociology of knowledge provides a rival approach to this issue. It discredits the "nugget of genius," the asocial nature of artists. It offers an alternative question,

"Why is so little known about great women artists of the past?" (Oren-stein, 1975:507). The sociology of knowledge directs our attention to the social conditions vital to the production of art:

> [In] the arts as in a hundred other areas, things remain
> stultifying, oppressing and discouraging to all those —
> women included — who did not have the good fortune
> to be born white, preferably middle class, and, above all,
> male (Nochlin, 1973:6).

As a result of these adverse conditions, the human experiences reflected in celebrated works of art have been either male experiences or men's conception of women's experiences (O'Kelly, 1983:145).[3] Considering the sex-typing of artistic endeavors as feminine in our culture, this is quite ironic!

What conditions have either made women artists amateurs or discouraged them completely? Even in the privileged classes, the "greedy institution of the family" (Coser, 1974) has demanded most of women's time and attention. A contemporary Prince Edward Island artist says:

> When we finally demand of ourselves to take . . . our
> own inherent creativity . . . seriously and make a studio
> of an upstairs room, attic or rent a space downtown, we
> still have to fight the automatic ground-in guilt that
> refuses time of a major sort to be spent in that space
> (MacKay, 1979; unpaginated).

Women have had great difficulty in getting artistic training. In the past, they were not free to take up a pursuit like painting without the approval and guidance of a male relative. Indeed, most women artists before the nineteenth century were daughters or wives of artists and were trained by these men to paint in their style. Accomplished artists require in-dependence of mind and freedom to develop a personal style. Neither of these qualities was emphasized in women's socialization (Hunter Collective, 1983:41).

For women artists to acquire a reputation for greatness, their accomplishments must survive with their names attached to them. Un-fortunately, women's work has had a tendency to disappear. For example, a catalogue of art exhibitions held in Halifax in the period 1830–1848 lists 17 Nova Scotia artists, 15 of them women. Today, the works of the two men are cherished in important collections, while the work of all the women has disappeared (Sparling, 1979:87). Why does men's work survive? For one thing, men's products are more highly valued than women's products.

> [There are] reviewers who repeatedly use the adjectives
> emotional, hysterical, and sensitive in their description of
> women's work — implying that women are incapable of
> serious intellectual involvement in the arts, are totally
> passive, substantially childlike, and sometimes uncon-
> scious in their behavior. When discussing important women
> artists, these critics are likely to center their attention on
> the women's teachers . . ., on their lovers, their salons,
> or on anecdotal narratives of their lives — rarely on the
> works themselves (Orenstein, 1975:512).

For years, the artistic achievement of American painter Georgia O'Keeffe was attributed to her husband, Alfred Stieglitz. A biographical note in an art book read: "Stieglitz discovered, developed, and married Georgia O'Keeffe, and first presented her in 1916" (Mitchell, 1978:686).

There is a second reason for women's invisibility in high culture: their work is erased from art history when it is taken over by men. Modern restoration techniques have uncovered a number of works by women which had, for centuries, been accepted as the work of notable male artists. Greer (1979) documents many cases where women artists turned over their work to fathers or husbands to be signed and sold by them. This takeover of women's ideas continues into the 1980s. For instance, in the 1970s, Miriam Schapiro began making collages that incorporated pieces of patterned and embroidered fabrics — tablecloths, curtains, aprons. She called them "femmages" to indicate their source in women's traditions. This experimentation became accepted and absorbed into mainstream art. Schapiro argues that "the real substance of the feminist contribution to the art of the seventies has never been acknowledged" (Harper, 1985:779).

The Male World of Art

The world of art has long been a masculine domain (O'Kelly, 1983:143). Artists, teachers, patrons, critics, gallery owners, and museum curators have been predominately male. When women do occupy these positions, they often feel constrained to follow masculine standards. Museums neglect the art of women artists, especially those now deceased (Russell, 1980:480).[4] Male gatekeepers define ideals of beauty and set the standards. In her autobiography *Through the Flower* (1975:5), Judy Chicago remarks upon the confusion this masculine world produces for female artists:

> When I was about eleven, I became fascinated with
> Toulouse-Lautrec and the way he used reds, dotting
> them around the painting so that your eye was forced to
> travel around and around until it had absorbed the entire
> picture. At the time, I gave no thought to the fact that,

> while I was studying the color, the images of women
> painted by artists like Lautrec were also penetrating my
> psyche, later to confuse me, the artist, who wanted to
> paint, with me, the woman, who, I learned through
> these paintings, was supposed to be the model.

As an adult, Chicago felt that "she had been thwarted by her male teachers, who had not understood the images she had tried to make and had imposed their own forms, artistic language, and subject matter on her" (Harper, 1985:762).

Male sponsorship puts the stamp of approval on women's art. Emily Carr (1871–1945), one of Canada's most famous painters, gave up painting for 15 years after critics rejected her stark, simplified landscapes. Carr (1946:228) speaks of the insult and scorn accorded her work by Vancouver's Fine Art Society:

> My pictures were hung either on the ceiling or on the
> floor and were jeered at, insulted; members of the "Fine
> Arts" joked at my work, laughing with reporters. Press
> notices were humiliating.

However, the Group of Seven, especially Lawren Harris, later admired and validated her work: "Your work is a joy to us here, a real vital contribution" (Carr, 1946:257).

Gender Differences in Art Content

The two-worlds proposition leads to the prediction that females and males should produce distinctive art. The implication is that differences in art products would reflect the unique socialization experiences of the sexes, especially the domestic versus the public sphere. In MacKay's (1979: unpaginated) words:

> Since the artist's exploration and creativity derive from
> kinaesthetic and psychic experience filtered through the
> intricate interplay of mind and body, it seems inevitable
> that the gender of the artist will be a vital component of
> the resulting art work.

However, female artists are often trained to negate or ignore their feminine experience (MacKay, 1979). Variations in social class and ethnic experiences may also mitigate gender differences in aesthetic style (Bernard, 1981:444).

A study of children's art (Reeves and Boyette, 1983) supports the two-worlds hypothesis. Children aged nine to twelve were asked to draw anything they wanted. The girls were more likely to depict quiet, domestic scenes, detailed eyes, and round shapes. The boys, on the other hand, were more likely to draw violent scenes, activity, mechanical devices, angular shapes, and humans in profile. A nine-year old girl drew a peaceful, bucolic landscape. No activity was present. Hills, mountain tops, sun and clouds were all round, soft shapes. By contrast, a boy the same age drew an exciting picture of an airplane in trouble with a broken propeller. People were being carried into the hospital. Geometric forms pervaded the picture. In view of research indicating no observable gender differentiation in drawings by toddlers, Reeves and Boyette (1983) conclude that girls and boys draw different kinds of things because their socialization exposes them to different social-psychological worlds.

In 1979, *Atlantis* (a Canadian women's studies journal) assembled a gallery of women's art from submissions from across the country. The jurors concluded that the gender of the artists was a vital component of the resulting work (MacKay, 1979). For example, there was use of traditional women's media, such as cloth or yarn, modified from craft to art form. There were scenes from women's traditional occupations "such as a woman trying to sew with a baby leaning on her back or a woman going through the frustration of trying to match the odd sock" (MacKay, 1979; unpaginated). There was exploration of female sexuality, through symbols of female sex organs — eggs, seeds, uteruses, breasts, nests, and embryos. A contributor of the *Atlantis* gallery commented that the women's movement had helped her to feel that women do not have to compete with male artists in "aggressive art content such as size and impersonal subject matter, or subject matter that contributes to a 'history' of art which conforms to the theories of male critics of how art should be . . ." (MacKay, 1979; unpaginated).

Our discussion of painting suggests that the symbols of high culture, like popular cultural forms, convey impressions of women's invisibility and subordination. However, feminism is finally beginning to reach the art world and exert some influence upon it (Bernard, 1981:442).

Erotica and Pornography: Symbols for Adults

Pornography: innocent entertainment or dangerous smut? Sexually explicit and violent symbols are currently the subject of bitter debate. The imagery is designed to appeal to males. In Canada, an average of four "men's" magazines are sold each year to every male over the age of 16 (Canadian Coalition Against Media Pornography, cited in Senn, 1985). However, the issue of pornography and censorship crosscuts the boundary between masculine and feminine worlds, and polarizes feminists, academics, and politicians. Feminists agree that pornography is distasteful and humiliating to women. Some regard it as downright dangerous. To Robin Morgan (1980), "pornography is the theory, rape is the practice." Gloria Steinem charged that "a woman who has *Playboy* in the house is like a Jew who has *Mein Kampf* on the table" (Lederer, 1980b:122).

Feminist strategies for dealing with pornography differ sharply. Civil libertarians advocate open discussion, education, consumer boycotts (Burstyn, 1985). They make a case for freedom of expression as a cornerstone of free societies (McCormack, 1984). According to this position, sweeping changes in Canadian legislation would not only allow prosecution of pornographic picture magazines, but it would also permit right-wing authoritarian groups to censor works of art, literature and science (*CAUT Bulletin*, February 1984:23). Manion's (1985:77) expression of this position is worth quoting at length:

> . . . I think we must be careful as women, who have
> never had the same "freedom of expression" as men,
> either because we were not allowed to speak in public
> forums, or because when we did speak our words carried
> no authority, were dismissed as hysterical ravings, we
> must be careful at this juncture, not to denigrate "freedom
> of expression," but to demand it, seize it, appropriate it,
> allow it to one another. Historically as women we have
> been silenced, and today we do not have the access or
> decision making power in relation to mainstream media
> we need. Pornography has become symbolic for us of the
> blatancy of male supremacy, acted out, represented and
> enjoyed. It seems particularly insidious because it directs
> its appeal to the most vulnerable areas of the psyche.
> The proliferation of pornography is certainly part of a
> whole cultural order that undermines our sense of
> security and authority, but displacing too much anxiety
> onto it may not only waste some of our time and energy,
> but also may encourage the state to think it can throw us
> a censorship sop and keep us happy, may even backfire
> in an unexpected wave of repression provoked by fears
> we've helped to generate.

> (Source: Eileen Manion, p. 77 in Marilouise Kroker et al.,
> *Feminism Now*, 1985. Used with the permission of New
> World Perspectives.)

Other feminists do look to the state and legislation for solutions. They demand that pornography be put back in the closet where it belongs (Brownmiller, 1980) and point out that:

> All kinds of limitations already exist on "freedom of
> speech": laws relating to libel, slander, perjury, copyright,
> advertising, incitement. We accept them; we acknowledge
> that this freedom is not absolute. Therefore, the "right"
> to produce and consume pornography must be curtailed

if our *women's* right to freedom from slander and injury
is to be respected (Kostash, 1982:51, emphasis in
original).

Images of Sexuality

Debate concerning images of male-female sexuality is at the heart of
the censorship question. Feminists advocating censorship tend to
polarize male-female sexuality, to assume male sexuality is essentially
different from women's and more pathological. Female sexuality is seen
as natural, gentle, egalitarian, and "good." Male constructions try to
transform women's sexuality into lewdness. (See Griffin, 1981.) Male
sexuality, according to this perspective, is "evil," violent, power-driven,
and controllable by pornography (Manion, 1985:72–73).

Civil libertarians posit no essential gender differences in sexuality that cannot be attributed to learning. They warn against a
gynocentric "good woman-bad man" dichotomy which sets women up
as moral superiors. The problem is patriarchy, not innate male-female
differences. They don't believe banning pornography will reform men
who bully women. Men hurt women because women are weak, not
because pornography gives them inspiration (Callwood, 1984:25).

Feminist Kathleen Mahoney (1984), who urges state intervention in the pornography issue, invokes Gilligan's (1982) proposition
(discussed in Chapter 4) that women's and men's morality differ to
analyze the conflict between advocates and opponents of censorship.
According to her, civil libertarians speak with the masculine "voice."
They embrace the morality of the ladder in their concern to protect the
rights of individual expression. Advocates of censorship, on the other
hand, guided by the feminine morality of the "web," focus on generalized responsibility to people connecting with one another. They
believe that all women are hurt by pornography.

Specifying Terminology

"Pornography" is an emotionally-charged word, used to label a variety
of phenomena. Some, but not all, of the disagreement among feminists disappears when the terminology is sorted out. "Erotica" comes
from the Latin root "eros" or passionate love. It signifies mutual pleasure
and shared sensuality. "Pornography," by contrast, begins with the
Greek root "porno," meaning prostitute or female captive. Here, the
subject is domination, not mutual love. The word ends with the root
"graphos" meaning to write about or to describe (Steinem, 1980:37).
The sexuality is externalized and objectified through its contemplation
by an outsider.

The inequality that is the essence of pornography may be quite
subtle. A woman is shown naked, off balance, with throat exposed,

mouth open, and eyes closed, while the man is fully clothed, standing over her, with feet firmly planted on the ground. At the other end of the scale is fusion of violence and sex into masochistic themes. A *Hustler* magazine cover depicts a woman being fed into a meat grinder. "Snuff," a movie billed as a pornographic thriller, allegedly shows a woman actually being tortured, mutilated, and murdered for sexual stimulation (Lederer, 1980a:15). After researching material circulating in Canada, author Margaret Atwood (1983:118) concluded:

> By "pornography," I meant women having their nipples snipped off with garden shears, having meat hooks stuck into their vaginas, being disemboweled; little girls being raped, men (yes, there are some men) being smashed to a pulp and forcibly sodomized. The cutting edge of pornography, as far as I could see, was no longer simple old copulation, hanging from the chandelier or otherwise: it was death, messy, explicit and highly sadistic.

The amount of sexually violent pornography available in this country is increasing (Malamuth and Spinner, 1980).

Feminists' Objections to Pornography

Most feminists have no objection to erotica, the "passionate celebration of sex between two equal partners" (Anderson, 1984:23). They regard pornography as the antithesis of love. It is a metaphor for the imbalance of power between the sexes; they fear the hostility that such an imbalance provokes (Kostash, 1982:46). Pornography is viewed as hate literature against women, which society would not tolerate against Jews, Indians, or blacks. Pornographic symbolism reinforces sexist attitudes, causing men to revile women. It is designed to reduce the female "to an object of sexual access" (Brownmiller, 1975:394). This dehumanization of women is illustrated by what Griffin (1981:40) calls the "quintessential form of pornography" — the pornographic doll:

> Pornography is replete with images and evocations of the "doll," an actual plastic copy of a woman, made to replace a woman, and to give a man pleasure without the discomfort of female presence . . . . Her vagina opens "on command," she is "ready to go, night after night," she does not talk back, she is perfectly controllable (Griffin, 1981:40, 41).

Similarly, the *Playboy* way of life portrays women as toys for boys. "Woman cannot be mate, companion and lover — she must be his thing, his pet, his chick, his 'bunny'. . ." (Lederer, 1980b:124).

Fusion of sexual and violent symbols encourages consumers to perceive women as enjoying rape and torture. According to psychologists Malamuth and Spinner (1980:228),

> the information conveyed in much of the sexually violent materials is that women are basically masochistic and in need of male dominance . . . .

This material suggests to the user that even if a woman seems un-interested or repulsed, she will eventually respond favorably to forceful advances.

Social scientists do not agree that pornography influences behavior.[5] However, pornographic symbols, like other symbols discussed in this chapter, contribute to a climate of opinion that normalizes male dominance and female submission. Pornographic symbols reflect and reinforce gender hierarchy. The equation of sexuality and violence in this "quintessential macho" cultural form (Manion, 1985:66) makes pornographic symbols particularly distasteful. Intense debate over the limits of freedom of expression in our society will continue for some time to come.

Symbols and the Politics of Gender in Everyday Life

The sexist structure of language and non-verbal communication, along with the "knowledge" about females and males reflected in popular and high culture, are central ingredients in the politics of gender. *Macropolitics* may be defined as the exercise of power in the public domain. Males have traditionally monopolized societal power and made the decisions and rules binding on both sexes. Women have been excluded from effective participation by myths, for example, that only men are equipped with the intellectual qualities needed to vote or the moral qualities to commune with the deity. By *micropolitics* is meant the dynamics of power and social control in the private sphere (Schur, 1984). Our present discussion is confined to the micropolitics of gender in everyday life. The significance of micropolitics is emphasized by Lipman-Blumen's (1984:177) argument that

> . . . the basis of most power relationships is the private, domestic relationship between individual women and men. It is echoed in the public relationship of male and female groups, as well as in power relationships among social groups, classes, and nations.

The main thrust of the micropolitics of gender is "the reproduction of male dominance" (Stockard and Johnson, 1980:11). Henley and Freeman (1974:474) elaborate:

> Social interaction is the battleground where the daily war
> between the sexes is fought. It is here that women are
> constantly reminded where their "place" is and that they
> are put back in their place should they venture out.

Male-female encounters draw upon symbolic resources of tacit understandings and well-practiced routines. The way people communicate reflects the background assumptions of patriarchal society. In turn, such communication reinforces the gender hierarchy. As we observed earlier, both sexes do not stand in the same relationship to language. However, they do share some of the same masculine rules for talk. The belief of both sexes that women talk too much is an excellent example of ideology and false consciousness. Spender (1985:106) explains:

> When a society is structured so that it permits male
> primacy and produces male dominance, it is quite
> reasonable to classify woman talk as dangerous because
> the whole fabric of that social order could be under-
> mined if the expression of the subordinates were allowed
> free choice.

Consequently, women limit their talk to escape negative appraisal (Lipman-Blumen, 1984:91). Certain topics, e.g. business, politics, sports are defined as male property, and women may be rebuked or ridiculed for trespassing. Male socialization teaches that power lies with those who do not disclose their vulnerability. Therefore, they may gain the upper hand over women by refraining from self-revelation or emotional displays (Spender, 1985:46–47). They augment their power by taking control of conversation, deciding which topics will be pursued and which dropped, and interrupting the other speaker (Kollock et al., 1985).

Women become adept at the techniques required of the powerless in intimate relationships (Lipman-Blumen, 1984:30–31). They limit their own talk to avoid criticism (Chapter 2). They are socialized to acquiesce, indeed, even cooperate, with aggressive, masculine communication tactics. They become well-versed in interpreting the body language and emotional states of the dominant males. Because most (not all) women lack authority in the public world, they (along with other low-status groups like children and minority ethnics) rely on manipulative, indirect, coy methods of dealing with the dominant group — charm, deceit, teasing, tears. These strategies are usually denigrated by males, if and when they become aware of them:

> [Women's] influence is often labelled as deviant or dis-
> ruptive and powerful women in modern societies are
> described as "bitches" and "castrating females" while

those in more traditional ones are thought of as witches
and sources of evil (Nielsen, 1979:332).

In symbolic interactionist terms, taking control of a situation
means imposing one's definition upon the other actors in that situation (Marshall, 1978-79:348). One strategy to accomplish this involves
invoking gender. Because gender is a salient[6] and sensitive social identity in our society, its invocation is an obvious power ploy. Moreover,
cultural evaluation of the sexes and gender stereotypes provide ready-
made definitions of the gender situation. In Goffman's (1974) language,
this *a priori* definition of reality serves to "frame" the interaction.[7] A
frame is an organizing definition of the situation that answers the question, "What is it that's going on here?" A husband and wife are discussing where to go on vacation. When the wife argues for her choice for
location, rather than accepting his, the husband becomes disturbed.
He applies a gender frame to the episode: "Isn't that just like a woman!
It must be your time of the month!"
    If this hypothetical scene is examined more closely, we see that
there are three levels at which the question, "What's going on here"
can be answered. The simplest answer is, "Gender is going on here."
Implicitly, the husband is saying to his wife, "The fact that you are
female explains your refusal to agree with my opinion." A more complex answer is that *typification* (Berger and Luckmann, 1966:31) is going
on. That is, the other in the interaction is perceived and dealt with as
a type. In our society, the male is normal and more highly valued; the
female is deviant or Other. At a yet more sophisticated level, altercasting
explains the episode. *Altercasting* means one person in an interaction
(ego) casting the other (alter) into a role that ego chooses for alter, in
order to manipulate the situation (Weinstein, 1969). Altercasting constrains the opponent's behavior. The husband treats the wife as someone whose behavior stems from female biology and irrationality. Even
in denial of the characterization, "there lies an acceptance of an issue — an implicit agreement that what is charged is worth talking about
and thus might actually be true" (Hewitt, 1984:171). Of course, women
also altercast men in gender micropolitics. For example, a woman in
need of help lifting a heavy object may persuade a man to volunteer
by referring to stereotypic masculine characteristics of strength and
chivalry. However, given male control of resources, altercasting is more
likely to work in their favor.
    Although it is difficult to establish scientifically direct effects
of mass communication,[8] it is reasonable to assume that the gender
imagery conveyed by the mass media serve as resource material for the
politics of everyday life. The media reinforce daily the relative worth
of females and males. They make "natural" female subordination and
the traditional division of labor. In addition, gender routines portrayed

in the media may be mimicked in real life. Women may feel guilty if they don't serve their men with Duncan Hines cakes, as television-ad wives do. Men may put pressure on their mates to engage in kooky sex acts portrayed in men's magazines. The media are a prolific source of stereotypical ammunition: female success is attributed to luck, male success to ability. Females lack the eye-hand coordination required to excel at video games. Women have failed to produce musical genius. Women are weak, men are strong. Powerful women in public life, such as Margaret Thatcher, Prime Minister of England, are really males in drag. The media also provide fuel for typification and altercasting of males. Although feminist ideas are beginning to enter the community of discourse, the media contribute to the imbalance of power between the sexes.

Conclusions

Chapter 6 has reviewed a selection of mediated and unmediated symbolic forms as one reply to the question, "How is the social reality of gender maintained?" In so doing, it provides descriptive content to theoretical generalizations about socialization presented in previous chapters. These include symbolic interactionist concepts of the "Me" and the Generalized Other, and sociology of knowledge propositions concerning the existential conditioning of thought and ruling ideas.

Perhaps the chapter's most important conclusion is the degree of consensus about gender definitions communicated by the various sources, mediated and unmediated, popular and high culture, mass media and informally disseminated. Male superiority and the traditional gender division of labor remain a dominant or hegemonic[9] ideology in Canadian society. According to Marchak (1975:1), ideologies serve as screens through which the social world is perceived. They provide "the ready references, the rules of thumb, . . . the glue that holds institutions together, the medium that allows members of the population to interact, predict events, understand their roles . . . ."

Nevertheless, the women's movement has begun to breach the false consciousness of the subordinate sex. Critics question the ideology. Significant numbers of women are beginning to understand that "all knowledge is knowledge from some point of view" (M. Fishman, 1978:531). Women's culture "created by and for women themselves" (Bernard, 1981:414) thrives as a low-status alternative to the dominant culture. Perhaps the most stunning recent example of women's culture is Judy Chicago's "The Dinner Party," a massive triangular table set for 39 guests — all women who have made significant contributions to Western society and the lives of other women. Some of the guests are famous (writer Virginia Woolf, painter Georgia O'Keeffe). Some are obscure — Egyptian Pharoah Hatshepsut. Others, such as primordial goddesses, are legendary. Chicago described her work as "a reinterpretation of the Last Supper from the point of view of women, who, throughout history, had prepared the meals and set the tables." "The Dinner Party" took Chicago and 400 needleworkers, ceramists, and researchers five years to complete. Since it opened in 1979, it has been "admired, and panned, criticized, condemned, praised and ignored more often and more fervently than any other individual work of contemporary art." When it opened in Montreal's Musée d'art contemporain in March, 1982, 75,000 people came to see it — 15,000 more than that museum's usual attendance in a year (Leaman, 1983).

NOTES

1. Humor can be mediated, as well as unmediated. Examples of the former include Bill Cosby tapes, Phyllis Diller live performances, TV sit-coms, published cartoons.
2. Wood (1980) describes the new musical scholarship which is currently documenting women's historical exclusion from classical music. For example, she remarks upon the "discovered pattern of the supportive, secondary roles that history allots to musical women: as wives of composers, as lesser siblings, as bearers rather than creators of musical traditions" (p. 287). Few works of women have been performed by major orchestras. Fewer women have produced opera and symphonies, forms that require time, money, and assurance of professional support to succeed. Finally, women have greater difficulty than their male colleagues in gaining commissions, performances, recordings, and publication of their work.
3. O'Kelly (1983) performed a content analysis of gender stereotypes in 971 highly acclaimed works of art selected for reproduction in three major Western art history textbooks. All of the works that depicted the human figure were included in her analysis. Only three of the artists were female. Males constituted 70 percent of the subjects, females only 30 percent. Males were shown as active, serious workers and leaders. The madonna and the idle nude were common female images. For example, in the Modern Period from 1750 to the 1930s: "War is a favorite theme and the soldier is the most common role for males. Men are pictured in a large number and wide variety of roles such as kings, gods, nobles, lawgivers, doctors, philosophers, priests, musicians, explorers, hunters, stonebreakers, gladiators and peasants. Females are mothers, slaves, peasants, dancers, prostitutes, harem girls and models. People involved in leadership roles or serious work are almost invariably male" (p. 140).
4. Rosenberg (1979) documents the representation of female artists in Canadian museums and art galleries.
5. McCormack (1979) identified a "machismo factor" in media research. In previous years, male researchers simultaneously condemned violence in the media and advocated its censorship, and condoned pornography as innocent pleasure without serious consequences. For example, the U.S. Government Commission on Obscenity and Pornography (1970) concluded that pornography was harmless and recommended unrestricted access. A year earlier, the U.S. Commission on the Causes and Preventions of Violence had concluded that media violence had deleterious effects. Researchers have used a catharsis theory to explain pornography and an imitation model to explain aggression unconnected with sex. "The catharsis model, when applied to pornography, assumes that the more you see the less you do. In contrast, the imitation model states that the more you see the more you do" (Bart and Jazsa, 1980:205).
6. As noted in Chapter 4, to possess a given identity means to be described by oneself and by others in social terms (Stone, 1962:93). Identity is further specified through the concept of identity salience. "Identity salience" refers to the internal organization of the differentiated self. Identities are related to one another in a salience hierarchy (Stryker, 1980:131). In Burke's (1980:19) words, "Each identity is more or less likely (relative to other identities which the individual has) to be enacted or portrayed or

taken into account, depending upon its position in the salience hierarchy." Some identities, such as gender, are at the center of the concern of ego and alter. Others are peripheral.

7. Frank (1979:176) says of Goffman's *Frame Analysis* (1974): "A frame . . . is an a priori definition of reality, within which certain constructions of the situation (the reality having already been constructed) are taken for granted. These constructions, being behaviors relevant to certain frames, will reinforce the sense of the validity of the original framing, which reinforces the propriety of the behavior, and so forth. Thus the frame becomes, in Berger and Kellner's [1970] phrase, massively objective."

8. It is inappropriate for sociologists simply to scrutinize cultural projects, such as novels or music, and *infer* their producers' motives, their effects upon people, and their connection to the mood of the times (Denzin, 1970). Instead, the analyst must establish the meanings of symbolic products for their producers and their audiences, as well as their actual circulation throughout the society. Take music as an example. A sociologist may carry out a very scholarly analysis of the lyrics of popular music in order to learn whether gender depictions are less stereotyped in the 1980s than in the 1960s. However, ideally, the analyst requires information on the intention of songwriters, interpretations of audiences in particular historical times, the actual popularity of the music, and so on. If the attraction of a piece of music was the beat and not the lyrics, or if the music had an extremely limited audience, or if the lyrics are ambiguous, or if the songwriters were not addressing themselves to gender at all, it is impossible to arrive at firm conclusions about whether music reflected or influenced society. Attempting to establish socialization effects of music *per se* is even more challenging. How does the sociologist isolate the impact of teenagers' musical diet from what they read, the movies they see, and their family and school experiences?

9. According to Williams (1977:110), quoted in Grayson (1983:383), "Hegemony is . . . not only the articulate upper level of 'ideology,' nor are its forms of control only those ordinarily seen as 'manipulation' or 'indoctrination.' It is a whole body of practices and expectations over the whole of living: our senses and assignments of energy, our shaping perceptions of ourselves and our world. It is a lived system of meanings and values . . . . It thus contributes a sense of reality for most people in the society, a sense of absolute because of experienced reality beyond which it is very difficult for most members of the society to move, in most areas of their lives. It is, that is to say, in the strongest sense a 'culture,' but a culture which has also to be seen as the lived dominance and subordination of particular classes."

Gender and Body, Self, and Emotion

Introduction

> [Smart Bunny] was a rabbit who lived like all the other
> wild rabbits, but who was as intelligent as Albert
> Einstein or William Shakespeare. It was a female
> rabbit . . . .
> She led a normal female rabbit's life, despite her
> ballooning intellect. She concluded that her mind was
> useless, that it was a sort of tumor, that it had no
> usefulness within the rabbit scheme of things.
> So she went hippity-hop, hippity-hop toward the city,
> to have the tumor removed. But a hunter named Dudley
> Farrow shot and killed her before she got there. Farrow
> skinned her and took out her guts, but then he and his
> wife Grace decided that they had better not eat her
> because of her unusually large head. They thought what
> she had thought when she was alive — that she must be
> diseased.
> (Excerpted from the book *Breakfast of Champions*
> by Kurt Vonnegut Jr. Copyright © 1973 by Kurt Vonnegut Jr.
> Reprinted by permission of Delacorte Press/Seymour
> Lawrence.[1])

Contained in Vonnegut's tale are the interconnected themes of this
chapter: gender and body, self, and emotion. Inside Smart Bunny's
female body is an unusual intellect. Rabbit society regards this combination as inappropriate. Smart bunnies are supposed to be male
bunnies. Smart Bunny's looking-glass self reflects her society's definition of the situation. She feels bad and her end is a sad one.

The human gender socialization story also begins with the
body. At birth, gender is assigned on the basis of the infant's external
genitals. Thus begins the sustained sorting process into different gender
socialization experiences. Through clothing choice, parents announce
their child's gender. According to gender stereotypes, females are soft
and weak, males strong and robust. The traditional gender division
of labor, the allocation of domestic tasks to women and public tasks
to men, likely originated in women's reproductive capacities and men's
superior strength. Certainly, "the oldest, most persistent, and most

pervasive explanation and justification for the division of labour by sex is biological" (Armstrong and Armstrong, 1984:107). In North American and Western European societies, male dominance and female subordination have their ultimate source in the relatively bigger, stronger male body.

In human society, like rabbit society, it is the social construction of the physical reality that counts. People "experience as real what they are taught is real" (Turner, 1976:1000). The shaping of the self lies at the heart of primary socialization. Since the self is social and reflexive, gender differences in self-imagery and self-esteem are to be expected. People of both sexes accept as "natural" the ruling dicta that males deserve more status, prestige, power, and resources.

Growing up male at the top of the hierarchy versus growing up female at the bottom of the hierarchy have distinctive emotional consequences. Although the fate of human beings is considerably more complicated than Smart Bunny's, lack of fit between idiosyncratic abilities and needs and the constraining cubby holes of gender produces problems for human and rabbit alike.

Previous chapters have often made reference to body, self, and emotion. However, treatment of these topics has been, for the most part, implicit, disconnected, or subordinate to other matters. In Chapter 7, we bring back female and male as whole persons — as biological, subjective, emotional, but above all, social beings. Symbolic interactionism and the sociology of knowledge guide our discussion of the interrelated aspects of gender's connection to body, self, and emotion.

Gender and the Body

Pictures of our bodies form in our minds. We see parts of the body surface. Mouth, hair, earlobes in mirrors. Knuckles, knees, toes when eyes cast downward. Posture and girth in chance reflections in store windows. We touch and smell our bodies. We experience heat, cold, pain, pleasure. Sensations come from muscles, viscera, and erogenous zones. Beyond these discrete impressions and sensations, there is perception of the body's unity (Schilder, 1968:107).

Knowledge of our own bodies would seem to be the most private of experiences. However, the meaning of the body emerges from interaction: *"Body-images are on principle social"* (Schilder, 1968:111; emphasis added). Children learn about their bodies through the talk and observations of others. Through adulthood, our opinions of our bodies and the ways we groom, clothe, and embellish them continue to be socially influenced.[2] Our bodies are altered through maturation, disease, accidents, aging, and pregnancy. Lynn Johnson, creator of the "For Better or Worse" cartoon, says of pregnancy: "Being lived in is a wierd experience. You feel like a duplex and you can't get rid of the tenant downstairs" (Zwarun, 1982a:30). Rossan's (1984) study of pregnant women shows that pregnancy, like other body transformations, is subject to social interpretation:

> A husband, for example, may tell his wife that he likes the way she looks, now that she is eight months pregnant, because she looks so feminine. His wife may feel pleased that her husband likes her current body shape. Or she may be pleased that he is pleased, but not certain that she wants to look feminine. Or she may wonder why he likes her fat, rather than slender. Or she may be unhappy that he prefers her temporary body shape to her permanent body shape. Or she may be angry that he likes her manifesting an aspect of woman's traditional role rather than her more usual competent role in a masculine milieu. Or she may not care what he thinks of her temporary shape, so long as he likes her permanent one. Or she may ignore the communication, because she does not care what he thinks! (p. 4).

Bodies are an important ingredient in self-imagery and self-esteem. As mentioned in Chapter 2, inhabiting a female, as opposed to a male, body likely contributes to the existential conditioning of thought. However, social interpretations color these idiosyncratic experiences. Because men are Subject and women Object (de Beauvoir, 1949), because males have the power to name female bodies, as well as their own, masculine opinions intrude on females' subjective experiences of their own bodies.

Symbolic interactionists (Stone, 1962) consider appearance (clothing, grooming, body shape and stance, etc.) to be just as important as discourse in social transactions. "Like it or not, looks are an instantly available measure of a person's value in our society" (Blumstein and Schwartz, 1983:246). By our presentation of self (Goffman, 1959), we indicate to others the kind of person we are, the line of action we intend to pursue. Others make inferences from our appearance to our personal traits, character and roles. Physical attractiveness is a major criterion in sizing up other people and their status (Berscheid and Walster, 1974; Webster and Driskell, 1983). Because each person is more or less aware that appearance is being judged by others, pressures to contrive one's appearance and manipulate others' impressions are strong (Lauer and Handel, 1983:296–297). Fashion behavior, for example, is by and large a very calculating act (Blumer, 1969a).

Appearance establishes gender in social transactions (Stone, 1962:90). Body size, hair length, clothing and the like communicate whether one is male or female. Beyond this basic categorization, appearance subtly communicates male superiority and female inferiority.

The female contrives an appearance that signals her interest in masculine attention. Those parts of the female body which are sexualized in our culture — face, breasts, legs, buttocks — "are subjected to special routines of display and enhancement" (Laws and Schwartz, 1977:43). Masculine standards determine which aspects of her body are enhanced, which concealed. A salesman's comments about his ex-wife's deviance indicate that masculine appearance norms continue after courtship:

> I think she forgot about being my lover. She got fat. She wouldn't listen to my complaints about that at all. She stopped dyeing her hair, and I got off on her being blond . . . . I put up with that horse manure for six years, if you can believe that. Not anymore! (Blumstein and Schwartz, 1983:247).

Males too are concerned about their appearance. A man writes Ann Landers:

> I am 36 years of age, depressed by the fact that I will be completely bald by the time I am 40. In the last 10 years I have spent nearly $8,000 on salves, injections and even sheep dung (*The Calgary Herald,* March 27, 1984).

Females want full bosoms and tiny waists, males muscular chests and big penises. Both sexes worry about their complexion. Nevertheless, the "tyranny of beauty" (Blumstein and Schwartz, 1983:246) falls disproportionately on females. Male value is influenced predominantly by the power and prestige they derive from their work and from simply being male. "Women, however, must rest their case largely on their bodies" (Bell, 1970:75). Our society limits females' ability to attain status in other ways and to translate that status into physical attractiveness. In other words, beautiful women are successful, and successful men "beautiful" in our society. This state of affairs is the result of ideology, not chance.

The Traditional Gender Ideology of the Body

> Next morning the prince went to his father, the King, and said to him: "No one shall be my wife but she whose foot this golden slipper fits." Then were the two sisters glad, for they had pretty feet. The eldest went with the shoe into her room and wanted to try it on, and her mother stood by. But she could not get her big toe into it, and the shoe was too small for her. Then her mother gave her a knife and said: "Cut the toe off, when thou art Queen thou wilt no more need to go on foot." The maiden cut the toe off, forced the foot into the shoe, swallowed the pain, and went out to the King's son.

> Then he took her on his horse as his bride and rode
> away with her.
> He was, alas, not an observant man. He galloped away
> with barely a glance at his prey; she might have been
> lame, for all he cared. But this was not the happy end;
> the Grimms' story continues with the discovery of the
> fraud. Blood, streaming from the bride's shoe, has dyed
> her white stockings red, making a mess . . . . Calling the
> bluff, the prince returns the misfit whereupon the
> mother, undaunted, fobs off her second daughter on the
> gullible bridegroom — not without first having shrunk
> her foot by amputating its heel. Again, the deceit is
> bloodily revealed, and the prince returns the wrong
> bride. This time he meets Cinderella. Virtue, equated by
> shoe size, triumphs when the prince finds the foot of his
> dreams.

Although Walt Disney's sanitized version of the Grimms' fairy tale has substituted glass slippers and pumpkin coaches for mangled feet, the moral of Cinderella's story still holds. The more powerful sex makes the rules, including standards of beauty. Both sexes learn the rules during childhood and adult socialization. Feminine subscription to this ideology is, of course, false consciousness.

The gender ideology of the body means that women "are *literally seen* as objects": men perpetually gape at their bodies (Schur, 1984:66, 42). "Men look at women. Women watch themselves being looked at" (Berger, 1977:47). Women's bodies have attracted an amazing amount of attention: they have "been mankind's most popular subject for adoration and myth, and also for judgment, ridicule, esthetic alteration and violent abuse" (Brownmiller, 1984:27).

Ideologies, by definition, serve to justify the status quo (Chapter 2). Women's bodies are not merely objectified; they are objectified in terms of male interests. Gender ideologies bolster male power and rationalize the traditional division of labor. If women can no longer be confined to the domestic sphere in the latter decades of the twentieth century, their attachment to the public sphere can be restricted to secondary participation.

More specifically, men have a stake in women's bodies as sexual objects, as incubators, as advertisements of masculine status, and as big business. First, gratifiers of men's sexual needs, women's bodies are often reduced to isolated parts: "breasts," "cunt," "pussy." Second, men have a vital interest in women's reproductive powers. As Lipman-Blumen (1984:33) notes, "the technological breakthrough of the Pill, which gave women virtually complete control over their sexuality and parenthood, introduced major changes in the power contest between men and women." Third, women's bodies serve to advertise and enhance the status of their men. For one thing, the contrast of a small, fragile, female body accentuates masculinity. For another, women's appearance has been employed traditionally to symbolize men's exalted position in the public domain. As Thorstein Veblen (1899:126) argued long ago, it has been woman's function to serve as the "chief ornament" of the household and "to put in evidence her household's ability to pay." Finally, women's preoccupation with cosmetics, fashionable clothing, weight loss clinics and the like is enormously profitable to the capitalist system. Even the profit-minded medical system has a financial stake in her body.

The traditional gender ideology of the body encompasses these five themes:

(1) *Traditionally, males, as the dominant sex, have controlled the production and dissemination of ideas concerning both female and male bodies.* This fact is the cornerstone of the ideology of the body. Until control of their own bodies became a central issue of the women's movement, masculine intellectual and moral authority in this area had gone unquestioned. In this, as in other areas, many, perhaps most women, continue to collaborate in their own subordination.

Male definition of female bodies has found expression in many modalities. Man-made language semantically derogates the female body. Religion has characterized women as physically, intellectually, and morally inferior. They are Peter's "weaker vessel" (1 Peter 3: 1-7) (Carmody, 1979:285). God the Father " 'gave birth' to the male Adam who in turn 'gave birth' to the female Eve" (Spender, 1985:167). The Roman Catholic and fundamentalist Protestant Churches continue to deny women's right to contraception and abortion. Painting, sculpture, literature, and pornography have presented male fantasies about women's bodies. With regard to the latter, "pornography forcefully suggests that the body is not a means to intimacy, but is rather a tool by which the subjugation of others can be perfected" (Ashley and Ashley, 1984:365).

The mass media have been powerful disseminators of the gender ideology of the body. Jane Fonda (1981:17) says she could hardly recognize herself in the mirror when movie makeup men were through with her: "winged eyebrows, false eyelashes, big pink lips, hair that looked as if it had been ironed. . . ." On one occasion,

> . . . a prominent film director suggested that I seriously consider having my back teeth pulled and my jaw broken. He told me that another baby-faced actress in search of cheekbones had had this done successfully (Fonda, 1981:17).

The cachet of science attaches to medical views of women's bodies. As mentioned in Chapter 2, the masculine medical profession edged out female lay healers and midwives (Ehrenreich and English, 1978). Feminists have charged the medical profession with misunderstanding their sexuality, diagnosing women's physical ills as psychogenic, dehumanizing pregnancy and childbirth, and performing unnecessary hysterectomies, mastectomies, and Caesarian sections (Armitage et al., 1980; Lewin and Olesen, 1985; Pearson and Clark, 1982). According to a medical authority quoted by Landsberg (1982:125), "It is the sheer *otherness* of women" that made them particularly prey to "medical and surgical overkill" (emphasis in original). The medical profession's emphasis on women's reproductive and maternal roles "provided what became a scientific rationale for woman's domestic place in society" (Mitchinson, 1980:118).

(2) *Women are valued for their bodies, men for their minds.* Quotations abound (Standard, 1971:197). "A woman has the form of an angel . . and the mind of an ass" (German proverb). "No woman is a genius; women are a decorative sex" (Oscar Wilde). Since our society values and rewards intellect and its products, women end up with the short end of the stick. According to Ortner (1974), women's procreative functions serve symbolically to associate them with nature. By contrast, men identify themselves with culture, which "naturally" subsumes and transcends nature:

> . . . woman's body seems to doom her to mere reproduction of life; the male, in contrast, lacking natural creative functions, must (or has the opportunity to) assert his creativity externally, "artificially," through the medium of technology and symbols. In so doing, he creates relatively lasting, eternal, transcendent objects, while the woman creates only perishables — human beings (Ortner, 1974:75).

Beauty and sexuality are women's most valuable assets (Lipman-Blumen, 1984:89–90). Becoming ambitious for knowledge and power "defeminizes them, endangers their beauty" (p. 89). Eve's intellectual curiosity earned her not praise, but eviction from the Garden of Eden. Her original sin allegedly inspired the Lord to assign all women the somatic penalty of pain in childbirth.

To succeed, women must cultivate their beauty and marry accomplished men. In this traditional bargain, such women as the late Princess Grace of Monaco achieve wealth, power, vicarious success, and the husband gains a status symbol who advertises his importance. Though no one, male or female, wants to be ugly, beauty and youth are critical for women. "Women learn early that if you are unlovely, you are unloved" (Stannard, 1971:195). The emphasis on women's looks implicitly devalues their other attributes and accomplishments. For women, appearance becomes a commodity and a key determinant of success or failure in life (Schur, 1984:68), to the end of life:

> She never gives up. Her blue hair waved, circles of rouge on her wrinkled cheeks, lipstick etching the lines around her mouth, still moisturizing her skin nightly, still corseted, she dies (Stannard, 1971:189).

(3) *Men's and women's bodies are quite different.* The first male gender socialization lesson is "don't be like girls/women because they are unequal, bad, and inferior" (Doyle, 1983:150). Clothing and cosmetics exaggerate the differences between female and male bodies. The ideal North American man is big, strong, and healthy. Women are small and delicate in comparison. The ideology emphasizes women's fragility, despite the average seven years' greater life expectancy of the latter (Statistics Canada, 1985:79). This "mythology of physical strength" (Pleck and Sawyer, 1974:126) explains the unique male ability to deal with challenges in the public domain and to protect women and children. Indeed, Nemerowicz (1979) discovered that children are convinced that only men are strong enough to handle the physical difficulties and dangers of many occupations (Chapter 3).

"Femininity pleases men because it makes them appear more masculine by contrast" (Brownmiller, 1984:16). Apparently, even the Prince of Wales requires this "extra portion of unearned gender distinction" (p. 16):

> Only a half-inch shorter than Prince Charles when she wore her flat heels, Lady Di was reduced in stature by a full head for the postage stamp that commemorated their royal wedding (Brownmiller, 1984:29).

(4) *Males have had the power to establish criteria of attractiveness for both sexes.* As a corollary, these beauty norms are unrealistic and ordinary people of both sexes suffer. Women, in particular, are apt to experience a sense of perpetual "deficiency" (Schur, 1984:68). Males whose bodies fail to match those of such "big bad wolf" heroes as John Wayne, Clint Eastwood, and Sylvester Stallone (Mellen, 1977) may feel inadequate. Physical strength becomes identified with moral strength (Gagnon, 1976). In a society where a big, robust body is an emblem of masculinity, a man with "effeminate" features is in trouble. Harding, a character in the novel *One Flew Over the Cuckoo's Nest* (Kesey, 1962), is afflicted with long, white dainty hands:

> While Harding's telling the story he gets enthusiastic and forgets about his hands, and they weave the air in front

> of him into a picture clear enough to see, dancing the
> story to the tune of his voice like two beautiful ballet
> women in white. . . . But as soon as the story's finished
> he notices McMurphy and his wife are watching the
> hands, and he traps them between his knees. He laughs
> about this, and his wife says to him, "Dale, when are
> you going to learn to laugh instead of making that
> mousy little squeak?" (Kesey, 1962:158).

Nevertheless, women are much more likely than men to feel permanently insecure about their bodies. The standards for female beauty are masculine. Take height, for example:

> "She looked up into his eyes" is more than a breathless
> phrase from a Gothic novel; it is an expression of the
> heterosexual relationship as we expect to find it. When a
> woman stands taller than a man she has broken a car-
> dinal feminine rule, for her physical stature reminds him
> that he may be too short — inadequate, insufficient — for
> the competitive world of men (Brownmiller, 1984:29).

Similarly, the ideal woman with large breasts, narrow waist, and generous hips reflects male sexual interests.[3] According to Bat-Ada (Lederer, 1980b:129), "Women hate themselves for not being like the magazine models they see men panting after." They know they don't fit the measurements touted in the magazines. She goes on to say,

> I have been conducting a field study now for six months.
> I carry a measuring tape around with me, and I measure
> the bust, waist, and hips of every woman who will
> cooperate. My findings are very interesting: *Not once* have
> I encountered a female who measures the 38-22-34-inch
> size that *Playboy* used to claim its centerfold was. I have
> not come across one female with a natural 22-inch waist!
> (Lederer, 1980b:130, emphases in original).

The billion-dollar fashion and cosmetic businesses tell women they are "monsters in disguise." Their beauty "needs lifting, shaping, dyeing, painting, curling, padding" (Stannard, 1971:192).

Across cultures and centuries, women have been encouraged (or obliged) to reconstruct their bodies to conform to male erotic expec-
tations (Hunter Collective, 1983:33): in the East, the bound feet of the Chinese, the Burmese neck ring, the Japanese obi; in the West, the steel-ribbed corset and whalebone stays. "Nineteenth-century belles even went to the extremity of having their lowest ribs removed so that they could lace their corsets tighter" (Greer, 1971:25). Each device of beauti-fication restricted women's freedom and sapped their strength (Brown-miller, 1984:33). Chinese women with three-inch stubs in place of nor-

mal feet were literally dainty ornaments. They could not move without assistance. Modern women pierce their ears, undergo silicone injections in their breasts and plastic surgery. Brownmiller (1984:35) argues:

> . . . whatever sartorial devices men have put on to bolster their body image — codpieces, elevated shoes, padded shoulders, a boxy jacket — these did not constrict or cause pain. The truth is, men have barely tampered with their bodies at all, historically, to make themselves more appealing to women.

When women undertake physical modification, it is intended to enhance their role as beautiful, passive object. Male physical alteration, however, has been intended to enhance their roles as actor. Witness U.S. President Ronald Reagan's 1986 presentation of self as a robust, competent 75-year old.

(5) *Women's sexuality is inexhaustible and potentially dangerous to men* (Lipman-Blumen, 1984:86). The differences between men's and women's sexuality have troubled men. Women's organs are internal, hidden, "shrouded in mystery" (Greer, 1971:29). Women, unlike men, are able to engage in intercourse with only minimal arousal. They can have multiple orgasms without a recovery period. Men fear they will not be able to satisfy women sexually (Schur, 1984:46). Dinnerstein (1976:62) writes of "their archetypal nightmare vision of the insatiable female." Male expressions of this fear range from the Bible story of the seductive Delilah who destroyed Samson to the recurring image of the vagina with teeth, to the "phantasmagorical specter of the engulfing superbreast" in the writings of Philip Roth and Woody Allen (Brownmiller, 1984:44). The aggressive challenge of feminism has been blamed for male impotence, his "failure to rise to the occasion" (Greer, 1984b:60). Women's seemingly boundless sexuality, combined with their capacity to bear children, has been a source of profound ambivalence for men. According to Dinnerstein (1976:125), "man has magic feelings of awe and fear, sometimes disgust . . . and destructive rage . . . toward all things that are mysterious, powerful, and not himself." She calls woman's fertile body "the quintessential incarnation of this realm of things" (p. 125).

Historically, men believed menstruation and childbirth to be contaminating. The Bible warns against socializing with menstruating women (Lipman-Blumen, 1984:87). Childbirth was similarly polluting. "If a woman have conceived seed, and born a man child, then she shall be unclean seven days; . . . But if she bear a maid child, then she shall be unclean two weeks. . ." (Leviticus 12: 2, 5). The Anglican Church ritual, "Churching of Women," supposedly purified women after childbirth.

In the context of the power relations of patriarchal society, women's bodies have been objects of social control. Methods of keeping women "in their place" vary from rhetoric to institutional and individual violence. Attempts to control women's awesome sexuality include the requirement in Muslim countries that women in public cover their bodies, hair, and often faces (Hunter Collective, 1983:39); ritual mutilation of female genitals in Africa and aboriginal Australia (Steinem, 1983); legal definition of girls' actual or suspected sexual behavior as "delinquency" (Smith, 1978); regulation of abortion and rape (Lipman-Blumen, 1984:86).

Although viewing all of men's brute force against women as conscious power strategy oversimplifies the problem (Lips, 1981:145), feminists locate the etiology of wife battering (Breines and Gordon, 1983) and rape (Brownmiller, 1975) in the everyday fabric of the relations between the sexes in patriarchal society. Individual men frequently use violence to maintain their power and privilege in the family (Dobash and Dobash, 1979). Similarly, the rapist's pleasure often derives from his sense of power over his victim. Therefore, rape has been described as "the ultimate metaphor for domination, violence, subjugation, and possession" (Morgan, 1980:134). The most basic fact of male-female relations is that "males are bigger than females and are able to bully them" (Hrdy, 1981:18).

Feminist Unmasking of the Patriarchal Ideology of the Body

The feminist movement has shown that "rebellious constructions of the mind" (Berger, 1963:133) are possible, that the "commonly agreed-upon

THE INTRUSION OF EXPERTS

After the first I didn't ever want to have another child, it was too much to go through for nothing, they shut you into a hospital, they shave the hair off you and tie your hands down and they don't let you see, they don't want you to understand, they want you to believe it's their power, not yours. They stick needles into you so you won't hear anything, you might as well be a dead pig, your legs are up in a metal frame, they bend over you, technicians, mechanics, butchers, students clumsy or snickering practicing on your body, they take the baby out with a fork like a pickle out of a pickle jar. After that they fill your veins up with red plastic, I saw it running down through the tube. I won't let them do that to me ever again.

(Source: *Surfacing*, Copyright © 1972 by Margaret Atwood. Published by McClelland and Stewart and Simon and Schuster. Reprinted by permission of the publishers.)

meanings are not omnipotent in their capacity to coerce" (p. 126). Feminists' appreciation of the political significance of masculine constructions of women's bodies dates from at least as early as the turn-of-the-century militant suffragist campaign in England:

> Making a stunning connection between the public celebration of the erotic feminine nude and the refusal of Britain's male Parliament to grant women the vote, [movement activist] Mary Richardson walked into the National Gallery with a small ax tucked into the sleeve of her jacket and broke the glass that protected the *Rokeby Venus* before she was dragged off by the guards (Brownmiller, 1984:24).

Nearly 60 years later, feminists remembered what they had forgotten and expressed similar sentiments by entering a sheep in the Miss America Beauty pageant (Wilson, 1973:234). The contemporary feminist challenge to male power over female bodies has taken a number of forms which are elaborated below:

Science and Female/Male Bodies. Feminists have consulted with science to discover whether women's biological equipment indeed "seals their fate" (Armstrong and Armstrong, 1984:107). Though the answer is complex (see Chapter 1), science has affirmed the basic similarity of male and female bodies (and minds). Needless to say, feminists found these findings congenial. As one woman put it, "I had always thought my brains were more beautiful than my body. It made me angry to think my personal appeal came from painted powerlessness" (Roth, 1982:182).

Women's Health Movement. In such publications as the Boston Women's Health Collective, *Our Bodies, Ourselves* (1973/1984), and McDonnell and Valverde, *The Healthsharing Book: Resources for Canadian Women* (1985) feminists began to reclaim from male experts the cognitive territory that had formerly been theirs.[4] They defied those medical authorities who held that women, dominated by their reproductive systems and their maternal role, "naturally" belonged in the home.

> Exposés of the hazards of the pill, intrauterine devices, and hormone treatments for menopausal women raised serious questions about the doctors' integrity, if not their basic competence. Doctors were found to be cutting into the female body with something of the same abandon which had characterized nineteenth-century gynecology. . . . Perhaps most shocking was the feminist dissection of professional obstetrical care: the routine use of anesthesia, and the common resort to forceps, chemical induction of labor, and Caesarian sections turned out to be hazardous for mother and child, though convenient and probably gratifying to the physician (Ehrenreich and English, 1978:315–316).

Sexuality and Reproduction. The struggle for control of women's sexuality and reproduction has been central to the power struggle between the sexes.[5] As mentioned in Chapter 2, some feminists (e.g., O'Brien, 1981) believe that male dominance over women originated in the sexual arena. They hold "that the discovery by men of their biological role in reproduction was succeeded by male property claims over female bodies and their offspring, and male control of reproduction" (Wine, 1985:58). This control is *not* ancient history. Speaking of the contemporary situation, MacKinnon (1982) describes sexuality as the "linchpin of gender inequality" (p. 533) and gender socialization as "the process through which women come to identify themselves as sexual beings, as beings that exist for men" (p. 531).

Issues relevant to male control of sexuality that have concerned feminists include rape, incest, prostitution, pornography, sexist advertising, and sexual harrassment in the workplace. In addition, phallocentric sex and the uneven distribution of orgasms became a political issue (Ehrenreich, 1983:115). During the permissive era of the 1970s, women campaigned for the right to exercise free will in sexual matters. Recently, such feminists as Germaine Greer (1984a) have had second thoughts about the wisdom of sexual permissiveness. Greer argues that women have been used, that automatic sexual accessibility has become a duty. She recommends chastity instead.[6]

Gaining control of their reproduction has been especially important to feminists (Oakley, 1980; Scully, 1980). "As long as sexuality led almost inevitably to maternity, the reins that kept women tied to hearth and home were short and stout" (Lipman-Blumen, 1984:33). Prior to the passage of the 1969 Canadian abortion law, mock funeral processions through city streets dramatized women's need for safe abortion as a legal and morally valid choice. Women dressed in black mourning garb formed a procession behind coffins symbolizing victims of back-alley abortionists. Piled on top of the coffin were abortionists' grisly tools.[7] Feminists have used less depressing symbolism to make the point that their bodies are their own. For example, several versions of this anecdote are in circulation:

> "Did you ever hear the story about Judy Holliday? . . .
> When she went for a movie interview, the head of the
> studio started chasing her around the desk. So she just
> reached into her dress, pulled out her falsies, and handed
> them to him. 'Here,' she said, 'I think this is what you
> want" (Steinem, 1983a:162).

The abortion issue continues to divide feminists and various counter-movements such as REAL Women.

Traditional Clothing. Gender norms of appearance have been bitterly attacked by the feminist movement. The symbolism of the movement has responded to " 'the way things are' by stressing the converse: 'not like this' (Cassell, 1974:91). The confining, uncomfortable, even dangerous nature of women's traditional clothing has been challenged:

> Take, for instance, the several hundred women who died at a South American party when a fire broke out in the 1800s. . . . In the rush for the door, their hoops became entangled. They went down in a writhing mass of humanity as impossible to disentangle as a pot of spaghetti (Zwarun, 1983).

Instead, women have been encouraged to wear safe, comfortable, utilitarian clothing. For outsiders, the well-publicized (but largely mythical) bra-burning proclivities of feminists came to symbolize the movement. Some changes have occurred. Pants are now considered appropriate for dress occasions, as well as picnicking and gardening. Many women, who expect to be in city streets and parking lots at night, now wear Adidas for speed, instead of the spiked heels of yesteryear.

From time to time, a few women engage in what Klapp (1972:330) terms *style rebellion*, "use of a fashion more or less deliberately as symbolic protest . . . ." According to the *Alberta Report* (October 21, 1985:34), University of Alberta student feminists were sufficiently inspired by the visit of Australian feminist Dale Spender that "all of them wore purple (the chosen color of turn-of-the-century British Suffragettes) from head to toe. . . ."

Attractiveness Attribute. The feminist movement also attempted to invert the attractiveness criterion for conventional female appearance (Cassell, 1974). "In our society, looking attractive is usually related to a woman's doing something to herself, as opposed to doing nothing. Time, effort, and equipment are needed" (Cassell, 1974:88). Movement literature teaches women not to disguise or constrain their natural bodies. The characteristic demeanor of extreme feminists a decade ago illustrates style rebellion or symbolic inversion of the attractiveness criterion:

> These women generally wear jeans, or workmen's denim overalls, the baggy kind that hides the shape of the wearer. The pants may be topped by a man's t-shirt or workshirt. It is generally clear they are not wearing bras. Their hair is not so much styled as *there*; they wear no makeup; steel-rimmed reading glasses or sunglasses are frequent; footgear is comfortable, with a predominance of men's workboots or sneakers; and jewelry is rare. . .
> (Cassell, 1974:87; emphasis in original).

At the same time, this feminist uniform constituted a symbolic nose-thumbing at the class conscious dress code of middle-class women.

Similarly, feminists argue that "fat is a feminist issue" (Orbach, 1978). Women's sex-object status in society is seen as causing them, much more often than men, to become fixated on their body weight, to become compulsive eaters, bulimics or anorexics. They view emaciated bodies as exaggerated striving to achieve stereotypical femininity (Boskind-Lodahl, 1976:346). Instead of self-castigation and dieting, women are encouraged to respect their fat which says,

> . . . 'screw you' to all who want her to be the perfect mom, sweetheart, maid and whore. Take me for who I am, not for who I'm supposed to be. If you are really interested in *me*, you can wade through the layers and find out who I am (Orbach, 1978:21).

The above discussion indicates that women's silence concerning "the body politic" (Ehrenreich, 1984) has ended. How effective has the challenge been?

The Bottom Line

The clash between traditional masculine and feminist ideologies has produced mixed results. Feminists have scored some significant victories in their fight for women's intellectual and somatic recognition. Regardless of their private thoughts, few dare say publicly that women have intuitive abilities, while men have abstract, analytical intelligence (Lipman-Bluman, 1984:78), or that women should be excluded from responsible positions because it is the wrong time of the month or the wrong time of life (Armstrong and Armstrong, 1984:122). Despite some victories, battles for jurisdiction over reproduction and health continue into the second half of the 1980s. The Boston Women's Health Collective (1984:xi) writes, "The more we learn, the less we believe that the medical system as it is structured today can or will alter to meet our needs."

So far as type of clothing is concerned, feminists have had some success in encouraging women and girls to present themselves in accordance with their personal values. According to Adler (1979:387), "there is more freedom in dress today than there has been for centuries in comfort, and more than ever in choice." Men too have softened their appearance with color and fragrance. In some circles, the elegant designer lines advertised in *Gentleman's Quarterly* carry more prestige than macho looks of earlier years. Nevertheless, fashion continues to matter more to females than to males. Also, it is important to keep in mind that fashion is a complex social process with many causes. Other influences on fashion, besides feminism, are discussed in the next section.

Despite feminist protest, the tyranny of beauty seems more pronounced than ever. Though the movement stimulated some appreciation of the energy, money, and pain produced by our society's emphasis on looking good and staying young, it "does not seem to have had much real impact on cultural standards of beauty and the industries which feed on these" (Laws and Schwartz, 1977:45). Weight-control clinics, plastic surgeons, cosmetic companies, fashion designers, and tanning salons all thrive. "I sometimes wish I had cancer," said a large, pretty woman in her early twenties at a diet workshop. . . . "I sometimes think I wouldn't mind dying, if only I could die thin" (Sternhell, 1985:142).

The reason for the tyranny of beauty? The inescapable fact is that the search for attractiveness pays off. It pays off for the capitalist economy. It pays off for the individual, as people change homes, jobs, and spouses more frequently. What is beautiful is assumed to be "good" (Dion et al., 1972). Attractive people are assumed to be intelligent, competent, popular, happy, kind and successful. Ugly, poorly dressed and poorly groomed individuals are also viewed and treated less positively (Agnew, 1984). All of these statements apply to both sexes. Beauty is yet more critical for female success. Though the traditional courtship bargain between men and women has been modified, males continue to dictate beauty standards. For example, many women invading the business world wear some variation of the uniform recommended by John Molloy's *Dress For Success* (1976): blue suit, tailored white shirt, scarf or little bow tie. Beauty is a billion-dollar industry. Feminist criticisms are rejected or co-opted and new "needs" created by an industry with enormous financial assets.

Additional Source of Body Ideas

The "culture of narcissism" (Lasch, 1979) has had a profound influence on philosophies of the body entertained by both sexes. After the political turmoil of the 1960s and early 1970s, North Americans retreated from politics to purely personal preoccupations: getting in touch with their feelings, eating health food, jogging, pumping iron (Lasch, 1979:29). Some of the motivation for "ego-screaming," "look-at-me!" fashions (Klapp, 1969:80) that defy traditional gender norms come from the same source. The middle-class male revolt of the 1970s was more a reflection of the narcissistic "me first" ethos than a reaction to feminist teachings. According to Ehrenreich (1983:140),

> The initial and irrefutable reason for men to transform
> themselves was . . . to save their lives. No treatise or
> document of men's liberation . . . failed to mention the
> bodily injuries sustained by role-abiding men, from
> ulcers and accidents to the most "masculine" of illnesses,
> coronary heart disease.

The middle class is currently caught up in a new obsession with health and physical fitness. Both sexes, but men particularly, are affected. Although Canadian women do not score quite as well on aerobic fitness, they have become almost as physically active as men (Statistics Canada, 1985:79). Oddly, beyond recommending self-defense classes, the feminist literature "is virtually devoid of discussions about sport" (Hall, 1980:51).

Good Habits and Their Gender Consequences

The growing preoccupation with health and fitness is influencing the gender definitions for both sexes. Men are becoming more conscious of appearance. Paul McCartney explains why he goes crazy when someone tries to snap a picture of him:

> So I go on holiday and I'm building sand castles with the kids, and I really hate having to hold my stomach in the whole time in case there's a photographer behind a bush. It drives me mad . . . I don't want my picture all over the world with my stomach hanging out (*People*, November 5, 1984).

As mentioned above, concern about their health is leading some men to question the wisdom of being a success machine (Ehrenreich, 1983).

The new body consciousness is having a number of gender-related consequences. First, abandoning the notion that "nice girls don't sweat," participating in sports (though not on an equal basis with men [Hall, n.d.]), is shifting the definition of femininity. Females need no longer be weak and delicate. Women bitten by "iron fever" say they enjoy the sensation of gaining strength and building muscles (Klein and Slater, 1985). For women, as for other excluded groups such as ethnic and racial minorities, "sport seems an important avenue to full citizenship . . ." (Beazley and Hobbes, 1983:42). However, males too are becoming more physically active. Does their increased interest in physicality and muscle-building carry implications for the future power balance between the sexes?

Second, the new concern with health and fitness is influencing children's sex-stereotyped play patterns. You will recall that in Chapter 4, children's play and games were described as microcosms of society. Therefore, as girls become more active in team sports, they are preparing for different sorts of participation in adult life than their mothers were (Hall, n.d.:51). In other words, girls' participation in "masculine" play may be anticipatory socialization for later performance in the public domain.

Third, the new emphasis on fitness and nutrition has lent prestige to the traditional feminine domains of food and cooking. Food has great emotional importance for women who associate it with nurturance of themselves or others:

> I like baked chicken, mashed potatoes, jellied cranberry
> sauce, salad, milk — they make me feel cared for. When
> I cook it for myself I become both my mother and me as
> a child (Rome, 1984:11).

Increasingly, "real men" can eat and cook quiche without being considered sissies, especially if they are young and middle class. However, since routine, daily cooking (as opposed to recreational, gourmet cooking) is hard work, men are unlikely to take it over from women.

Fourth, the new emphasis on health and fitness may be a counter-influence to traditional gender norms which encourage males to abuse their bodies. Goldberg (1976:103) describes the traditional situation that teaches boys

> that it is "sissy behavior" to complain of body pains and
> also encourages him to deny and resist the fact of illness
> and injuries as long as possible. One cultural definition
> of being a "real boy" or a hero is that he carries on,
> whether in a football game, a fight . . . *in spite* of his injuries and symptoms (emphasis in original).

The same sort of mentality encourages risk taking behind the wheel of automobiles. This bravado was epitomized by Evel Knievel, the motorcycle daredevil who jumped over 13 trucks at the 1974 Toronto Canadian National Exhibition.

Finally, the physical fitness craze is increasing the pressure on both sexes, but especially women to be attractive. One serious result of rising standards for the body beautiful is the recent prevalence of severe eating disorders, with their "total emotional and moral investment in a thin body" (Caspar and Ostrov, 1981:98). These disorders are primarily, but not exclusively, female conditions (Boskind-Lodahl, 1976; Kaplan, 1980). Another consequence is the relatively recent female interest in the male as esthetic/sexual object. Are such phenomena as male strip shows, *Playgirl* magazine, "Buns" calendars, scantily clad waiters at "Ladies Only" nights in taverns passing fads? Or do they signify substantial change in both sexes' perception of male bodies? In general, we conclude good body habits are blurring gender norms.

Bad Habits and Gender

The rewards of physical fitness cannot compete with the status, money, and power that derive from public-sphere accomplishment in capitalist society. Moreover, activity in the public domain has been hard on men's bodies. As women seek opportunities in that sphere, are they emulating men's bad habits and dying like men? According to Veevers (1982:9), one factor contributing to narrowing discrepancies in male-female accident rates "may be an increased propensity of women to drive 'like a man' — to be assertive, to take risks, to drink and drive." Tobacco advertising has tried to equate women's emancipation with a pack-a-day habit. An ad for Viceroy shows a vivacious young woman sports reporter taking a cigarette break during a motor race. The copy reads: "She covers the fastest men on wheels, tours the world throughout the year. . . . She isn't about to smoke a boring cigarette" (Tait, 1983:A17). The alcohol industry has also been quick to take advantage of women's changing social and economic status with aggressive campaigns geared to the "female market" (Sandmaier, 1984:33).

Though women drink and smoke less than men, the gap is lessening in younger age cohorts (Statistics Canada, 1985:80). Lung cancer rates among women continue to rise (Nathanson, 1984:194). Women's use of alcohol and drugs elicits more extreme and negative reactions than substance use by men (Marsh et al., 1982). The labeling of these behaviors as "unladylike" has contributed to the hidden addiction of women. In general, however, liberated women are *not* losing their survival advantage and dying like men (Verbrugge, 1985). In Nathanson's (1984:208) words:

> One of the most tenaciously held hypotheses in the current literature is that sex mortality differentials will gradually disappear as women gain increasing equality with men, particularly in employment. The available evidence concerning the effects of employment on the sex mortality differential provides little support for this hypothesis.

Not only are the death rates of employed women lower than those of employed men, they are substantially lower than those of housewives (Nathanson, 1984:209). For both sexes,

> it's healthier to be rich and successful and in control of your life than to be poor and a failure and helpless. To the degree that the women's revolution has put more women in the former category and taken millions from the latter, it's a profound health benefit (Rodgers, 1985:60).

Despite rising female death rates from lung cancer and accidents, the largest contributor to the sex differential in mortality is cardiovascular disease. Mortality from this source is declining among both sexes (Nathanson, 1984:194). However, women have higher morbidity rates. That is, they get sick more often than men. However, women's higher rates entail relatively mild forms of illness (Gove and Hughes, 1979): "women get sick and men die" (Nathanson, 1977). These "milder" conditions include anemia, thyroid problems, arthritis and rheumatism, and difficulties related to pregnancy and reproductive organs (Statistics Canada, 1985:81). Although gender and mortality present an extremely complicated topic for research, Nathanson (1984:210) suggests this intriguing hypothesis:

> . . . it is altogether possible that sex differences in patterns of socialization and in the normative and structural constraints associated with their respective positions in society cause *men and women to respond quite differently* to potentially "risky" or "stressful" situations, in part because these *situations have different meanings for men and women.* (Emphases added.)

Again we see that biology is mediated by social and cultural organization. In sum, bad habits are *not* the price of changing gender norms. We turn now from the body to the second basic dimension of the individual — the self.

Gender and the Self

Symbolic interactionists have paid considerable theoretical attention to the self. According to them, self-conceptions emerge from and are sustained in social relationships. One's sense of self as a meaningful object arises from taking the role of specific, primary others, and then the generalized other. Here, one sees oneself from the perspective of the larger community (Thoits, 1985:222). Self-development is closely linked with language development. The self-conception may be further specified as "self-image" or "self-esteem." *Self-image* is descriptive, what sort of person one thinks one is, while *self-esteem* is evaluative, how favorably one regards oneself (Lauer and Handel, 1983:256). The self-image may be further differentiated into *social identities,* or internalized positional designations that vary in their importance to the individual (Chapter 4).

The *reflected-appraisals proposition,* "one of the most basic ideas of symbolic interactionism" (Felson, 1985:71), holds that we come to see ourselves as we imagine others see us. Indeed, research shows a strong and consistent association between our self-conception and our *perception* of others' opinions of us. What we *believe* others think of us is more closely related to our self-conception than what they *actually* think of us (Rosenberg, 1981:597–598). In other words, self-appraisals tend to be idealized (Felson, 1985).

The sociology of knowledge concurs with symbolic interactionism in emphasizing the connection between self and social order. That perspective assumes that intellectual activity, including thought about the self, reflects the actor's social location. Recalls Bernard's (1981:3) claim that "most human beings live in single-sex worlds, women in a female world and men in a male world," which differ "both *subjectively* and *objectively*" (emphasis added). Both perspectives lead us to predict first, that gender will be an especially salient dimension of the self, and second, that female and male self-conceptions will differ in important ways.

The Impact of Gender upon the Content of Self-imagery

A study carried out by the author (Mackie, 1980a) in the research tradition of Kuhn (1960), explored the relationship between gender and self-imagery. Data were collected, by means of a questionnaire, from 355 social science students at the University of Calgary. The student sample does restrict the generalizability of the findings. Gender should be particularly salient for people of this age who face courtship and career decisions. Self-imagery was measured by a technique called the semantic differential (Osgood, Suci and Tannenbaum, 1957). Sample members rated the concept MYSELF on a series of 44 bipolar adjectival scales, e.g.,

MYSELF

Warm	1	:	2	:	3	:	4	:	5	:	6	:	7	Cold
Bad	7	:	6	:	5	:	4	:	3	:	2	:	1	Good
Cruel	7	:	6	:	5	:	4	:	3	:	2	:	1	Kind

In each case, respondents checked off the position on the scale which they felt best described themselves. The numbers labeling these positions were inserted later. The direction of scale polarity was varied according to a randomly designed pattern. Female and male means were calculated and compared statistically by "t" tests. Means centering around "4" indicate neutral responses. Low means generally signify the socially desirable pole of the scale.

The results are shown on Table 7.1. Of the 44 gender comparisons, 17 (39 percent) are statistically significant. In general, the women described themselves in terms of the pole of the scale listed first on Table 7.1. Usually, this was the socially desirable end of the scale. That is, the female students described themselves as significantly kinder, warmer, more honest, hardworking, loved and harmless than the males. There were exceptions, however. The women viewed themselves as *less* fearless, guiltless, relaxed, superior, and thin than the men. (Note the significantly different reference to the body.) Although the women did describe themselves as *less* superior than the males, they also described

TABLE 7.1
Gender Comparisons of Semantic Differential
Concept "Myself", N = 355**

Semantic Differential Scales	Females		Males	
	Mean	S.D.	Mean	S.D.
Sex Differences Significant*				
Conventional–Eccentric	3.65	1.47	4.05	1.64
Fearless–Fearful	3.78	1.28	3.18	1.30
Feminine–Masculine	1.99	1.20	5.99	1.01
Guiltless–Guilty	3.85	1.23	3.54	1.23
Hardworking–Lazy	2.46	1.12	3.00	1.41
Harmless–Dangerous	2.54	1.32	3.22	1.45
Honest–Dishonest	2.04	0.85	2.35	1.22
Important–Unimportant	1.97	0.93	2.24	1.18
Kind–Cruel	2.19	1.10	2.66	1.24
Loved–Unloved	1.84	1.19	2.26	1.21
Relaxed–Tense	3.92	1.52	3.40	1.55
Religious–Nonreligious	3.91	2.03	4.39	2.05
Responsible–Irresponsible	2.00	1.04	2.36	1.17
Sexually Moral–Immoral	2.67	1.41	3.08	1.47
Superior–Inferior	3.37	1.06	3.08	1.17
Thin–Fat	3.39	1.33	3.00	1.25
Warm–Cold	2.06	1.02	2.43	1.23
Sex Differences Non-significant				
Beautiful–Ugly	3.06	1.00	3.05	1.22
Capable–Helpless	2.14	1.08	2.22	1.05
Certain–Uncertain	3.19	1.42	2.96	1.33
Clean–Dirty	1.89	1.04	2.08	1.03
Conservative–Radical	3.46	1.51	3.72	1.68
Emotionally Stable–Unstable	2.46	1.47	2.48	1.40
Ethnic–Non-ethnic	4.04	1.77	4.37	1.78
Free–Enslaved	2.40	1.34	2.27	1.14
Friendly–Unfriendly	2.07	0.94	2.22	0.99
Good–Bad	2.30	1.12	2.27	1.03
Happy–Sad	2.28	1.12	2.40	1.25
Healthy–Sick	2.01	1.05	2.09	1.07
Humble–Arrogant	3.57	1.17	3.49	1.33
Humorous–Serious	2.88	1.35	2.90	1.40
Intelligent–Stupid	2.15	0.94	2.24	1.03
Interesting–Dull	2.44	1.07	2.54	1.18
Lenient–Severe	3.16	1.25	3.42	1.46
Lucky–Unlucky	2.98	1.34	2.95	1.39
Materialistic–Nonmaterialistic	3.27	1.42	2.98	1.41
Mature–Immature	2.26	1.07	2.39	1.06
Open-minded–Dogmatic	2.49	1.29	2.59	1.43
Outgoing–Shy	3.17	1.67	3.52	1.59
Right–Wrong	3.05	0.98	2.89	1.06
Saved–Sinful	3.64	1.19	3.84	1.23
Strong–Weak	2.77	1.23	2.72	1.10
Subdued–Flashy	3.86	1.29	3.86	1.46
Valuable–Worthless	2.00	0.94	2.17	1.14

*Two-tailed t-test, significant at .05 level
**Females, N = 232; Males, N = 123

themselves as *more* important. (We will return to this matter at the end of this section.) The pattern of difference shown in Table 7.1 makes some sense in terms of society's view of females as expressive creatures. However, sex differences did *not* occur in 61 percent of the scales.

Gender and the Material Self

Strauss (1969:36) tells us that "self-regard is linked with what is owned, with what is one's own." He goes on to say that a person's possessions are a fair index of what he/she is, provided that the researcher takes the trouble to distinguish what a person owns by chance and what he/she really cherishes.[9] Treasured objects should provide some clues about male versus female self-conceptions. Therefore, gender differences in the material self were explored (Mackie, 1986a). Following Csikszentmihalyi and Rochberg-Halton (1981), another sample of 140 University of Calgary students were asked to respond in writing to this question: "What are the things in your home which are special to you? Please list three special things." Then, we requested that they explain why each object was special.

Table 7.2 shows favorite objects, mentioned by at least 5 percent of the students, for the total sample and for male and female respondents. Electronic entertainment was top priority for both sexes.

TABLE 7.2
Gender and the Material Self, N=140

Treasured Objects	Percentage Mentioning		
	Total Sample	Females, N=100	Males, N=40
Stereo, Walkmans, radios	52.9%	41.0%	82.5%*
Photographs	27.1	33.0	12.5 *
Television set	23.6	18.0	37.5 *
Bed	19.3	19.0	20.0
Other furniture	17.1	21.0	7.5 *
Books	17.1	16.0	20.0
Clothing & accessories	16.4	16.0	17.5
Collectibles, ornaments	13.6	14.0	12.5
Jewellery	12.9	17.0	2.5 *
Musical instruments	10.0	12.0	4.0
Stuffed animals, dolls	7.9	11.0	— *
Telephone	7.1	8.0	5.0
Sports equipment	7.1	5.0	12.5
Appliances	6.4	6.0	7.5
Visual Art	5.0	6.0	2.5

*Chi-square, one-tailed, one d.f., p. < .05

According to Csikszentmihalyi and Rochberg-Halton (1981), who reported the same result for a Chicago sample, this preference is related to age. (The parental generation in the Chicago sample mentioned furniture first; photographs were most important to grandparents.) Gender differences emerged for six of 15 cherished objects. Stereos, etc. and TV were mentioned by significantly more males. Photographs, furniture, jewelry, and stuffed toys were mentioned by significantly more females. The feminine material self reflects components of gender stereotypes, i.e. feminine concern with relationships, nurturing, and self-adornment. The analysis of reasons for choices strengthens this impression.

TABLE 7.3
Reasons for Choice of Cherished Objects, N=76

Reason	Percentage Mentioning		
	Total Sample	Females, N=51	Males, N=25
Entertainment/relaxation	60.5%	52.9%	76.0%*
Utilitarian	42.1	41.2	44.0
Sentimental	35.5	43.1	20.0 *
Connection with self	30.3	29.4	32.0
Kinship ties	26.3	33.0	12.0 *
Friendship ties	25.0	31.4	12.0 *
Financial investment	22.4	19.6	28.0
Aesthetic	17.1	23.5	4.0 *

*Chi–square, one–tailed, one d.f., p. < .05

Table 7.3 shows the reasons volunteered by the students. Thirty percent of both sexes spontaneously acknowledged the connection between treasured object and self:

My closet because it contains my wardrobe that helps create my image.

This blanket is something I made, it represents a part of me.

As the Table 7.2 results lead us to expect, "entertainment/relaxation" is relevant for many people, and for males more than females:

The ghetto blaster is important to me because I can't live without music.

No sex difference emerged for the utilitarian reason:

> Without a desk, it would be pretty uncomfortable doing
> homework on the floor.

Sentiment and memories were significantly more important for the females:

> My photographs are important because they help bring
> to life many of the happiest moments of my life.

Kinship, friendship ties, and esthetic reasons were all more important to the women:

> This baby quilt is important to me because it was a gift
> from my grandfather to me when I was born. It is
> important because he never had gone out to buy a gift
> by himself before.

> My telephone is important because I can't stand to be
> isolated from my friends.

> My prints and graphics enhance my home.

Although more men mentioned the financial investment involved ("I had to work hard to get the money to purchase these items"), the difference could not have been produced by chance. The material self, then, shows the impact of gender. However, once again, male and female self-conceptions share many commonalities.

The Salience of Social Identities

Identity salience refers to the internal organization of the differentiated self. Identities are related to one another in a salience hierarchy. In Burke's (1980:19) words:

> Each identity is more or less likely (relative to other iden-
> tities which the individual has) to be enacted or por-
> trayed or taken into account, depending upon its posi-
> tion in the salience hierarchy.

Some identities are at the center of the individual's concerns, while others are peripheral (Rosenberg, 1981:601). Rowbotham, for example, says, "the work of a housewife . . . is not just something you do, it's somebody you are" (1973:76), and it "sucks you into itself as a person rather than a 'worker' " (p. 71). As circumstances and settings change, the priority of a given identity may shift. The identity "student" is more salient when a student is at the university than when she is enjoying a movie. When circumstances require people to describe themselves on a questionnaire, we get one kind of indication about the hierarchy of social identities.

The University of Calgary study results referred to in Table 7.1 supported the symbolic interactionist prediction that gender is an important axis of the self-conception. When sample members were asked to choose among the identities of gender, religion, ethnicity, Canadian citizenship, and provincial residence as the most important aspect of self, gender was the most salient. Gender was cited by 62.3 percent (versus 17 percent Canadian citizenship, 12.5 percent religion, 4.4 percent ethnicity, and 3.7 percent provincial residence). Although provision of other identities would change the percentages, it is reasonable to assume that gender would continue to be extremely important.

The two-worlds proposition would lead us to expect gender differences in identity salience. To test this hypothesis, a probability sample of 797 Calgary, Alberta adults was asked to complete the Twenty Statements Test (Mackie, 1983a). This test asks respondents to write 20 different answers to the question, "Who Am I?" (Kuhn and McPartland, 1954). Content analysis focused on mention of these identities: gender, marital status, parental status, work inside and outside the home. It was hypothesized that gender would be more salient for males than for females, on the ground that a status that enjoys cultural esteem should be more prominent in the individual's self-conception. Hartley (1959:231) long ago argued "that masculinity is more important to men than femininity is to women." Marital and parental statuses and housework should be more salient for females. According to traditional gender norms, outside work should be more salient in the self-imagery of men than in that of employed women. In general, it was expected that while family would be the more salient dimension of women's self-conception, work would take priority over family for men. Relative salience of identities was measured in two ways. First, if an identity was mentioned more *frequently* by one sex than other, we assumed it is higher in the salience hierarchy of that sex. Second, the *order* of mention of an identity among the total number of statements volunteered by a person tells us something about its relative importance. Other research (Gordon, 1968:123) has found identities mentioned earlier to be more salient.

As Table 7.4 shows, gender was mentioned spontaneously by 34.5 percent of the males and 34.3 percent of the females. Moreover, the mean rank for males was 2.66 and for females 3.24. (The lower the

TABLE 7.4
The Salience of Social Identities
Females = 417   Males = 380

Categories	% Mention	Significance Level Chi–Square[a]	Mean Order	S.D.	Significance Level t[a]
Gender					
Males	34.5	0.50	2.66	3.56	0.25
Females	34.3		3.24	3.60	
Marital Status					
Males	75.0	0.025*	3.38	3.37	0.10
Females	80.8		2.99	3.23	
Parental Status[b]					
Males	85.0	0.0005*	3.34	2.81	0.005*
Females	94.3		2.77	2.11	
Family Generally					
Males	88.2	0.0005*	1.89	1.15	0.0005*
Females	94.7		2.40	1.40	
Household Work					
Males	36.8	0.0005*	0.66	1.16	0.0005*
Females	75.1		2.12	2.26	
Outside Work					
Males	85.5	0.10	1.76	1.37	0.0005*
Females[c]	80.8		1.25	1.00	

[a]One–tailed significance level, significant .05 level.
[b]Males = 300, Females = 335.
[c]Females in labor force, N = 192.
(Source: Marlene Mackie, "The Domestication of Self," *Social Psychology Quarterly*, Vol. 46, 1983, p. 346. Reprinted with permission.)

mean, the earlier the mention of gender.) Therefore, the hypothesis is *not* supported: gender is equally important to both sexes. Similarly, when the university students described the most important aspect of self, no sex difference emerged in the mention of gender.

The rest of the hypotheses are supported. Marriage, parenthood, the family, and household work are more salient for women than men. Outside work was more salient for men than for women in the labor force. As Gilligan (1982) has argued so persuasively, connectedness with others is more important for women. Nevertheless, men also define themselves in terms of their relationships with the women and children in their lives. Eighty-one percent of the married women mentioned their marriage, but so did 75 percent of the married men. For the third time, we find similarity, as well as differences, in the self-conceptions of females and males.

Self-esteem

Theoretically speaking, females *ought* to have lower self-esteem than males. Our society belittles femininity. Evidence documenting "substantial" devaluation of women in our society is "massive" (Schur, 1984:35). Men command more power, prestige, and resources. Cultural symbolism communicates the derogation of females to both sexes. Women share with men admiration of masculine qualities and achievements and devaluation of their own unique capacities. Acquisition of money and power and the production of things are rewarded. Creation of life and cultivation of relationships are less esteemed (Bardwick and Douvan, 1971:234). Boys and men are taught to be selfish, while girls and women are taught that self-sacrifice and immersion in other people's lives and accomplishments are "naturally" feminine (Lipman-Blumen, 1984:83; Gilligan, 1982:66 ff.). "Society has never impressed on women as it has on men the absolute necessity of putting yourself first" (Brothers, 1972:136). Television interviewer Phil Donahue (quoted in Steinem, 1983a:182) makes the same point:

> If you're in a social situation, and women are talking to each other, and one woman says, "I was hit by a car today," all the other women will say, "You're kidding! What happened? Where? Are you all right?" In the same situation with males, one male says "I was hit by a car today." I guarantee you that there will be another male in the group who will say, "Wait till I tell you what happened to *me* '." (Emphasis in original.)

According to Lipman-Blumen (1984:83):

> Learning to put oneself second (or third, or even last) is the proper feminine way to play the gender power game, where being weaker, having less, is somehow construed as better. By making one's own needs secondary, one becomes first in goodness and morality.

Selflessness wins females a "moral gold star," but an unequal share in the resources valued in our society (Lipman-Blumen, 1984:85). If the symbolic interactionist assumption that self mirrors society is correct, then the conclusion that female self-esteem should be severely impaired seems inescapable.[10]

Many writers on gender relations have apparently found the above reasoning persuasive. As Whitehurst (1979:76) has observed, "there seems to be a basic assumption in much recent feminist literature that women have 'negative self concepts' . . . ." For instance, Bernard (1975:10) claims "women themselves have accepted their own inferiority; they have accepted the low value placed on them." According to Gornick and Moran (1971:xx):

> Sexism has made of women a race of children, a class of
> human beings utterly deprived of self-hood, of auto-
> nomy, of confidence. . . . As a result, women have long
> suffered from an image of the self that paralyzes the will
> and short circuits the brain, that makes them deny the
> evidence of their senses and internalize self-doubt to a
> fearful degree.

Schur (1984) has recently described femaleness as a stigmatized status
and concluded that "systematic devaluation implies a strong likelihood
of impaired self-esteem" (p. 39).

Despite the appeal of the reflected appraisals proposition, empirical data fail to establish sex differences in global self-esteem (Maccoby
and Jacklin, 1974; Whitehurst, 1979). The data in Table 7.1 do not show
damaged self-esteem in the women students. Recall that the lower
means are the more positive or socially desirable ones. The female
means are more positive than the males' on two-thirds of the adjectival scales. In only five of 44 cases did male students register significantly more positive self-imagery. Table 7.1 includes four purely evaluative scales: good–bad; valuable–worthless; important–unimportant;
superior–inferior. No sex differences emerged on the first two scales.
Women's self-imagery was significantly higher on the third, and men's
on the fourth.

The adult sample referred to in Table 7.4 completed the widely
used Rosenberg (1965) Self-esteem Scale (Mackie, 1983a). This instru-
ment records maximum self-esteem as 10. When females' (X = 8.82,
S.D. = 1.34) and males' (X = 8.86, S.D. = 1.46) mean responses were
compared, sex differences in self-esteem were *not* found.

This "counterintuitive" finding (Gecas, 1982:8) is consistent with
studies of other groups suffering categorical inferiority, such as Canadian Indians (Clifton, 1975) and American blacks (Rosenberg and Simmons, 1972). Indeed, Rosenberg's (1981:605) review of the literature concludes that race, ethnicity, gender, and religion "show virtually no
association with global self-esteem. . . ."

This puzzling failure of self to reflect social structure has
stimulated considerable debate in the context of race relations and social
class (Adam, 1978; Gecas, 1982:8; Rosenberg, 1981:605; Rosenberg and
Simmons, 1972; Rosenberg and Pearlin, 1978; Simmons, 1978). By comparison, few attempts have been made to explain the anomaly in the
case of gender. Moreover, the explanations for race and social class have
limited applicability to gender. For instance, to explain why blacks do
not have lower self-esteem than whites, Simmons (1978:56) says:

> One major line of reasoning is that an individual's
> negative or positive attitude toward himself is influenced
> less by the larger society and more by opinions of signifi-

cant others in his immediate environment. The black, particularly the black child, tends to be surrounded by other blacks. Thus, those persons who matter most to him — parents, teachers and peers — tend to be black and to evaluate him as highly as white parents, teachers, and peers evaluate the white child. In addition, although his race, family structure or socioeconomic status may be devalued in the larger society, in his immediate context most others share these characteristics.

Since females are not segregated from males, the above reasoning does not apply to gender. Reference group behavior may partly explain why women think more highly of themselves than they theoretically should. That is, women may be comparing themselves with other women, not men (Rosenberg and Simmons, 1972). They may be giving women's opinions more credibility. Alternatively, women may find other ways to interpret society's devaluation of them, rather than to seeing it for what it is (Stockard and Johnson, 1980:76). All people, female as well as male, need to feel worthy.

This enigma has led some sociologists to wonder whether the looking-glass self is the sole mechanism in the development of self-esteem (Gecas and Schwalbe, 1983; Reitzes, 1980). Two processes seem to be involved: (1) the reflected appraisals of significant others, i.e. the looking-glass self, and (2) the individual's feelings of efficacy and competence (Franks and Marolla, 1976:325). The first process, which is concerned with relationships, other people's opinions, and physical appearance, appears to be more important for females. Bardwick and Douvan (1971:231) say, "the loss of love remains for her the gravest source of injury to the self." Also, research suggests that good looks are more closely related to the self-esteem of women than of men (Al-Issa, 1980:289).

Efficacy, where "one's sense of self-esteem derives from the experience of self as an active agent — of making things actually happen . . ." (Franks and Marolla, 1976:326) seems more pertinent for males. Data show that females do not approach tasks with confidence equal to that of males (Maccoby and Jacklin, 1974:155). While men and women actually perform equally well in such problem-solving situations as anagrams, men think they do better than women. Also, men are more likely than women to attribute their own success to ability rather than luck (Deaux and Emswiller, 1974). However, women are more prone to blame their failures on their own lack of ability, while men blame external circumstances (Deaux and Farris, 1974). Women would rather play a game of chance, like slot-machines, than a game involving some strategy, such as blackjack (Deaux, 1976:43). Why? Men expect to do better at skill games than women, and losing is not so hard on their egos. Nevertheless, women do not fear success more than men

(Henley, 1985:104). Although this hypothesis (Horner, 1969) has received a great deal of media attention, it did not stand up to subsequent research (Tresemer, 1977).

A further point in support of greater male efficacy: in comparison with men, women feel less in control of their own destiny than men (Maccoby and Jacklin, 1974:157). Their sense of powerlessness seems reasonable in view of the fact that they truly have less power to control their fate. Though Gecas and Schwalbe (1983:82) do not refer specifically to gender, they observe that

> . . . individuals located near the bottom of the power hierarchy, whose degree of autonomous action is more circumscribed, may be more dependent upon the opinions of others (especially of those who have power over them) for their self-esteem. In short, *the looking-glass self as a process in the development of self-esteem may be most relevant to those in subordinate status;* whereas efficacy-based self-esteem may be most salient for those in positions of dominance within specific social structures . . . (emphasis added).

To summarize, the components of self-esteem appear to mirror social organization, even if the level of self-esteem does not. Though females do not regard themselves as less worthy than do males, socioemotional success is more central to their self-evaluation than achievement. In the language of symbolic interactionism, perhaps the vital "I" overrides the socially-constrained 'Me." In a parallel fashion, shared aspects of the human condition seem to override disparities between male and female worlds. Chapter 7 has considered relations between gender and first, the body and, second, self-conceptions. The last aspect of the individual to be examined is his/her feelings.

Gender and Emotion

> Marriage, chaos, unreal, completely different in many ways than I imagined. Unfortunately we rehearsed the morning of our wedding at eight o'clock. The wedding was to be at eleven o'clock. It wasn't like I thought (everyone would know what to do). They didn't. That made me nervous. My sister didn't help me get dressed or flatter me (nor did anyone in the dressing room until I asked them). I was depressed. I wanted to be so happy on our wedding day. I never dreamed how anyone would cry at their wedding. A wedding is "the happy day" of one's life. I couldn't believe that some of my best friends couldn't make it to my wedding and that added to a lot of little things. So I started out to the church and all these things that I always thought would not happen

at my wedding went through my mind. I broke down —
I cried going down. "Be happy" I told myself. Think of
the friends and relatives that are present. (But I finally
said to myself, "Hey, people aren't getting married, you
are. It's for Rich — my husband — and you.") From
down the pretty long aisle we looked at each other's
eyes. His love for me changed my whole being. From
that point on we joined arms. I was relieved and the
tension was gone. In one sense it meant misery — but in
the true sense of two people in love and wanting to
share life — it meant the world to me. It was beautiful. It
was indescribable.

(Source: Arlie Russell Hochschild, "Emotion work,
feeling rules, and social structure," *American Journal of
Sociology,* Vol. 85, 1979, pp. 551-575. Reprinted with
permission of The University of Chicago Press.)

Social rules apply to emotion or feelings as well as thought and behavior
(Hochschild, 1979:551).[12] We are supposed to feel happy at weddings
(especially our own), subdued and attentive in class, gay at parties, and
sad at funerals. In Chapter 5, we talked about people falling in love
when it's time to fall in love. *Feeling rules* specify which emotion (if any)
is appropriate to a situation, the intensity of the emotion, and the
manner of its expression. When we don't feel as we believe we should
feel, we do *emotion work* to try to move experience to coincide with
feeling rules (Hochschild, 1983a:252). We try to convince ourselves,
other people, or both:

I *psyched myself* up . . . . I *squashed* my anger down . . . .
I *tried hard* not to feel disappointed . . . . I *made* myself
have a good time . . . . I *tried* to feel grateful . . . .
I *let myself* finally feel sad (Hochschild, 1979:561,
emphases in original).

Internal bodily states and cues do not, in themselves, establish
emotion. Because the physiological states accompanying various emotions often resemble one another (Shott, 1979:1321), emotions are
amenable to social interpretation. Indeed, emotions *are* social interpretation. *Emotion norms* — proper ways of interpreting and expressing feelings — vary from society to society, and are learned along with other
socialization lessons. Since feeling rules guide thinking, "channel the
stream of subjective experience" (Hochschild, 1975b:290), and "since
feeling is a form of pre-action" (Hochschild, 1983b:56), emotion norms
are a matter of some importance. Indeed, societies have an enormous
stake in them (Shibutani, 1961:383 ff.). Rules about feelings are the foundation for the large part of social control that is self-control. "Since it
is impossible for a society to monitor and sanction everyone's behavior

all the time, self-regulation must be the basis of much social control" (Shott, 1979:1329). Rules for managing feelings are the "bottom side" of ideology (Hochschild, 1979:566). People's emotional investment in playing their traditional roles bolsters the status quo. On the other hand, when an ideology begins to lose its hold, subordinates begin to challenge and ignore the feeling rules.

For example, a feeling rule in our society is that anger should "normally" be aimed down at people with less power, not up at the more powerful. Hochschild (1975b:297) suggests we take seriously

> . . . the proverbial case of the boss who blows up at the worker, the worker who blows up at his wife, the wife who gets angry at her children, and the children who take it out on the dog.

When actors begin to understand the power structure and their place in it, the targets for anger may change. For example, when women begin to understand that the "personal is political" (Mills, 1959:187), to emerge from false consciousness, their anger becomes redirected from such scapegoats as small children to agents of the social structure.[13]

Masculine Ideology of Emotions

Gender, the "pervasive network of interrelated norms and sanctions through which female (and male) behavior is evaluated and controlled" (Schur, 1984:11), includes feeling rules. Like other dimensions of gender, these emotion rules are viewed as "moral facts," which *ought* to be obeyed because they are "naturally" and "eternally" true. They originated with the ruling sex to motivate both sexes to uphold the status quo. Therefore, the feminist movement has implications for many of the "old-fashioned" ideas about proper masculine and feminine emotionality (Hochschild, 1979:567). What are some of these feeling rules and how do they serve to control female and male behavior?

As one might expect, our society's gender feeling norms are grounded upon the assumption that female and male natures are profoundly and innately different (Hochschild, 1979:567). A division of emotional labor between the sexes parallels the traditional gender specialization into domestic and public spheres. The content of gender stereotypes (Chapter 3) reflects this fact. Women are the sentimental sex. They "bear the chief emotional burden of caring for human life from the cradle to the grave . . . " (Brownmiller, 1984:218). Men, on the other hand, "have the tough mental fiber, the intellectual muscle, to stay in control" (Brownmiller, 1984:208). Anger is an exception to male inexpressiveness. Because competitive action and physical aggression often flow from angry feelings, they are understood in a man. However, anger in a woman isn't nice. "An angry woman is hard, mean and nasty; she is unreliably, unprettily out of control" (Brownmiller, 1984:210). Historically, our society has regarded the cognitive or rational dimensions of experience as superior to sentiment. Emotions have been an "impediment to getting things done" (Hochschild, 1975b:281).

Men *don't* cry? or men *can't* cry? Although the paucity of male tears has become the hallmark of male inexpressiveness in recent years, a controversy surrounds the origins of this phenomenon. Is inexpressiveness a deeply socialized and unfortunate inability to show tenderness, sadness, and vulnerability that many males would like to remedy when its costs to their relationships and health are pointed out to them (Balswick and Peck, 1971)? Or is keeping cool a deliberate micropolitical strategy for keeping the upper hand? Sattel (1983:243) takes the latter position:

> My argument is that one reason little boys become inexpressive is not simply because our culture expects boys to be that way — but because our culture expects little boys to grow up to hold positions of power and prestige. What better way is there to exercise power than *to make it* appear — to dissemble a style — in which *all* one's behavior seems to be the result of unemotional rationality. Being impersonal and inexpressive lends to one's decisions and position an apparent autonomy and "rightness" (emphasis in original).

Be that as it may, research reports no sex differences in the crying of children (Maccoby and Jacklin, 1974). Moreover, male inexpressiveness is not a constant (Ross and Mirowsky, 1984). Some men cry more than others. Those who adhere to traditional gender roles are less likely to cry than are non-traditional men. Thus, younger, better-educated, and richer men cry less than older, less well-educated, and poorer men. Men in the higher socioeconomic positions are more likely to cry even though they have less to cry about.

Traditional gender feeling rules, i.e. the masculine ideology of emotions, control the behavior of both sexes. Whether they like it or not, individual males are socialized to be cool and tough, to monopolize the public sphere, to operate as the dominant sex in public and private. Lethal aspects of the masculine role have been associated with the non-expression of emotions other than anger (Jourard, 1964). It is easier yet to see how emotion rules have served to keep women "in their place." "Our culture invites women . . . to focus on feeling rather than action . . ." (Hochschild, 1983b:57). After all, action pays off in power, prestige, and money. Women's specialization in emotion is used against them. Real or alleged emotional upsets and mood swings associated with menstruation and menopause are invoked to disqualify women from important work and political roles. Women who do make it into the professional and corporate elite are expected to play by male rules and be affectively neutral.

Specific emotions are similarly useful in propping up the gender status quo. For example, all females are supposed to like babies. This norm supports the "motherhood mystique," which teaches that a woman must experience maternity in order to find true happiness and feminine self-actualization (Veevers, 1977). Women are not supposed to envy male accomplishments. Instead, they are expected to withdraw from competition and appear at their husbands' occupational cere-monies and to share symbolically in their glory (Hochschild, 1975b:292). Finally, ruling out anger as an expressive possibility for women preserves the status quo from attack. As noted above, social movements that challenge ideology carry implications for feelings. Gender libera-tion movements have legitimated anger and envy for women and tender feelings for men. It is not surprising that gender activists have been charged with inappropriate emotional displays: the dried-up (unemo-tional, unmotherly), angry (castrating) woman; the weak, sissy (homosexual) man. Appropriate and inappropriate emotionality takes us to the topic of mental health and ill health.

The Social Construction of Mental Health and Mental Illness

Mental health and ill health are matters of interpretation and labeling (Scheff, 1966). Just as language conditions our perception of reality, psychiatric language — the language of madness — defines, indeed creates, a particular reality. Smyth (1979:295) speaks of "the need to understand the pervasive and corrosive influence of language when dealing with the irrational as manifested in so-called madness." In our society, the authority to establish criteria of illness, to interpret behavior as deviant, and to label given individuals as mentally ill has been in-vested in the masculine institution of psychiatry (Schur, 1984:197). In Smith's (1975b:4) words, psychiatric ideologies "are part of the ideologies constructed by men from their perspective of the world."

Women are vulnerable to being labeled mentally ill. Indeed, they are in the classic double-bind situation. If they obey the gender scripts, they may be in deep trouble (Broverman et al., 1970). What men are appears to set the clinical standards for mental health; stereotypically feminine traits contradict these standards. For example, a study of per-ceptions of Canadian mental health practitioners found that their defini-tion of ideal mental health involved relatively less emotionality than our culture expects of females (Smyth and McFarlane, 1985).

The other side of the "catch-22" is that women who deviate from gender norms may also be judged mentally ill. As Goffman (1971:355) notes, mental illness labeling is likely to occur when the persons with whom an individual interacts concludes that he or she is not prepared to keep his or her place. Female rebels and eccentrics have been labeled (and mistreated) as witches, crazies, neurotics, and psychotics.

Pinning the label of mental illness on a woman discredits her complaints about her subordinate status. "In psychiatric terms what is wrong is identified as what is wrong *with her*" (Smith, 1975b:7). Sex-typing is assumed to be necessary and normal (Carmen et al., 1981). Psychiatric theories have been advanced to explain women who are too fat, too thin, too passive, too aggressive, unmarried mothers, voluntarily childless, heterosexually "promiscuous" or lesbians. Even when a woman has been obviously victimized, psychological theorizing focuses on *her* behavior. Why did she allow herself to be raped? Why did the battered wife stay with her husband? (Schur, 1984:200). In therapy, what are really collective problems become problems of the individual. The remedy is talk, not action (Chesler, 1972). Mental illness, then, is an extreme example of how the masculine ideology of emotion is used to control women. As Schur (1984:199) points out:

> The general tendency to treat women as being emo-
> tionally disturbed is always present in the background as
> a ground for dismissing what a woman says or does and
> as an implicit "threat" should she seriously step out of
> line.

Psychiatry also keeps men in line (Pleck:1984). Mental health professionals often assume that traditional masculinity is normal and label as "sick" or "effeminate" males who deviate from these norms. Gay men are especially vulnerable here.

The labeling of behavior as deviant, odd, or expressive of mental illness is frequently self-imposed. (Thoits, 1985). In other words, well-socialized individuals need not depend on the presence and reactions of others to define behavior as out of line. Rather, people who have internalized the perspectives of their society bear witness against themselves. When they note norm violation in their own feelings, thoughts or behavior, they may label themselves as ill. For example, a woman who dislikes children or experiences a great deal of anger, or a man who doesn't feel like "keeping a stiff upper lip" or being competitive, may judge his or her feelings as "strange" and seek help voluntarily.

Gender and the "True" Incidence of Mental Illness

What reliable conclusions can be reached about gender differences in mental disturbances? Obviously, the fact that the power to define, diagnose, and treat mental illness has been in male hands makes the question complex and controversial. Additional complicating factors exist. For one thing, mental illness is fundamentally inchoate and "indeterminate as a phenomenon" (Smith, 1975b:16). Mental health practitioners have varying interpretations of what constitutes illness and who is ill. Further, many persons do not seek treatment, and this also makes mental illness statistics suspect. Men are reluctant to admit psychological difficulties. However, women are encouraged by our culture to label their unhappiness in these terms and to view themselves as candidates for psychotherapy (Schur, 1984:205).

Researchers agree that women use mental health services more than men (Greenglass, 1982:213). Women also take more mood-altering drugs than men (Cooperstock, 1978; Statistics Canada, 1985:82). In addition, more women than men receive treatment for mental disorders from physicians without special psychiatric training (Williams, 1983:371). Though these gender differences in incidence do not necessarily mean that females are crazier than males, Gove and Tudor (1973:54) are probably correct in their conclusion that differing rates are grounded in the fact that "women find their position in society to be more frustrating and less rewarding than do men . . . ." The issue here is sex differences in *style of reaction* to stress rather than *amount* of stress (Al-Issa, 1982:98).

Attending to female-male differences in the forms that mental disturbance take tells us more about the gender system than debates over "true" incidence. The diagnoses of female patients tend to be grouped into categories that focus on emotional states. Women seem to be prone to neuroses and depression. Men's diagnoses, on the other hand, are more sociopathic. Male patients are more assaultive, more likely to act out "antisocial urges such as robbery, rape, and homicide" (Greenglass, 1982:214). In addition, males, more than females, receive diagnoses of personality disorders (psychopathy, alcoholism, addiction) and such physiological disorders as ulcers (Al-Issa, 1980:331). While women are sad and passive, men act out their unhappiness.

When we examine male-female differences by marital status, the role played by gender in mental illness becomes even clearer. Studies (Gove, 1972; Gove, 1980) report that it is married women who are most likely to be mentally ill. Single, divorced, and widowed women have fewer problems than either married women or men in these same categories. Married women who are not employed are at the highest risk for psychological disorders (Verbrugge, 1985:169).

What is the explanation? Both social stimulation of rewarding adult relationships and efficacy (versus powerlessness) seem to be involved. Marriage provides men with an intimate relationship they may not find elsewhere (Greenglass, 1982:214). Therein lies the greater psychological benefit of marriage for men. Married women, however, have other friendship resources. However, they are *more* likely to feel powerless in the face of demands of husbands and children. Greenglass (1982:216) concludes that "being continually immersed in the world of children with their continual demands and the relative lack of meaningful adult contacts . . . can lead to a greater vulnerability to psychiatric symptoms." Employed women have more protection from these symptoms (and from suicide [Cumming et al., 1975]). They apparently experience more social stimulation on the job *and* feel more in control of their destiny.

The study of suicide strengthens the impression that the two-worlds proposition carries into mental illness. Although women attempt suicide more often, men are two to three times more "successful" at it, depending on age (Barnes, 1985). For example, in 1982, the suicide rate for men aged 15 to 24 was five and a half times that of women the same age (Statistics Canada, 1985:83). Over the past century, American men's suicide rates have responded to major political and economic events, rising in times of economic depression and falling in times of war. However, suicide rates among women have remained relatively stable over the same time span (Barnes, 1985:466). Typically, men use violent methods, such as firearms, explosives and cutting instruments, while women prefer pills or gas (Greenglass, 1982:234).

Self-destructive behavior appears to have different meanings for men and women. While men injure themselves as a step towards the instrumental goal of suicide, women hurt themselves as a "cry for help," a dramatic expression of feelings, or in an indirect way of controlling others (Barnes, 1985; Stengel, 1964). These behaviors are consistent with gender socialization. Though expression of feelings and seeking help are more hopeful motivations than wanting to die, the medical profession has more respect for the masculine mode (Barnes, 1985:472). Whether male and female forms of psychopathology will become more similar as (and if) societal conditions become more egalitarian is an interesting question.

Feminist Therapy

In the past, troubled women were usually treated by male therapists. People of both sexes perceived males to be authorities and preferred them (Greenglass, 1982:246). Typically, women were subordinate and dependent in the therapeutic relationship, which assumed the validity of the traditional gender system. Treatment emphasized overmedication and women's adjustment to their traditional roles (Chesler, 1972). Smith (1975b:13) argued that psychiatry

> . . . relies upon women's lack of authority to speak; it relies upon their subservience to the abstracted modes of social control; it relies upon not knowing them and upon not listening to what they might have to say.

Criticism of psychiatry has been part of the feminist movement since the 1960s. Consciousness-raising groups helped women to understand the structural source of their problems and to develop a critique of the medical and psychiatric professions as discriminatory agents of a sexist society. Grass-roots crisis intervention organizations emerged to help women who had been battered, sexually abused, or needed abortion or contraceptive advice. In the 1970s, as an outgrowth of the women's movement, feminist mental health practitioners began to formulate a feminist approach to professional help. This approach is really a set of attitudes, not a set of formal credentials. In addition to training in various accredited programs, such therapists recognize the equality of the sexes and the right of each person "to strive for self-fulfillment in keeping with the rights of others" (Valentich, 1986:4).

Feminist therapy recognizes the role of oppressive social structures, such as marriage and the workplace, and the masculine ideology of the body in producing women's unhappiness. This stance contradicts traditional therapy, which points to defects in women's nature and promotes adjustment to the existing order (Carmen et al., 1981:1324). The therapist, aware of power imbalances in traditional therapy, tries to use respectfully the power she has (Hawley and Sanford, 1984:74). She uses her first name, discloses information about her own personal experiences, and involves the client in decision making. Feminist therapy acknowledges women's distinctive nature and problems. For example, such therapists respond positively to the expression of affectivity or emotionality in the therapeutic process (Toukmanian, 1985). They have brought up and responded sympathetically to such mental health issues as battering, incest, child abuse, alcoholism, and compulsive eating which traditional therapists have ignored. Moreover, models of career counselling designed specifically for women have been developed (Cammaert and Larsen, 1979). Feminist therapy's goals for the client are "self-esteem, independence, power over one's life, achievement of individual growth free of traditional sex-role stereotypes" (Collier, 1982:13). In short, feminist therapy understands how gender is constructed and treats *both* sexes with respect.

Conclusions

Chapter 7 returned to the person, who is, after all, the object of gender socialization lessons. Three central aspects of the individual — body, self, and feelings — were considered. The main conclusion is that masculine-derived rules concerning these three facets of the person serve to support gender as a "natural," inevitable phenomenon. Since these particular norms touch the person's very core of being, they are *the* most critical dimensions of gender ideology.

A second conclusion is the interwoven nature of the gender norms concerning body, self, and emotions. Space limitations preclude a full exploration of these interconnections. However, as an example, the traditional ideology of the body influences self-esteem and happiness. The impact is different for females and males. It was an overweight woman, not an overweight man, who made the following remark to Millman (1980:74):

> I always felt that the first thing anyone would notice is that I was fat. And not only that I was fat, but that they would know *why* I was fat. They would know I was neurotic, that I was unsatisfied, that I was a pig, that I had problems. They could tell immediately that I was out of control. I always looked around to see if there was anyone as fat as me. I always wondered when I saw a fat woman, "Do I look like *that*?" (Emphases in original.)

Beautiful women tend to be happier, more satisfied with themselves and more emotionally stable than unattractive women. However, good looks are not related to the happiness, self-esteem, and emotional adjustment of men (Al-Issa, 1980:289). The fading of beauty (the quintessentially traditional feminine asset) is one reason aging is more difficult for women than for men.

A second example. An important gender norm regarding the self holds that females should be self-sacrificing. A woman whose behavior is labeled selfish by herself or other people, who gives her own interests priority, is more likely to experience guilt than a man in similar circumstances. As Shott (1979) has emphasized, feeling rules such as these translate social control into self-control. Despite feminist critique of these traditional norms, they continue to be part of contemporary gender socialization.

NOTES

1. Deaux (1976:36) cites Vonnegut's (1973) fable of Smart Bunny in the context of women's self-evaluations.
2. Canadians may be especially vulnerable to other people's evaluations of their bodies. Whitehurst and Booth (1980:64) say, "As a society we hve been singularly uncreative about teaching children positive acceptance of their bodies."
3. Germaine Greer (1971:23) remarks: "When the life of the party wants to express the idea of a pretty woman in mime, he undulates his two hands in the air and leers expressively. The notion of a curve is so closely connected to sexual semantics that some people cannot resist sniggering at road signs. The most popular image of the female despite the exigencies of the clothing trade is all boobs and buttocks, a hallucinating sequence of parabolae and bulges."
4. Barbara Ehrenreich (1984:52) writes: "When I think of the beginnings of the women's health movement, I think, above all, of the stories women told. Stories, like my own, of humiliation and helplessness: for example, of being diagnosed as "difficult" for asking questions or "neurotic" for possessing a symptom for which the doctors did not yet have a disease. Stories of terrible insult: like that of the teenage black woman

who had been subjected to a dozen serial pelvic exams for teaching purposes because she was a "charity case." Stories of unbearable loss: like that of a Missouri woman who told me she had been sterilized, at her doctor's discretion, just after delivering her first baby — stillborn. And some stories told in the third person, because the protagonists had not survived to tell them: stories of wombs perforated by unsafe — actually, experimental — IUDs; stories of sleazy black-alley abortionists who left women hemorrhaging or fatally infected." For the comments of a Canadian journalist on the same topic, see Landsberg (1982).

5. Margaret Atwood's *The Handmaid's Tale* (1985a) gives recognition, in science fiction form, to the fact that "sexuality is the linchpin of gender inequality" (MacKinnon, 1982:533). Her book is a post-catastrophe novel set in the near future in an oppressive, theocratic regime. Abortionists and homosexuals are publicly hanged. The narrator is one of a category of women, certified genetically healthy, whose role it is to be surrogate wombs and to produce children for the new regime. Handmaids who fail to conceive are declared to be "unwomen" and expelled from the society to die. The society is ordered on the anti-feminist principle: "from each according to her ability; to each according to his needs" (Goddard, 1985:7).

6. In *Sex and Density* (1984a), Germain Greer argues that women do not have control over their own sexuality. "Some might say that we had that right already, but as long as saying no causes unpleasantness or tension or recriminations or guilt, we do not have it. As long as a woman is economically, emotionally, and socially dependent on the man in her life she is not really free to say no. The quality of her life depends upon keeping him happy."

7. McDaniel (1985:89), in a recent overview, concludes: "Abortion policy as it is presently implemented in Canada has enormous implications for women's lives. The structure of abortion policy permits medical doctors on therapeutic abortion committees to serve as gate-keepers . . . In Canada today, abortion policy implementation is a random system in which the well-to-do can benefit but the poor, particularly the single, young and deprived suffer from severe, crippling biases in the abortion adjudication process. It is an idiosyncratic, locally controlled system for which no one seems willing to take responsibility. It is a male-dominated system in which women's appropriate roles are defined by men for their own purposes."

8. Symbolic interactionism has been divided historically into two main schools of thought. The "Chicago School," associated with Herbert Blumer continues the ideas of Mead discussed in Chapter 2. The Chicago tradition emphasizes the "indeterminant, unpredictable, and subjective aspects" of social behavior (Burr et al., 1979:44). It holds that sociologists should use sensitizing concepts, not hypotheses or variables to explore their subject matter. By contrast, the Iowa School, associated with the late Manford Kuhn, holds that symbolic interactionism should be studied with the same methods used to test other theories in the natural and social sciences. The parts of Chapter 7 that focus on the operationalization of the self-conception are in the Iowa tradition.

9. William James (1910; 1968) was probably the first scholar to recognize the material self. He wrote: "Between what a man calls *me* and what he simply calls *mine* the line is difficult to draw . . . . *In its widest possible sense . . . a man's Me is the sum total of all that he can call his,* not only his body, and his psychic powers, but his clothes and his house, his wife and children, his ancestors and friends, his reputation and works, his lands and horses, and yacht and bank-account" (1910:1968:41), emphasis in original). Presumably, James would also have granted women a material self, if he had thought about it. Goffman (1961a:18) also observed that "persons invest self feelings in their possessions."

10. The Freudian perspective also leads to the conclusion of low female self-esteem. After all, the "woman's self is . . . only . . . a poor version of a man — a woman is like a man, but with something missing" (Whitehurst, 1979:76).

11. Empirical work on these ideas is currently being carried out. See Mackie and Brinkerhoff, "The crack in the mirror: The enigma of female self-esteem" (University of Calgary, manuscript in progress), 1986.

12. In earlier years, symbolic interactionism was frequently criticized for neglecting the emotional dimension of social behavior. Following the lead of the "self-feeling" aspect of Cooley's (1902) looking-glass self, the social emotions of shame and embarrass-

ment had been examined (Goffman, 1967; Gross and Stone, 1964). Also, Shibutani (1961:383 ff.) had described the social control of sentiments. However, such emotions as love, hate, anger, joy, sorrow, and envy had received little attention (Meltzer, Petras and Reynolds, 1975:93). Recent impetus from feminist scholars, especially Hochschild (1975b), has produced a growing theoretical literature on the symbolic interactionism of emotion. See Shott (1979), Gordon (1981), Hochschild (1979; 1983). Shott (1979:1323) concludes that, "symbolic interactionism is well suited for bringing out the interplay of impulse, definition, and socialization that is central to the construction of feelings."

13. For an analysis of the connection between child abuse and patriarchy, see Lahey (1984).

Epilogue

Large introductory sociology classes have the reputation among instructors for being tough to teach. Some students, perhaps the majority, are
serious scholars. They politely write down their instructors' words of
wisdom and do their best to make sense of them. Others, however,
seem to believe Woody Allen's maxim that eighty percent of life is simply
showing up. Plunking their bottoms into classroom seats, they listen
when the proceedings catch their fancy, and daydream or visit when
they don't.

Whatever else one might say about introductory level classes,
they provide excellent feedback to their teachers. Throughout the term,
sociology instructors offer a smorgasbord of topics. Sometimes the
students are interested, sometimes not; at least, the instructor knows
where she stands. However, when the topic of gender relations comes
along, the situation changes. The emotional thermometer rises. While
some students appear intensely interested, others are angry, and still
others sullen and resentful. If the instructor is a woman, there is an
eyeballs-to-ceiling ("Oh God, there she goes again!") attitude in some
quarters. Girlfriends reassure boyfriends that they personally don't
subscribe to this stuff. But no one seems to find gender boring.

What's going on here? What exactly does the sociology of
gender relations mean to students? The whole business is a matter of
enormous importance to their instructors, my contemporaries, who
were adults when the feminist movement came along to revolutionize
their thoughts about themselves and their lives. However, in 1969, when
our thinking began to change, most of our current students were pre-
schoolers. So in good symbolic interactionist fashion, I began talking
to students about *their* definitions of the situation. I asked, "How do
you feel when you encounter the sociology of gender relations?" I want
to describe (with some poetic license) my conversation with a sociology
class in the hope that this encounter will help eventual readers to see
this book's relevance for them.

As the two-worlds proposition would lead us to expect, female
and male reactions to the sociology of gender differ. The women's sentiments also varied by age. Young women, nineteen- and twenty-year-
olds at the peak of their power, have not yet had their consciousness
raised. Attempting to make gender more meaningful for them, I asked,
"Will all the men please raise their hands?" One hundred percent of
the males, but none of the females complied. The women agreed that

females do feel excluded by masculine generic terms. Still, many young women remain unconvinced that the disadvantages of gender will eventually happen to *them*. The few older women in the class who had been in the labor market, married, or produced children, do understand. They experience a mixture of emotions: anger at having been duped and relief that social structure, not they personally, are to blame. They monopolize class discussions. One woman, white-faced from the strain of coping with courses, young children, and a messy divorce confided in me, "There's so many things I want to tell the class."

The reaction of men of all ages, encountering the sociology of gender relations for the first time, is quite different. Many feel guilty and they resent it. After a few brave fellows articulated these thoughts, the class discussion took two directions. First, we talked about personal responsibility, collective responsibility, and social change. I remarked that I feel very badly about such historical events as the abuse of the Indians and the World War II relocation of the Japanese from Canada's West Coast. However, I feel guilty only when I personally mistreat people. When I see institutionalized injustice in our society, I may join with others in social movements to bring about both ideational and structural changes.

As a second response to male guilt, I reminded them that patriarchy is a dual system in which men oppress women *and* men oppress each other. In Pleck's (1981:239) words, "men do not just happily bond together to oppress women. In addition to hierarchy over women, men create hierarchies and rankings among themselves according to criteria of 'masculinity.'" In a sense, the sociology of gender relations really has more to do with males and their competition with one another than with females. For one thing, escorting a "good-looking chick" to a party wins status in the male hierarchy. For another, the sheer existence of the feminine "underclass" mitigates the intensity of male competition; there is a lowest possible level to which males cannot fall (Pleck, 1981:241).

A true story illustrates this "underclass" idea. Last summer, my 76-year-old father, who takes his golf very seriously, was out on the golf course with a crony. They met and formed a threesome with an 89-year-old woman, visiting from Florida where people golf year around. An excellent golfer, she gave the two men pointers about their games and soundly beat them. Weeks later, my father was still digesting the experience. He felt reassured about his own golfing future. Still, to be beaten by a woman and an 89-year-old woman at that!

At the macro-level, the dual nature of patriarchy helps keep the wheels of capitalism turning (Pleck, 1981:242). Traditionally, many men have devoted their lives to onerous, intrinsically meaningless jobs. Their payoff has been in the coin of gender. As breadwinners, they derived satisfaction from thinking, "I put bread on the table and a roof over my family's head." Here is a major reason why women's public domain participation threatens men. From the intent looks on their faces, the men in my class seemed to find these ideas intriguing, if not comforting.

A young woman expressed a third reaction to the sociology of gender:

> I don't like the "we-them" feeling. It's always the women
> who do the complaining. Couldn't we look at gender
> from some neutral position?

We agreed that gender, an issue that touches our most intimate rela-tionships, arouses considerably more anxiety than social issues we can keep at arm's length. Moreover, the essence of gender is power and that has consequences for how we analyze it. Although some males benefit more than others from the gender system, as mentioned earlier, all males derive some benefit from their power over females. An analysis of gender that omitted the tension and strain between the sexes would be sterile. Complaints come from "have nots," i.e., women, not from "haves." It is the disadvantaged sex which seeks to expand its options through new social arrangements. Though gender constrains both sexes, the more privileged males did not understand gender's negative im-plications for them until after the women had organized.

How can I make the concept of masculine power meaningful to young people? Perhaps examples will help. Being powerless is women doing a disproportionate share of the crummy jobs in the home and labor force, for a fraction of male pay. It is women feeling they have to make love in return for dinner. It is women silent, convinced that what they have to say is not important. It is the medical profession labeling unhappy women "neurotic," and prescribing IUDs that kill. It is wife battering and rape. It is demeaning depictions of females in television advertising and pornography. It is women complaining about all these things and nothing happening.

> When one reads the new feminists side by side with the
> ones from previous generations, and even centuries, one
> is struck by the fact that, of what is being currently said
> and written, very little is new: it is an ever-repeating
> script (Ambert, 1976:170).

A final reaction came from the class:

> What's all the fuss about? The sexes are already equal.
> After all, in 1986, we have Section 15 of the Canadian
> Charter of Rights and Freedoms and Jeanne Sauvé as
> Governor General. Our university has lots of women in
> the Faculties of Engineering, Business, Medicine, and

Law (and two men in the Faculty of Nursing). Men are
wearing pink shirts and learning to cry. Why, my
brother-in-law sometimes changes diapers and micro-
waves the dinner.

Has feminist utopia truly arrived? Has women's false consciousness
evaporated? Does our society now accord men's and women's perspectives equal respect? Do the sexes enjoy equal control over their own
bodies? Do they even like their own bodies? Does no one fret about
being too short, too fat, or too flat? When they leave school, do young
people anticipate equal access to challenging work and fair return for
that work? How will gender impinge on the families they eventually
establish? Will he still be an "iron man," while she carries a double load
of work inside and outside the home? Will the socialization of their
children recapitulate the traditional construction of their own gender?
Or is gender transcendence a real possibility? Rhetorical questions,
surely.

   Our discussion ended on a sober note. The decade of the 1980s
is not hospitable to the achievement of equality of the sexes. Although
the conditions that necessitated the feminist movement have been continuously present in our society, the movement for improving women's
status has flourished only in periods "when sensitivity to moral injustice, discrimination, and social inequality was widespread in the
society as a whole" (Taylor, 1983:435). The social conservatism of the
1980s — the swing to the right in political and religious thought, the
anti-feminist countermovement — threatens both feminists' gains of the
1970s and their hopes for the future.

   Several years ago, I had an experience that taught me to be
humble about the long-term impact of sociology courses upon students.
One day, after a lecture that had gone particularly well, I had been
ruminating over what students might take away from my course.
Although I knew the sociological jargon and the details would soon
be forgotten, I expected some key generalizations, perhaps a clever anecdote or two, to remain with them. By chance, that very evening, I
encountered a former student waiting on tables in a restaurant. He
recognized me and remarked that he had once taken a course from me.
But he couldn't recall which one! Nonetheless, I still like to think that
he took away one or two worthwhile ideas from my class, even if he
has forgotten the source. I am especially optimistic that students incorporate some ideas from the sociology of gender relations into their
own thinking. Courses end and textbooks gather dust. However,
blinders once removed usually stay off permanently.

References

Abbey, Antonia. 1982. "Sex differences in attributions for friendly behavior: Do males mis-perceive females' friendliness?" *Journal of Personality and Social Psychology* 42:830–838.

Abu-Laban, Sharon McIrvin. 1980a. "The family life of older Canadians." Pp. 125–134 in Victor W. Marshall (ed.), *Aging in Canada*. Don Mills, Ontario: Fitzhenry and Whiteside.

———. 1980b. "Social supports in older age: The need for new research dimensions." *Essence* 4:195–210.

———. 1981. "Women and aging: A futurist perspective." *Psychology of Women Quarterly* 6:85–98.

Acock, Alan C. 1984. "Parents and their children: The study of inter-generational influence." *Sociology and Social Research* 68:151–171.

Adam, Barry D. 1978. "Inferiorization and 'self-esteem'." *Social Psychology* 41:47–53.

Adler, Shane. 1979. "Dressing up." Pp. 387–397 in Claire B. Kopp (ed.), *Becoming Female: Perspectives on Development*. New York: Plenum Press.

Agnew, Robert. 1984. "The effect of appearance on personality and behaviour: Are the beautiful really good?" *Youth & Society* 15:285–303.

Albrecht, Milton C. 1954. "The relationship of literature and society." *American Journal of Sociology* 59:425–436.

Al-Issa, Ihsan. 1980. *The Psychopathology of Women*. Englewood Cliffs, N.J.: Prentice-Hall.

———. 1982. *Gender and Psychopathology*. New York: Academic Press.

Allgeier, E.R. 1981. "The influence of androgynous identification on heterosexual relations." *Sex Roles* 7:321–330.

Allport, Gordon W. 1961. *Pattern and Growth in Personality*. New York: Holt, Rinehart and Winston.

Ambert, Anne-Marie. 1976. *Sex Structure*. Second Edition. Don Mills, Ontario: Longman Canada.

———. 1980. *Divorce in Canada*. Don Mills, Ontario: Academic Press Canada.

———. 1983. "Separated women and remarriage behavior: A comparison of financially secure women and financially insecure women." *Journal of Divorce* 6:43–54.

———, and Maureen Baker. 1984. "Marriage dissolution: Structural and ideological changes." Pp. 85–103 in Maureen Baker (ed.), *The Family: Changing Trends in Canada*. Toronto: McGraw-Hill Ryerson.

———, and Gladys Symons Hitchman. 1976. "A case study of status differential: Women in academia." Pp. 113–146 in Anne-Marie Ambert, *Sex Structure*. Second Edition. Toronto: Longman Canada.

Andersen, Margaret L. 1983. *Thinking About Women: Sociological and Feminist Perspectives*. New York: Macmillan Publishing Co.

Anderson, C.H. 1971. *Toward a New Sociology: A Critical View*. Homewood, Illinois: Dorsey Press.

Anderson, Doris. 1984. "The real problems behind controlling pornography." *CAUT Bulletin* (February):23–24.

Archibald, Kathleen. 1970. *Sex and the Public Service*. Ottawa: Queen's Printer.

Ardener, Edwin. 1975. "The 'problem' revisited." Pp. 19–27 in Shirley Ardener (ed.), *Perceiving Women*. London: Malaby Press.

Argyle, M., V. Salter, H. Nicholson, M. Williams, and P. Burgess. 1970. "The communica-tion of inferior and superior attitudes by verbal and nonverbal signals." *British Jour-nal of Social and Clinical Psychology* 9:222–231.

Ariès. Philippe. 1962. *Centuries of Childhood: A Social History of Family Life*. New York: Vintage Books.

Armitage, Karen J., Lawrence J. Schneiderman and Robert A. Bass. 1980. "Response of physicians to medical complaints in men and women." *International Journal of Women's Studies* 3:111–116.

Armstrong, Pat, and Hugh Armstrong. 1978. *The Double Ghetto: Canadian Women and Their Segregated Work*. Toronto: McClelland and Stewart.

———. 1983. *A Working Majority: What Women Must Do For Pay*. Ottawa: Canadian Advisory Council on the Status of Women.

———. 1984. *The Double Ghetto: Canadian Women and Their Segregated Work*. Revised Edition. Toronto: McClelland and Stewart.

Ashley, Barbara Renchkovsky, and David Ashley. 1984. "Sex as violence: The body against intimacy." *International Journal of Women's Studies* 7:352–371.

Atchley, Robert C. 1982. "The process of retirement: Comparing women and men." Pp. 153–168 in Maximiliane Szinovacz (ed.), *Women's Retirement: Policy Implications of Recent Research*. Beverly Hills: Sage.

Atchley, R.C. and S.L. Corbett. 1977. "Older women and jobs." In L.E. Troll, J. Israel, and K. Israel (eds.), *Looking Ahead: A Woman's Guide to the Problems and Joys of Growing Older*. Englewood Cliffs, N.J.: Prentice-Hall.

Atkinson, Jane Monnig. 1982. "Anthropology," *Signs* 8:236–258.

Atwood, Margaret. 1972. *Surfacing*. New York: Simon and Schuster.

———. 1983. "Atwood on pornography." *Chatelaine* (September): 61, 118, 126, 128.

———. 1985. *The Handmaid's Tale*. Toronto: McClelland and Stewart.

Badgley, R. (Chairman). 1984. *Report of the Committee on Sexual Offences against Children*. Ottawa: Government of Canada.

Bakan, David. 1966. *The Duality of Human Existence: An Essay on Psychology and Religion*. Chicago: Rand McNally.

Baker, Maureen. 1983. "Divorce: Its consequences and meanings." Pp. 289–300 in K. Ishwaran (ed.), *The Canadian Family*. Toronto: Gage.

———. 1984. "His and her divorce research: New theoretical directions in Canadian and American research." *Journal of Comparative Family Studies* 15:17–28.

———. 1985. *"What Will Tomorrow Bring? . . ." A Study of the Aspirations of Adolescent Women*. Ottawa: Canadian Advisory Council on the Status of Women.

———, and J.I. Hans Bakker. 1980. "The double-bind of the middle class male: Men's liberation and the male sex role." *Journal of Comparative Family Studies* 11:547–561.

Ball, Donald W. 1969. "The definition of the situation: Some theoretical and methodological consequences of taking W.I. Thomas seriously." Paper presented to the Canadian Sociology and Anthropology Association meetings, Toronto.

Balswick, J.O. and C.W. Peek. 1971. "The inexpressive male: A tragedy of American society." Pp. 237–244 in A. Skolnick and J.H. Skolnick (eds.), *Intimacy, Family and Society*. Boston: Little, Brown.

Barash, David. 1979. *The Whisperings Within*. New York: Penguin.

Bardwick, Judith M. 1979. *In Transition*. New York: Holt, Rinehart and Winston.

———, and Elizabeth Douvan. 1971. "Ambivalence: The socialization of women." Pp. 225–241 in Vivian Gornick and Barbara K. Moran (eds.), *Woman in Sexist Society*. New York: Signet Books.

Barfield, Ashton. 1976. "Biological influences on sex differences in behavior." Pp. 62–121 in Michael S. Teitelbaum (ed.), *Sex Differences: Social and Biological Perspectives*. Garden City, N.Y.: Anchor Books.

Barnes, Rosemary. 1985. "Women and self-injury." *International Journal of Women's Studies* 8:465–474.

Barnett, Rosalind C., and Grace K. Baruch. 1978. "Women in the middle years: A critique of research and theory." *Psychology of Women Quarterly* 3:187–197.

Barol, Bill. 1985. "Women in a video cage." *Newsweek*, March 4:54.

Baron, Robert A., and Donn Byrne. 1984. *Social Psychology: Understanding Human Interaction*. Fourth Edition. Boston: Allyn and Bacon.

Bart, Pauline B., and Margaret Jozsa. 1980. "Dirty books, dirty films and dirty data." Pp. 204–217 in Laura Lederer (ed.), *Take Back the Night: Women on Pornography*. New York: William Morrow.

Basow, Susan A. 1980. *Sex-Role Stereotypes: Traditions and Alternatives*. Monterey, California: Brooks/Cole.

Becker, Gary S. 1981. *A Treatise on the Family.* Cambridge, Massachusetts: Harvard University Press.

Becker, Howard S. 1970. "Personal change in adult life." Pp. 583–593 in Gregory P. Stone and Harvey A. Farberman (eds.), *Social Psychology through Symbolic Interaction.* Waltham, MA.: Ginn-Blaisdell.

———. 1972. "A school is a lousy place to learn anything." Pp. 89–109 in Blanche Geer (ed.), *Learning to Work.* Beverly Hills: Sage.

Beezley, William H. and Joseph P. Hobbs. 1983. " 'Nice girls don't sweat: Women in American sport." *Journal of Popular Culture* 16:42–53.

Bell, Inge Powell. 1970. "The double standard: Age." *Trans-action* 8 (November-December): 75–80.

Bell, Richard O, and Lawrence V. Harper. 1977. *Child Effects on Adults.* New York: John Wiley.

Bell, Robert R. 1981. *Worlds of Friendship.* Beverly Hills: Sage.

Bem, Sandra L. 1974. "The measurement of psychological androgyny." *Journal of Consulting and Clinical Psychology* 42:155–162.

———. 1976. "Probing the promise of androgyny." Pp. 48–62 in Alexandra G. Kaplan and Joan P. Bean (eds.), *Beyond Sex-role Stereotypes: Readings toward a Psychology of Androgyny.* Boston: Little, Brown.

———. 1981. "Gender schema theory: A cognitive account of sex typing." *Psychological Review* 88:354–364.

———. 1983. "Gender schema theory and its implications for child development: Raising gender-aschematic children in a gender-schematic society." *Signs* 8:598–616.

———, and Daryl J. Bem. 1971. "Training the woman to know her place: The power of a nonconscious ideology." Pp. 84–96 in Michele Hoffnung Garskof (ed.), *Roles Women Play: Readings toward Women's Liberation.* Belmont, CA.: Brooks/Cole.

Bem and Bem. 1984. "Homogenizing the American woman: The power of unconscious ideology." Pp. 10–22 in Alison M. Jaggar and Paula S. Rothenberg (eds). *Feminist Frameworks.* Second Edition. New York: McGraw-Hill.

Benjamin, Harry. 1966. *The Transsexual Phenomenon.* New York: Julian Press.

Benston, Margaret. 1969. "The political scenery of women's liberation." *Monthly Review* 21:13–27.

———, 1982. "Feminism and the critique of scientific method." Pp. 47–66 in Angela R. Miles and Geraldine Finn (eds.), *Feminism in Canada: From Pressure to Politics.* Montreal: Black Rose Books.

Ben-Yehuda, Nachman. 1980. "The European witch craze of the 14th to 17th centuries: A sociologist's perspective." *American Journal of Sociology* 86:1–31.

Berenstain, Stan and Jan Berenstain. 1984. *The Berenstain Bears and Mama's New Job.* New York: Random House.

Berger, Brigitte, and Peter L. Berger. 1984. *The War Over the Family: Capturing the Middle Ground.* Garden City, N.Y.: Doubleday Anchor.

Berger, Charlene and Dolores Gold. 1976. "The relation between sex-role identification and problem-solving performance in young boys and girls." Paper presented at "Research on Woman-Current Projects and Future Directions, an Interdisciplinary Conference." Mount Saint Vincent University, Halifax, Nova Scotia.

Berger, John. 1977. *Ways of Seeing.* New York: Penguin Books.

Berger, Peter L. 1963. *Invitation to Sociology: A Humanistic Perspective.* Garden City, N.Y.: Doubleday Anchor.

———, and Brigitte Berger, 1975. *Sociology: A Biographical Approach.* Second Edition. New York: Basic Books.

———, and Hansfried Kellner. 1970. "Marriage and the construction of reality: An exercise in the microsociology of knowledge." Pp. 50–72 in Hans Peter Dreitzel (ed.), *Recent Sociology No.2: Patterns in Communicative Behavior.* New York: Macmillan.

———, and Thomas Luckmann. 1966. *The Social Construction of Reality.* Garden City, New York: Doubleday Anchor.

Berger, Thomas. 1964. *Little Big Man.* New York: Fawcett Crest Books.

Berk, Bernard. 1977. "Face-saving at the singles dance." *Social Problems* 24:530–544.

Berman, Ronald. 1981. *Advertising and Social Change.* Beverly Hills: Sage.

Bernard, Jessie. 1972. *The Future of Marriage.* New York: Bantam Books.

———. 1973. "My four revolutions: An autobiographical history of the ASA." *American Journal of Sociology* 78:773–791.

———. 1975. *Women, Wives, Mothers: Values and Options*. Chicago: Aldine.

———. 1976. "Sex differences: An overview." Pp. 10–26 in Alexandra G. Kaplan and Joan P. Bean (eds.), *Beyond Sex-role Stereotypes: Readings toward a Psychology of Androgyny*. Boston: Little, Brown.

———. 1981a. *The Female World*. New York: Free Press.

———. 1981b. "The good-provider role: its rise and fall." *American Psychologist* 36:1–12.

Berscheid, Ellen and Elaine Walster. 1974. "Physical attractiveness." Pp. 157–215 in L. Berkowitz (ed.), *Advances in Experimental Social Psychology*, Vol. 7. New York: Academic Press.

Best, D.L., Williams, J.E., Cloud, J.M., Davis, S.W., Robertson, L.S., Edwards, J.R., Giles, H., and Fowles, J. 1977. "Development of sex-trait stereotypes among young children in the United States, England and Ireland." *Child Development* 48:1375–1384.

Best, Raphaela. 1983. *We've All Got Scars*. Bloomington, IN.: Indiana University Press.

Beuf, Ann. 1974. Doctor, lawyer, household drudge." *Journal of Communication* 24:142–145.

Bibby, Reginald W. and Donald C. Posterski. 1985. *The Emerging Generation: An Inside Look at Canada's Teenagers*. Toronto: Irwin.

Biller, H. 1971. *Father, Child and Sex Role*. Lexington, MA.: Heath Lexington.

Birdwhistell, Ray L. 1970. *Kinesics and Context*. Philadelphia: University of Pennsylvania Press.

Blackwood, Evelyn. 1984. "Sexuality and gender in certain native American tribes: The case of cross-gender females." *Signs* 10:27–42.

Blau, Zena Smith. 1970. "Changes in status and age identification." Pp. 513–619 in Gregory P. Stone and Harvey A. Farberman (eds.), *Social Psychology through Symbolic Interaction*. Waltham, MA.: Ginn-Blaisdell.

———. 1973. *Old Age in a Changing Society*. New York: Watts.

Blaubergs, Marja. 1980. "An analysis of classic arguments against changing sexist language." *Women's Studies International Quarterly* 3:135–147.

Bleier, Ruth. 1979. "Social and political bias in science: An examination of animal studies and their generalizations to human behavior and evolution." Pp. 49–70 in Ruth Hubbard and Marion Lowe (eds.), *Genes and Gender II*. Staten Island, N.Y.: Gordian Press.

Bliss, Michael. 1974. "Pure books on avoided subjects: Pre-Freudian sexual ideas in Canada." Pp. 326–346 in Michiel Horn and Ronald Sabourin (eds.), *Studies in Canadian Social History*. Toronto: McClelland and Stewart.

Block, Jeanne H. 1978. "Another look at sex differentiation in the socialization behaviors of mothers and fathers." Pp. 29–87 in Julia A. Sherman and Florence L. Denmark (eds.), *The Psychology of Women: Future Directions in Research*. New York: Psychological Dimensions.

Blumer, Herbert. 1969a. "Fashion: From class differentiation to collective selection." *Sociological Quarterly* 10:275–291.

Blumer, Herbert. 1969b. *Symbolic Interactionism: Perspective and Method*. Englewood Cliffs, N.J.: Prentice-Hall.

Blumstein, Philip, and Pepper Schwartz. 1983. *American Couples*. New York: William Morrow.

Boras, Alan. 1985. "Brave new world." *The Calgary Herald*, June 15th, p. G1.

Boskind-Lodahl, Marlene. 1976. "Cinderella's stepsisters: A feminist perspective on anorexia nervosa and bulimia." *Signs* 2:342–356.

Boston Women's Collective. 1984. *The New Our Bodies, Ourselves*. New York: Simon and Schuster.

Bowlby, John. 1952. *Maternal Care and Maternal Health*. Geneva: World Health Organization.

Boyd, Monica. 1975. "English-Canadian and French-Canadian attitudes towards women: Results of the Canadian Gallup polls." *Journal of Comparative Family Studies* 6:153–169.

———. 1977. "The forgotten minority: The socioeconomic status of divorced and separated women." Pp. 47–71 in Patricia Marchak (ed.), *The Working Sexes*. Vancouver: University of British Columbia.

———. 1984. *Canadian Attitudes Toward Women: Thirty Years of Change*. Ottawa: Labour Canada.

Braithwaite, Max. 1969. *Never Sleep Three in a Bed*. Toronto: McClelland and Stewart.

Brandt, Anthony. 1984. "The partnership." *Esquire* 101 (June):227–233.
Breines, Wini, and Linda Gordon. 1983. "The new scholarship on family violence." *Signs* 8:490–531.
Brenton, Myron. 1974. *Friendship.* New York: Stein and Day.
Briggs, Jean L. 1974. "Eskimo women: Makers of men." Pp. 261–304 in Carolyn J. Matthiasson (ed.), *Many Sisters: Women in Cross-Cultural Perspective.* New York: Free Press.
Brim, Orville G., Jr. 1968. "Adult socialization." Pp. 182–226 in John A. Clausen (ed.), *Socialization and Society.* Boston: Little, Brown.
——. 1976. "Theories of the male mid-life crisis." *Counselling Psychologist* 6:2–9.
——, and Jerome Kagan. 1980. "Constancy and change: A view of the issues." Pp. 1–25 in Orville G. Brim, Jr., and Jerome Kagan (eds.), *Constancy and Change in Human Development.* Cambridge, MA.: Harvard University Press.
Brodzinsky, David M., Karen Barnet, and John R. Aiello. 1981. "Sex of subject and gender identity as factors in humor appreciation." *Sex Roles* 7:561–573.
Bronfenbrenner, Urie. 1961. "Some familial antecedents of responsibility and leadership in adolescents." In Luigi Petrullo and Bernard M. Bass (eds.), Leadership and Interpersonal Behavior. New York: Holt, Rinehart and Winston.
Broschart, Kay Richards. 1978. "Female sex roles and middle age." *International Journal of Women's Studies* 1:259–262.
Brothers, Joyce. 1972. *The Brothers' System for Liberated Love and Marriage.* New York: Avon Books.
Broverman, I.K., D.M. Broverman, F.E. Clarkson, P. Rosenkrantz, and S.R. Vogel. 1970. "Sex-role stereotypes and clinical judgments of mental health." *Journal of Consulting and Clinical Psychology* 34:1–7.
——, Susan Raymond Vogel, Donald M. Broverman, Frank E. Clarkson, and Paul S. Rosenkrantz. 1972. "Sex-role stereotypes: A current appraisal." *Journal of Social Issues* 28:59–78.
Brownmiller, Susan. 1975. *Against Our Will: Men, Women and Rape.* New York: Simon and Schuster.
——. 1980. "Let's put pornography back in the closet." Pp. 252–255 in Laura Lederer (ed.), *Take Back the Night: Women on Pornography.* New York: William Morrow.
——. 1984. *Femininity.* New York: Linden Press, Simon and Schuster.
Bryden, M.P. 1979. "Evidence for sex-related differences in cerebral organization." Pp. 121–143 in M.A. Wittig and A.C. Petersen (eds.), *Sex-Related Differences in Cognitive Functioning: Developmental Issues.* New York: Academic Press.
Buckland, Lin. 1985. "Education and training: Equal opportunities or barriers to employment?" Pp. 133–156 in Rosalie Silberman Abella, *Equality in Opportunity: A Royal Commission Report.* Ottawa: Supply and Services Canada.
Bulliet, C.J. 1927. *Apples and Madonnas.* Chicago: Pascal Covici.
Burke, Peter J. 1980. "The self: Measurement requirements from an interactionist perspective." *Social Psychology Quarterly* 43:18–29.
Burr, Wesley R., Geoffrey K. Leigh, Randall D. Day and John Constantine. "Symbolic interaction and the family." 1979. Pp. 42–111 in Wesley R. Burr, Reuben Hill, F. Ivan Nye and Ira L. Reiss (eds.), *Contemporary Theories about the Family.* Vol. II. New York: The Free Press.
Burstyn, Varda (ed.), 1985. *Women Against Censorship.* Vancouver: Douglas & McIntyre.
Burwell, Elinor J. 1984. "Sexism in social science research on aging." Pp. 185–208 in Jill McCalla Vickers (ed.), *Taking Sex into Account.* Ottawa: Carleton University Press.
Bush, Diane Mitsch and Roberta G. Simmons. 1981."Socialization processes over the life course." Pp. 133–164 in Morris Rosenberg and Ralph H. Turner (eds.), *Social Psychology: Sociological Perspectives.* New York: Basic Books.
Cahill, Spencer E. 1980. "Directions for an interactionist study of gender development." *Symbolic Interaction* 3:123–138.
Caine, Lynn. 1985. *What Did I do Wrong? Mothers, Children, Guilt.* Toronto: Fitzhenry & Whiteside.
Callender, Charles and Lee M. Kochems. 1983. "The North American Berdache." *Current Anthropology* 24:443–456.
Callwood, June. 1984. "Pornography and the law: A delicate problem." *CAUT Bulletin* (February):25.

Calzavara, Liviana. 1985. "Trends in the employment opportunities of women in Canada, 1930–1980." Pp. 517–536 in Rosalie Silberman Abella, *Equality in Opportunity: A Royal Commission Report.* Ottawa: Supply and Services Canada.

Cammaert, Lorna P., and Carolyn C. Larsen. 1979. *A Woman's Choice: A Guide to Decision Making.* Brossard, Quebec: Research Press.

Campbell, Colin. 1976. "What happens when we get . . . the manchild pill?" *Psychology Today* (August): Pp. 86, 88, 90, 91.

Campbell, Ernest Q. 1969. "Adolescent socialization." Pp. 821–860 in David A. Goslin (ed.), *Handbook of Socialization Theory and Research.* Chicago: Rand McNally.

———. 1975. *Socialization: Culture and Personality.* Dubuque, Iowa: Wm. C. Brown.

Campbell, Maria. 1973. *Half-Breed.* Toronto: McClelland and Stewart.

Canadian Radio-television and Telecommunications Commission. 1982. *Images of Women: Report of the Task Force on Sex-Role Stereotyping in the Broadcast Media.* Hull, Quebec: Supply and Services Canada.

Cancian, Francesca M. 1985. "Gender politics: Love and power in the private and public spheres." Pp. 253–264 in Alice S. Rossi (ed.), *Gender and the Life Course.* New York: Aldine.

Cantor, Joanne R. 1976. "What is funny to whom? The role of gender." *Journal of Communication* 26:164–172.

Caplan, Paula J. 1985. "Anti-feminist women." *International Journal of Women's Studies* 8:351–355.

Carlson, Rae. 1971. "Sex differences in ego functioning: Exploratory studies of agency and communion." *Journal of Consulting and Clinical Psychology* 37:267–277.

———. 1972. "Understanding women: Implications for personality theory and research." *Journal of Social Issues* 28:17–32.

Carmen, Elaine Hilberman, Nancy Felipe Russo, and Jean Baker Miller. 1981. "Inequality and women's mental health: An overview." *American Journal of Psychiatry* 138:1324.

Carmody, Denise Lardner. 1979. "Women and religion: Where mystery comes to center stage." Pp. 262–295 in Eloise C. Snyder (ed.), *The Study of Women: Enlarging Perspectives of Social Reality.* New York: Harper and Row.

Carr, Emily. 1946. *Growing Pains: The Autobiography of Emily Carr.* Toronto: Clarke, Irwin.

Carrigan, Tim, Bob Connell, and John Lee. 1985. "Towards a new sociology of masculinity." *Theory and Society* 14:551–604.

Carson, Rachel. 1962. *Silent Spring.* Boston: Houghton Mifflin.

Carter, Betsy. 1984. "Liberation's next wave, according to Gloria Steinem." *Esquire* (June): 202–206.

Caspar, R. and E. Ostrov. 1981. "The self-image of adolescents with acute anorexia nervosa." *The Journal of Pediatrics* 98:656.

Cassell, Joan. 1974. "Externalities of change: Deference and demeanor in contemporary feminism." *Human Organization* 33:85–94.

Cassin, A. Marguerite and Alison I. Griffith. 1981. "Class and ethnicity: Producing the difference that counts." *Canadian Ethnic Studies* 13:109–129.

Chafetz, Janet Saltzman. 1974. *Masculine/Feminine or Human?* Itasca, Il.: Peacock.

Charon, Joel M. 1979. *Symbolic Interactionism: An Introduction, An Interpretation, An Integration.* Englewood Cliffs, N.J.: Prentice-Hall.

Cherlin, Andrew and Pamela Barnhouse Walters. 1981. "Trends in United States men's and women's sex-role attitudes 1972 to 1978." *American Sociological Review* 46:453–460.

Chesler, Phyllis. 1972. *Women and Madness.* New York: Avon Books.

Chicago, Judy. 1975. *Through the Flower: My Struggle as a Woman Artist.* Garden City, N.Y.: Doubleday.

Chodorow, Nancy. 1971. Being and doing: A cross-cultural examination of the socialization of males and females." Pp. 259–291 in Vivian Gornick and Barbara K. Moran (eds.), *Woman in Sexist Society.* New York: New American Library.

———. 1974. "Family structure and feminine personality." Pp. 43–66 in Michelle Zimbalist Rosaldo and Louise Lamphere (eds.), *Woman, Culture and Society.* Stanford, CA.: Stanford University Press.

———. 1978. *The Reproduction of Mothering.* Berkeley, CA.: University of California Press.

Cicourel, Aaron W. 1970. "The acquisition of social structure: Toward a developmental sociology of language and meaning." Pp. 136–168 in Jack D. Douglas (ed.), *Understanding Everyday Life.* Chicago: Aldine.

Clark, Susan and Andrew S. Harvey. 1976. "The sexual division of labour: The case of time." *Atlantis* 2:46–66.

Clausen, John A. 1968. "Perspectives on childhood socialization." Pp. 130–181 in John A. Clausen (ed.), *Socialization and Society.* Boston: Little, Brown.

Clement, Wallace. 1975. *The Canadian Corporate Elite: An Analysis of Economic Power.* Toronto: McClelland and Stewart.

Clifton, Rodney A. 1975. "Self-concept and attitudes: A comparison of Canadian Indian and non-Indian students." *The Canadian Review of Sociology and Anthropology* 12, Part 2:577–584.

Cloyd, Gerald W. 1976. "The market-place bar: The interrelation between sex, situation, and strategies in the pairing ritual of *homo ludens.*" Urban Life 5:293–312.

Cole, Jonathan. 1979. *Fair Science: Women in the Scientific Community.* New York: Free Press.

Coleman, James S. 1976. "Learning through games." Pp. 460–463 in Jerome S. Bruner, Alison Jolly and Kathy Sylva (eds.), *Play: Its Role in Development and Education.* Harmondsworth, Middlesex, England: Penguin Books.

Collier, Helen V. 1982. *Counseling Women: A Guide for Therapists.* New York: Free Press.

Collins, H.M. 1983. "The sociology of scientific knowledge: Studies of contemporary science." *Annual Review of Sociology* 9:265–285.

Colwill, Nina L. 1982. *The New Partnership: Women and Men in Organizations.* Palo Alto, CA.: Mayfield.

Condry, John and Douglas Keith. 1983. "Educational and recreational uses of computer technology." *Youth and Society* 15:87–112.

Connell, R.W. 1985. "Theorising gender." *Sociology* 19:260–272.

Connelly, Patricia. 1978. *Last Hired, First Fired: Women and the Canadian Work Force.* Toronto: The Women's Press.

———, and Linda Christiansen-Ruffman. 1977. "Women's problems: private troubles or public issues?" *Canadian Journal of Sociology* 2:167–178.

Cooley, Charles H. 1902. *Human Nature and the Social Order.* New York: Scribner's.

Cooperstock, R. 1978. "The epidemiology of psychotropic drug use in Canada." *Canadian Family Physician* 24: 889–893.

Coser, Lewis A. 1968. "Sociology of knowledge." Pp. 428–435 in David L. Sills (ed.), *International Encyclopedia of the Social Sciences.* New York: Macmillan.

———. 1974. *Greedy Institutions: Patterns of Undivided Commitment.* New York: Free Press.

———, with Rose Leah Coser. 1974. "The housewife and her 'greedy family'." In Lewis A. Coser, *Greedy Institutions: Patterns of Undivided Commitment.* New York: Free Press.

Coser, Rose Laub. 1959. "Some social functions of laughter: A study of humor in a hospital setting." *Human Relations* 12:171–182.

———. 1960. "Laughter among colleagues." *Psychiatry* 23:81–89.

———, and Gerald Rokoff. 1971. "Women in the occupational world: Social disruption and conflict." *Social Problems* 18:535–554.

Courtney, Alice E. and Thomas W. Whipple. 1978. *Canadian Perspectives on Sex Stereotyping in Advertising.* Ottawa: Advisory Council on the Status of Women.

Cox, Sue. 1976. *Female Psychology: The Emerging Self.* Chicago: Science Research Associates.

Coyne, James C., Richard C. Sherman, and Karen O'Brien. 1978. "Expletives and woman's place." *Sex Roles* 4:827–835.

Csikszentmihalyi, Mihaly, and Eugene Rochberg-Halton. 1981. "Object lessons." *Psychology Today* 15 (December): 79–85.

Cumming, Elaine, Charles Lazer, and Lynne Chisholm. 1975. "Suicide as an index of role strain among employed and not employed married women in British Columbia." *Canadian Review of Sociology and Anthropology* 12, Part I:462–470.

———, and Charles Lazer. 1981. "Kinship structure and suicide: A theoretical link." *The Canadian Review of Sociology and Anthropology,* 18:271–282.

Daly, Mary. 1978. *Gyn/Ecology: The Metaethics of Radical Feminism.* Boston: Beacon Press.

Daniels, Arlene Kaplan. 1975. "Feminist perspectives in sociological research." Pp. 340–380 in Marcia Millman and Rosabeth Moss Kanter (eds.), *Another Voice: Feminist Perspectives on Social Life and Social Science.* Garden City, N.Y.: Doubleday Anchor.

Danneer, Dale. 1984. "Adult development and social theory: A paradigmatic reappraisal." *American Sociological Review* 49:100–116.

Darling, Jon. 1977. "Bachelorhood and late marriage: An interactionist interpretation." *Symbolic Interaction* 1:44–55.

Davies, Mark and Denise B. Kandal. 1981. "Parental and peer influences on adolescents' educational plans: Some further evidence." *American Journal of Sociology* 87:363–387.

Davis, Jay M. and Amerigo Farina. 1970. "Humor appreciation as social communication." *Journal of Personality and Social Psychology* 15:175–178.

Davis, Kingsley. 1940. "The sociology of parent-youth conflict." *American Sociological Review* 5:523–535.

Dawkins, Richard. 1976. *The Selfish Gene.* London: Oxford University Press.

Deaux, Kay. 1976. *The Behavior of Women and Men.* Monterey, CA.: Brooks/Cole.

———. 1984. "From individual differences to social categories: Analysis of a decade's research on gender." *American Psychologist* 39:105–116.

———. 1985. "Sex and gender." *Annual Review of Psychology* 36:49–81.

———, and Tim Emswiller. 1974. "Explanations of successful performance on sex-linked tasks: What is skill for the male is luck for the female." *Journal of Personality and Social Psychology* 29:80–85.

———, and Elizabeth Farris. 1974. "Attributing causes for one's own performance: The effects of sex, norms, and outcome." Unpublished paper, Purdue University.

——— and Lawrence S. Wrightsman. 1984. *Social Psychology in the 80s.* Fourth Edition. Monterey, CA.: Brooks/Cole.

de Beauvoir, Simone. 1949. *The Second Sex.* New York: Bantam Books.

———. 1970. *Old Age.* Harmondsworth, England: Penguin Books.

De Mause, Lloyd. 1982. "The evolution of childhood." Pp. 48–59 in Chris Jenks (ed.), *The Sociology of Childhood.* London: Batsford.

Denisoff, R. Serge and Richard A. Peterson. 1972. "Introduction: Theories of culture, music, and society." Pp. 1–12 in R. Serge Denisoff and Richard A. Peterson (eds.), *The Sounds of Social Change.* Chicago: Rand McNally.

Denmark, Florence L. and Helen M. Goodfield. 1978. "A second look at adolescence theories." *Sex Roles* 4:375–379.

Denzin, Norman K. 1970. "Problems in analyzing elements of mass culture: Notes on the popular song and other artistic productions." *American Journal of Sociology* 75:1035–1038.

———. 1972. "The genesis of self in early childhood." *The Sociological Quarterly* 13:291–314.

———. 1975. "Play, games, and interaction: The context of childhood socialization." *Sociological Quarterly* 16:458–478.

———. 1979. "Children and their caretakers." Pp. 36–51 in Peter I. Rose (ed.), *Socialization and the Life Cycle.* New York: St. Martin's Press.

Deutsch, Morton, and Robert M. Krauss. 1965. *Theories in Social Psychology.* New York: Basic Books.

De Vries, Hilary. 1984. "Advertisers focus in on image of women." *The Calgary Herald,* July 9:D4.

Dietz, Mary Lorenz. 1981. "Managing a deviant identity: The case of the male dancer in ballet." Paper presented at the annual meeting of the Canadian Sociology and Anthropology Association, Halifax, Nova Scotia.

Dill, Bonnie Thornton, Evelyn N. Glenn and Bettina J. Huber. 1983. "Women in departmental administrative positions." *ASA Footnotes* (August):10–11.

Dinnerstein, Dorothy. 1976. *The Mermaid and the Minotaur: Sexual Arrangements and Human Malaise.* New York: Harper and Row.

Dion, K.K., E. Berscheid and E. Walster. 1972. "What is beautiful is good." *Journal of Personality and Social Psychology* 24:285–290.

Dixon, Marlene. 1971. "Why women's liberation." Pp. 165–178 in Michele Hoffnung Garskof (ed.), *Roles Women Play: Readings Toward Women's Liberation.* Belmont, CA.: Brooks/Cole.

Dixon, Richard D., and Diane E. Levy. 1985. "Sex of children: a community analysis of preferences and predetermination attitudes." *The Sociological Quarterly* 26:251–271.

Dobash, R. Emerson and Russell Dobash. 1979. *Violence Against Wives: A Case Against the Patriarchy.* New York: Free Press.

Dominick, Joseph R. 1979. "The portrayal of women in prime time, 1953-1977." *Sex Roles* 5:405–411.

Douvan, E. 1969. "Sex differences in adolescent character processes." Pp. 437–445 in D. Rogers (ed.), *Issues in Adolescent Psychology.* New York: Appleton-Century-Crofts.

Doyle, James A. 1983. *The Male Experience.* Dubuque, IO.: Wm. C. Brown.

——. 1985. *Sex and Gender: The Human Experience.* Dubuque, IO.: Wm. C. Brown.

Dubinsky, Karen. 1985. *Lament For a "Patriarchy Lost?": Anti-Feminism, Anti-Abortion and REAL Women in Canada.* Ottawa: Canadian Research Institute for the Advancement of Women.

Dulude, Louise. 1978. *Women and Aging: A Report on the Rest of Our Lives."* Ottawa: Canadian Advisory Council on the Status of Women.

Dunbar, Roxanne. 1970. "Female liberation as the basis for social revolution." Pp. 477–492 in Robin Morgan (ed.), *Sisterhood is Powerful.* New York: Vintage Books.

Durden-Smith, Jo and Diane deSimone. 1983. *Sex and the Brain.* New York: Arbor House.

Eagly, A.H. and L.L. Carli. 1981. "Sex of researchers and sex-typed communications as determinants of sex differences in influenceability: A meta-analysis of social influence studies." *Psychological Bulletin* 90:1–20.

——, and Valerie J. Steffen. 1984. "Gender stereotypes stem from the distribution of women and men into social roles." *Journal of Personality and Social Psychology* 46:735–754.

Eakins, Barbara Westbrook and R. Gene Eakins. 1978. *Sex Differences in Human Communication.* Boston: Houghton Mifflin.

Eder, Donna, and Maureen T. Hallinan. 1978. "Sex differences in children's friendships." *American Sociological Review* 43:237–250.

Edwards, John R. and J.E. Williams. 1980. "Sex-trait stereotypes among young children and young adults: Canadian findings and cross-national comparisons." *Canadian Journal of Behavioral Science* 12:210–220.

Ehrenreich, Barbara. 1981. "The women's movement: Feminist and anti-feminist." *Radical America* 15(Spring).

——. 1983. *The Hearts of Men.* Garden City, N.Y.: Doubleday Anchor.

——. 1984. "The body politic." *Ms.* (May) 12:52–53.

——, and Deirdre English. 1978. *For Her Own Good: 150 Years of the Experts' Advice to Women.* Garden City, N.Y.: Doubleday Anchor.

Eichler, Margrit. 1978. "Women's unpaid labour." *Atlantis* 3, Part 2:52–62.

——. 1980. *The Double Standard: A Feminist Critique of Feminist Social Science.* New York: St. Martin's Press.

——. 1983. *Families in Canada Today: Recent Changes and Their Policy Consequences.* Toronto: Gage.

——. 1984. "Sexism in research and its policy implications." Pp. 17–39 in Jill McCalla Vickers (ed.), *Taking Sex Into Account: The Policy Consequences of Sexist Research.* Ottawa: Carleton University Press.

——, and Jeanne Lapointe. 1985. *On the Treatment of the Sexes in Research.* Ottawa: Social Sciences and Research Council of Canada.

Elkin, Frederick, and Gerald Handel. 1984. *The Child and Society: The Process of Socialization.* Fourth Edition. New York: Random House.

Ellis, Godfrey J. 1983. "Youth in the electronic environment: An introduction." *Youth & Society* 15:3–12.

Ellmann, Mary. 1968. *Thinking about Women.* New York: Harcourt Brace Jovanovich.

Engels, Friedrich. 1902. *Origins of the Family, Private Property and the State.* Chicago: Charles H. Kerr.

English, Deirdre. 1982. "The war against choice: Inside the anti-abortion movement." *Mother Jones* (February/March):16–32.

Epstein, Cynthia F. 1981. "Women in sociological analysis: New scholarship versus old paradigms." Pp. 149–62 in Elizabeth Langland and Walter Gove (eds.), *A Feminist Perspective in the Academy.* Chicago: University of Chicago Press.

——, and Rose F. Coser (eds.), 1980. *Access to Power: Cross-National Studies of Women and Elites.* London: George Allen and Unwin.

Erikson, Erik H. 1963. *Childhood and Society.* Second Edition. New York: W.W. Norton.

——. 1968. *Identity: Youth and Crisis.* New York: W.W. Norton.

Exline, R.V., S. Ellyson, and B. Long. 1974. "Visual behavior as an aspect of power role relationships." Pp. 21–52 in P. Pliner, L. Kramer, and T. Alloway (eds.), *Nonverbal Communication in Aggression.* New York: Plenum.

Farrell, Barry. 1971. "You've come a long way, buddy." *Life,* August 27:51.

Farrell, Warren. 1974. *The Liberated Man.* New York: Random House.

Fasteau, Marc Feigen. 1975. *The Male Machine.* New York: Dell.

Fausto-Sterling, Anne. 1985. *Myths of Gender: Biological Theories About Women and Men.* New York: Basic Books.

Felson, Richard B. 1985. "Reflected appraisal and the development of self." *Social Psychology Quarterly* 48:71–78.

Festinger, Leon, Henry W. Riecken and Stanley Schachter. 1956. *When Prophecy Fails.* New York: Harper & Row.

Fine, Gary Alan. 1977. "Popular culture and social interaction: Production, consumption, and usage." *Journal of Popular Culture* 11:453–466.

Finlayson, Judith. 1984. "Gender." *Homemaker's Magazine,* 19 (October):10–21.

Finn, Jeremy D., Loretta Dulberg, and Janet Reis. 1979. "Sex differences in educational attainment: A cross-national perspective." *Harvard Educational Review* 49:477–503.

Firestone, Melvin M. 1978. "Socialization and interaction in a Newfoundland outport." *Urban Life* 7:91–110.

Firestone, Shulamith. 1971. *The Dialectic of Sex: The Case for Feminist Revolution.* New York: Bantam Books.

Firth, R.R. 1973. *Symbols: Public and Private.* Ithaca, N.Y.: Cornell University Press.

Fishman, Mark. 1978. "Crime waves as ideology." *Social Problems* 25:531–543.

Fishman, Pamela M. 1978. "Interaction: The work women do." *Social Problems* 25:397–406.

Fonda, Jane. 1981. *Jane Fonda's Workout Book.* New York: Simon and Schuster.

Foote, Audrey C. 1982. "The kids who won't leave home." Pp. 357–363 in Jeffrey P. Rosenfeld (ed.), *Relationships: The Marriage and Family Reader.* New York: Random House.

Ford, Catherine. 1983. "Leave-me-alone-group tunes out." *The Calgary Herald* (July 23).

Fouts, Gregory T. 1980. "Parents as censors of TV content for their children." *Journal of the Canadian Association for Young Children* 6:20–31.

Fowke, Edith. 1969. *Sally Go Round the Sun.* Toronto: McClelland and Stewart.

Fox, Bonnie (ed.), 1980. *Hidden in the Household: Women's Domestic Labour Under Capitalism.* Toronto: Women's Educational Press.

Fox, Greer Litton. 1977. " 'Nice girl': social control of women through a value construct." *Signs* 2:805–817.

Frances, S.J. 1979. "Sex differences in nonverbal behavior." *Sex Roles* 5:519–535.

Frank, Anne. 1952. *The Diary of a Young Girl.* New York: Washington Square Press.

Frank, Arthur W. III. 1979. "Reality construction in interaction." *Annual Review of Sociology* 5:167–191.

Franks, David D. and Joseph Marolla. 1976. "Efficacious action and social approval as interacting dimensions of self-esteem: A tentative formulation through construct validation." *Sociometry* 39:324–341.

Freedman, Daniel G. 1979. *Human Sociobiology.* New York: Free Press.

Freeman, Derek. 1983. *Margaret Mead and Samoa.* Cambridge, MA.: Harvard University Press.

Freimuth, Marilyn J., and Gail A. Hornstein. 1982. "A critical examination of the concept of gender." *Sex Roles* 8:515–532.

French, Marilyn. 1977. *The Women's Room.* New York: Summit Books.

Freud, Sigmund. 1927/1975. "Some psychological consequences of the anatomical distinction between the sexes." Reprinted in Rhoda Kesler Unger and Florence L. Denmark (eds.), *Women: Dependent or Independent Variable?* New York: Psychological Dimensions.

Friedan, Betty. 1963. *The Feminine Mystique.* Harmondsworth, England: Penguin Books.

———. 1981. *The Second Stage.* New York: Summit Books.

Friedl, Ernestine. 1975. *Women and Men: An Anthropologist's View.* New York: Holt, Rinehart and Winston.

———. 1978. "Society and sex roles." *Human Nature* (April):70.

Frieze, Irene H., Jacquelynne E. Parsons, Paula B. Johnson, Diane N. Ruble, and Gail L. Zellman. 1978. *Women and Sex Roles: A Social Psychological Perspective.* New York: W.W. Norton.

Fromm, Erich. 1961. *Marx's Concept of Man.* New York: Frederick Ungar.

Gacslay, Sari, and Cheryl Borges. 1979. "The male physique and behavioral expectancies." *Journal of Psychology* 101:97–102.

Gagnon, John H. 1976. "Physical strength, once of significance." Pp. 169–178 in Deborah S. David and Robert Brannon (eds.), *The Forty-nine Percent Majority: The Male Sex Role.* Reading, MA.: Addison-Wesley.

Gagnon, John H., and Cathy S. Greenblat. 1982. "Rehearsals and realities: Beginning to date." Pp. 125–135 in Jeffrey P. Rosenfeld (ed.), *Relationships: The Marriage and Family Reader*, New York: Random House.

Gans, Herbert J. 1966. "Popular culture in America: Social problems in a mass society or social asset in a pluralist society?" Pp. 549–620 in Howard S. Becker (ed.), *Social Problems: A Modern Approach*. New York: Wiley.

Garfinkel, Harold. 1967. *Studies in Ethnomethodology*. Englewood Cliffs, N.J.: Prentice-Hall.

Garn, Stanley M. 1966. "Body size and its implications." Pp. 529–561 in Lois W. Hoffman and Martin L. Hoffman (eds.), *Review of Child Development Research*. Vol. 2. New York: Russell Sage Foundation.

Garnets, Linda, and Joseph H. Pleck. 1979. "Sex role identity, androgyny, and sex role transcendence: A sex role strain analysis." *Psychology of Women Quarterly* 3:270–283.

Gecas, Viktor. 1981. "Contexts of socialization." Pp. 165–199 in Morris Rosenberg and Ralph H. Turner (eds.), *Social Psychology: Sociological Perspectives*. New York: Basic Books.

———. 1982. "The self-concept." *Annual Review of Sociology* 8:1–33.

———, and Michael Schwalbe. 1983. "Beyond the looking-glass self: Social structure and efficacy-based self-esteem." *Social Psychology Quarterly* 46:77–88.

Geer, James, Julia Heiman, and Harold Leitenberg. 1984. *Human Sexuality*. Englewood Cliffs, N.J.: Prentice-Hall.

Gerbner, George. 1978. "The dynamics of cultural resistance." Pp. 46–50 in G. Tuchman, A.K. Daniels, and J. Benet (eds.), *Hearth and Home*. New York: Oxford University Press.

———, and Larry Gross. 1976. "The scary world of TV's heavy viewer." *Psychology Today* 9 (April):41–45, 89.

Gerson, Mary-Joan, Judith L. Alpert, and Mary Sue Richardson. 1984. "Mothering: The view from psychological research." *Signs* 9:434–453.

Gerth, H. and C.W. Mills. 1953. *Character and Social Structure*. New York: Harcourt, Brace and World.

Gibbins, Roger, J. Rick Pointing, and Gladys L. Symons. 1978. "Attitudes and ideology: Correlates of liberal attitudes towards the role of women." *Journal of Comparative Family Studies* 9:19–40.

Gilligan, Carol. 1979. "Woman's place in man's life cycle." *Harvard Educational Review* 49:431–446.

———. 1982. *In a Different Voice*. Cambridge, MA.: Harvard University Press.

Gillis, John R. 1974. *Youth and History*. New York: Academic Press.

Gilman, Charlotte Perkins. 1935/1975. *The Living of Charlotte Perkins Gilman: An Autobiography*. New York: Harper & Row.

Glaser, Barney G., and Anselm L. Strauss. 1967. *The Discovery of Grounded Theory*. Chicago: Aldine.

Glazer, Nona. 1977. "Introduction to part two," in Nona Glazer and Helen Youngelson Waehrer (eds.), *Woman in a Man-Made World*. Second Edition. Chicago: Rand McNally.

Glick, Ira, Robert Weiss, and C. Murray Parkes. 1974. *The First Year of Bereavement*. New York: John Wiley and Sons.

Goddard, John. 1985. "Lady oracle." *Books in Canada* 14 (November):6–8,10.

Goffman, Erving. 1952. "On cooling the mark out: some aspects of adaptation to failure." *Psychiatry* 15:451–463.

———. 1959. *The Presentation of Self in Everyday Life*. Garden City, N.Y.: Doubleday Anchor.

———. 1961a. *Asylums*. Garden City, New York: Doubleday Anchor.

———. 1961b. *Encounters*. Indianapolis: Bobbs-Merrill.

———. 1963. *Stigma: Notes On the Management of Spoiled Identity*. Englewood Cliffs, N.J.: Prentice-Hall.

———. 1967. *Interaction Ritual*. Garden City, N.Y.: Doubleday Anchor.

———. 1971. *Relations in Public*. New York: Basic Books.

———. 1974. *Frame Analysis: An Essay on the Organization of Experience*. Cambridge, MA.: Harvard University Press.

———. 1976. *Gender Advertisements*. New York: Harper and Row.

———. 1977. "The arrangement between the sexes." *Theory and Society* 4:301–331.

Gold, D. and Andres, D. 1978. "Developmental comparisons between ten-year-old children with employed and nonemployed mothers." *Child Development* 49:75–84.

Goldberg, Herb. 1976. *The Hazards of Being Male: Surviving the Myth of Masculine Privilege*. New York: Signet.

Goode, William J. 1960. "A theory of role strain." *American Sociological Review* 25:483–496.

Goodenough, E.W. 1957. "Interest in persons as an aspect of sex differences in the early years." *Genetic Psychology Monographs* 55:287–323.

Goodman, Paul. 1956. *Growing up Absurd.* New York: Vintage Book, Random House.

Gordon, Chad. 1968. "Self-conceptions: Configurations of content." Pp. 115–136 in Chad Gordon and Kenneth J. Gergen (eds.), *The Self in Social Interaction.* New York: John Wiley & Sons.

Gordon, Steven L. 1981. "The sociology of sentiments and emotion." Pp. 562–592 in Morris Rosenberg and Ralph H. Turner (eds.), *Social Psychology: Sociological Perspectives.* New York: Basic Books.

Gornick, Vivian and Barbara K. Moran. 1971. "Introduction." Pp. xiii–xxxii in Vivian Gornick and Barbara K. Moran (eds.), *Woman in Sexist Society.* New York: New American Library.

Gould, Lois. 1972. "X: A fabulous child's story." *Ms.* (December):74–76, 105–106.

Gould, Meredith. 1980. "Review essay: The new sociology." *Signs* 5:459–467.

———, and Rochelle Kern-Daniels. 1977. "Toward a sociological theory of gender and sex." *The American Sociologist* 12:182–189.

Gove, Walter R. 1972. "Sex, marital status, and suicide." *Journal of Health and Social Behavior* 13:204–213.

———. 1980. "Mental illness and psychiatric treatment among women." *Psychology of Women Quarterly* 4:345–362.

———, and Michael Hughes. 1979. "Possible causes of the apparent sex differences in physical health: An empirical investigation." *American Sociological Review* 44:126–146.

———, and Jeannette F. Tudor. 1973. "Adult sex roles and mental illness." *American Journal of Sociology* 78:812–835.

Gray, J. Patrick. 1979. "The universality of the female witch." *International Journal of Women's Studies* 2:541–550.

Grayson, J. Paul. 1983. "Culture, ideology and social control." Pp. 372–409 in J. Paul Grayson (ed.), *Introduction to Sociology: An Alternate Approach.* Toronto: Gage.

Green, Richard. 1979. *Human Sexuality.* Second Edition. Baltimore: Williams & Wilkins.

———, and John Money. 1969. *Transsexualism and Sex Reassignment.* Baltimore: Johns Hopkins Press.

Green, S.K., and P. Sandos. 1980. "Perceptions of male and female initiators of relationships." Paper presented at meeting of the American Psychological Association, Montreal.

Greenberger, E., and L. Steinberg. 1981. "The workplace as a context for the socialization of youth." *Journal of Youth and Adolescence* 10:185–210.

———, and L. Steinberg. 1983. "Sex differences in early labor force experience: Harbinger of things to come." *Social Forces* 62:467–486.

Greenglass, Esther R. 1982. *A World of Difference: Gender Roles in Perspective.* Toronto: John Wiley & Sons.

Greer, Germaine. 1971. *The Female Eunuch.* New York: McGraw Hill.

———. 1979. *The Obstacle Race: The Fortunes of Women Painters and Their Work.* New York: Farrar, Straus, & Giroux.

———. 1984a. *Sex and Destiny.* New York: Harper and Row.

———. 1984b. "The uses of chastity and other paths to sexual pleasure." *Ms.* 12(April):53, 58–60, 96.

Greif, Esther Blank. 1976. "Sex role playing in pre-school children." Pp. 385–391 in Jerome S. Bruner, Alison Jolly and Kathy Sylva (eds.), *Play: Its Role in Development and Education.* Harmondsworth, Middlesex, England: Penguin Books.

———. 1979. "Sex differences in parent-child conversations: Who interrupts whom." Paper presented at meetings of the Society for Research on Child Development, San Francisco. (March).

Griffin, Susan. 1971. "Rape: The all-American crime." *Ramparts* 10 (September):26–35.

———. 1981. *Pornography and Silence: Culture's Revenge Against Nature.* New York: Harper & Row.

Groch, A.S. 1974. "Generality of response to humor and wit in cartoons, jokes, stories, and photographs." *Psychological Reports* 35:835–838.

Gross, Edward, and Gregory P. Stone. 1964. "Embarrassment and the analysis of role requirements." *American Journal of Sociology* 70:1–15.

Gusfield, Joseph R. and Jerzy Michalowicz. 1984. "Secular symbolism: Studies of ritual, ceremony, and the symbolic order in modern life." *Annual Review of Sociology* 10:417–435.

Haas, Adelaide. 1979. "Male and female spoken language differences: Stereotypes and evidence." *Psychological Bulletin* 86:616-626.

Haas, Jack and William Shaffir. 1978. *Shaping Identity in Canadian Society.* Scarborough, Ontario: Prentice-Hall.

Haas-Hawkings, Gwen, Sandra Sangster, Michael Ziegler and David Reid. 1985. "A study of relatively immediate adjustment to widowhood in later life." *International Journal of Women's Studies* 8:158–166.

Hacker, Helen Mayer. 1951. "Women as a minority group." *Social Forces* 30:60–69.

Hall, Edward T. 1959. *The Silent Language.* New York: Fawcett World Library.

Hall, M. Ann. (n.d.) *Sport and Gender: A Feminist Perspective on the Sociology of Sport.* Ottawa: Canadian Association for Health, Physical Education and Recreation.

———. 1980. "Rarely have we asked why: Reflections on Canadian women's experience in sport." *Atlantis* 6:51–60.

Hall, Elizabeth. 1980. "Acting one's age: New rules for old." (Interview of Bernice Neugarten.) *Psychology Today* 13 (April):66–80.

Hall, G. Stanley. 1904. *Adolescence* (2 volumes). New York: Appleton.

Halvorson, Marilyn. 1984. *Cowboys Don't Cry.* Toronto: Clarke Irwin.

Hamilton, Roberta. 1978. *The Liberation of Women.* London: George Allen & Unwin.

Hanisch, Carol. 1971. "Male psychology: A myth to keep women in their place." *Women's World* 1 (July–August):2.

Harding, Deborah and Emily Nett. 1984. "Women and rock music." *Atlantis* 10:60-76.

Harper, Paula. 1985. "The first feminist art program: A view from the 1980s." *Signs* 10:762–781.

Harris, D.A. 1974. "Androgyny: The sexist myth in disguise." *Women's Studies* 2:171–184.

Harris, Marvin. 1981. "Why it's not the same old America." *Psychology Today* 15 (August): 22–51.

Hartley, Ruth E. 1959. "Sex-role pressures in the socialization of the male child." *Psychological Reports* 5:457–468.

———. 1964. "A developmental view of female sex-role definition and identification." *Merrill-Palmer Quarterly* 10:3–16.

Hartmann, Heidi I. 1981. "The family as the locus of gender, class, and political struggle: The example of housework." *Signs* 6:366–394.

Hawley, Nancy P., and Wendy Sanford. 1984. "Psychotherapy." Pp. 73–76 in the Boston Women's Health Book Collective, *The New Our Bodies, Ourselves.* New York: Simon & Schuster.

Hebdige, Dick. 1979. *Subculture: The Meaning of Style.* London: Methuen.

Hefner, R., M. Rebecca and B. Oleshansky. 1975. "Development of sex-role transcendence." *Human Development* 18:143–156.

Henley, Nancy M. 1975. "Power, sex, and nonverbal communication." Pp. 184–203 in Barrie Thorne and Nancy Henley (eds.), *Language and Sex: Difference and Dominance.* Rowley, MA: Newbury House.

———. 1977. *Body Politics: Power, Sex and Nonverbal Communication.* Englewood Cliffs, N.J.: Prentice-Hall.

———. 1985. "Psychology and gender." *Signs* 11:101–119.

———, and Jo Freeman. 1979. "The sexual politics of interpersonal behavior." Pp. 474–486 in Jo Freeman (ed.), *Women: A Feminist Perspective.* Second Edition. Palo Alto, CA.: Mayfield.

———, Mykol Hamilton, and Barrie Thorne. 1985. "Womanspeak and manspeak: Sex differences and sexism in communication, verbal and nonverbal." Pp. 168–185 in Alice G. Sargent (ed.), *Beyond Sex Roles.* Second Edition. St. Paul, Minnesota: West Publishing.

Herold, Edward S. 1984. *Sexual Behavior of Canadian Young People.* Markham, Ontario: Fitzhenry & Whiteside.

———, D. Mantle, and O. Zemitis. 1979. "The study of sexual offenses against females." *Adolescence* 14:65–72.

Hess, Beth B. 1985. "Aging policies and old women: The hidden agenda." Pp. 319–331 in Alice S. Rossi (ed.), *Gender and the Life Course.* New York: Aldine.

Hetherington, E.M., M. Cox, and R. Cox. 1979. "The aftermath of divorce." In J.H. Stevens and M. Matthews. (eds.), *Mother-Child, Father-Child Relations.* Washington, D.C.: National Association for Education.

Hewitt, John P. 1984. *Self and Society: A Symbolic Interactionist Social Psychology.* Third Edition. Boston: Allyn and Bacon.

Hobart, Charles W. 1981. "Sources of egalitarianism in young unmarried Canadians." The Canadian Journal of Sociology 6:261–282.

Hochschild, Arlie Russell. 1975a. "Disengagement theory: A critique and proposal." *American Sociological Review* 40:553–569.

———. 1975b. "The sociology of feeling and emotion: Selected possibilities." Pp. 280–307 in Marcia Millman and Rosabeth Moss Kanter (eds.), Another Voice: Feminist Perspectives on Social Life and Social Science. Garden City, N.Y.: Doubleday Anchor.

———. 1979. "Emotion work, feeling rules, and social structure." *American Journal of Sociology* 85:551–575.

———. 1983a. "Attending to, codifying and managing feelings: Sex differences in love." Pp. 250–262 in Laurel Richardson and Verta Taylor (eds.), *Feminist Frontiers: Rethinking Sex, Gender, and Society.* Reading, MA.: Addison-Wesley.

———. 1983b. *The Managed Heart: Commercialization of Human Feeling.* Berkeley: University of California Press.

Hoffman, D.M. and L.S. Fidell. 1979. "Characteristics of androgynous, undifferentiated, masculine, and feminine middle-class women." *Sex Roles* 5:765–781.

Horner, Matina. 1969. "Fail: Bright women." *Psychology Today* 3 (November):36,38,62.

Howard, Jane. 1984. *Margaret Mead: A Life.* New York: Simon and Schuster.

Hrdy, Sarah Blaffer. 1981. *The Woman that Never Evolved.* Cambridge, MA.: Harvard University Press.

Huber, Joan. 1976. "Toward a socio-technological theory of the women's movement." *Social Problems* 23:371–388.

Huber, Joan and Glenna Spitze. 1980. "Considering divorce: An expansion of Becker's theory of marital instability." *American Journal of Sociology* 86:75–89.

Hughes, Everett C. 1958. *Men and Their Work.* Glencoe, Il.: Free Press.

Hunter, Alfred A. 1981. *Class Tells: On Social Inequality in Canada.* Toronto: Butterworth & Co.

Hunter College Women's Studies Collective. 1983. *Women's Realities, Women's Choices: An Introduction to Women's Studies.* New York: Oxford University Press.

Huston, Aletha C. 1983. "Sex typing." Pp. 387–467 in Paul H. Mussen (ed.), *Handbook of Child Psychology,* Volume IV. (E. Mavis Hetherington, Volume Editor). New York: John Wiley & Sons.

Huston-Stein, A. and A. Higgins-Trenk. 1977. "The development of females: Career and feminine role aspersions." In P.B. Baltes (ed.), *Life-span Development and Behavior.* Vol. I. New York: Academic Press.

Hyde, Janet S. 1981. "How large are cognitive gender differences?" *American Psychologist* 36:892–901.

———, and B.G. Rosenberg. 1980. *Half the Human Experience.* Second Edition. Lexington, MA.: D.C. Heath.

———, B.G. Rosenberg and J. Behrman. 1977. "Tomboyism." *Psychology of Women Quarterly* 2:73–75.

Inglis, J. and J. Lawson. 1981. "Sex differences in the effects of unilateral brain damage on intelligence." *Science* 212:693–695.

Ishwaran, K. 1979. "An overview of theory and research." Pp. 3–36 in K. Ishwaran (ed.), *Childhood and Adolescence in Canada.* Toronto: McGraw-Hill Ryerson.

Israel, Lee. 1984. "Joan Rivers—and how she got that way." *Ms.* 13(October):108–114.

Jacklin, C.N. and Maccoby, E.E. 1978. "Social behavior at 33 months in same-sex and mixed-sex dyads." *Child Development* 49:557–569.

Jaggar, Alison. 1986. "The feminist challenge to Western political theory." Paper delivered at the University of Calgary, March 6th.

———, and Paula S. Rothenberg. 1984. *Feminist Frameworks: Alternative Theoretical Accounts of the Relations Between Women and Men.* Second Edition. New York: McGraw-Hill.

James, William. 1910/1968. *Psychology: The Briefer Course.* Pp. 41–49 reprinted in Chad Gordon and Kenneth J. Gergen (eds.), *The Self in Social Interaction.* New York: John Wiley & Sons.

Janeway, E. 1974. *Between Myth and Morning: Women Awakening.* New York: Morrow.

Jardine, Alice. 1979. "Interview with Simone de Beauvoir." *Signs* 5:224–236.

Jenkins, Mercilee M. and Chris Kramarae. 1981. "A thief in the house: Women and language." Pp. 11–22 in Dale Spender (ed.), *Men's Studies Modified: The Impact of Feminism on the Academic Disciplines.* Oxford: Pergamon Press.

Jenks, Chris. 1982. "Introduction: Constituting the child." Pp. 9–24 in Chris Jenks (ed.), *The Sociology of Childhood.* London: Batsford.

Jorgensen, Christine. 1968. *A Personal Autobiography.* New York: Bantam Books.

Jourard, Sidney M. 1964. *The Transparent Self.* New York: Van Nostrand, Reinhold.

Jung, Carl G. 1926. *Psychological Types.* New York: Harcourt, Brace.

Juteau-Lee, Danielle and Barbara Roberts. 1981. "Ethnicity and femininity: (d')aprés nos experiences." *Canadian Ethnic Studies* 13:1–23.

Kando, Thomas. 1973. *Sex Change: The Achievement of Gender Identity Among Feminized Transsexuals.* Springfield, Il.: Charles C. Thomas.

Kane, Thomas R., Jerry Suls, and James T. Tedeschi. 1977. "Humour as a tool of social interaction." Pp. 13–16 in Anthony J. Chapman and Hugh C. Foot (eds.), *It's A Funny Thing, Humour.* Oxford: Pergamon Press.

Kanter, Rosabeth Moss. 1976. "The impact of hierarchical structures on the work behavior of women and men." *Social Problems* 23:415–430.

―――. 1977a. *Men and Women of the Corporation.* New York: Basic Books.

―――. 1977b. "Some effects of proportions on group life: skewed sex ratios and responses to token women." *American Journal of Sociology* 82:965–990.

Kaplan, Jane Rachel. 1980. *A Woman's Conflict: The Special Relationship between Women and Food.* Englewood Cliffs, N.J.: Prentice-Hall.

Katz, Michael and Ian E. Davey. 1978. "Youth and early industrialization in a Canadian city." Pp. S81–S119 in John Demos and Sarane Spence Boocock (eds.), *Turning Points: Historical and Sociological Essays on the Family.* Chicago: University of Chicago Press.

Katz, Phyllis A. 1979. "The development of female identity." Pp. 3–28 in Claire B. Kopp (ed.), *Becoming Female: Perspectives on Development.* New York: Plenum Press.

―――, and S.R. Zalk. 1974. "Doll preferences: An index of social attitudes." *Journal of Educational Psychology* 66:663–668.

Kealey, Linda. 1979. "Introduction." Pp. 1–14 in Linda Kealey (ed.), *A Not Unreasonable Claim: Women and Reform in Canada, 1880s–1920s.* Toronto: The Women's Press.

Keasey, C.B. and C.I. Tomlinson-Keasey. 1971. "Social influence in a high-ego-involvement situation: A field study of petition signing." Paper presented at meeting of the Eastern Psychological Association, New York City, April.

Kerber, Linda K., et al. 1986. "On *In a Different Voice*: An interdisciplinary forum." *Signs* 11:304–333.

Kesey, Ken. 1962. *One Flew over the Cuckoo's Nest.* New York: Viking Press (Signet).

Kessler, Suzanne J., and Wendy McKenna. 1978. *Gender: An Ethnomethodological Approach.* New York: John Wiley and Sons.

Kimball, Meredith M. 1981. "Women and science: A critique of biological theories." *International Journal of Women's Studies* 4:318–338.

Kincaid, Pat J. 1982. *The Omitted Reality: Husband-Wife Violence in Ontario and Policy Implications for Education.* Maple, Ontario: Publishing and Printing Services.

Kinsella, W.P. 1982. *Shoeless Joe.* New York: Ballantine Books.

Kinsey, Alfred C., et al. 1953. *Sexual Behavior in the Human Female.* Philadelphia: W.B. Saunders.

Klapp, Orrin E. 1969. *Collective Search for Identity.* New York: Holt, Rinehart and Winston.

―――. 1972. *Currents of Unrest: An Introduction to Collective Behavior.* New York: Holt, Rinehart and Winston.

Klein, Alan M. and Jan Slater. 1985. "Pumping iron." *Society* 22 (Sept/Oct):68–75.

Knill, Barbara J., Marina Pesch, George Pursey, Paul Gilpin, and Richard M. Perloff. 1981. "Still typecast after all these years? Sex role portrayals in television advertising." *International Journal of Women's Studies* 4:497–506.

Kochman, Thomas. 1969. " 'Rapping' in the black ghetto." *Trans-action* 6: (February):26–34.

Kohlberg, Lawrence. 1966. "A cognitive-developmental analysis of children's sex-role concepts and attitudes." Pp. 82–172 in Eleanor Maccoby (ed.), *The Development of Sex Differences.* Stanford, CA.: Stanford University Press.

Kollock, Peter, Philip Blumstein, and Pepper Schwartz. 1985. "Sex and power in inter-action: Conversational privileges and duties." *American Sociological Review* 50:34–46.

Komarovsky, Mirra. 1946. "Cultural contradictions and sex roles." *American Journal of Sociology* 52:184–189.

———. 1976. *Dilemmas of Masculinity: A Study of College Youth.* New York: W.W. Norton.

Kome, Penney. 1983. *The Taking of Twenty-eight: Women Challenge the Constitution.* Toronto: Women's Press.

Konopka, G. 1973. "Replacements for healthy development of adolescent youth." *Adolescence* 8:291–316.

Kopinak, Kathryn M. 1983. "Polity." Pp. 401–431 in Robert Hagedorn (ed.), *Sociology, Second Edition.* Toronto: Holt, Rinehart and Winston.

Kostash, Myrna. 1982. "Whose body? Whose self? Beyond pornography." Pp. 43–54 in Maureen Fitzgerald, Connie Guberman and Margie Wolfe (eds.), *Still Ain't Satisfied! Canadian Feminism Today.* Toronto: The Women's Press.

Kamer, Cheris, Barrie Thorne and Nancy Henley. 1978. "Perspectives on language and communication." *Signs* 3:638–651.

Kuhn, Manford H. 1960. "Self-attitudes by age, sex, and professional training." *Sociological Quarterly* 9:39–55.

Kuhn, Manford H., and Thomas S. McPartland. 1954. "An empirical investigation of self-attitudes." *American Sociological Review* 19:68–76.

Kuklick, Henrika. 1983. "The sociology of knowledge: Retrospect and prospect." *Annual Review of Sociology* 9:287–310.

Kunkel, John H. 1977. "Sociobiology vs. biosociology." *The American Sociologist* 12:69–73.

Lahey, Kathleen A. 1984. "Research on child abuse in liberal patriarchy." Pp. 156–184 in Jill McCalla Vickers (ed.), *Taking Sex Into Account.* Ottawa: Carleton University Press.

Lakoff, Robin. 1975. *Language and Woman's Place.* New York: Harper and Row.

Lamb, M.E. 1978. "Influence of the child on marital quality and family interaction during the prenatal, natal, and infancy periods." Pp. 137–164 in R. Lerner and G. Spanier (eds.), *Child Influences on Marital and Family Interaction.* New York: Academic Press.

Lamb, Theodore A. 1981. "Nonverbal and paraverbal control in dyads and triads: Sex or power differences?" *Social Psychology Quarterly* 44:49–53.

Lambert, Ronald D. 1971. *Sex Role Imagery in Children: Social Origins of Mind.* Royal Commission on the Status of Women in Canada, Study 6. Ottawa: Information Canada.

Lambert, Wallace E., Josiane F. Hamers, and Nancy Frasure-Smith. 1980. *Child-Rearing Values: A Cross-National Study.* New York: Praeger.

Lamphere, Louise. 1977. "Anthropology." *Signs* 2:612–627.

Landsberg, Michele. 1982. *Women & Children First.* Markham, Ontario: Penguin Books.

Lanser, Susan Smader and Evelyn Torton Beck. 1979. "[Why] are there no great women critics?: And what difference does it make?" Pp. 79–91 in Julia A. Sherman and Evelyn Torton Beck (eds.), *The Prism of Sex: Essays in the Sociology of Knowledge.* Madison, WI.: The University of Wisconsin Press.

Laron, Elaine. 1974. "What are little boys made of?" P. 38 in Ms. Foundation, Inc., *Free to Be . . . You and Me.* New York: McGraw-Hill.

LaRossa, R. and M.M. LaRossa. 1981. *Transition to Parenthood.* Beverly Hills: Sage.

Larson, Reed, and Robert Kubey. 1983. "Television and music: Contrasting media in adolescent life." *Youth & Society* (15):13–31.

Lasch, Christopher. 1979. *The Culture of Narcissism.* New York: W.W. Norton.

Lauer, Robert H., and Warren H. Handel. 1983. *Social Psychology: The Theory and Application of Symbolic Interactionism.* Second Edition. Englewood Cliffs, N.J.: Prentice-Hall.

Laws, Judith Long. 1979. *The Second X: Sex Role and Social Role.* New York: Elsevier.

———, and Pepper Schwartz. 1977. *Sexual Scripts: The Social Construction of Female Sexuality.* Hinsdale, Il.: Dryden.

Leacock, Eleanor. 1978. "Women's status in egalitarian society: Implications for social evolution." *Current Anthropology* 19:247–275.

Leaman, Dana. 1983. "The Dinner Party." *Glenbow* 3(January-February):4–5.

Lederer, Laura. 1980a. "Introduction," Pp. 15–20 in Laura Lederer (ed.), *Take Back the Night: Women on Pornography.* New York: William Morrow.

———. 1980b. "Playboy isn't Playing: An interview with Judith Bat-Ada." Pp. 121–133 in Laura Lederer (ed.), *Take Back the Night: Women on Pornography.* New York: William Morrow.

Lee, John Alan. 1982. "Three paradigms of childhood." *The Canadian Review of Sociology and Anthropology* 19:591–608.
Leo, John. 1985. "Bringing Dr. Spock up-to-date." *Time* Magazine, (April 8):65,67–68.
Lessing, Doris. 1962. *The Golden Notebook.* London: Michael Joseph.
Lester, Julius. 1973. "Being a boy." *Ms.* 2(July):112–113.
Lever, Janet. 1976. "Sex differences in the games children play." *Social Problems* 23:478–487.
———. 1978. "Sex differences in the complexity of children's play." *American Sociological Review* 43:471–483.
Levin, Jack, and Arnold Arluke. 1985. "An exploratory analysis of sex differences in gossip." *Sex Roles* 12:281–286.
Levinson, D.J. 1978. *The Seasons of a Man's Life.* New York: Alfred A. Knopf.
Lewin, Ellen, and Virginia Olesen (eds.). 1985. *Women, Health and Healing.* New York: Tavistock.
Lewis, Michael. 1972. "Culture and gender roles: There's no unisex in the nursery." *Psychology Today,* 5(May):54–57.
Liebert, Robert M., Joyce N. Sprafkin, and Emily S. Davidson. 1982. *The Early Window: Effects of Television on Children and Youth.* Second Edition. New York: Pergamon Press.
Lifshin, Lyn (ed.). 1982. *Ariadne's Thread: A Collection of Contemporary Women's Journals.* New York: Harper & Row.
Lindemann, Eric. 1944. "Symptomology and management of acute grief." *American Journal of Psychiatry* 101:141–148.
Lindesmith, Alfred, and Anselm Strauss. 1968. *Social Psychology.* New York: Holt, Rinehart and Winston.
———, Anselm L. Strauss, and Norman K. Denzin. 1977. *Social Psychology.* Fifth Edition. New York: Holt, Rinehart and Winston.
Lipman-Blumen, Jean. 1984. *Gender Roles and Power.* Englewood Cliffs, N.J.: Prentice-Hall, Inc.
———, and Ann R. Tickamyer. 1975. "Sex roles in transition: A ten-year perspective." *Annual Review of Sociology* 1:297–337.
Lippmann, Walter. 1922. *Public Opinion.* New York: Harcourt and Brace.
Lips, Hilary M. 1981. *Women, Men, and the Psychology of Power.* Englewood Cliffs, N.J.: Prentice-Hall.
———. 1983. "Attitudes toward childbearing among women and men expecting their first child." *International Journal of Women's Studies* 6:119–129.
Lofland, Lyn H. 1975. "The 'thereness' of women: A selective review of urban sociology." Pp. 44–170 in Marcia Millman and Rosabeth Moss Kanter (eds.), *Another Voice: Feminist Perspectives on Social Life and Social Science.* Garden City, N.Y.: Doubleday Anchor.
Long, Karen R. 1983. "Desire for sons may have dangerous results." Newhouse News Service: November 3.
Longino, Helen and Ruth Doell. 1983. "Body, bias, and behavior: A comparative analysis of reasoning in two areas of biological science." *Signs* 9:206–227.
Lopata, Helena Z. 1971. *Occupation: Housewife.* New York: Oxford University Press.
———. 1973. "Self-identity in marriage and in widowhood." *The Sociological Quarterly* 14:407–418.
———. 1979. *Women as Widows: Support Systems.* New York: Elsevier North-Holland.
———. 1984. "The self-concept, identities and traumatic events: The death of a husband." Paper presented at the International Conference on Self and Identity, Cardiff, Wales.
Lothstein, Leslie M. 1982. "Sex reassignment surgery: Historical, bioethical, and theoretical issues." *American Journal of Psychiatry* 139:417–425.
Lott, Bernice. 1981. "A feminist critique of androgyny: Toward the elimination of gender attributions for learned behavior." Pp. 171–180 in Clara Mayo and Nancy M. Henley (eds.), *Gender and Nonverbal Behavior.* New York: Springer-Verlag.
Lowe, Graham S. 1980. "Women, work and the office: The feminization of clerical occupations in Canada, 1901–1931." *Canadian Journal of Sociology* 5:361–381.
———, and Harvey J. Krahn. 1984. "Work values and job satisfaction: Editors' introduction." Pp. 1–3 in Graham S. Lowe and Harvey J. Krahn (eds.), *Working Canadians: Readings in the Sociology of Work and Industry.* Toronto: Methuen.
———, and Harvey Krahn. 1985. "Where wives work: The relative effects of situational and attitudinal factors." *Canadian Journal of Sociology* 10:1–22.
Lowenthal, M.M. et al. 1975. *Four Stages of Life.* San Francisco: Jossey-Bass.

Lundberg, Ferdinand, and Marynia F. Farnham. 1947. *Modern Woman: The Last Sex*. New York: Harper and Bros.

Lupri, Eugene, and Donald L. Mills. 1983. "The changing roles of Canadian women in family and work: An overview." Pp. 43–77 in Eugene Lupri (ed.), *The Changing Roles of Women in Family and Society: A Cross-Cultural Comparison*. Leiden, Netherlands: E.J. Brill.

———, and Donald L. Mills. 1987. "The household division of labour in young dual-earner couples: The case of Canada." *International Review of Sociology* 23 (forthcoming).

Luxton, Meg. 1980. *More Than a Labour of Love: Three Generations of Women's Work in the Home*. Toronto: The Women's Press.

Lyman, Stanford M., and Marvin B. Scott. 1970. *A Sociology of the Absurd*. New York: Appleton-Century Crofts.

Lynn, David B. 1959. "A note on sex differences in the development of masculine and feminine identification." *Psychological Review* 66:126–135.

———. 1969. *Parental and Sex-role Identification: A Theoretical Formulation*. Berkeley, CA.: McCutchan.

Lyon, Nancy. 1972. "Toys: More than child's play." *Ms.* (December):54–56, 58–63.

Maccoby, Eleanor E. 1980. *Social Development: Psychological Growth and the Parent-Child Relationship*. New York: Harcourt Brace Jovanovich.

———, and Carol Nagy Jacklin. 1974. *The Psychology of Sex Differences*. Stanford, CA.: Stanford University Press.

MacFarlane, Jeanie. 1984. "Stories of sex change." *The Calgary Sunday Sun*, April 1: S19.

MacKay, Donald G. 1980. "Psychology, prescriptive grammar, and the pronoun problem." *American Psychologist* 35:444–449.

MacKay, Susanne. 1979. "Women artists in Canada: An Atlantis Gallery of women's art." *Atlantis* 5:unpaginated.

Mackie, Marlene. 1971. "The accuracy of folk knowledge concerning Alberta Indians, Hutterites, and Ukrainians." Unpublished Ph.D. dissertation, University of Alberta (Edmonton).

———. 1973. "Arriving at 'truth' by definition: The case of stereotype inaccuracy." *Social Problems* 20:431–447.

———. 1976. "Role constraints and married women." Paper presented at symposium on "The Working Sexes," University of British Columbia, Vancouver, British Columbia.

———. 1977a. "On congenial truths: A perspective on women's studies." *Canadian Review of Sociology and Anthropology* 14:117–128.

———. 1977b. "Professional women's collegial relations and productivity: Female sociologists' journal publications, 1967 and 1973." *Sociology and Social Research* 61:277–293.

———. 1978. "Ethnicity and nationality: How much do they matter to Western Canadians?" *Canadian Ethnic Studies* 10:118–129.

———. 1979. "Gender socialization in childhood and adolescence." Pp. 136–160 in K. Ishwaran (ed.), *Childhood and Adolescence in Canada*. Toronto: McGraw-Hill Ryerson.

———. 1983a. "The domestication of self: Gender comparisons of self-imagery and self-esteem." *Social Psychology Quarterly* 46:343–350.

———. 1983b. *Exploring Gender Relations: A Canadian Perspective*. Toronto: Butterworths.

———. 1984a. "Gender and self-imagery: A critique of the 'two worlds' metaphor." Paper presented at the British Psychological Society Conference on Self and Identity, Cardiff, Wales, July 1984.

———. 1984b. "Socialization: Changing views of child rearing and adolescence." Pp. 35–62 in Maureen Baker (ed.), *The Family: Changing Trends in Canada*. Toronto: McGraw-Hill Ryerson.

———. 1985. "Female sociologists' productivity, collegial relations, and research style examined through journal publications." *Sociology and Social Research* 69:189–209.

———. 1986a. "The material self and the blemished self: Gender and self-conceptions." The University of Calgary, unpublished study.

———. 1986b. "Socialization." Pp. 63–97 in Robert Hagedorn (ed.), *Sociology*. Third Edition. Toronto: Holt, Rinehart and Winston.

———, and Merlin B. Brinkerhoff. 1984. "Measuring ethnic salience." *Canadian Ethnic Studies* 16:114–131.

———, and Merlin B. Brinkerhoff. 1986. "A crack in the looking glass: The enigma of female self-esteem." The University of Calgary: unpublished manuscript.

MacKinnon, Catharine A. 1982. "Feminism, Marxism, method, and the state: An agenda for theory." *Signs* 7:515–544.

Madsen, Jane. 1979. "Women and children's literature: We read what we are and we are what we read." Pp. 207–227 in Eloise C. Snyder (ed.), *The Study of Women: Enlarging Perspectives of Social Reality.* New York: Harper & Row.

Mahoney, Kathleen. 1984. "Obscenity, morals and the law: A feminist viewpoint." *The University of Calgary Gazette* (November 21): 4, 6.

Maines, David R. 1977. "Social organization and social structure in symbolic interactionist thought." *Annual Review of Sociology* 3:235–259.

———. 1981. "Recent developments in symbolic interaction." Pp. 461–486 in Gregory P. Stone and Harvey A. Faberman (eds.), *Social Psychology through Symbolic Interaction.* Second Edition. New York: John Wiley & Sons.

Malamuth, Neil M. and Barry Spinner. 1980. "A longitudinal content analysis of sexual violence in the best-selling erotic magazines." *The Journal of Sex Research* 16:226–237.

Manion, Eileen. 1985. "We objects object: Pornography and the women's movement." Pp. 65–80 in Marilouise and Arthur Kroker, Pamela McCallum, and Mair Verthay (eds.), *Feminism Now: Theory and Practice.* Montreal: New World Paperbacks.

Manis, Jerome G. and Bernard N. Meltzer. 1978. "Intellectual antecedents and basic propositions of symbolic interactionism." Pp. 1–9 in Jerome G. Manis and Bernard N. Meltzer (eds.), *Symbolic Interaction: A Reader in Social Psychology.* Third Edition. Boston: Allyn and Bacon.

Mannheim, Karl. 1936. *Ideology and Utopia.* New York: Harcourt, Brace & World.

———. 1952. "The problem of generations." In P. Kectskemeti (ed.), *Karl Mannheim: Essays in the Sociology of Knowledge.* London: Routledge and Kegan Paul.

Marchak, M. Patricia. 1975. *Ideological Perspectives on Canada.* Toronto: McGraw-Hill Ryerson.

Marini, Margaret Mooney, and Ellen Greenberger. 1978. "Sex differences in occupational aspirations and expectations." *Sociology of Work and Occupations* 5:147–178.

Marks, Julie. 1979. " 'On the road to find out': The role music plays in adolescent development." Pp. 333–362 in Claire B. Kopp (ed.), *Becoming Female: Perspectives on Development.* New York: Plenum Press.

Marks, Stephen R. 1977. "Multiple roles and role strain: Some notes on human energy, time, and commitment." *American Sociological Review* 42:921–936.

Marsden, Lorna R., and Edward B. Harvey. 1979. *Fragile Federation: Social Change in Canada.* Toronto: McGraw-Hill Ryerson.

Marsh, Jeanne C., Mary Ellen Colten, and M. Belinda Tucker. 1982. "Women's use of drugs and alcohol: New perspectives." *Journal of Social Issues* 38:1–8.

Marshall, Victor W. 1978-79. "No exit: A symbolic interactionist perspective on aging." *International Journal of Aging and Human Development* 9:345–358.

Marshall, Victor W. 1980. *Last Chapters: A Sociology of Aging and Dying.* Monterey. CA.: Brooks/Cole.

Martel, Angeline, and Linda Peterat. 1984. "Naming the world: Consciousness in a patriarchal iceberg." Pp. 43–56 in Jill McCalla Vickers (ed.), *Taking Sex Into Account: The Policy Consequences of Sexist Research.* Ottawa: Carleton University Press.

Martin, Elaine. 1984. "Power and authority in the classroom: Sexist stereotypes in teaching evaluations." *Signs* 9:482–492.

Martin, M. Kay, and Barbara Voorhies. 1975. *Female of the Species.* Toronto: Methuen.

Martyna, Wendy. 1980. "Beyond the 'he/man' approach; the case for nonsexist language." *Signs* 5:482–493.

Marx, Karl. 1963 (1846–47). *The Poverty of Philosophy.* New York: International.

———. 1859/1913. *A Contribution to the Critique of Political Economy.* Chicago: Kerr.

———, and Friedrich Engels. 1932/1947. *The German Ideology.* New York: International.

Maslow, Abraham. 1954. *Motivation and Personality.* New York: Harper & Row.

Masters, W., and V. Johnson. 1966. *Human Sexual Response.* Boston: Little, Brown.

Matalene, Carolyn. 1978. "Women as witches." *International Journal of Women's Studies* 1:573–587.

Matthews, Anne Martin. 1980. "Women and widowhood," in Victor W. Marshall (ed.), *Aging in Canada: Social Perspectives.* Don Mills: Fitzhenry and Whiteside.

Matthews, Sarah H. 1979. *The Social World of Old Women: Management of Self-identity.* Beverly Hills: Sage.

——. 1982. "Rethinking sociology through a feminist perspective." *The American Sociologist* 17:29–35.

Maynard, Fredelle. 1985. *The Child Care Crisis.* Markham, Ontario: Penguin Books.

Maynard, Rona. 1984. "Women and men: Is the difference brain-deep?" *Chatelaine* 57(October):76,86,88,90,98.

McCall, George J., and J.L. Simmons. 1978. *Identities and Interactions.* Revised Edition. New York: Free Press.

McClelland, David C. 1961. *The Achieving Society.* New York: Free Press.

McClung, Nellie L. 1915/1972. *In Times Like These.* Toronto: University of Toronto Press.

McCormack, Thelma. 1978. "Machismo in media research: A critical review of research on violence and pornography." *Social Problems* 22:544–555.

——. 1981. "Good theory or just theory? Toward a feminist philosophy of social science." *Women's Studies International Quarterly* 4:1–12.

——. 1984. "Censorship may not be answer to porn." *CAUT Bulletin* (February):27.

McCormick, Naomi B., and Clinton J. Jesser. 1983. "The courtship game: Power in the sexual encounter." Pp. 64–86 in Elizabeth R. Allgeier and Naomi B. McCormick (eds.), *Changing Boundaries: Gender Roles and Sexual Behavior.* Palo Alto, CA.: Mayfield.

McDaniel, Susan A. 1985. "Implementation of abortion policy in Canada as a women's issue." *Atlantis* 10:74–91.

McDonnell, Kathleen, and Mariana Valverde (eds.). 1985. *The Healthsharing Book: Resources for Canadian Women.* Toronto: Women's Press.

McGhee, Paul E. 1979. "The role of laughter and humor in growing up female." Pp. 183–206 in Claire B. Kopp (ed.), *Becoming Female: Perspectives on Development.* New York: Plenum Press.

McKie, D.C., B. Prentice, and P. Reed. 1983. *Divorce: Law and the Family in Canada.* Ottawa: Statistics Canada.

McNulty, Faith. 1982. "Children's books for Christmas." *The New Yorker* (December 6): 176–182.

McVey, Wayne W., Jr., and Barrie W. Robinson. 1981. "Separation in Canada: New insights concerning marital dissolution." *Canadian Journal of Sociology* 6:353–366.

Mead, George Herbert. 1934. *Mind, Self, and Society.* Chicago: University of Chicago Press.

Mead, Margaret. 1928. *Coming of Age in Samoa.* New York: Mentor (The New American Library of World Literature).

——. 1935. *Sex and Temperament in Three Primitive Societies.* New York: Mentor Books (reprint of original edition by William Morrow and Company).

Meade, Marion. 1972. "The degradation of women." Pp. 173–177 in R. Serge Denisoff and Richard A. Peterson (eds.), *The Sounds of Social Change.* Chicago: Rand McNally.

Meissner, Martin, Elizabeth W. Humphreys, Scott M. Meis, and William J. Scheu. 1975. "No exit for wives: Sexual division of labour and the cumulation of household demands." *Canadian Review of Sociology and Anthropology* 12, Part 1:424–439.

Mellen, J. 1977. *Big Bad Wolves: Masculinity in the American Film.* New York: Pantheon.

Meltzer, Bernard N. 1978. "Mead's social psychology." Pp. 15–27 in Jerome G. Manis, and Bernard N. Meltzer (eds.), *Symbolic Interaction: A Reader in Social Psychology.* Third Edition. Boston: Allyn and Bacon.

——, John W. Petras, and Larry T. Reynolds. 1975. *Symbolic Interactionism: Genesis, Varieties and Criticism.* London: Routledge & Kegan Paul.

Menzies, Heather. 1984. "Women and microtechnology." Pp. 290–297 in Graham S. Lowe and Harvey J. Krahn (eds.), *Working Canadians.* Toronto: Methuen.

Merton, Robert K. 1957. *Social Theory and Social Structure.* Glencoe, Il.: Free Press.

Meyer, J.K., and D.J. Reter. 1979. "Sex reassignment: Follow-up." *Archives of General Psychiatry* 36:1910–1915.

Miles, Angela. 1982. "Introduction." Pp. 9–23 in Angela R. Miles and Geraldine Finn (eds.), *Feminism in Canada: From Pressure to Politics.* Montreal: Black Rose Books.

Miller, Jim, et al. 1985. "Rock's new women." *Newsweek,* March 4th:48–57.

Miller, Joanne, and Howard Garrison. 1982. "Sex roles: The division of labor at home and in the workplace." *Annual Review of Sociology* 8:237–262.

Miller, Patricia Y., and Martha R. Fowlkes. 1980. "Social and behavioral constructions of female sexuality." *Signs* 5:783–800.

Millett, Kate. 1970. *Sexual Politics*. New York: Avon Books.

Millman, Marcia. 1980. *Such a Pretty Face: Being Fat in America*. New York: Berkley Books.

———, and Rosabeth Moss Kanter. 1975. "Editorial Introduction." Pp. vii–xvii in Marcia Millman and Rosabeth Moss Kanter (eds.), *Another Voice: Feminist Perspectives on Social Life and Social Science*. Garden City, N.Y.: Doubleday Anchor.

Mills, C. Wright. 1940. "Situated actions and vocabularies of motive." *American Sociological Review* 5:904–913.

———. 1951. *White Collar*. New York: Oxford University Press.

———. 1959. *The Sociological Imagination*. New York: Grove Press.

Mitchell, Martyn Hall. 1978. "Sexist art criticism: Georgia O'Keeffe—a case study." *Signs* 3:681–687.

Mitchinson, Wendy. 1980. Review of Barbara Ehrenreich and Deirdre English, *For Her Own Good: 150 Years of the Experts' Advice to Women*. *Atlantis* 6:118–119.

Molloy, John T. 1976. *Dress for Success*. New York: Warner Books.

Molotch, Harvey L. 1978. "The news of women and the work of men." Pp. 176–185 in Gaye Tuchman, Arlene Kaplan Daniels, and James Benet (eds.), *Hearth and Home: Images of Women in the Mass Media*. New York: Oxford University Press.

———, and Deirdre Boden. 1985. "Talking social structure: Discourse, domination, and the Watergate hearings." *American Sociological Review* 50:273–288.

Money, John, and A.A. Ehrhardt. 1972. *Man and Woman, Boy and Girl: The Differentiation and Dimorphism of Gender Identity from Conception to Maturity*. Baltimore, MD.: Johns Hopkins University Press.

Morgan, A.J. 1978. "Psychotherapy for transsexual candidates screened out of surgery." *Archives of Sexual Behavior* 7:273–283.

Morgan, Michael, and Nancy Rothschild. 1983. "Impact of the new television technology: Cable TV, peers, and sex-role cultivation in the electronic environment." *Youth & Society* 15:33–50.

Morgan, Robin. 1980. "Theory and practice: Pornography and rape." Pp. 134–140 in Laura Lederer (ed.), *Take Back the Night: Women on Pornography*. New York: William Morrow.

Morris, Cerise. 1980. "'Determination and thoroughness: The movement for a Royal Commission on the Status of Women in Canada." *Atlantis* 5:1–21.

Morris, Jan. 1974. *Conundrum*. New York: Harcourt Brace Jovanovich.

Mortimer, Jeylan T., and Roberta G. Simmons. 1978. "Adult socialization." *Annual Review of Sociology* 4:421–454.

Munro, Alice. 1968. *The Dance of the Happy Shades*. Toronto: McGraw-Hill Ryerson.

Murdock, Graham. 1974. "Mass communication and the construction of meaning." Pp. 205–220 in Nigel Armistead (ed.), *Reconstructing Social Psychology*. Harmondsworth, England: Penguin Books.

Murphy, G., L. Murphy, and T. Newcomb. 1937. *Experimental Social Psychology*. New York: Harper & Row.

Nathanson, Constance. 1977. "Sex, illness and medical care: A review of data, theory and method." *Social Science and Medicine* 111:13–25.

———. 1984. "Sex differences in mortality." *Annual Review of Sociology* 10:191–213.

Nemerowicz, Gloria Morris. 1979. *Children's Perceptions of Gender and Work Roles*. New York: Praeger.

Nett, Emily M. 1978. "A research note: On reviewing the Canadian literature on marital interaction, 1967–77." *Journal of Comparative Family Studies* 9:373–383.

———. 1981a. "Canadian families in social-historical perspective." *Canadian Journal of Sociology* 6:239–260.

———. 1981b. "Gender and the Canadian introductory sociology textbook." *Atlantis* 7, 127–133.

Nettler, Gwynn. 1978. *Explaining Crime*. Second Edition. New York: McGraw-Hill.

Neugarten, B.L. 1968. "The awareness of middle age." Pp. 93–98 in B.L. Neugarten (ed.), *Middle Age and Aging: A Reader in Social Psychology*. Chicago: University of Chicago Press.

———. 1974. "Age groups in American society and the rise of the young-old." *Annals of the American Academy of Political and Social Science* 415:189–198.

———, and N. Datan. 1974. "Sociological perspectives on the life cycle." Pp. 53–69 in P.B. Bates and K.W. Schaie (eds.), *Life-span Development Psychology: Personality and Socialization*. New York: Academic Press.

————, and D.C. Garron. 1965. "Attitudes of middle-aged persons toward growing older." Pp. 12–17 in C.D. Vedder (ed.), *Problems of the Middle Aged.* Springfield, II.: Charles C. Thomas.

————, et al. 1968. "Women's Attitudes toward the menopause." Pp. 195–200 in B.L. Neugarten (ed.), *Middle Age and Aging: A Reader in Social Psychology.* Chicago: University of Chicago Press.

Newcomb, Paul R. 1982. "Cohabitation in America: An assessment of consequences." Pp. 143–152 in Jeffrey P. Rosenfeld (ed.), *Relationships: The Marriage and Family Reader.* New York: Random House.

Nicholson, John. 1984. *Men and Women: How Different Are They?* New York: Oxford University Press.

Nielsen, Joyce McCarl. 1979. "From corrective to creative progress in sex stratification: Sociological and anthropological contributions." *International Journal of Women's Studies* 2:324–339.

Nochlin, Linda. 1971. "Why are there no great women artists?" Pp. 480–510 in Vivian Gornick and Barbara K. Moran (eds.), *Women in Sexist Society.* New York: Basic Books.

————. 1973. "Why have there been no great women artists." in Thomas Hess and Elizabeth Baker (eds.), *Art and Sexual Politics,* New York: Collier Books.

Novak, Mark. 1985. *Successful Aging: The Myths, Realities and Future of Aging in Canada.* Markham, Ontario: Penguin Books.

Nowotny, H. 1980. "Women in public life in Austria." Pp. 147–156 in C.F. Epstein, and R.L. Coser (eds.), *Access to Power: Cross-National Studies of Women and Elites.* London: George Allen and Unwin.

Nugent, Andrea. 1982. "Canada's silenced communicators: A report on women in journalism and public relations." *Atlantis* 7:125–135.

Oakley, Ann. 1972. *Sex, Gender and Society.* New York: Harper & Row.

————. 1974. *The Sociology of Housework.* London: Martin Robertson.

————. 1980. *Women Confined: Towards a Sociology of Childbirth.* London: Martin Robertson.

O'Brien, Mary. 1979. "Reproducing Marxist man." In L. Clark and L. Lange (eds.), *The Sexism of Social and Political Theory.* Toronto: University of Toronto.

————. 1981. *The Politics of Reproduction.* London: Routledge and Kegan Paul.

O'Kelly, Charlotte G. 1983. "Gender role stereotypes in fine art: A content analysis of art history books." *Qualitative Sociology* 6:136–148.

Olesen, Virginia, and Ellen Lewin. 1985. "Women, health, and healing: a theoretical introduction." Pp. 1–24 in Ellen Lewin and Virginia Olesen (eds.), *Women, Health and Healing.* New York: Tavistock.

Orbach, Susie. 1978. *Fat Is a Feminist Issue.* New York: Berkley.

Orenstein, Gloria Feman. 1975. "Art history." *Signs* 1:505–525.

Ortner, Sherry B. 1974. "Is female to male as nature is to culture?" Pp. 67–87 in Michele Zimbalist Rosaldo and Louise Lamphere (eds.), *Woman, Culture, and Society.* Stanford, CA.: Stanford University Press.

————, and Harriet Whitehead. 1981. "Introduction: Accounting for sexual meanings," Pp. 1–27 in Sherry B. Ortner and Harriet Whitehead (eds.), *Sexual Meanings: The Cultural Construction of Gender and Sexuality.* Cambridge: Cambridge University Press.

Osgood, C.E., G.J. Suci, and P.H. Tannenbaum. 1957. *The Measurement of Meaning.* Urbana, II.: University of Illinois Press.

Palmore, Erdman. 1971. "Attitudes toward aging as shown by humor." *The Gerontologist* 25–26 (Autumn):181–186.

Panelas, Tom. 1983. "Adolescents and video games: Consumption of leisure and the social construction of the peer group." *Youth & Society* 15:51–65.

Papanek, H. 1973. "Men, women and work: Reflections on the two-person career." *American Journal of Sociology* 78:90–110.

Parker, Stanley. 1982. *Work and Retirement.* London: George Allen & Unwin.

————. 1983. *Leisure and Work.* London: George Allen & Unwin.

Parsons, Talcott. 1954. "Age and sex in the social structure of the United States." In *Essays in Sociological Theory.* Revised Edition. New York: Free Press of Glencoe.

————. 1955. "Sex roles and family structure." In Talcott Parsons and Robert F. Bales (eds.), *Family Socialization and Interaction Process.* Glencoe, II.: Free Press.

Pearson, Judy Cornelia. 1985. *Gender and Communication.* Dubuque, IO.: Wm. C. Brown.

298   *Constructing Women & Men*

Pearson, Willie, Jr., and Maxine L. Clark. 1982. "The Mal(e) treatment of American women in gynecology and obstetrics." *International Journal of Women's Studies* 5:348–362.
Peplau, Letitia Anne. 1983. "Roles and gender." Pp. 220–264 in Harold H. Kelley et al., *Close Relationships*. New York: W.H. Freeman.
Peters, John. 1982. "Children as socialization agents through the parents' middle-years." Paper presented at the Canadian Sociology and Anthropology Association meetings, April. Ottawa, Ontario.
———. 1983. "Divorce: The disengaging, disengaged, and re-engaging process." Pp. 277–288 in K. Ishwaran (ed.), in *The Canadian Family*. Toronto: Gage.
Peterson, Richard A. 1977. "Where the two cultures meet: Popular culture." *Journal of Popular Culture* 11:385–400.
Pfeiffer, John. 1985. "Girl talk, boy talk." *Science* 85, Vol. 6(Jan/February):58–63.
Phillips, Paul, and Erin Phillips. 1983. *Women and Work: Inequality in the Labour Market*. Toronto: James Lorimer.
Phillips, Susan U. 1980. "Sex differences and language." *Annual Review of Anthropology* 9:523–544.
Piaget, Jean. 1928. *Judgment and Reasoning in the Child*. New York: Harcourt.
———. 1932/1965. *The Moral Judgment of the Child*. New York: The Free Press.
Pierson, Ruth. 1977. "Women's emancipation and the recruitment of women into the labour force in World War II." Pp. 125–145 in Susan Mann Trofimenkoff and Alison Prentice (eds.), *The Neglected Majority*. Toronto: McClelland and Stewart.
———, and Alison Prentice. 1982. "Feminism and the writing and teaching of history." *Atlantis* 7:37–46.
Pleck, Joseph H. 1977. "The work-family role system." *Social Problems* 24:417–427.
———. 1981a. *The Myth of Masculinity*. Cambridge, MA.: MIT Press.
———. 1981b. "Men's power with women, other men, and society: A men's movement analysis." Pp. 234–244 in Robert A. Lewis (ed.), *Men in Difficult Times*. Englewood Cliffs, N.J.: Prentice-Hall.
———. 1984. "How psychology constructed masculinity: The theory of male sex-role identity." Pp. 278–286 in Alice G. Sargent (ed.), *Beyond Sex Roles*. Second Edition. St. Paul, Minnesota: West.
———, and Jack Sawyer. 1974. *Men and Masculinity*. Englewood Cliffs, N.J.: Prentice-Hall.
Polk, Barbara Bovee. 1972. "Women's liberation: Movement for equality." Pp. 321–330 in Constantina Safilios–Rothschild (ed.), *Toward a Sociology of Women*. Lexington, MA.: Xerox College Publishing.
Posner, Judith. 1975. "Dirty old women: Buck Brown's cartoons." *Canadian Review of Sociology and Anthropology* 12:471–473.
———. 1979. "It's all in your head: Feminist and medical models of menopause (strange bedfellows)." *Sex Roles* 5:179–190.
———. 1980. "Old and female: The double whammy." Pp. 80–87 in Victor W. Marshall (ed.), *Aging in Canada*. Don Mills, Ontario: Fitzhenry and Whiteside.
Press, Andrea. 1985. "The differential effects of liberal feminism on working-class and middle-class women." Paper presented at the Pacific Sociological Association meeting, Albuquerque, New Mexico, April.
Prince, Virginia. 1978. "Transsexuals and pseudotranssexuals." *Archives of Sexual Behavior* 7:263–272.
Proefrock, David W. 1981. "Adolescence: Social fact and psychological concept." *Adolescence* 16:851–858.
Propper, Alice. 1984. "The invisible reality: Patterns and power in family violence." Pp. 104–128 in Maureen Baker (ed.), *The Family: Changing Times in Canada*. Toronto: McGraw-Hill Ryerson.
Pyke, S.W. 1975. "Children's literature: Conceptions of sex roles." Pp. 51–73 in Robert M. Pike and Elia Zureik (eds.), *Socialization and Values in Canadian Society*, Vol. 2. Toronto: McClelland and Stewart.
———. 1980. "Androgyny: A dead end or a promise?" Pp. 20–32 in Cannie Stark-Adamec (ed.), *Sex Roles: Origins, Influences, and Implications for Women*. Montreal: Eden Press.
———, and J.C. Stewart. 1974. "This column is about women: Women and television." *The Ontario Psychologist* 6:66–69.
Rabkin, Brenda. 1985. *Loving & Leaving*. Toronto: McClelland and Stewart.

Ramu, G.N. 1983. "Courtship and marriage." Pp. 246–262 in K. Ishwaran (ed.), *The Canadian Family*. Toronto: Gage.

Raymond, Janice G. 1979. *The Transsexual Empire*. Boston: Beacon Press.

Reeves, Joy B., and Nydia Boyette. 1983. "What does children's art work tell us about gender? *Qualitative Sociology* 6:322–336.

Reinstein, P. Gila. 1984. "Sex roles in recent picture books." *Journal of Popular Culture* 17:116–123.

Reitzes, Donald C. 1980. "Beyond the looking glass self: Cooley's social self and its treatment in introductory textbooks." *Contemporary Sociology* 9:631–640.

Remmling, Gunter W. 1973. "Existence and thought." Pp. 3–43 in Gunter W. Remmling (ed.), *Towards the Sociology of Knowledge: Origin and Development of a Sociological Thought Style*. London: Routledge & Kegan Paul.

Restak, Richard M. 1979. "The sex-change conspiracy." *Psychology Today* (December):20–25.

Rheingold, Harriet L. 1966. "The development of social behavior in the human infant." In H.W. Stevenson (ed.), *Concept of Development: A Report of a Conference Commemoration of the 40th Anniversary of the Institute of Child Development, University of Minnesota*. Monographs of the Society for Research in Child Development:31(5, whole No. 107.).

———. 1969. "The social and socializing infant." Pp. 779–790 in David A. Goslin (ed.) *Handbook of Socialization Theory and Research*. Chicago: Rand McNally.

———, and K. Cook. 1975. "The content of boys' and girls' rooms as an index of parent behavior." *Child Development* 46:459–463.

Rich, Adrienne. 1976. *Of Woman Born*. New York: Bantam Books.

Richards, Renée. 1983. *Second Serve*. New York: Stein and Day.

Richardson, Laurel Walum. 1981. *The Dynamics of Sex and Gender*. Second Edition. Boston: Houghton Mifflin.

Richer, Stephen. 1979. "Sex-role socialization and early schooling." *The Canadian Review of Sociology and Anthropology* 16:195–205.

———. 1983. "Sex role socialization: Agents, content, relationships, and emotions." Pp. 117–125 in K. Ishwaran (ed.), *The Canadian Family*. Toronto: Gage.

———. 1984. "Sexual inequality and children's play." *The Canadian Review of Sociology and Anthropology* 21:166–180.

Richmond-Abbott, Marie. 1983. *Masculine and Feminine: Sex Roles Over the Life Cycle*. Reading, MA.: Addison-Wesley.

Rickel, Annette U., and Lynn R. Anderson. 1981. "Name ambiguity and androgyny." *Sex Roles* 7:1057–1066.

———, and Linda M. Grant. 1979. "Sex role stereotypes in the mass media and schools: five consistent themes." *International Journal of Women's Studies* 2:164–179.

Riley, Matilda White. 1985. "Women, men, and the lengthening life course." Pp. 333–347 in Alice S. Rossi (ed.), *Gender and the Life Course*. New York: Aldine.

———, Anne Foner, Beth Hess, and Marcia L. Toby. 1969. "Socialization for the middle and later years." Pp. 951–982 in David A. Goslin (ed.), *Handbook of Socialization Theory and Research*. Chicago: Rand McNally.

Riley, Susan. 1985. "Anti-feminist group incensed over lack of funding." *The Calgary Herald* (July 2).

Rinehart, James W. 1975. *The Tyranny of Work*. Don Mills, Ontario: Academic Press Canada.

Roberts, Helen (ed.). 1981. *Doing Feminist Research*. London: Routledge and Kegan Paul.

Robertson, Heather. 1975. "The honourable Judy." Pp. 1–17 in Myrna Kostash et al., *Her Own Woman: Profiles of Ten Canadian Women*. Toronto: Macmillan of Canada.

Robinson, Barbara. 1972. *The Best Christmas Pageant Ever*. New York: Avon.

Robinson, Gertrude Joch. 1983. "The media and social change: Thirty years of magazine coverage of women and work (1950–1977)." *Atlantis* 8:87–111.

Rodgers, Joann Ellison. 1985. "The best health kick of all." *Ms.* 13 (May):57–60, 140–141.

Rogers, Dorothy. 1981. *Adolescents and Youth*. Fourth Edition. Englewood Cliffs, N.J.: Prentice-Hall.

Roman, Neil, and William Haddad. 1978. *The Disposable Parent: The Case for Joint Custody*. Harmondsworth, England: Penguin Books.

Rome, Esther. 1984. "Food." Pp. 2–32 in the Boston Women's Health Book Collective, *The New Our Bodies, Ourselves*. New York: Simon & Schuster.

Romer, Nancy, and Debra Cherry. 1980. "Ethnic and social class differences in children's sex-role concepts." *Sex Roles* 6:245–263.

Ropers, Richard. 1973. "Mead, Marx, and social psychology." *Catalyst* 7:42–61.

Rosaldo, Michelle Zimbalist. 1974. "Woman, culture, and society: A theoretical overview." Pp. 17–42 in Michelle Zimbalist Rosaldo and Louise Lamphere (eds.), *Woman, Culture and Society.* Stanford, CA.: Stanford University Press.

———. 1980. "The use and abuse of anthropology: Reflections on feminism and cross-cultural understanding." *Signs* 5:389–417.

Rose, Peter I. (ed.). 1979. *Socialization and the Life Cycle.* New York: St. Martin's Press.

Rosenberg, Avis Lang. 1979. "Women artists and the Canadian art world." *Atlantis* 5:107–126.

Rosenberg, Bernard, and Norris Fliegel. 1971. "Prejudice against female artists." Pp. 660–665 in Athena Theodore (ed.), *The Professional Woman.* Cambridge, MA.: Schenkman.

Rosenberg, F., and R.G. Simmons. 1975. "Sex differences in the self-concept in adolescence." *Sex Roles* 1:147–159.

Rosenberg, Morris. 1965. *Society and the Adolescent Self-image.* Princeton, N.J.: Princeton University Press.

———. 1981. "The self-concept: Social product and social force." Pp. 593–624 in Morris Rosenberg and Ralph H. Turner (eds.), *Social Psychology: Sociological Perspective.* New York: Basic Books.

———, and Leonard I. Pearlin. 1978. "Social class and self-esteem among children and adults." *American Journal of Sociology* 84: 53–77.

———, and Roberta Simmons. 1972. *Black and White Self-esteem: The Urban School Child.* Washington, D.C.: American Sociological Association.

Rosow, I. 1974. *Socialization to Old Age.* Berkeley: University of California Press.

Ross, Aileen D. 1982. *The Lost and the Lonely: Homeless Women in Montreal.* Montreal: Canadian Human Rights Foundation.

Ross, Catherine E., and John Mirowsky. 1984. "Men who cry." *Social Psychology Quarterly* 47:138–146.

Ross, Val. 1983. "The joys of a bountiful season." *Maclean's* (December 19):40–48.

Rossan, Sheila. 1984. "Identity and its development in adulthood." Paper presented at British Psychological Society Self and Identity Conference, Cardiff, Wales (July).

Rossi, Alice. 1964. "Equality between the sexes." Pp. 98–143 in Robert Jay Lifton (ed.), *The Woman in America.* Boston: Houghton Mifflin.

Rossi, Alice S. (ed.), 1973. *The Feminist Papers.* New York; Bantam Books.

———. 1980. "Life-span theories and women's lives." *Signs* 6:4–32.

———. 1984. "Gender and parenthood." *American Sociological Review* 49:1–19.

Roth, Geneen. 1982. *Feeding the Hungry Heart: The Experience of Compulsive Eating.* New York: New American Library.

Rowbotham, Sheila. 1972. *Women, Resistance and Revolution.* New York: Vintage Books.

———. 1973. *Woman's Consciousness, Man's World.* Markham, Ontario: Penguin Books.

Roy, William G. 1984. "Class conflict and social change in historical perspective." *Annual Review of Sociology* 10:483–506.

Royal Commission on the Status of Women in Canada. 1970. *Report of the Royal Commission on the Status of Women in Canada.* Ottawa: Information Canada.

Rubin, J.Z., F.J. Provenzano, and Z. Luria. 1974. "The eye of the beholder: parents' views on sex of newborns." *American Journal of Orthopsychiatry* 44:512–519.

Rubin, Lillian B. 1976A. "Editorial." *Social Problems* 23:369–370.

———. 1976B. *World of Pain: Life in the Working-class Family.* New York: Basic Books.

———. 1979. *Women of a Certain Age: The Midlife Search for Self.* New York: Harper & Row.

———. 1983. *Intimate Strangers: Men and Women Together.* New York: Harper Colophon Books.

Ruble, Diane N., Terry Balaban, and Joel Cooper. 1981. "Gender constancy and the effects of sex-typed televised toy commercials." *Child Development* 52:667–673.

Rudofsky, Bernard. 1971. *The Unfashionable Human Body.* New York: Doubleday Anchor.

Russell, H. Diana. 1980. "Art history." *Signs* 5:468–481.

Ryan, William. 1971. *Blaming the Victim.* New York: Random House.

Sacks, Karen. 1974. "Engels revisited: Women, the organization of production, and private property." Pp. 207–222 in Michelle Zimbalist Rosaldo and Louise Lamphere (eds.), *Woman, Culture, and Society.* Stanford, CA.: Stanford University Press.

———. 1979. *Sisters and Wives: The Past and Future of Sexual Equality.* Westport, CT.: Greenwood Press.

Safilios-Rothschild, Constantina. 1974. *Women and Social Policy.* Englewood Cliffs, N.J.: Prentice-Hall.

Sales, Esther. 1978. "Women's adult development." Pp.157–190 in Irene H. Frieze et al., *Women and Sex Roles: A Social Psychological Perspective.* New York: W.W. Norton.

Sandmaier, Marian. 1984. "Alcohol, mood-altering drugs and smoking." Pp. 33–40 in the Boston Women's Health Book Collective, *The New Our Bodies, Ourselves.* New York: Simon & Schuster.

Sanford, Stephanie, and Donna Eder. 1984. "Adolescent humor during peer interaction." *Social Psychology Quarterly* 47:235–243.

Santrock, John W. 1984. *Adolescence.* Second Edition. Dubuque, IO.: Wm. C. Brown.

Sargent, Lydia (ed.). 1983. *Women and Revolution: A Discussion of the Unhappy Marriage of Marxism and Feminism.* Montreal: Black Rose Books.

Sassen, Georgia. 1980. "Success anxiety in women: A constructivist interpretation of its source and its significance." *Harvard Educational Review* 50:13–24.

Sattell, Jack W. 1983. "Men, inexpressiveness, and power." Pp. 242–246 in Laurel Richardson and Verta Taylor (eds.), *Feminist Frontiers.* Reading, MA.: Addison-Wesley.

Sayers, Janet. 1982. *Biological Politics: Feminist and Anti-Feminist Perspectives.* London: Tavistock.

Scanzoni, John, and Greer Litton Fox. 1980. "Sex roles, family and society: The seventies and beyond." *Journal of Marriage and the Family* 42:743–756.

Scheff, Thomas. 1966. *Being Mentally Ill.* Chicago. Aldine.

Schilder, Paul. 1968. "The image and appearance of the human body." Pp. 107–114 in Chad Gordon and Kenneth J. Gergen (eds.), *The Self in Social Interaction,* Vol. I. New York: John Wiley & Sons.

Schlesinger, Benjamin. 1970. "Remarriage as family reorganization for divorced persons: A Canadian study." *Journal of Comparative Family Studies* 1:101–118.

——. 1985. *The One-Parent-Family in the 1980s.* Toronto: University of Toronto Press.

Schneider, Joseph W., and Sally L. Hacker. 1973. "Sex role imagery and the use of the generic "man" in introductory texts: the case in the sociology of sociology." *The American Sociologist* 8:12–18.

Schudson, Michael. 1984. *Advertising, The Uneasy Persuasion.* New York: Basic Books.

Schuetz, Stephen, and Joyce N. Sprafkin. 1978. "Spot messages appearing within Saturday morning television programs." Pp. 69–77 in Gaye Tuchman, Arlene Kaplan Daniels, and James Benet (eds.), *Hearth and Home: Images of Women in the Mass Media.* New York: Oxford University Press.

Schulz, Muriel R. 1975. "The semantic derogation of woman." Pp. 64–75 in Barrie Thorne and Nancy Henley (eds.), *Language and Sex: Difference and Dominance.* Rowley, MA.: Newbury House.

Schur, Edwin M. 1984. *Labelling Women Deviant: Gender, Stigma, and Social Control.* New York: Random House.

Schutz, A. 1967. *The Phenomenology of the Social World.* Evanston, Il.: Northwestern University Press.

Schwendinger, Julia, and Herman Schwendinger. 1971. "Sociology's founding fathers: Sexists to a man." *Journal of Marriage and the Family* 33:783–799.

Scott, Joan Pinner. 1981. "Science subject choice and achievement of females in Canadian high schools." *International Journal of Women's Studies* 4:348–361.

Scully, Diana. 1980. *Men Who Control Women's Health: The Miseducation of Obstetrician-Gynecologists.* Boston: Houghton Mifflin.

——, and Pauline Bart. 1973. "A funny thing happened on the way to the orifice: Women in gynecology textbooks." *American Journal of Sociology* 78:1045–1050.

Senn, Charlene Y. 1985. "A comparison of women's reactions to non-violent pornography, violent pornography, and erotica." Unpublished Masters thesis, Department of Psychology, University of Calgary.

Serbin, L.A., I.J. Tonick, and S. Steinglanz. 1977. "Shaping cooperative cross-sex play." *Child Development* 48:924–929.

Shames, Lawrence. 1984. "New, revised (if not improved) rules of dating." *Esquire* 101 (June):254.

Shapiro, Judith. 1981. "Anthropology and the study of gender." Pp. 110–129 in Elizabeth Langland and Walter Gove (eds.), *A Feminist Perspective in the Academy.* Chicago: University of Chicago Press.

302   *Constructing Women & Men*

Shaw, Marvin E., and Philip R. Costanzo. 1982. *Theories in Social Psychology.* Second Edition. New York: McGraw-Hill.

Sheehy, Gail. 1974. *Passages.* New York: E.P. Dutton.

Sheinin, Rose. 1981. "The rearing of women for science, engineering and technology." *International Journal of Women's Studies* 4:339–347.

Sherif, Carolyn Wood. 1982. "Needed concepts in the study of gender identity." *Psychology of Women Quarterly* 6:375–398.

Shibutani, Tamotsu. 1955. "Reference groups as perspectives." *American Journal of Sociology* 60:562–569.

———. 1961. *Society and Personality.* Englewood Cliffs, N.J.: Prentice-Hall.

———. 1962. "Reference groups and social control." Pp. 128–147 in Arnold M. Rose (ed.), *Human Behavior and Social Processes: An Interactionist Approach.* Boston: Houghton Mifflin.

Shore, Valerie. 1982. "Woman steered away from science, says council." *University Affairs* (April) 23:4.

Shott, Susan. 1979. "Emotion and social life: A symbolic interactionist analysis." *American Journal of Sociology* 84:1317–1334.

Shulman, Alix Kates. 1980. "Sex and power: Sexual bases of radical feminism." *Signs* 5:590–604.

Sieber, Sam D. 1974. "Toward a theory of role accumulation." *American Sociological Review* 39:567–578.

Silverman, Elaine Leslau. 1982. "Writing Canadian women's history, 1970–82: An historiographical analysis." *Canadian Historical Review* 63:513–533.

———. 1984. *The Last Best West: Women on the Alberta Frontier 1880–1930.* Montreal: Eden Press.

Simmons, Roberta G. 1978. "Blacks and high self-esteem: A puzzle." *Social Psychology* 41:54–57.

Singer, J. 1976. *Androgyny.* Garden City, N.Y.: Doubleday Anchor.

Smith, C.W. 1985. "Uncle Dad." *Esquire,* 103 (March) 73–85.

Smith, Dorothy E. 1973. "Women, the family and corporate capitalism." Pp. 2–35 in Marylee Stephenson (ed.), *Women in Canada.* Toronto: new press.

———. 1974. "Women's perspective as a radical critique of sociology." *Sociological Inquiry* 44:7–13.

———. Smith, Dorothy E. 1975a. "An analysis of ideological structures and how women are excluded: Considerations for academic women." *Canadian Review of Sociology and Anthropology* 12, Part 1, 353–369.

———. 1975b. "Women and psychiatry." Pp. 1–19 in Dorothy E. Smith, and Sara J. David (eds.), *Women Look at Psychiatry.* Vancouver, B.C.: Press Gang Publishers.

———. 1979. "A sociology for women." Pp. 135–187 in Julia A. Sherman and Evelyn Torton Beck (eds.), *The Prism of Sex: Essays in the Sociology of Knowledge.* Madison, WI.: University of Wisconsin Press.

———. 1983. "Women, the family and the productive process." Pp. 312–344 in J. Paul Grayson (ed.), *Introduction to Sociology.* Toronto: Gage.

———. 1984. "The renaissance of women." Pp. 1–14 in Ursula Martius Franklin et al., *Knowledge Reconsidered: A Feminist Overview.* Ottawa: Canadian Research Institute for the Advancement of Women.

Smith, Goldwin. 1957. *A History of England.* Second Edition. New York: Charles Scribner's Sons.

Smith, Lesley A. 1978. "Sexist occupations and female delinquency: An empirical investigation." Pp. 74–88 in Carol Smart and Barry Smart (eds.), *Women, Sexuality and Social Control.* London: Routledge & Kegan Paul.

Smyth, Donna E. 1979. "Metaphors of madness: Women and mental illness." *Atlantis* 4:287–299.

Smyth, Michael, and Gregory McFarlane. 1985. "Sex-role stereotyping by psychologists and psychiatrists: A further analysis." *International Journal of Women's Studies* 8:130–139.

Snodgrass, J. (ed.), 1977. *For Men Against Sexism.* Albion: Times Change Press.

Snyder, Eloise C. 1979. "That half of 'mankind' called women: Introduction to women's studies." Pp. 1–12 in Eloise C. Snyder (ed.), *The Study of Women: Enlarging Perspectives of Social Reality.* New York: Harper & Row.

Sparling, Mary. 1979. "The lighter auxiliaries: Women artists in Nova Scotia in the early nineteenth century." *Atlantis* 5:83–106.

Special Committee on Pornography and Prostitution. 1985. *Pornography and Prostitution in Canada*. Ottawa: Supply and Services Canada.

Spence, Janet T. 1981. "Changing conceptions of men and women: A psychologist's perspective." Pp. 130–148 in Elizabeth Langland and Walter Gove (eds.), *A Feminist Perspective in the Academy*. Chicago: University of Chicago Press.

———. R.L. Helmreith, and J. Strapp. "Ratings of self and peers on sex-role attributes and their relation to self-esteem and conceptions of masculinity and femininity." *Journal of Personality and Social Psychology* 32:29–39.

Spender, Dale. 1981a. "The gatekeepers: a feminist critique of academic publishing." Pp. 186–202 in Helen Roberts (ed.), *Doing Feminist Research*. London: Routledge and Kegan Paul.

———. 1981B. "Introduction," Pp. 1–9 in Dale Spender (ed.), *Men's Studies Modified*. Oxford: Pergamon Press.

———. 1982. *Women of Ideas and What Men Have Done to Them*. London: Ark Paperbacks.

———. 1985. *Man Made Language*. Second Edition. London: Routledge & Kegan Paul.

Spock, Benjamin. 1976. *Baby and Child Care*. Fourth Edition. New York: Pocket Books.

Sprecher, Susan. 1985. "Sex differences in bases of power in dating relationships." *Sex Roles* 12:449–462.

Spreitzer, Elmer, Eldon E. Snyder, and David L. Larson. 1979. "Multiple roles and psychological well-being." *Sociological Focus* 12:141–148.

St. David, Lynne. 1983. " 'Tootsie brings out the artist in Dustin Hoffman." *The Calgary Herald* (January 4).

Stacey, Judith, and Barrie Thorne. 1985. "The missing feminist revolution in sociology." *Social Problems* 32:301–316.

Stanley, Julia. 1973. "Paradigmatic woman: The prostitute." Paper presented to South Atlanta Modern Language Association, 1972, *Linguistic Society of America*, 1973.

Stanley, Liz, and Sue Wise. 1983. *Breaking Out: Feminist Consciousness and Feminist Research*. London: Routledge & Kegan Paul.

Stannard, Una. 1971. "The masks of beauty." Pp. 187–203 in Vivian Gornick and Barbara K. Moran (eds.), *Woman in Sexist Society*. New York: New American Library.

Statistics Canada. 1984. *Survey News*. Vol. 1, No. 2 (October-November).

Statistics Canada. 1985. *Women in Canada: A Statistical Report*. Ottawa: Minister of Supply and Services Canada.

Stebbins, Robert A. 1967. "A theory of the definition of the situation." *The Canadian Review of Sociology and Anthropology* 4:148–164.

———. 1975. "Role distance, role distance behavior and jazz musicians." Pp. 133–141 in Dennis Brissett and Charles Edgley (eds.), *Life as Theater: A Dramaturgical Handbook*. Chicago: Aldine.

Stein, Dorothy K. 1978. "Women to burn: Suttee as a normative institution." *Signs* 4:253–268.

Steinem, Gloria. 1980. "Erotica and pornography: A clear and present difference." Pp. 35–39 in Laura Lederer (ed.), *Take Back the Night: Women on Pornography*. New York: William Morrow.

———. 1983a. *Outrageous Acts and Everyday Rebellions*. New York: Holt, Rinehart, and Winston.

———. 1983b. "Perspectives on women in the 1980s: The Baird Poskanzer Memorial Lecture." Pp. 14–27 in Joan Turner and Lois Emery (eds.), *Perspectives on Women in the 1980s*. Winnipeg: The University of Manitoba Press.

Stengel, E. 1984. *Suicide and Attempted Suicide*. Baltimore: Penguin.

Sternhell, Carol. 1985. "Some of us will always be fat, but fat can be fit." *Ms.* 13(May):66–68, 142–146, 154.

Stockard, Jean, and Miriam M. Johnson. 1980. *Sex Roles: Sex Inequality and Sex Role Development*. Englewood Cliffs, N.J.: Prentice-Hall.

Stogdill, Ralph. 1974. *Handbook of Leadership*. New York: Free Press.

Stoller, Robert J. 1968. *Sex and Gender: On the Development of Masculinity and Femininity*. New York: Science House.

Stone, Gregory P. 1962. "Appearance and the self." Pp. 86–118 in Arnold M. Rose (ed.), *Human Behavior and Social Processes*. Boston: Houghton Mifflin.

———. 1970. "The play of little children." Pp. 545–553 in Gregory P. Stone and Harvey A. Farberman (eds.), *Social Psychology Through Symbolic Interaction*. Waltham, MA.: Ginn-Blaisdell.

———, and Harvey A. Farberman. 1970. *Social Psychology Through Symbolic Interaction*. Waltham, MA.: Ginn-Blaisdell.

Strauss, Anselm L. 1969. *Mirrors and Masks: The Search for Identity*. San Francisco, CA.: The Sociology Press.

Strong-Boag, Veronica. 1972. "Introduction," to Nellie McClung, *In Times Like These*. Toronto: University of Toronto Press.

———. 1979. "Canada's women doctors: Feminism constrained." Pp. 109–129 in Linda Kealey (ed.), *Women and Reform in Canada, 1880s–1920s*. Toronto: The Women's Press.

———. 1982. "Intruders in the nursery: Child care professionals reshape the years one to five, 1920–1940." Pp. 160–178 in Joy Parr (ed.), *Childhood and Family in Canadian History*. Toronto: McClelland and Stewart.

———. 1983. "Mapping women's studies in Canada: Some signposts." *The Journal of Educational Thought* 17:94–111.

Stryker, Sheldon. 1964. "The interactional and situational approaches." Pp. 125–170 in Harold T. Christensen (ed.), *Handbook of Marriage and the Family*. Chicago: Rand McNally.

———. 1980. *Symbolic Interactionism: A Social Structural Version*. Menlo Park. CA.: Benjamin Cummings Publishing Company.

———. 1981. "Symbolic interactionism: Themes and variations." Pp. 3–29 in Morris Rosenberg and Ralph H. Turner (eds.), *Social Psychology: Sociological Perspectives*. New York: Basic Books.

Sutton-Smith, Brian. 1979. "The play of girls." Pp. 229–257 in Claire B. Kopp (ed.), *Becoming Female: Perspectives on Development*. New York: Plenum Press.

Swatos, William H.J., and Cynthia McCauley. 1984. "Working-class sex-role orientation." *International Journal of Women's Studies* 7:136–143.

Sydie, Rosalind. 1980. "Women painters in Britain: 1768–1848." *Atlantis* 5:144–175.

———. 1983. "Sociology and gender." Pp. 185–223 in M. Michael Rosenberg et al. (eds.), *An Introduction to Sociology*. Toronto: Methuen.

Symons, D. 1979. *The Evolution of Human Sexuality*. New York: Oxford University Press.

Symons, G.L. 1981. "Her view from the executive suite: Canadian women in management." Pp. 337–353 in Katherina L.P. Lundy and Barbara D. Warme (eds.), *Work in the Canadian Context*. Toronto: Butterworths.

Synnott, Anthony. 1983. "Little angels, little devils: A sociology of children." *The Canadian Review of Sociology and Anthropology* 20:79–95.

Tait, Mark. 1983. "Tobacco ads set feminists fuming." *The Calgary Herald* (July 15):A17.

Tancred-Sheriff, Peta, 1985. "Women's experience, women's knowledge and the power of knowledge." *Atlantis* 10:106–117.

Tanner, Julian. 1981. "Pop music and peer groups: A study of Canadian high school students' responses to pop music." *Canadian Review of Sociology and Anthropology* 18:1–13.

Tavris, Carol, and Carole Offir. 1977. *The Longest War: Sex Differences in Perspective*. New York: Harcourt Brace Jovanovich.

Taylor, Verta. 1983. "The future of feminism in the 1980s: a social movement analysis." Pp. 434–451 in Laurel Richardson and Verta Taylor (eds.), *Feminist Frontiers: Rethinking Sex, Gender, and Society*. Reading, MA.: Addison-Wesley.

Terry, R.L., and S.L. Ertel. 1974. "Exploration of individual differences in preferences for humor." *Psychological Reports* 34:1031–1037.

Theodore, Athena (ed.). 1971. "The professional woman: Trends and prospects." Pp. 1–35 in Athena Theodore (ed.), *The Professional Woman*. Cambridge, MA.: Schenkman.

Thoits, Peggy A. 1983. "Multiple identities and psychological well-being." *American Sociological Reveiw* 48:174–187.

———. 1985. "Self-labelling processes in mental illness: The role of emotional deviance." American Journal of Sociology 91:221–249.

Thomas, Darwin L., David D. Franks, and James M. Calonico. 1978. "Role-taking and power in social psychology." Pp. 128–137 in Jerome G. Manis and Bernard N. Meltzer (eds.), *Symbolic Interaction: A Reader in Social Psychology*. Third Edition. Boston: Allyn and Bacon.

Thomas, W.I. 1937. *Primitive Behavior*. New York: McGraw-Hill.

————, and D.S. Thomas. 1928. *The Child in America*. New York: Knopf.

Thompson, Mary K., and Julia S. Brown. 1980. "Feminine roles and variations in women's illness behaviors." *Pacific Sociological Review* 23:405–422.

Thorne, Barrie. 1983. "An analysis of gender and social groupings." Pp. 61–63 in Laurel Richardson and Verta Taylor (eds.), *Feminist Frontiers: Rethinking Sex, Gender, and Society* Reading, MA.: Addison-Wesley.

————, and Nancy Henley. 1975. "Difference and dominance: An overview of language, gender, and society." Pp. 5–42 in Barrie Thorne and Nancy Henley (eds.), *Language and Sex: Difference and Dominance*. Rowley, MA.: Newbury House.

————, and Nancy Henley (eds.), 1975. *Language and Sex: Difference and Dominance*. Rowley, MA.: Newbury House.

Thornton, Arland, Duane F. Alwin, and Donald Camburn. 1983. "Causes and consequences of sex-role attitudes and attitude change." *American Sociological Review* 48:211–227.

————, and Deborah Freedman. 1979. "Changes in the sex-role attitudes of women, 1962–1977: Evidence from a panel study." *American Sociological Review* 44:832–842.

Thorsell, Siv. 1967. "Employer attitudes to female employees." Pp. 135–169 in Edmond Dahlstrom (ed.), *The Changing Roles of Men and Women*. London: Unwin Brothers.

Tindale, Joseph. 1980. "Identity maintenance processes of old poor men." Pp. 88–94 in Victor W. Marshall (ed.), *Aging in Canada*. Don Mills, Ontario: Fitzhenry & Whiteside.

Tolson, Andrew. 1977. *The Limits of Masculinity*. London: Tavistock.

Toukmanian, Shake G. 1985. "Women and therapy: A research perspective." *International Journal of Women's Studies* 8:102–110.

Tousley, Nancy. 1985. "Little Mermaid graces terrace." *The Calgary Herald* (November 3): E3.

Tresemer, David W. 1975. "Assumptions made about gender roles." Pp. 308–339 in Marcia Millman and Rosabeth Moss Kanter (eds.), *Another Voice: Feminist Perspectives on Social Life and Social Science*. Garden City, N.Y.: Doubleday Anchor.

————. 1977. *Fear of Success*. New York: Plenum Publishing Corp.

Tuchman, Gaye. 1975. "Women and the creation of culture." Pp. 171–202 in Marcia Millman and Rosabeth Moss Kanter (eds.), *Another Voice: Feminist Perspectives on Social Life and Social Science*. Garden City, N.Y.: Doubleday Anchor.

————. 1978a. "Introduction: The symbolic annihilation of women by the mass media." Pp. 3–38 in Gaye Tuchman, Arlene Kaplan Daniels, and James Benet (eds.), *Hearth and Home: Images of Women in the Mass Media*. New York: Oxford University Press.

————. 1979. "Women's depiction by the mass media." *Signs* 4:528–542.

————, and Nina Fortin. 1980. "Edging women out: Some suggestions about the structure of opportunities and the Victorian novel." *Signs* 6:308–325.

————, and Nina E. Fortin. 1984. "Fame and misfortune: Edging women out of the great literary tradition." *American Journal of Sociology* 90:72–96.

Turkle, Sherry. 1984. *The Second Self: Computers and the Human Spirit*. New York: Simon and Schuster.

Turner, Jonathan H. 1978. *The Structure of Sociological Theory*. Revised Edition. Homewood, Il.: Dorsey Press.

Turner, Ralph H. 1962. "Role-taking: Process versus conformity." Pp. 20–40 in Arnold M. Rose (ed.), *Human Behavior and Social Processes: An Interactionist Approach*. Boston: Houghton Mifflin.

————. 1970. *Family Interaction*. New York: Wiley.

————. 1976. "The real self: From institution to impulse." *American Journal of Sociology* 81:989–1016.

————. 1978. "The role and the person." *American Journal of Sociology* 84:1–23.

Turrittin, Anton H., Paul Anisef, and Neil J. Mackinnon. 1983. "Gender differences in educational achievement: A study of social inequality." *The Canadian Journal of Sociology* 8:395–419.

Twain, Mark. *The Adventures of Huckleberry Finn*. 1884/1966. Harmondsworth, England: Penguin Books.

Unger, Rhoda Kesler. 1978. "The politics of gender: A review of relevant literature." In Julia A. Sherman and Florence L. Denmark (eds.), *The Psychology of Women: Future Directions in Research*. New York: Psychological Dimensions.

————, and Florence L. Denmark (eds.), 1975. *Women: Dependent or Independent Variable?* New York: Psychological Dimensions, Inc.

Valadez, Joseph J., and Remi Clignet. 1984. "Household work as an ordeal: Evidence of standards reverses standardization of culture." *American Journal of Sociology* 89:812–835.

Valentich, Mary. 1986. "Feminism and social work practice." In F.J. Turner (ed.), *Social Work Treatment*. Third Edition. New York: Free Press (forthcoming).

Van Gelder, Lindsy. 1984. "Carol Gilligan: Leader for a different kind of future." *Ms.* (January):37–40, 101.

———. 1985. "Help for technophobes: Think of your computer as just another appliance." *Ms.* 13 (January) :89–91.

Veblen, Thorstein. 1899. *The Theory of the Leisure Class*. New York: New American Library.

Veevers, J.E. 1977. "The child-free alternative: Rejection of the motherhood mystique." Pp. 90–108 in Marylee Stephenson (ed.), *Women in Canada*. Revised Edition. Don Mills, Ontario: General Publishing.

———. 1979. "Voluntary childlessness: A review of issues and evidence." *Marriage and Family Review* 2:1–26.

———. 1982. "Women in the driver's seat: Trends in sex differences in driving and death." *Population Research and Policy Review* 1:1–12.

———, and Susan M. Adams. 1982. "Bringing bodies back in: the neglect of sex differences in size and strength." Paper presented at the Canadian Sociology and Anthropology Association Meeting, Ottawa.

Verbrugge, Lois M. 1985. "Gender and health: an update on hypotheses and evidence." *Journal of Health and Social Behavior* 26:156–182.

Vipond, Mary. 1977. "The image of women in mass circulation magazines in the 1920s." Pp. 116–124 in Susan Mann Trofimenkoff and Alison Prentice (eds), *The Neglected Majority*. Toronto: McClelland and Stewart.

Vogel, I. 1968. *When I Grow Up*. New York: Western Publishing.

Vonnegut, Kurt, Jr. 1973. *Breakfast of Champions*. New York: Dell Publishing Co.

Walker, Nancy. 1981. "Do feminists ever laugh? Women's humor and women's rights." *International Journal of Women's Studies* 4:1–9.

Waller, W. 1937. "The rating and dating complex." *American Sociological Review* 2:727–734.

Walster, Elaine and G. William Walster. 1978. *A New Look at Love*. Reading, MA.: Addison-Wesley.

Walum, Laurel Richardson. 1974. "The changing door ceremony." *Urban Life and Culture* 2:506–515.

Ward, Kathryn B., and Linda Grant. 1985. "The feminist critique and a decade of published research in sociology journals." *The Sociological Quarterly* 26:139–157.

Warren, Denise. 1978. "Commercial liberation." *Journal of Communication* 28:169–173.

Wax, Judith. 1979. *Starting in the Middle*. New York: Holt, Rinehart and Winston.

Waxman, Stephanie. 1976. *What Is A Girl? What Is A Boy?* Toronto: The Women's Press.

Weber, Max. 1930. *The Protestant Ethic and The Spirit of Capitalism*. Translated by Talcott Parsons. New York: Scribner's.

Webster, Murray J., and James E. Driskell, Jr. 1983. "Beauty as status." *American Journal of Sociology* 89:140–165.

Weinstein, Eugene A. 1969. "The development of interpersonal competence." Pp. 753–775 in David A. Goslin (ed.), *Handbook of Socialization Theory and Research*. Chicago: Rand McNally.

Weisstein, Naomi, and Virginia Blaisdell. 1972. "Feminist rock: No more balls and chains. *Ms.* 1(December):25–27.

Weitzman, Lenore J. 1979. *Sex Role Socialization*. Palo Alto, CA.: Mayfield Publishing.

———, Deborah Eifler, Elizabeth Hokada, and Catherine Ross. 1972. "Sex-role socialization in picture books for preschool children." *American Journal of Sociology* 77:1125–1150.

West, Candy. 1973. "Sexism and conversation: Everything you always wanted to know about Sachs (but were afraid to ask)." Unpublished M.A. thesis, Department of Sociology, University of California, Santa Barbara.

West, Candace, and Don H. Zimmerman. 1977. "Women's place in everyday talk: reflections on parent-child interaction." *Social Problems* 24:521–529.

Weyant, Robert G. 1979. "The relationship between psychology and women." *International Journal of Women's Studies* 2:358–385.

Wharton, William. 1981. *Dad*. New York: Avon Books.

White, Lynn K., and David B. Brinkerhoff. 1981. "The sexual division of labor: Evidence from childhood." *Social Forces* 60:170–181.

Whitehead, Harriett. 1981. "The bow and the burden strap: A new look at institutionalized homosexuality in native North America." Pp. 80–115 in Sherry B. Ortner and Harriet Whitehead (eds.), *Sexual Meanings: The Culture Construction of Gender and Sexuality*. Cambridge: Cambridge University Press.

Whitehurst, Carol A. 1979. "An empirical investigation of women's self-evaluation." *International Journal of Women's Studies* 2:76–86.

Whitehurst, R.N., and G.V. Booth. 1980. *The Sexes: Changing Relationships in a Pluralistic Society*. Toronto: Gage.

Whorf, B. 1949. *Four Articles on Metalinguistics*. Washington, D.C.: Foreign Service Institute, Department of State.

Wikler, Norma. 1976. "Sexism in the classroom." Paper delivered at American Sociological Association Meeting, New York.

Wilensky, Harold L. 1964. "The professionalization of everyone?" *American Journal of Sociology* 70:137–158.

Williams, John E., and Deborah L. Best. 1982. *Measuring Sex Stereotypes: A Thirty-Nation Study*. Beverly Hills: Sage.

Williams, Juanita H. 1983. *Psychology of Women*. Second Edition. New York: Norton & Company.

Williams, Raymond. 1977. *Marxism and Literature*. London: Oxford University Press.

Wilson, Edward O. 1975. *Sociobiology: The New Synthesis*. Cambridge: Harvard University Press.

Wilson, John. 1973. *Introduction to Social Movements*. New York: Basic Books.

Wilson, Robert A. 1966. *Feminine Forever*. New York: M. Evans & Co.

Wilson, Sam, Bryan Strong, Leah Clarke and Thomas Johns. 1977. *Human Sexuality*. St. Paul: West.

Wilson, Susannah J. 1981. "The image of women in Canadian magazines." Pp. 231–245 in Elihu Katz and Tamas Szeckso (eds.), *Mass Media and Social Change*. Beverly Hills: Sage.

———. 1982. *Women, the Family and the Economy*. Toronto: McGraw-Hill Ryerson.

Wilson, Sue. 1984. "Nontraditional and living arrangements." Pp. 198–218 in Maureen Baker (ed.), *The Family: Changing Trends in Canada*. Toronto: McGraw-Hill Ryerson.

Wine, Jeri Dawn. 1985. "Women's sexuality." *International Journal of Women's Studies* 8:58–63.

Wolf, Margery. 1974. "Chinese women: Old skills in a new context." Pp. 157–172 in Michele Zimbalist Rosaldo and Louise Lamphere (eds.), *Woman, Culture, and Society*. Stanford, CA.: Stanford University Press.

Wolfe, Margie. 1982. "Working with words: Feminist publishing in Canada." Pp. 265–273 in Maureen Fitzgerald, Connie Guberman and Margie Wolfe (eds.), *Still Ain't Satisfied! Canadian Feminism Today*. Toronto: The Women's Press.

Wolfenstein, Martha. 1954. *Children's Humor*. Glencoe, II.: Free Press.

———. 1968. "Children's humor: Sex, names, and double meanings." Pp. 266–284 in Tony Talbot (ed.), *The World of the Child*. New York: Doubleday Anchor.

Wolff, Kurt H. 1959. "The sociology of knowledge and sociological theory." Pp. 567–602 in Llewellyn Gross (ed.), *Symposium on Sociological Theory*. New York: Harper & Row.

Wolinsky, Howard. 1983. "Gender selection elusive." Independent Press Service: December 31st.

Wollstonecraft, Mary. 1792/1967. *A Vindication of the Rights of Women*. New York: W.W. Norton.

Wood, Elizabeth. 1980. "Women in music." *Signs* 6:283–297.

Woolf, Virginia. 1928. *A Room of One's Own*. Harmondsworth, England: Penguin Books.

Wrightsman, Lawrence S., and Kay Deaux, 1981. *Social Psychology in the 80s*. Third Edition. Belmont, CA.: Wadsworth.

Wrong, Dennis H. 1961. "The oversocialized conception of man in modern sociology." *American Sociological Review* 26:183–193.

Wylie, Betty Jane. 1982. *Beginnings: A Book for Widows*. Revised Edition. Toronto: McClelland and Stewart.

Yoels, William C., and David A. Karp. 1978. "A social psychological critique of 'over-socialization': Dennis Wrong revisited." *Sociological Symposium* 24:27–39.

Zelizer, Viviana A. 1981. "The price and value of children: the case of children's insurance." *American Journal of Sociology* 86:1036–1056.

Zellman, Gail L. and Jacqueline D. Goodchilds. 1983. "Becoming sexual in adolescence." Pp. 49–63 in Elizabeth R. Allgeier and Naomi B. McCormick (eds.), *Changing Boundaries: Gender Roles and Sexual Behavior.* Palo Alto, CA.: Mayfield.

Zentner, Henry. 1982. "Durkheim's conception of time, space, and the theory of knowledge as a theory of change." *Indian Journal of Social Research* 23:212–223.

Zetterberg, Hans L. 1965. *On Theory and Verification in Sociology.* Third Edition. Totowa, N.J.: Bedminster Press.

Zimbardo, Philip G., and Wendy Meadow. 1974. "Becoming a sexist—in one easy laugh: sexism in the Reader's Digest." Paper presented at the Annual Meetings of the Western Psychological Association, San Francisco.

Zwarun, Suzanne. 1982a. "The lady is a champ." *Quest* (June/July/August):25–34.

———. 1982b. "Women frightened by messages in advertising today." *The Calgary Herald.* December 20th.

———. 1983. "Fashion still enslaves women." *The Calgary Herald.* March 25th.

Index

To the owner of this book:

We are interested in your reaction to Marlene Mackie's **Constructing Women and Men: Gender Socialization**

Through feedback from you, we can help improve this book in future editions.

1. What was your reason for using this book?

____ university course   ____ continuing education course
____ college course   ____ personal interest
                                ____ other (specify)

2. Which school? _____
3. Approximately how much of the book did you use?
   ____ ¼   ____ ½   ____ ¾   ____   ____ all
4. What is the best aspect of the book?
5. Have you any suggestions for improvement?
6. Is there anything that should be added?

_____ **Fold here** _____